War girls

MANCHESTER
1824

Manchester University Press

War girls

The First Aid Nursing Yeomanry
in the First World War

JANET LEE

Manchester University Press
Manchester and New York   2006

distributed exclusively in the USA by Palgrave

Copyright © Janet Lee 2005

The right of Janet Lee to be identified as the author of this work has been
asserted by her in accordance with the Copyright, Designs and Patents Act 1988.

Published by Manchester University Press
Oxford Road, Manchester M13 9NR, UK
and Room 400, 175 Fifth Avenue, New York, NY 10010, USA
www.manchesteruniversitypress.co.uk

Distributed exclusively in the USA by
Palgrave, 175 Fifth Avenue, New York, NY 10010, USA

Distributed exclusively in Canada by
UBC Press, University of British Columbia, 2029 West Mall,
Vancouver, BC, Canada V6T 1Z2

British Library Cataloguing-in-Publication Data
A catalogue record for this book is available from the British Library

Library of Congress Cataloging-in-Publication Data applied for

ISBN   0 7190 6712 X   *hardback*
EAN   978 0 7190 6712 9
ISBN   0 7190 6713 8   *paperback*
EAN   978 0 7190 6713 6

First published 2005

14 13 12 11 10 09 08 07 06 05   10 9 8 7 6 5 4 3 2 1

Typeset in Ehrhardt with Chianti display
by Northern Phototypesetting Co. Ltd, Bolton
Printed in Great Britain
by Bell & Bain Ltd, Glasgow

For Edith and Herbert

Contents

List of plates

Acknowledgements

This book began as a 'back burner project' and has become my most favourite research and writing project to date. This is thanks largely to the FANY and their fabulous stories of courage and ingenuity that held my fascination throughout the various stages of the book's completion. I am indebted to them for providing me with such wonderful material. In this spirit I want to acknowledge their service and hope this account provides some measure of their work and commitment during this period. I also want to thank present FANY, especially Ailsa Camm and Lynda Rose for their assistance in the archives and Lynette Beardwood for helping me with some historical details and interpretation of FANY materials. As an outsider I have done my best to capture the nuances of the organization but regret any inaccuracies or omissions. I am especially indebted to the late Grace McDougall, Commandant of the FANY throughout the First World War, whose papers and memoirs I have used extensively and whose courage and ambition blazed the trail, so to speak, in terms of the development of the FANY and in giving me the motivation to write this history. I would also like to thank key people in the various archives who assisted with this project. Richard Davies at the Brotherton Library, University of Leeds, was extremely gracious and helped me navigate the FANY material in the Liddle Collection; I am indebted to him for his assistance. Thanks also to Mary Wilkinson at the Imperial War Museum and to the editorial team at Manchester University Press, especially Alison Welsby.

I would also like to thank my colleagues here at Oregon State University who gave emotional and professional support as well as feedback on drafts of the book. Thanks especially to Rebecca Warner, Susan Shaw, Vicki Tolar Burton, Bob Nye and Maria Olaya, as well as to Joan Gross who was always most gracious about helping me translate French. Also thanks to my colleagues at the Center for the Humanities, especially Janet Winston, Franny Nudelman, Laura Belmonte, David Robinson and Wendy Madar, as well as to my special riding buddies, Sally, Dale and Barb. Appreciation is also given for office support from Lisa Lawson and Mandi Dolecheck. Completion of the manuscript was made possible by research assistance from the College of Liberal Arts and from the Center for the Humanities at Oregon State University. Last but not least, thanks to my mother Leti Halvorsen whose example has always given me an appreciation for dazzling women, and to Gary Barnes and our children Liam, Fiona and Edyth.

List of abbreviations

ASC	Army Service Corps
ATS	Auxiliary Territorial Service
BEF	British Expeditionary Force
BRCS	British Red Cross Society
FA	First Aid Nursing Yeomanry (FANY) Archives
IWM	Impeial War Museum
LC	Liddle Collection, Special Collections of the Brotherton Library, University of Leeds
PRVC	Princess Royal's Volunteer Corps
RAMC	Royal Army Medical Corps
SOE	Special Operations Executive
SS	*Sections Sanitaires* [Sanitary Sections]
SSBM	Société de Secours aux Blessés Militaires [Society to Aid Wounded Soldiers]
TAT	Temporary Ambulance Trains
TFNS	Territorial Forces Nursing Service
VAD	Voluntary Aid Detachment
WAAC	Women's Army Auxiliary Corps
WRAF	Women's Royal Air Force
WRNS	Women's Royal Naval Service
WSPU	Women's Social and Political Union
WTS	Women's Transport Service
WVR	Women's Volunteer Reserve
YMCA	Young Men's Christian Association
YWCA	Young Women's Christian Association

Introduction

There's the girl who clips your ticket for the train,
      And the girl who speeds the lift from floor to floor,
There's the girl who does a milk-round in the rain,
      And the girl who calls for orders at your door.
          Strong, sensible, and fit,
          They're out to show their grit,
    And tackle jobs with energy and knack.
          No longer caged and penned up,
          They're going to keep their end up
Till the khaki soldier boys come marching back.

There's the motor girl who drives a heavy van,
      There's the butcher girl who brings your joint of meat,
There's the girl who cries 'All fares, please!' like a man,
      And the girl who whistles taxis up the street.
          Beneath each uniform
          Beats a heart that's soft and warm,
    Though of canny mother-wit they show no lack;
          But a solemn statement this is,
          They've no time for love and kisses
Till the khaki soldier boys come marching back.

                                Jessie Pope[1]

Written by patriotic pro-war poet Jessie Pope, this poem carries the reminder that while the war girls are 'strong, sensible, and fit', and 'out to show their grit', still beneath each uniform beats 'a heart that's soft and warm'. Such verse with its multiple gendered messages suggests how women might relate their gendered lives to possible wartime roles and highlights the complex tangle of intersections between war and early twentieth-century womanhood. Although I love the empowerment implied in such refrains as 'no longer caged and penned up, they're going to keep their end up', my delight at this awkward pathos is always tempered by the final refrain that brings these 'war girls' of the First World War squarely back to earth: the time will come when 'the khaki soldier boys come marching back'. The poem (whose title, 'War Girls', I have borrowed for the title of this book) encourages us to think about the ways this war subverted existing gender arrangements and encouraged personal and social autonomy for women at the very same time that it relied on traditional tropes of gender to stabilize the war effort and contain women's independence.

In this book I focus on these wartime renegotiations of gender and explore the everyday lives of a group of British women volunteers named the FANY (First Aid Nursing Yeomanry)[2] who found themselves, as did many young middle- and upper-class women of the period, 'straight out of Edwardian drawing rooms into the manifold horrors of the First World War'.[3] Approximately 450 FANY worked as nurses and driver-mechanics on the Western Front with the Belgian, British and French Armies during the war.[4] Described as 'one of the most picturesque, as well as useful and dauntless organisations of women',[5] they were fiercely independent and quite audacious, and while they threw themselves into their hard and gruelling work, they are also remembered for their propensity for fun and adventure. In addition, they were one of the most decorated volunteer organizations and amassed an outstanding number of honours and medals.[6] As the first women's voluntary corps in Great Britain and still the only such corps to have survived two world wars and still be in business, the FANY was renamed the Women's Transport Service after the First World War and thrives today as the First Aid Nursing Yeomanry (Princess Royal's Volunteer Corps).[7]

War Girls is part of a scholarship that gives voice to women and to stories that were increasingly silenced in the years after the war. As a feminist I am enthralled and intrigued by FANY adventures, especially their motivation to claim a space for themselves at the battlefront and to write about it with such feminine bravado. As a feminist I am also, of course, disappointed by them and irked by their sometimes snobbish behaviour and their strong allegiances to military and political elites. A colleague once told me he could never write biography about someone toward whom he felt indifference: liking or disliking someone motivated writing, but indifference, never. I can say at this point I definitely agree: I mostly liked the FANY and occasionally disliked them, but never did I feel indifference and much of the time I was in awe of their accomplishments. I own horses and love to ride and it was the 'horsey' aspect of the FANY that first attracted my attention. I recognized that the FANY life offered both rewards and constraints: terrific opportunities, harsh working conditions and poignant witness to one of the most brutal of human experiences. Imagining myself in their shoes was in some ways easy: as an independent woman who enjoys the company of other women (especially on horseback), I could imagine myself a First World War FANY quite easily. In other ways it was more difficult: certainly it is difficult to conceive of such a war when one has never lived through it, and given my geographic and class background I know my contribution to the war effort would most likely have been in one of the munitions factories. Indeed, my grandmother lived through this war and spent it raising my aunt and uncle in a pit community in Yorkshire; my grand-father, a coal miner, was a Lance Corporal in the King's Own Yorkshire Light Infantry and lived through the horrors of the trenches. It's to them that I dedicate this book, especially to my grandmother who I think would have loved to have been a FANY if she had been able.

Although *War Girls* seeks to give voice to women's muted narratives, it also explores how war redefines notions of femininity and masculinity as well as how gender encourages the reformulation of discourses about war. This means studying war as a gendering activity: not only asking questions about the impact of women's military service on women, making women visible as historical agents, but also reading the First World War through the lens of gender.[8] A central question then is how femininity is constituted in relation to war and how it is modified by structures of difference. Since women have never been, and certainly were not during this war, a clearly defined coherent group, femininity must be recognized as a contested site of meaning. I am using the term 'women' to imply members of a discursive category or people structurally positioned or assigned to the category female who are encouraged to take up certain discourses and indulge in certain material practices and behaviours. These practices and discourses are historically and politically con-textualized in social relations of power (that include class, sexual orientation, race and colonial status) that shape and mould what any given notion of the feminine might entail.[9]

In other words, while women share similarities of experience based upon their position in gendered systems of power in society and are affected by the discourses associated with femininity in any given historical moment, these discourses are by no means universal, coherent or consistently experienced by all. This was especially the case during the First World War as class back-ground framed the kind of war work women might perform. Working- and lower-middle-class women needed to work for a wage whereas others were privileged enough to volunteer their services. Volunteer nursing was framed as an extension of the charitable and philanthropic activities of middle- and upper-class women, just as driving, an elite masculine activity in Edwardian Britain, was off-limits to all but relatively privileged women.[10] Class status, however, also informed notions of sexual morality as women's work challenged established lines of gender stratification. Women's entry into the war caused a sense of moral panic and a challenge to a social order where men fought to protect women, and, as a result, those who dared to transgress and go against public mandate for womanly behaviour were often morally and sexually suspect. While all women faced this, working-class women were especially accused of sexual deviance compared to middle- and upper-class women whose 'respectability' or 'good breeding' protected them to some extent from suspicion and harassment.[11]

In this way, acting as a 'woman' is an interplay between subjectivity and discourse such that gender as a set of social identities is constantly being performed against a complex cultural backdrop. Language is integral to this performance; the meanings within language are cultural constructions that frame how we think and therefore act and certainly shape how we make sense of our experiences and organize them as stories and recollections. *War Girls* constructs the history of the FANY through the historicization of such stories and recollections. What this recognizes is that narratives mobilize the relationship between individuals and cultural landscapes and there is always some distance between individuals as experiencing subjects and their accounts of this lived experience.[12] FANY members drew upon cultural myths to organize their lives and represent their experiences, and their narratives are inevitably expressions of dominant ideologies and cultural mythologies. Their stories are also entangled with the 'legend' or collective identity of the FANY organization itself. This is the cultural and socio-political context of their lived experience. The FANY experienced themselves as women at a cultural moment when gender anxiety was high: although the imperialist cultural imagination linked virile, martial manhood with British nationalist interest and relegated women to the domestic sphere, women were seeking agency in the public world and disenfranchised groups were rocking the status quo. The war would provide both opportunities and constraints and facilitate a negotiation of gender relations. This context therefore encouraged contradictory discourses and the opportunity for the appropriation and subversion of traditional cultural myths. The FANY were able to appropriate and subvert these discourses and integrated them into their narratives in new and potentially emancipatory ways.

Central in the exploration of these narratives is the question of voice and rhetoric. I do not assume some notion of unified subjectivity or absolute 'truth' on the part of the women and their stories; authors construct rather than represent biographical subjects and subjects themselves re-narrate their lives and experiences in the telling. At the level of the subject, narrative work is a negotiation between cultural scripts and scenarios that provide individuals with stories of how events should unfold and both interpersonal and personal/ intrapsychic scripts and understandings. Telling a story of wartime experiences (either at the moment or later as recollections of the event) is a way of account- ing for these cultural scripts, the experience of the event, and (especially in the case of recollections) the processes and practices informing everyday life since the event or experience. As such it is a strategy for managing the event that can include reconciling contradictory feelings such as fear, frustration or joy. As Karin Martin explains, narrative work is 'a method of balancing what happened, how things are "supposed" to happen (according to cultural and interpersonal scripts), and how one wants them to be'.[13]

This does not mean, of course, that I dispute the truthfulness of the sto- ries written and spoken by the FANY, only that I assume their stories are self- interested, as all our stories inevitably are (including the 'objective' facts created by academics). Despite the fact that one anonymous reviewer of this book was concerned about the potentially unreliable aspect of using the FANY's own stories because of this self-interested aspect, I believe these sto- ries are central not only for 'giving voice' to these women but for the very reason that it *is* the legend or collective identity of the FANY that I want to capture. As Alistair Thomson in his research on ANZAC (Australian and New Zealand Army Corps) explains, organizational legends arise in part 'by not excluding contradictory versions of experience, but by representing them in ways that fit the legend and flatten out contradictions'.[14] I see my role as a writer of FANY history to represent this legend in the context of the culture, politics and wider historical forces that gave rise to it and to pay attention to the rhetorical devices used as FANY members made sense of their war expe- riences. And, in addition, I try to be cognizant of my own interpretive frame- work, which produces a variety of meanings that have as much to do with me as the stories themselves. In this way, biography and textual analysis are prac- tices and conscious products of human action: a retelling and not a realist interpretation of past lives. The cultural memory involved is always shaped in a contested field. This means that the historical moment is essentially produc- tive in providing the cultural context for the narratives the women tell about their own lives, for biography as the interpretation of these narratives, and for the act of reading itself at this very moment. Ultimately I make the case for a relatively humble history that assumes it occurred that way, reminding us that we transform the past by reconstructing it as the past of a different present.[15]

A country at war

Although the beginning of the First World War can be traced to the assassination of the Archduke Franz Ferdinand, heir to the Austrian throne, and his wife Sophie during a state visit to Sarajevo in June 1914, war had been brewing for several years. European dynasties and nations stewed in resentment over past battles, and nationalism fuelled an intense patriotism that offered military solutions to contemporary problems, uniting a populace in Britain threatened by increasing poverty and economic strife, the demands of the unenfranchised, and secularization and the growth of scientific thought. British nationalism was imperial in nature, incorporating a world view that embraced a notion of cultural and racial superiority and which disguised its greed for new markets and raw materials. The period 1880–1914 has been labelled the Age of Empire when large parts of Africa were annexed and Britain consolidated its hold on India. As many historians have noted, this imperialist nationalism was a key part of the general popular imagination and certainly fuelled an enthusiasm for war in 1914.[16] In this way, a belief in war as a test of national character (and especially British manhood) and proof of national superiority was central in the culmination of events leading up to Britain's entry into the war.

After the assassination, Austria–Hungary joined with its ally Germany in swift retaliation against the Serbs, who in turn were supported by the Russians. Russia then looked to its ally France, who hoped for the support of Britain. In August 1914 after Germany demanded unrestricted passage of its armies through Belgium, Britain ordered mobilization and issued an ultimatum to Germany that unless guarantees for Belgian neutrality were given, Britain would also be at war. At this point the British Foreign Secretary Sir Edward Grey delivered his famous quote, 'the lamps are going out all over Europe; we shall not see them again in our lifetime', and the British Expeditionary Force (BEF) entered the struggle.[17]

In August 1914 when Britain first became involved in the war, this belligerence that was only supposed to last until Christmas, the nation's understanding of war was steeped in Victorian and Edwardian notions of glory and honour wound up in the racist project of Empire-building. Queen Victoria had been known as the imperial matriarch and Social Darwinism and proselytizing Christianity united to provide justification for 'civilizing' huge regions of the globe. 'Britishness' (or more specifically 'Englishness') as John MacKenzie explains, was presented as a 'complex of historical, moral, and heroic values'.[18] The defence of Empire involved pride, self-denial, commitment and determinism, as well as demonstration of that important British quality: pluck.

'War was a glorious affair and the British always won', was one social observer's interpretation.[19] It is not surprising therefore that so many rushed to volunteer their services in August 1914 since it was 'to that high noon of power and Empire, of prosperity and expansion, of national pride and security, that they owed their unshakeable confidence, their patriotism and the unquestioning sense of duty that went with it'.[20]

In addition, some believed that war might provide a cleansing or purifying force. This reflected the gender and racial anxiety about cultural and eugenic degeneration, self-absorption and narcissism, as well as waywardness from spiritual values of an earlier period. Included as evidence for this weakening were the near losses as a result of the Boer War, suffrage demands, various avant-garde artistic movements and the general spiritual vacuum implicit in bourgeois society. Also implicated were diminished birth rates, high rates of emigration and the fear that an increasing proportion of each generation would be the offspring of the lower class.[21] As a result, some embraced war as a means of regeneration and purification: a form of spiritual cleansing.[22] The darling war poet Rupert Brooke symbolized this cleansing as an antidote to both spiritual degeneration and the monotony of bourgeois life when he declared the war a chance to dive 'as swimmers into cleanness leaping, glad from a world grown old and cold and weary'.[23]

In this way, as the twentieth century opened and Britain reflected the mechanical and scientific advances that were slowly moving it into a new era, the roots of the generation who would be most affected by this war were still embedded in a Victorian age where war represented some form of heroic pageantry with chivalrous and religious overtones. Not only were England and her tranquil green pastures at stake, but civilization itself. Alice Meynell's poem 'Summer in England, 1914' expresses the glory of that last summer before war – and, in effect, tells us that war was necessary to protect this pastoral English life:

Most happy year! And out of town
The hay was prosperous, and the wheat;
The silken harvest climbed the down:
Moon after moon was heavenly sweet,
Stroking the bread within their sheaves,
Looking 'twixt apples and their leaves.

Who said 'No man hath greater love than this,
To die to serve his friend'?
So these have loved us all unto no end.[24]

Sentimentality and patriotism went hand in hand as this war unfolded, as did religious metaphors of Christian salvation. The work of building and maintaining empires of course had long involved colonization as a Christian-izing force. Men might sacrifice themselves in battle against the infidels like Christ on the cross, and women for their part could identify with Mary as Christ's mother or as Mary Magdalene who lived in obedience to the values for which Christ died. 'To question those values is to question the Sacrifice itself – impossible. For then his death must become not only horrible but meaning-less.'[25] Mary H. J. Henderson's poem, 'The Incident', illustrates this senti-ment well. The last stanza reads:

> And still on the battlefield of pain
> Christ is stretched on His Cross again;
> And the Son of God in agony hangs,
> Womanhood striving to ease His pangs.
> For each son of man is a son divine,
> Not just to the mother who calls him 'mine',
> As he stretches out his stricken hand,
> Wounded to the death for the Mother Land.[26]

This was a holy war where young men's sacrifice was equated with the cruci-fixion of Jesus and the defence of the Christian Empire was the most hon-ourable cause.[27]

It is generally agreed that a generation of innocent young men ('the lost generation') who believed in such nineteenth-century notions as valour, honour, glory and the Empire, went off to war and were killed in pointless bat-tles incompetently staged by generals whose military tactics belonged in another era and who were out of touch with the daily slaughter of trench war-fare. No one was prepared for such an event as 800 men killed in one trench in three minutes.[28] Scholars such as Paul Fussell and Samuel Hynes emphasize that surviving soldiers became embittered, were horrified at the hypocrisy and stupidity of those in power as well as those at home who supported and encouraged such a war, and turned against the generation that had betrayed them.[29] This disjuncture or unfolding of events, it is suggested, helps con-struct what we understand as the modern period and facilitated the appear-ance of irony as the dominant form of modern understanding. And, while Robert Wohl and others have rightly criticized this myth of the lost generation as an elitist notion based upon the losses of men of socio–economic privilege, it has come to frame British understanding of this historical period.[30]

The First World War was thus a decisive political and cultural episode in British history that resulted in both huge destruction and loss of life as well as a shifting of the cultural terrain toward the beginning of the modern period. At the signing of the Armistice in 1918, Europe could look back at the tragedies of this war with almost 9 million people dead and countless millions injured physically and emotionally; it left a deep scar in British national consciousness, perceived as a force of radical change in society and culture.[31] While it is too strong to say that it brought to an end the cultural values of the Victorian and Edwardian era since there is evidence of their continuity in the postwar or interwar period,[32] certainly British society was substantially transformed by the realities of this war and would never again be the same. Women would also be transformed by this war. It had important consequences for their everyday lives and would frame the expectations they held for a future in the postwar period.

Gendering war

Women and men did not share the same experiences of the First World War even though they both participated in it. Men were the ones who experienced conscription and the direct brutalities of combat and who endured what Joanna Bourke calls the inhumanity of war: the threats of field punishment, the firing-squad, and the training in killing.[33] Still, to read traditional texts about the First World War that frame it as trench warfare, one is struck by the absence of women and their exclusion from the war's collective memory.[34] Huge treatises about the war and its role in the development of modern culture and consciousness have in the past given little or no mention of women, except in a footnote or chapter subheading, or in separate discussion of issues concerning the home front.[35] War has traditionally been conceptualized as an exclusively male zone that legitimates men's full citizenship in society.[36] This is not, of course, news. As Peggy McCracken emphasizes, 'the gendering of the blood of war has a long history' and only men's blood is shed in war. 'To be sure women are hurt, killed, raped, and wounded, but women's wounds and women's deaths are usually classified under the heading of atrocities; they are the result of illegitimate violence that takes place outside the battlefield. Legitimate violence authorized by a higher good that requires heroic struggle and sacrifice is traditionally the domain of men in most cultures: only men should die in combat; the blood of war is men's bloodshed.'[37]

In the last several decades new scholarship has shown that women played crucial roles at home and abroad during the First World War despite a gendering of war work underscored by assumptions that women are programmed to nurture rather than kill and be killed. As well as being mobilized into the many different aspects of the industrial labour force, and munitions in particular, women worked in farming and agriculture, nursing, clerical and communications work, transport, and various other types of service work that had hitherto been performed by men. Indeed, in 1914 Britain had just over 3 million women working in the labour force and by 1918 there were 5 million working outside the home.[38] In addition, more than a 100,000 women served in volunteer corps and in the women's services of the military.

Among the volunteer corps were the Voluntary Aid Detachments (VAD) who worked under the auspices of the Red Cross and performed nursing duties as well as cooking, cleaning, and later driving. The General Service VADs did clerical work and other tasks. Voluntary groups also included the Women's Volunteer Reserve, the Home Service Corps, Women's Emergency Corps, the Signaller's Territorial Corps, and of course the FANY.[39] Most of these voluntary groups were established to aid in home defence and to replace male labour; the VADs and the FANY were two organizations that worked in the battle zone. The women's services with the military included the Women's Army Auxiliary Corps (WAAC) established in 1917, and the Women's Royal Naval Service (WRNS) and the Women's Royal Air Force (WRAF) founded soon thereafter.[40] By the end of the war the women's services had enrolled more than 90,000 women.[41] Although these women were not, of course, allowed into combat positions, they developed 'masculine' skills as engineers, electricians and mechanics. The volunteer groups attracted middle- and upper-class women who did not need to support themselves financially. Less affluent middle-class and working-class women joined the official military service corps towards the end of the war when these agencies were founded.

Enveloped in this focus on gender and the First World War is the question of whether the war changed the material status of women. Did it enhance liberatory trends or did it renegotiate gender and ultimately end up reinforcing gender hierarchies? Early work such as that by Gordon Wright and Arthur Marwick emphasized that women's status improved as a result of the war since it provided new opportunities for women and eventually led to the extension of the franchise as women were rewarded for their service.[42] These studies underscore how living conditions improved, technological advancements helped raise the standard of living generally, and disparities between the rich and the poor were reduced in the postwar period. Among this scholarship that sees the war in terms of its emancipation for women is the classic article 'Soldier's Heart: Literary Men, Literary Women, and the Great War' by Sandra Gilbert. She suggests that women were sexually liberated by the war: 'As young men became increasingly alienated from their prewar selves, increasingly immured in the muck and blood of No Man's Land, women seemed to become, as if by some uncanny swing of history's pendulum, ever more powerful.'[43] She writes that the war temporarily dispossessed men from their power in society at the same time that it released women from patriarchal authority, transforming the last vestiges of nineteenth-century femininity at the cusp of a modern world. The revival and reprinting of memoirs and literature of women who worked in or resisted war (such as works by Kate Finzi, May Sinclair, Enid Bagnold, Mary Borden, Rebecca West and Vera Brittain) have also been used as evidence for the Great War as a liberatory force for women.[44]

While the First World War provided opportunities to move beyond traditional gendered scripts, recent scholarship on women's roles during the war and after it has doubted the persistence of much meaningful change outside of improvements in women's working and living conditions.[45] These more sobering accounts have emphasized that gender relations were not permanently altered by the First World War (or the Second, come to that) since war is a stabilizing force that puts things and people back into their 'natural' places and tends to reinscribe gender rather than transform it. During the war, traditionally gendered maternal scripts provided overriding metaphors for women's role since patriotic duty was linked to women's work as mothers cheerfully sending sons off to war and maintaining domestic constancy. Women's war effort was conceptualized in the context of traditionally feminine healing and nurturing roles and the masculine domain of the battlefront received social and economic priority.[46]

On the home front, policies of dilution were in effect whereby skilled men were replaced by unskilled or semi-skilled women and these women had to fight hard for decent pay and recognition of their labour. Much of their work in munitions was very dangerous and hazardous to their health and well-being.[47] Also, the government, unions, and factory owners agreed to a process whereby women would be dismissed from much of this work after the war was over – part of the strategy of realigning gender and moving women back into the home. About two-thirds of all women who had been employed during the war had left their jobs by 1920. These imperatives were accompanied by a glorification of male heroism and the expectation for women to subordinate themselves to the needs of the returning men. Women who did not do this were seen as selfish and unappreciative of the great sacrifice made in their name. Women were often told that during the war they had been merely acting like men; their new roles were to be accepted as a temporary expedient. Now they could return to their 'natural' state. In addition, while popular sentiment often assumes that the war facilitated suffrage for women, a case has been made that the war actually hampered women's suffrage demands and set the movement back in terms of its momentum.[48] Jane Marcus, for example, has argued that the war was a stunning setback to the struggle for liberty at home. She suggests that the images of women used to promote the war effort encompassed a backlash against the endeavours of the suffragettes and that the insistent depiction of women as nurses and mothers illustrated the ways the propagandists 'had to work particularly hard to erase the powerful new images created by women at the height of the movement'.[49]

Margaret Higonnet and Patrice L.-R. Higonnet call this process of progress and regress in wartime the 'double helix' and emphasize that women do not 'advance' by access to previously held masculine jobs, since men move into the most masculine jobs of war itself.[50] What all this 'evidence' illustrates is the ambiguous position of women during wartime. It also reveals other issues intrinsic to the debate: whether political (such as legislative or economic) or cultural (like hemlines and women smoking in public) markers are used to demonstrate women's advancement as well as an acknowledgement of differences between contemporary analysis and the subjective perception of people who actually lived through this period. The wartime mobilization of women 'bore the appearance both of an alignment between women and men and of a blurring of the visual boundary between masculinity and femininity' even if historians are less optimistic of permanent change.[51]

Total war tends to create a situation that falls back on established social and cultural discourses and institutional arrangements at the same time that it provides the opportunity for a shifting and renegotiation of these arrangements. This is the ambiguous cultural paradox experienced by women during such a period as the state attempts both to use and to rework existing discourses of femininity to support the war effort. Although the government found it important to maintain notions of late Victorian and Edwardian womanhood in cultural propaganda precisely because these values provided key foundations for the justification of British involvement in the European conflict (the 'peace worth fighting for'), the authorities would come to need this new breed of independent women at home and abroad to support the war. The title of this book *War Girls* underscores these paradoxes: the FANY and others like them might be women transforming the public space and claiming their right to serve; nonetheless, as Jessie Pope reminded them, they were war 'girls' and still 'beneath each uniform / Beats a heart that's soft and warm'. The FANY called themselves girls and were referred to as girls. It has always been difficult for girls to claim power and citizenship, but, as the FANY would have said, if anyone could do it, then it would be the FANY.

I am particularly interested in understanding how the FANY drew upon, and/or subverted cultural mythologies to make sense of their wartime service, how as a paramilitary organization they crafted their identity in the context of class and gendered social relations and how they were ultimately able to rene-gotiate gender in the context of wartime service. This book focuses on this renegotiation of gender and examines seven key themes implicit in this process. The first theme concerns the ways women's military organizations utilized traditional notions of genteel femininity and its accompanying nurtu-rance, cheerfulness and devotion in their promise of service, yet went beyond the parameters of such cultural mythologies. The second focuses on the gen-dering of military heroism. It explores women's participation in the dangers of war and the creation of feminine stories of personal heroism that aligned women alongside male combatants, thus marking their place as participants in the war. The third theme addresses the context of female military service in terms of the preparation women received, the opportunities they were given and the risks they took, and focuses on their coping behaviours. Although such coping behaviour was grounded in traditional femininity, it allowed women opportunities to push against the boundaries of feminine war service and transgress into masculine space. Theme four focuses specifically on women's transgression into the masculine terrain of driving and mechanics and shares the ways they developed skills and competencies previously off-limits for women. Such transgressions almost invariably led to women having to nego-tiate masculine authority and develop skills in autonomy, independence and assertiveness – the focus of theme five.

The last two themes discussed in the book address the integration and consolidation of women's organizations as the war progressed and their serv-ice became indispensable. Theme six focuses on the ways women found them-selves routinely taking over men's roles, participating in the dangers of war in an official capacity and being recognized as militarized personnel. Finally, theme seven explores the development of comradeship that encouraged a col-lective feminine solidarity. Through all these processes and developments women renegotiated gender and made a place for themselves as women within masculine space. Their presence here as militarized women made the impor-tant case for their full citizenship.[52] No longer could women be denied this on the grounds that only men participate in war.

Organization of the book

War Girls is organized chronologically by time period and substantively in terms of the different FANY units that served in Europe during the war. What this means in practice is that each chapter focuses on a specific time period and a specific FANY unit in order to maintain a continuity that follows the history of the war and avoids the chaos of a narrative that moves between different time periods and different FANY units. Every year new FANY units would be organized in various locations with differing missions and work expectations. Although this featuring of one unit in one time period encourages (hopefully!) a more fluent and less confusing account of FANY activities, it does tend to disguise the fact that the various FANY units often spanned many years beyond the year featured in the various chapters. In addition, each chapter highlights one of the seven key themes outlined above, although invariably all chapters also touch on themes other than the one featured in any specific chapter.

The book begins with a focus on the founding of the FANY Corps in 1907. Chapter 1 historicizes the Corps' beginnings in social and cultural changes at the turn of the century that encouraged women's patriotic call to service amidst a growing nationalist and militarist discourse. It records FANY prewar activities and focuses on the first theme discussed above: the utilization of a class-based, gendered identity that provided both opportunities and constraints for a women's organization determined to enter masculine space. Chapter 2 begins with the outbreak of war and analyses the service and adventures of Grace Ashley-Smith, future Commanding Officer of the FANY and one of its fledgling leaders, who worked as a FANY in Belgium in the autumn of 1914. The chapter focuses on the second theme in the negotiation of gender: the gendering of military heroism. It explains the ways participation in the dangers of war and the creation of feminine stories of personal heroism aligned women with male combatants and gave them a subjectivity and narrative authority as participants in this war. Chapter 3 examines the first collective FANY war service in Calais and their work with the Belgians at the Lamarck Hospital during late 1914 through 1915. It focuses on the third theme and traces the ways the FANY carved out their niche in this war by accepting traditional roles as well as taking on new opportunities that stretched them beyond anything they could ever have imagined. Chapter 4 describes the success of the FANY as the first women drivers and mechanics for the British Army during 1916, a time when war casualties increased and the euphoria that characterized the beginning of the belligerence subsided into a grim determined nationalism that kept all in deadlock. The chapter examines theme four: women transgressing into masculine space through their work in driving and mechanics.

Known for their competence and flair, the FANY sought to expand during 1917 and took on new work. Their development of a convoy for the Belgians in Calais and a hospital for the French at Port à Binson is the topic of Chapter 5. The chapter focuses on theme five: the ways the FANY dealt with masculine authority and especially the red tape established by the various Allied armies and governments during the war. Although these governments were anxious about the role of women in war, the FANY managed to use various arguments to establish their claim to serve. They were also able to maintain their identity and independence. Chapter 6 explores the many new FANY units that evolved as a result of this expansion and focuses in particular on 1917 through early 1918 with the development of a series of convoys for the French and the British. The FANY of these new units illustrate theme six: women's official militarization. Working in areas of heavy fighting, often transporting wounded under fire in the most difficult and dangerous conditions, the FANY helped prove at last the indispensability and competence of women as official militarized personnel.

When the Armistice was declared in November 1918, many FANY had mixed feelings about demobilization and hoped to keep working in France during this period of reconstruction. Chapter 7 highlights the activities of the FANY in the year following the Armistice and focuses on theme seven, the ways the FANY enjoyed their identity as non-traditional women with a propensity for fun and a keen sense of solidarity and collective friendship. The book ends with a 'Postscript' that summarizes the development of the FANY Corps through and beyond the interwar years and traces the lives of key FANY featured throughout the book, briefly exploring their activities once the war was over.

Feminist historians have emphasized that a history of the twentieth century has most often been constructed as the story of masculine subjectivity with war a central discourse. As we embark on the twenty-first century we are again reminded of the ways wars are created and fought as masculist and capitalist imperatives and the impact of these antagonisms on the lives of ordinary people. Ashley-Smith, who became Grace McDougall upon her marriage in 1915, well understood this masculine predilection for war and women's part in it.

[H]uman nature being what it is, I think the rising generation will be interested [in war]. I should like to think it will be a generation that seeks peace above all things – but I doubt it. Can we keep the ring out of our voices, the glow from our eyes, when we forget the present and tell them of our uncles who were killed, their fathers who were wounded – or when we meet other FANYs and forget even our children in recalling old jests, the old loyalties, the old comrades? Soldiers, toy cannons, bombardments are the games of our sons, and the little girls ask for dolls dressed as nurses. I am afraid the glamour that blinded us will blind our children. Pray God it be not so.[53]

Notes

1 Jessie Pope, 'War Girls', in Catherine Reilly (ed.), *The Virago Book of Women's War Poetry and Verse* (London: Virago, 1997), p. 90.
2 FANY materials are located in various archives that include the FANY Headquarters, recently moved from the Duke of York's Headquarters to TA Centre, 95 Horseferry Road, London SW (abbreviated as [FA]), the Imperial War Museum, Department of Printed Books, Lambeth Road, London SE (abbreviated as [IWM]), and the Liddle Collection, Special Collections of Brotherton Library, University of Leeds (abbreviated as [LC]). All references to primary sources are used with kind permission of the FANY archives, the Liddle Collection at the University of Leeds, and the Trustees of the Imperial War Museum. Attempts were made to contact the McDougall family without success. All materials used or obtained by the author from the FANY archives remain the worldwide copyright of the FANY (PRVC) and should not be reproduced in any form without its written permission.
3 Lyn Macdonald, *The Roses of No Man's Land* (London: Michael Joseph, 1980), p. 11.
4 Lecture of Corps History, lecture notes General Course – Grade II, 1961, p. 9. [FA]
5 Undated magazine clipping, *British Journal of Nursing*. [IWM]
6 They received 135 decorations and various medals during the war. From the British this included eighteen Military Medals and an OBE; from the French a *Legion d'Honneur*, a *Croix de Guerre* with Palm, thirty-two *Croix de Guerre* (two with silver stars); and from the Belgians an *Ordre de Leopold* 1st Class, an *Ordre de la Couronne de Belgique*, six *Ordres de Leopold* 2nd Class, several *Medailles de l'Ordre de la Reine Elisabeth* and several *Croix Civiques*.
7 The current Corps Commander at the time of writing is Lynda Rose, and HRH Princess Anne is the Honorary Commandant-in-Chief.
8 Joan Wallach Scott makes this point in 'Rewriting History', in Margaret R. Higonnet (with Jane Jenson, Sonya Michel and Margaret C. Weitz) (eds), *Behind the Lines: Gender and the Two World Wars* (New Haven: Yale University Press, 1987), pp. 19–30. Other texts that have done this pioneering work include Nicoletta F. Gullace. *'The Blood of Our Sons': Men, Women, and the Renegotiation of British Citizenship During the Great War* (New York: Palgrave Macmillan, 2002); Billie Melman (ed.), *Borderlines: Genders and Identities in War and Peace, 1870–1930* (New York: Routledge, 1998); Sharon Ouditt, *Fighting Forces, Writing Women: Identity and Ideology in the First World War* (London: Routledge, 1994); Miriam Cooke and Angela Woollacott (eds), *Gendering War Talk* (Princeton, New Jersey: Princeton University Press, 1993); Jean Gallagher, *The World Wars through the Female Gaze* (Carbondale: Southern Illinois Press, 1998); Krisztina Robert, 'Gender, Class and Patriotism: Women's Paramilitary Units in First World War Britain', *The International History Review* 19: 1 (1997), 52–3; Janet K. Watson, 'Khaki Girls, VADs and Tommy's Sisters: Gender and Class in First World War Britain', *The International History Review* 19: 1 (1997), 32–51; and Susan R. Grayzel, *Women's Identities at War: Gender, Motherhood, and Politics in Britain and France During the First World War* (Chapel Hill: University of North Carolina Press, 1999). Writings that focus on women's literary contributions to make this point include Angela K. Smith, *The Second Battlefield: Women, Modernism and the First World War* (Manchester: Manchester University Press, 2000); Claire M. Tylee (ed.), *The Great War and Women's Consciousness: Images of Militarism and Womanhood in Women's Writings, 1914–64* (London: Macmillan, 1990); Dorothy Goldman (ed.), *Women and World War I: The Written Response* (New York: St Martin's Press, 1993) and Dorothy Gold-

man (with Jane Gledhill and Judith Hattaway), *Women Writers and the Great War* (New York: Twayne, 1995); Susanne Raitt and Trudi Tate (eds), *Women's Fiction and the Great War* (Oxford: Clarendon Press, 1997); and the 'Afterwords' written by Jane Marcus in Helen Zenna Smith (a.k.a. Evadne Price) *Not So Quiet . . . Stepdaughters of War* (New York: The Feminist Press, [1930] 1989) and Irene Rathbone, *We That Were Young* (New York: The Feminist Press, [1932] 1989). For an early account of women's fiction see Mary Cadogan and Patricia Craig, *Women and Children First: The Fiction of Two Wars* (London: Gollancz, 1978). For an anthology see Margaret R. Higonnet (ed.), *Lines of Fire: Women Writers of World War I* (New York: Penguin, 1999).

9 Denise Riley, *'Am I That Name?' Feminism and the Category of 'Women' in History* (Minneapolis: University of Minnesota Press, 1980); Joan Wallach Scott, 'Gender: A Useful Category of Historical Analysis', in Joan Wallach Scott (ed.), *Feminism and History* (Oxford: Oxford University Press, 1996); Judith Butler, *Gender Trouble: Feminism and the Subversion of Identity* (London: Routledge, 1990).

10 Jane Lewis, *Women in England, 1870–1950* (Brighton, Sussex: Wheatsheaf Books, 1984), pp. 92-7; Sean O'Connell, *The Car and British Society: Class, Gender and Motoring, 1896–1939* (Manchester: Manchester University Press, 1998).

11 Watson, 'Khaki Girls, VADs and Tommy's Sisters'. See also Angela Woollacott, '"Khaki Fever" and its Control: Gender, Class, Age and Sexual Morality on the British Homefront', *Journal of Contemporary History* 29 (1994); and Grayzel, *Women's Identities at War*, ch. 4.

12 Janet S. K. Watson contrasts war as lived experience with war as memory in *Fighting Different Wars: Experience, Memory, and the First World War in Britain* (New York: Cambridge University Press, 2004). See also Bridget Byrne, 'Reciting the Self: Narrative Representations of the Self in Qualitative Interviews', *Feminist Theory* 4: 1 (2003), 29–49; Laurel Graham, 'Archival Research in Intertextual Analysis: Four Representations of the Life of Dr. Lillian Moller Gilbreth', in Carolyn Ellis and Michael G. Flaherty (eds), *Investigating Subjectivity* (Newbury Park: Sage, 1992), pp. 31–52; D. E. Polkinghorne, 'Narrative and Self-Concept', *Journal of Narrative and Life History* 1 (1999), 135–53. See also Penny Summerfield, *Reconstructing Women's Wartime Lives: Discourse and Subjectivity in Oral Histories of the Second World War* (Manchester: Manchester University Press, 1998).

13 Karin Martin, '"I Couldn't Ever Picture Myself Having Sex . . .": Gender Differences in Sex and Sexual Subjectivity', in Christine L.Williams and Arlene Stein (eds), *Sexuality and Gender* (Malden, MA: Blackwell, 2002), p. 161.

14 Alistair Thomson, *ANZAC Memories: Living with the Legend* (Oxford: Oxford University Press, 1994), p. 12.

15 Texts that explore writing of women's life stories include Jo Burr Margadant (ed.), *The New Biography: Performing Femininity in Nineteenth-Century France* (Berkeley: University of California Press, 2000); Liz Stanley, *The Auto/biographical I* (Manchester: Manchester University Press, 1992); Sara Alpern, Joyce Antler, Elisabeth Israels Perry, and Ingrid Winther Scobie (eds), *The Challenge of Feminist Biography: Writing the Lives of Modern American Women* (Urbana: University of Illinois Press, 1992); Susan Groag Bell and Marilyn Yalom (eds), *Revealing Lives: Autobiography, Biography and Gender* (Albany: State University of New York, 1990); Dennis Petrie (ed.), *Ultimately Fiction: Design in Modern American Literary Biography* (West Lafayette: Purdue University Press, 1981); Mary Rhiel and David Suchoff (eds), *The Seductions of Biography* (New York: Routledge, 1996). I have found Carolyn Steedman's work very useful: see *Landscape for a Good Woman* (London: Virago Press, 1986); *Childhood,*

Culture and Class in Britain: Margaret McMillan, 1860–1931 (London: Virago Press, 1990); and *Past Tenses: Essays on Writing, Autobiography and History* (London: Rivers Oram Press, 1992). Sources on biography in the context of situating subjectivities include Kathleen Barry, 'Biography and the Search for Women's Subjectivity', *Women's Studies International Forum* 12 (1989), 561–77; Mary Jean Corbett, *Representing Femininity: Middle-Class Subjectivity in Victorian and Edwardian Women's Autobiographies* (New York: Oxford University Press, 1992); and Regina Gagnier, *Subjectivities: A History of Self-Representation in Britain, 1832–1920* (New York: Oxford University Press, 1991). See also my book, *Comrades and Partners: The Shared Lives of Grace Hutchins and Anna Rochester* (Lanham, MD: Rowman and Littlefield, 2000).

16 J. A. Hobson, *Imperialism: A Study* (New York: J. Pott and Co., 1902); Catherine Hall, *Cultures of Empire: A Reader. Colonizers in Britain and the Empire in the Nineteenth and Twentieth Centuries* (Manchester: Manchester University Press, 2000); John MacKenzie (ed.), *Imperialism and Popular Culture* (Manchester: Manchester University Press, 1986) and *Propaganda and Empire: The Manipulation of British Public Opinion, 1880–1960* (Manchester: Manchester University Press, 1984). See also Anne Summers, 'Edwardian Militarism', in Raphael Samuel (ed.), *Patriotism: The Making and Unmaking of British National Identity* (London: Routledge, 1989).

17 John Terraine, *The Great War* (Ware, Hertfordshire: Wordsworth, 1998), p. 11.

18 MacKenzie, *Imperialism and Popular Culture*, p. 10. See also Samuel Hynes, *A War Imagined: The First World War and English Culture* (New York: Collier, 1990) for an extensive discussion of this cultural context at the eve of the First World War.

19 Quoted in John Stevenson's *British Society, 1914–1945* (London: Penguin, 1984), p. 49.

20 Macdonald, *The Roses of No Man's Land*, pp. 26–7.

21 Richard A. Soloway, *Demography and Degeneration: Eugenics and the Declining Birthrate in Twentieth-Century Britain* (Chapel Hill: University of North Carolina Press, 1990).

22 Jane Potter, '"A Great Purifier": The Great War in Women's Romances and Memoirs, 1914–1918', in Raitt and Tate (eds), *Women's Fiction and the Great War*, pp. 85–106.

23 Cited in Robert Wohl, *The Generation of 1914* (Cambridge, MA: Harvard University Press, 1979), p. 89.

24 Alice Meynell, 'Summer in England, 1914', in Reilly (ed.), *The Virago Book of Women's War Poetry*, pp. 73-4.

25 Judith Kazantsis, 'Preface', in Reilly (ed.), *The Virago Book of Women's War Poetry*, p. xxv.

26 Mary H. J. Henderson, 'An Incident', in Reilly (ed.), *The Virago Book of Women's War Poetry*, p. 52. Another poem in this genre is Lucy Whinemell's 'Christ in Flanders', reprinted in the same collection, p. 127.

27 Vera Brittain used this symbolism. See Alan Bishop and Terry Smart (eds), *Chronicle of Youth: War Diary 1913–17* (London: Gollancz, 1981). See also Janet Montefiore, '"Shining Pins and Wailing Shells": Women Poets and the Great War', in Goldman (ed.), *Women and World War I*, pp. 51–72. May Wedderburn Cannan's poems 'Lamplight', and 'Rouen' reprinted in Reilly (ed.), *The Virago Book of Women's War Poetry*, pp. 16–18, demonstrate this Christian imperialism. Australian writer Mabel Brookes wrote three war novels that were preoccupied with maintaining white supremacy. See Jan Bassett, '"Untravelled Minds": The War Novels of Mabel Brookes', in Goldman (ed.), *Women and World War I*, pp. 113–27.

28 Tylee, *The Great War and Women's Consciousness*, p. 38.
29 Texts that focus on the relationship between the war, psychology and culture include Reginald Pound, *The Lost Generation* (London: Constable, 1964); Paul Fussell, *The Great War and Modern Memory* (Oxford: Oxford University Press, 1975); Hynes, *A War Imagined*; Eric J. Leed, *No Man's Land: Combat and Identity in World War I* (Cambridge: Cambridge University Press, 1979); Wohl, *The Generation of 1914*; Ellis Hawley, *The Great War and the Search for a Modern Order* (New York: St Martin's Press, 1992); and Modris Eksteins, *Rites of Spring: The Great War and the Birth of the Modern Age* (New York: Anchor Doubleday, 1990). Also see J. M. Winter, *The Great War and the British People* (Houndsmills, Hampshire: Macmillan, 1986) and Jay Winter and Blaine Baggett, *The Great War and the Shaping of the Twentieth Century* (New York: Penguin, 1996). For a focus on European culture and the arts in the First World War see Aviel Roshwald and Richard Stites (eds), *European Culture in the Great War: The Arts, Entertainment, and Propaganda, 1914–1918* (Cambridge: Cambridge University Press, 1999).
30 Wohl, *The Generation of 1914*; Hynes, *A War Imagined*.
31 Catherine Reilly makes this point in her introduction to *The Virago Book of Women's War Poetry*, p. vii.
32 J. M. Winter, *Sites of Memory, Sites of Mourning: The Great War in European Cultural History* (Cambridge: Cambridge University Press, 1995). He looks at the British response to the war through memorials and eulogies and focuses on the continuities of Edwardian cultural tropes of meaning in the postwar era in the ways the war has popularly been remembered.
33 Joanna Bourke, *Dismembering the Male: Men's Bodies, Britain and the Great War* (Chicago: University of Chicago Press, 1996) and *An Intimate History of Killing: Face-to-Face Killing in Twentieth Century Warfare* (London: Basic Books, 1999).
34 As Melman writes in her introduction to *Borderlines*, total war involves 'not only the varying degrees of mobilization of the Western home front, but also occupation, the dislocation of civilians, and degrees of persecution – both random and systematic' (p. 4). This gendered perspective blurs the borderlines between 'front' and 'rear'. Note that the British historical perspective has exacerbated these divisions between the battle and home fronts since Great Britain was not under military occupation and its civilian populations were not dislocated and turned into refugees. In addition, it is probably safe to say that the emphasis of women historians (and, indeed, of my book too) to focus on the feminine equivalent of the combatant male – ambulance drivers and nurses – tends to reinscribe these distinctions between home and battlefront in the determination to locate women in the latter.
35 Tylee, *The Great War and Women's Consciousness*, p. 8.
36 For a sample of the books that focus on masculine voices in wartime see the following books and anthologies of poetry of the war: E. L. Black (ed.), *1914–18 in Poetry* (London: Hodder and Stoughton, 1970); Brian Gardner (ed.), *Up the Line to Death: The War Poets 1914–18* (London: Metheun, 1964); Maurice Hussey (ed.), *Poetry of the First World War* (London: Longmans, 1967); I. M. Parsons (ed.), *Men Who March Away: Poems of the First World War* (London: Heinemann, 1965); Martin Stephen (ed.), *Never Such Innocence: A New Anthology of Great War Verse* (London: Buchanan and Enright, 1988); Jon Silkin (ed.), *The Penguin Book of First World War Poetry* (Harmondsworth: Penguin, 1979, rep. 1981); Peter Vansittart (ed.), *Voices from the Great War* (Harmondsworth: Penguin, 1983); and John Lehman, *English Poets of the First World War* (London: Thames and Hudson, 1981). Academic analysis of soldier

poetry and writing include Bernard Bergonzi, *Heroes' Twilight: A Study of the Literature of the Great War* (London: Constable, 1965, rep. 1980); Stanley Cooperman, *World War I and the American Novel* (London: Johns Hopkins University Press, 1967, rep. 1970); M. Greicus, *Prose Writers of World War One* (London: Longmans, 1973); J. H. Johnston, *English Poetry of the First World War* (Princeton, NJ: Princeton University Press, 1964); and Holger Klein (ed.), *Promise of Greatness: The War of 1914–18* (London: Cassell, 1968).

For discussions of the home front see Arthur Marwick, *The Explosion of British Society 1914–62* (London: Pan, 1963) and *The Deluge: British Society and the First World War* (London: Bodley Head, 1965). The Imperial War Museum's 1977 exhibition on the role of women in the war was very influential in educating about women's wartime roles. Another book by Arthur Marwick coincided with this exhibition: *Women at War, 1914–1918* (London: Fontana, 1977). An accessible overview of women in the First World War is Gill Thomas's *Life on All Fronts* (Cambridge University Press, 1989).

37 Peggy McCracken, 'The Amenorrhea of War', *Signs: Journal of Women in Culture and Society* 28: 2 (2002), 625.

38 For women working in domestic industries see Deborah Thom, *Nice Girls and Rude Girls: Women Workers in World War I* (London: I. B. Tauris, 1998); Gail Braybon, *Women Workers in the First World War: The British Experience* (London: Croom Helm, 1981); Gail Braybon and Penny Summerfield, *Out of the Cage: Women's Experiences in Two World Wars* (London: Pandora, 1987); and Claire A. Cullerton, *Working-Class Culture, Women, and Britain, 1914–1922* (New York: St Martin's Press, 1999). *On Her Their Lives Depend: Munitions Workers in the Great War* (Berkeley: University of California Press, 1994) by Angela Woollacott documents the lives of munition workers.

39 Robert, 'Gender, Class and Patriotism', pp. 52–3.

40 Jenny Gould, 'Women's Military Services in First World War Britain', in Higonnet et al. (eds), *Behind the Lines*, pp. 114–25; Julia Cowper, *A Short History of Queen Mary's Army Auxiliary Corps* (Guildford, 1967); K. Beauman, *Partners in Blue: The Story of Women's Service with the Royal Air Force* (London: Leo Cooper, 1971); Ursula Mason, *Britannia's Daughters: The Story of the Women's Royal Navy Service* (London: Leo Cooper, 1977).

41 Robert, 'Gender, Class and Patriotism', p. 53.

42 Marwick, *The Deluge*; Gordon Wright, *The Ordeal of Total War* (New York: Harper and Row, 1968).

43 Sandra Gilbert, 'Soldier's Heart: Literary Men, Literary Women, and the Great War', *Signs: Journal of Women in Culture and Society* 8: 3 (1983), 422–50, 425. See also Sandra Gilbert and Susan Gubar, *No Man's Land: The Place of the Woman Writer in the Twentieth Century* (London: Yale University Press, 1987).

44 Such memoirs and travel writing include Kate Finzi, *Eighteen Months in the War Zone: A Record of a Woman's Work on the Western Front* (London: Cassell, 1916); May Sinclair, *A Journal of Impressions in Belgium* (New York: Macmillan, 1915); Enid Bagnold, *A Dairy Without Dates* (London: Heinemann, 1918, rep. Virago, 1978); and *The Happy Foreigner* (London: Heinemann, 1920, rep. Virago, 1987); Rebecca West, *War Nurse: The True Story of a Women Who Lived, Loved, and Suffered on the Western Front* (New York: Cosmopolitan Book Corporation, 1930); Helen Zenna Smith (a.k.a. Evadne Price), *Not So Quiet*; and Mary Borden, *The Forbidden Zone* (London: Heinemann, 1929). *Nurses at the Front: Writing the Wounds of the Great War* (Boston: Northeastern University Press, 2001), edited by Margaret R. Higonnet, focuses on the writings of

Mary Borden and Ellen N. La Motte. La Motte wrote *The Backwash of War*, originally published in 1916 by G. P. Putnam's Sons, New York.

    See Vera Brittain, *Testament of Youth* for the classic pacifist account of the war written by a woman, as well as Ann Wiltshire, *Most Dangerous Women: Feminist Peace Campaigners of the Great War* (London: Pandora, 1985). Lyn Bicker, 'Public and Private Choices: Public and Private Voices', in Goldman (ed.), *Women and World War I*, pp. 92–112, writes about the work of pacifist Helena Swanwick. See also Swanwick's autobiography, *I Have Been Young* (London: Gollancz, 1935).

45 For a summary of this literature see Melman (ed.), *Borderlines*, pp. 1–25. Braybon makes this point in *Women Workers in the First World War*, as does Margaret H. Darrow in *French Women and the First World War: War Stories of the Home Front* (New York: Oxford University Press, 2000) and Michelle Perrot in 'The New Eve and the Old Adam: French Women's Condition at the Turn of the Century', in Higonnet et al. (eds), *Behind the Lines*, pp. 51–60. Referring to the US experience, Leila Rupp in *Mobilizing Women for War: German and American Propaganda, 1939–1945* (Princeton: Princeton University Press, 1978) also emphasizes that no real changes in women's status occurred as a result of the Second World War.

46 Kathleen Kennedy focuses on the state's role in enforcing patriotic motherhood *in Disloyal Mothers and Scurrilous Citizens: Women and Subversion During World War I* (Bloomington, IN: Indiana University Press, 1999). See also Jean Bethke Elshtain, *Women and War* (New York: Basic Books, 1987).

47 Since munitions factories were key sites for enemy shelling, they were often very dangerous places to work. In addition, munitions work often involved contact with such hazardous chemicals as TNT. Workers who had TNT poisoning were referred to as 'canaries' because it turned their skin yellow. See Cullerton, *Working-Class Culture*, p. 81.

48 See Barbara Caine, *English Feminism, 1780–1980* (Oxford: Oxford University Press, 1997), pp. 178–82; and Sandra Stanley Holton, *Feminism and Democracy: Women's Suffrage and Reform Politics in Britain, 1900–1918* (New York: Cambridge University Press, 1986). In 'Politicians and the Women's Vote, 1914–18', *History* 59 (1974), 372, Martin Pugh writes that 'when one remembers that the 1918 Act actually enfranchised boys of nineteen if they had served in the forces, the limit on women was almost an insult'. In 1918 only women over thirty years of age were enfranchised and the vote was not extended to women over twenty-one years until 1921. See also Pugh's *The March of Women: A Revisionist Analysis of the Campaign for Women's Suffrage, 1866–1914* (Oxford: Oxford University Press, 2002). In *The Cause* (London: 1928, rep. Virago, 1978), Ray Strachey links women's role in the war with the franchise for women, using information from the writings of suffragist Millicent Fawcett, President of the National Union of Woman Suffrage Societies (NUWSS). However, Sylvia Pankhurst's account in *The Home Front* (London: Hutchinson, 1932, rep. 1987) suggests that the war did not hasten the franchise and it has been argued that woman suffrage would have come sooner had the war not occurred. Steven Hause in 'More Minerva than Mars: The French Women's Rights Campaign and the First World War', in Higonnet et al (eds), *Behind the Lines*, pp. 99–113, makes this point about the French experience. For a succinct account of the double bind experienced by the suffragettes who might abhor war yet feel the need to be patriotic and support men, as well as the political lead-up to the war in terms of suffrage activity, see Lyn Bicker in Goldman (ed.), *Women and World War I*, pp. 94–5.

49 Jane Marcus, 'The Asylums of Antaeus: Women, War, and Madness – Is There a Fem-

inist Fetishism?', in H. Aram Veeser (ed.), *The New Historicism* (London, 1990), pp. 140–1.

50 Higonnet et al., 'Introduction', in Higonnet et al. (eds), *Behind the Lines*, p. 6. See also Margaret Higonnet and Patrice L.-R. Higonnet, 'The Double Helix', in the same collection, pp. 31–47.

51 Penny Summerfield, 'Gender and War in the Twentieth Century', *The International History Review* 19: 1 (1997), 5. See also Summerfield, *Reconstructing Women's Wartime Lives*, ch. 1.

52 See Maureen Healey, 'Becoming Austrian: Women, the State, and Citizenship in World War I', *Central European History* 35: 1 (2002), 1–35, for a discussion of the complexity of citizenship for women (and for Austrian women in particular) during this period.

53 Grace McDougall, 'Five Years with the Allies, 1914–1919: The Story of the FANY Corps', p. 1. [IWM]

1

Aristocratic amazons in arms
The founding of the FANY
1907–14

In 1908 the London *Daily Graphic* featured a new ladies' volunteer organization in training to provide first aid to the fallen heroes of the battlefield. It was
the First Aid Nursing Yeomanry (FANY) and they were starting to attract
public attention. Alongside the newsworthiness of women breaking new
ground, many FANY had aristocratic connections and a good number were
young and attractive and looked quite dashing in their uniforms. As a result,
the press loved to cover their activities and often sensationalized their exploits:
'A mere male member of the staff yesterday invaded the sanctum of the First
Aid Nursing Yeomanry Corps', wrote the *Daily Graphic* reporter, giving the
password to the 'pretty sentinel' and finding himself among a 'busy band of
aristocratic amazons in arms'.[1] Alongside such popular titillation, this excerpt
illustrates the anxiety and condescension among 'mere males' for 'aristocratic
amazons' who dare to tread on masculine turf. It also portrays the masculine
desire to return to normal gendered relations with the mention of the 'pretty'
sentinel at the door.

The FANY were organizing themselves as an independent paramilitary
organization to aid in the nation's defence through the transportation of the
wounded and the administering of first aid. They saw themselves riding into
areas of potential fighting, stabilizing the wounded, and transporting them to
regimental aid posts or first aid facilities. Imagine this in 1908: a paramilitary
group of women, daring to claim expertise to enter the war zone. Here were
several dozen women who might more likely be found in the fashionable
London shops or at debutante balls, subverting masculine space. What kinds
of cultural changes were happening to make space for such developments, and
how were these women able to use their class privilege and modify existing
notions of gender and militarism in order to practise such behaviours? This
chapter addresses these questions by exploring the first theme of the book, the
ways the FANY utilized and subverted traditional notions of genteel femininity. It explores the origins of the FANY and historicizes their founding in the
social and cultural forces of the day.

Edwardian womanhood and the call to service

Edwardian society was stratified into relatively rigid classes with a small number of powerful elites, a growing middle class, and a large mass of working people. The upper-class gentry included the great landed families of the aristocracy who owned the greater part of Britain through their land holdings and inherited titles, the landed gentry with substantial holdings, and the lesser gentry or squires with less extensive estates. The middle class or *bourgeoisie* included the wealthy upper-middle class or *haute bourgeoisie* who were involved in finance and commerce and often intermarried with the aristocracy and landed gentry; the wealthy industrialists who tended to have a less cosy relationship with the elites and were mostly in the cities in the north; the middle class of more modest means that included various professionals and clergy; and the lower-middle class of shopkeepers and small business owners, teachers and clerks. The working classes made up about 75 percent of the population and included craft and trades workers, industrial and farm labourers, miners, mill, foundry and factory workers, laundresses, and domestic servants.[2] A key feature of the Edwardian era involved the fusing of the landed elite with the *nouveaux riches* from industry and commerce.[3] Another feature was the huge divide between the wealthy and the poor, exacerbated by increasing urbanization, the economic depression that characterized the period between 1873 and 1896 and the tapering off of real wages after the turn of the century. While Chartism and various Reform Bills of the late nineteenth century had produced a gradual extension of the franchise, property holding and residence requirements meant that in 1911 less than 30 per cent of the adult population was enfranchised and political power was invariably held by landowning elites and wealthy industrialists.[4] Of course although women were members of the middle and upper classes, their power was circumscribed by the social relations of gender during this period.[5]

According to ideal notions of late-nineteenth-century womanhood, feminine nature was passive, submissive, emotional, irrational and self-sacrificing: ideals deeply rooted in biological, anthropological and medical theories of innate female inferiority. They justified woman's 'natural' concern with reproduction and mothering and made the case for her subordinate position in society. Female illness was invariably diagnosed as problems associated with women's reproductive organs at the same time that sexual attitudes encouraging female ignorance, chastity and the double standard of sexual conduct were well-entrenched. 'Scientific' theories, while being barely-disguised justification for patriarchal domination, circumscribed women's lives squarely within the confines of domesticity: the home was a haven, separate from the vicissitudes of the public world.[6] Although recent scholarship has challenged the impermeability of separate gendered spheres of existence, it is still true that women were encouraged to remain in relatively separate areas of gendered activity that placed their legal and political identity in relation to husbands, fathers and sons. Important differences of course existed in the construction of ideal femininity for economically privileged as opposed to working-class women with the former being seen as delicate, fragile, more sensitive, and more morally advanced than their working-class sisters. It was these essentialized, biologically based qualities that made women unfit for war, yet 'experts in nurturing and "drying tears"'.[7] Women came to represent home, security, and the good things in life for which men were willing to fight.

Men on the other hand were understood as naturally fitted for the demands of the public world, industry, and of course the battlefield, although men of the landed gentry preserved and justified their power through styles and codes of behaviour that encouraged leisure and often disdained involvement in industry. As new peerages were granted to men whose fortunes had been made in commerce and manufacturing and the sons of the wealthy industrialists were educated at elite public schools, more men from the upper levels of the middle class aspired to become 'gentlemen' with lives patterned on the basic premises of assured income and leisure. In this process 'culture' replaced the hereditary principle and provided 'the terms in which social and economic differences were encoded'.[8] This was true also for women whose family wealth was not of the 'old' inherited kind but still were launched into Society (with a capital 'S') and learned skills associated with managing large households with many servants and entertaining with appropriate style and glamour. The middle classes were especially vulnerable to aspirations of 'respectability' associated with the ideal notions of femininity and often placed a very high premium on feminine moral purity, working hard to 'keep up appearances' even though this might stretch their economic resources.

This ideology of the 'womanly woman' was being contested by the turn of the century and never adequately described the real lives of most Edwardian women. First, almost 40 per cent of women in 1900 were involved in paid labour (mostly very low paid, depressed by the concept of the 'family wage' that assumed women were taken care of by a man's wage). Most British women during this period (as they are today) were members of the working class and toiled inside and outside the home to provide for their families, often in the face of great poverty. A large majority of working-class women worked in domestic service and many worked in the mills and factories of industrial cities.[9] For lower-middle-class women there was some widening of employment opportunities as a consequence of technological advancements like the typewriter and telephone and the expansion of an economy that needed more white-collar workers.[10]

Ideal notions of 'the angel in the house' were also contested by the acceptance of companionate marriage among some groups where spouses functioned as potential partners/companions and there was a movement away from the rigid patriarchal spousal union that kept privileged women in the separate sheltered domestic sphere.[11] Campaigns to extend women's rights in marriage were also important in the transformation of women's lives: the Married Women's Property Act of 1882 removed much of the common law disabilities associated with married women owning property, and earnings and legislation made divorce accessible for middle-class women and later facilitated legal separation and maintenance for abused wives. In addition, in 1907 (the year the FANY was formed) the Qualification of Women Act allowed women to take such public office as chair, alderman, or mayor on local, county or borough councils. The backdrop to all this was the ongoing organized resistance to women's inferior status through various suffrage campaigns and the claim for the full citizenship of women.[12]

Educational opportunities for women also contested the separate-spheres ideology of the Victorian period as women claimed their right to education, if only to be better wives and mothers. The Education Acts through the late nineteenth and early-twentieth century that attempted to consolidate education for the working classes helped foster some awareness of girls' education. In 1900, full-time schooling was compulsory for all girls aged five to twelve years, although working-class girls tended to enter the workplace (most often as domestic servants) soon thereafter. Young upper- and upper-middle-class Edwardian girls moved between the nurseries and schoolrooms of their parental homes, taught by governesses and sometimes sharing a tutor with the offspring of other privileged families; others attended exclusive day or boarding schools for young ladies.[13] The less affluent middle classes also tended to educate their daughters at home and some might attend a variety of independent schools.[14] The development of women's colleges in the late nineteenth century also opened doors to some women. The number of women students in British universities rose after the 1890s with the development of teacher education and women's colleges. Women were not admitted as members of Oxford and Cambridge (or conferred degrees until 1920 and 1948 respectively), although women could take classes and degree examinations and were affiliated with the women's colleges at these universities from the late nineteenth century onwards.[15]

These social and cultural changes helped create the phenomenon of the 'New Woman', a discursive obsession with the crisis of gender. She triggered anxiety about the instability of women's domestic destiny and the 'new women' themselves (educated, independent, and critical of the social and economic constraints of marriage) were often caricatured as 'blue stockings', dried-up 'old maids' or, alternatively, whores.[16] Despite these cultural anxieties, the New Woman or *femme nouvelle* provided new templates for women and challenged the notion that women's maternal role was a biological imperative.

In this way, while the middle-class ideal of femininity inherited from the Victorian era might locate respectable womanhood in the leisured activities of the domestic household and see it as unnatural for women to function outside this sphere except in the role of hostess and philanthropist, in reality the extension of women's rights and the structural and economic changes associated with industrialization and urbanization loosened bonds of family and kinship and were eroding spheres of public/masculine and private/feminine activity and beginning to transform what women might negotiate for themselves as they sought to enter the public world. Jessica Gerard has made the case that upper-class women of the landed classes were not useless, decorative creatures but instead relatively autonomous and hard-working members of a vibrant community that relied on their skills in management and philanthropy.[17] Following M. Jeanne Peterson who challenges the stereotype of Victorian women and emphasizes the ways gentlewomen moved outside feminine spheres, Gerard suggests that birth and rank allowed some women access to estate management and politics. In addition, their expected role as 'Lady Bountiful' meant that upper- and upper-middle-class women were very engaged in social work and often ran various institutions for the poor and needy.[18] This work was seen as the obligation of landed women and an extension of their 'natural' role as guardians of the moral order.

Another opportunity for upper-middle- and upper-class women that allowed a small few some freedom was driving the new motor cars starting to frequent the British roads at the turn of the century. In his study of the consumption of the car and its social impact on British society, Sean O'Connell emphasizes the ways class and gender relations were inscribed on this machine. Motoring was a relatively elite activity in Edwardian England and few could afford the purchase and upkeep associated with automobiles. In addition, motoring's focus on machines and technology produced it as a masculine activity and the physically exacting tasks of using a starting handle or mending a puncture were assumed to be off-limits to women. There were also social pressures to relegate women to the passenger seat: the car's 'arrival at the time of great controversy over the issues of women's place in society, with the debate over women's suffrage raging, made the woman driver a powerful

symbol of potential equality.'[19] Still, some women in families privileged
enough to own a motor car learned to drive and learned new skills that would
frame their service in the war and in society.

As middle- and upper-class women moved increasingly into the public
arena they justified their work as a reflection of the essentialized feminine
attributes of care and domesticity, extending these into a form of 'municipal
housekeeping' or 'civic' or 'social maternalism'. Feminine virtues were thus
broadened from the nurturance and management of the family, household and
local community to society at large and the traits associated with femininity
were translated into a call for public service. In this way full-time social work
'provided an acceptable sublimation for many women of ambitions otherwise
thwarted'.[20] Women served in local government and on school boards where
they helped run local charities and worked in volunteer social agencies,
stretching rather than breaking the parameters of normative gender relations
and claiming rather than rejecting traditional notions of femininity.

Given the ideals associated with Edwardian womanhood, it is not surprising that women's duty in wartime was the care and service of the home and
family and the giving of life and not its taking: a feminine patriotism where
sons were birthed, offered and sacrificed in the name of Empire (or what Margaret Darrow in the French context has named 'spartan motherhood').[21] While
working-class women of course might also be expected to work in the factories
and other industries, more privileged women could claim the acceptance of
voluntary social work and extend this into charitable war service: raising
funds, collecting supplies for hospitals and agencies, helping refugees and
needy soldiers and knitting woollens. The other option for women seeking a
'respectable' place in the war effort was nursing, although this had not always
been the case.

Nursing was one profession that allowed women service opportunities
while still maintaining this guardian angel role; still, there had long been negative connotations associated with the profession, especially in terms of its
association with the military. This was because many paid nurses were drawn
from the lower-working class, hospitals were often squalid, inhospitable places
to work and much manual labour was involved. In addition, nursing required
women to perform personalized services in the care of male strangers' bodies
at a time when a high proportion of men in military hospitals were admitted
with venereal disease. These realities prevented 'respectable' women from
seeking these roles.[22] Prior to the First World War, while most wounded soldiers were cared for by male orderlies, paid female nurses were sometimes
attached to military services and army wives did their share of nursing. On the
whole, the number of women in military hospitals throughout the nineteenth

and early-twentieth century was low. However, Florence Nightingale's work during the Crimean War and the development of Queen Alexandra's Imperial Military Nursing Service that replaced the Army Nursing Service in 1902 did much to change these negative connotations and helped nursing develop as a field where women of all classes worked, participating through a variety of medical, philanthropic and religious movements for the care of the sick, including, to some extent, the military.

The cultural model used to persuade British authorities to consider middle- and upper-class women as military nurses was again the manipulation of the genteel feminine virtues associated with 'Lady Bountiful' and the replication of the middle- and upper-class domestic household: nurses would show deference to the male boards of governors, doctors and surgeons ('husbands'), supervise the work of the lower-class male orderlies ('servants'), and care for wounded soldiers ('children'). As another variation of social maternalism or civic housekeeping, this role allowed these women to experience the adventures and opportunities of the public sphere without overly disturbing the moral order. It enabled them to imagine combining the feminine and the patriotic in ways that did not transgress Edwardian notions of womanly behaviour and might help the nation in time of need.

Although it is important not to overestimate the presence of professional and volunteer nurses in military positions during the Edwardian period, there were cultural changes afoot that helped provide a context for an increased acceptance of women military nursing staff. These included threats to Empire and generalized insecurities concerning military readiness as well as deeper anxieties about the state of British manhood. In some areas of Britain half of all men who attempted to enlist in 1897 at the start of the Boer War were declared physically unfit for service. The near-defeat in South Africa and various invasion scares encouraged a popular movement for readying the nation in case of war and called for male military conscription and an 'arms-bearing' notion of citizenship.[23] These cultural anxieties helped facilitate the passing of the Territorial and Reserve Forces Act of 1907, hoping to ready the nation in case of invasion and helping found the Territorial Forces Nursing Service (TFNS) and the Voluntary Aid Detachments (VAD). The TFNS and VAD movements established the presence of volunteer nurses in Britain to care for wounded citizens and reflected the growing understanding of the likelihood of total war where all citizens would be involved as well as combatant soldiers. New technologies of militarism, the increase in war's scope and scale, and increasing tensions in Europe as the new century progressed, all encouraged the development of this notion of total war, and opened a space for the consideration of how women might best serve the Empire.

Yeomanry to the rescue

This discussion of the ideals of Edwardian femininity and the role of middle- and upper-class women in the public sphere is central in understanding the context for the founding of the FANY in 1907, as is the transformation of military nursing as an appropriate venue for such women. In addition, while the nationalist arms-bearing notion of citizenship discussed above helped encourage nursing as a component of territorial defence, it also helped mobilize yeomanry groups and various kinds of nationalist youth and adult organizations.[24] This was a time when a discourse of bravery, heroism and glory in battle abounded and the idea of working for 'King and Country' tapped intense loyalty and patriotism. Yeomanry groups were imagined in this scenario as volunteer cavalry forces aiding the nation's defence.[25] The Yeoman of the Guard attended and defended the British sovereign and royal family and the British Yeomanry was a volunteer cavalry unit that was incorporated into the Territorial Army in its defence of the Empire. It is important to emphasize that the FANY imagined themselves not merely as a nursing corps but as an independent paramilitary 'yeomanry' group whose job was to rescue the wounded as well as administer first aid. As such they combined the notions of a volunteer cavalry force with their role as nurses into the job of ambulance transport. Eventually horses would be replaced by motorized vehicles, but it was the mounted, cavalry aspect of their work that framed their yeomanry organization. Yeomanry groups had a tradition of being male; it was here that the FANY were transgressing gender. Mary Baxter-Ellis, FANY Commanding Officer from 1932 to 1947, summed this up on the occasion of the FANY Jubilee in 1957 when the organization celebrated fifty years of service:

The FANY Corps, that small pioneering band of women, was created out of the Old World. It belonged to the age of the horse. Its members, primarily horsewomen, took as their standard the *élan* and daring of their cavalry and hunting fathers and brothers. To this fundamental characteristic they added the very feminine idealism centred round that great Victorian heroine, Florence Nightingale; and made of the combination something quite new – a Mobile Unit of mounted nurses and first-aiders.[26]

Yeomanry groups during this period were connected in spirit and motivation to the Edwardian youth movement and its focus on preparation for service through healthy forms of exercise and summer camps. Formed to masculinize male youths it also had the unforeseen consequences of masculinizing some girls too. Designed to regenerate the nation and maintain readiness in case of war, the male youth movement also hoped to contain potential working-class militancy as the threat of socialism grew. These groups had their ori-

gins in the cultural perception that modern social and national life had a dis-
integrating and decaying effect on the British character, and men were at risk
of becoming soft, selfish and undisciplined: the same cultural anxieties associated with the call-for-arms notion of citizenship that facilitated defence in case
of invasion and the build-up for war. Alongside political threats to the status
quo from labour and suffragist movements, fear was also generated by changes
in the nature of work and in the gender of the worker. As the expanding middle
class settled into white collar, sedentary positions that discouraged such traits
as independence and self-reliance, the forces of industrialization and bureau-
cratization reduced opportunities for entrepreneurship, risk-taking and other
'masculine' ventures, and women were entering the labour force in expanded
numbers. On an individual level, these perceived forces of feminization
included the closer mother–son relationship (resulting from both the profes-
sionalization and sanctification of motherhood and the reduction in the
number of servants who might buffer this relationship) and the increase in
numbers of women teaching young males in the schools and in higher education. If modern life was encouraging women to act more like men, then misog-
ynous fears that men might become more like women were a widespread
concern.

Boys' organizations like the Boy Scouts and the Boys' Brigade were
formed to counter these forces of feminization and maintain traditional
British manhood.[27] They taught traditional virtues of courage, bravery and
chivalry through outdoor pursuits aimed at building a rugged endurance
among male youth. Boys wore pseudo-military uniforms and learned to
march, drill and carry rifles.[28] Ironically, while the scouting movement was
picking up pace and attempting to re-masculinize men and boys, girls' groups
(such as the Girls' Guildry, the Girl Scouts and the Girls' Life Brigade) were
also founded. The Girls' Guildry was the first, established in 1900 with a mission to develop 'capacities of womanly helpfulness' in adolescent girls.[29] However like the girls' youth groups that would come later, although the focus was
on teaching the feminine arts of home nursing and hygiene, they also required
quasi-military uniform, marching and drill instruction. The Girl Scout
groups were the most popular and their ranks soon swelled. Modelled after the
Boy Scouts founded by Baden-Powell, the girls were initially involved in
scouting activities and healthy outdoor recreation. Since this was not what the
leaders of the boys' scouting movement had anticipated, the Girl Scouts was
transformed and co-opted by Baden-Powell and his sister Agnes Baden-Powell
into the Girl Guides: a movement that would not disrupt existing gender hierarchies and would instead function to reinforce traditional gender socialization through the teaching of womanly skills. The Girl Guides thus became a

way to impose character training on girls and help them to become better mothers and wives for 'the future manhood of the country'.[30] Indeed, Agnes Baden-Powell's *The Handbook of the Girl Guides* revealed its gender and class-based motives with the subtitle *How Girls Can Help to Build Up the Empire*.[31]

Many girls were disappointed by this co-optation; they had formed scouting groups modelled on the boys' groups and looked forward to being involved in outdoor fun. 'Having been Peewits and Kangaroos, we thought it a great come-down to become White Roses and Lilies-of-the-Valley' recalled one former Girl Guide in Rose Kerr's *The Story of the Girl Guides*.[32] Nonetheless, despite the intent of the authorities, the popularity of scouting and yeomanry groups trickled down into the popular culture, and girls, especially those privileged girls who had been raised to ride and follow the hunt, took to it immediately, recognizing possible adventures and horsey amusements they might pursue. Given the ideals associated with Edwardian womanhood, it made sense that girls might want to escape the constraints of this normative femininity. Whether in the form of scouting groups or horse-back riding nursing yeomanry, these groups gave young women opportunities to experience fun and adventure while still remain within the confines of duty and service.

The formation of the FANY as a yeomanry group also represented the ways that, in order to compensate for men's perceived softness, 'the right sort of women' were allowed to be strong.[33] It was precisely the middle- and upper-class origins of these women that allowed them to be part of a re-masculinization process. They had ties to the aristocratic and military establishment and their political ideologies were non-threatening in grounding their service in devotion to the Empire. As such they were able to soften the disruption of gendered social hierarchies: they were allies in the patriotic call for service to keep Britain and the Empire strong. Still, even with these alliances, the FANY risked transgressing notions of appropriate womanly behaviour in forming themselves as a yeomanry corps. Activities where women stepped outside traditional bounds of 'womanly' behaviour, as Susan Grayzel explains, were invariably interpreted as linked to women's struggle for political rights as well as to issues of morality and sexuality.[34]

'Fresh laurels for the brow of womanhood': FANY is born

It was Captain Edward Baker, an eccentric ex-cavalryman, who formed the FANY Corps in 1907 with visions of courageous horsewomen in scarlet uniform galloping side-saddle onto the battlefield to tend to the wounded and transport them to military dressing stations.[35] His idea was born out of personal experience in the Boer War where saddle horses had the best chances of reaching wounded soldiers before the slower horse-drawn ambulance wagons on the harsh terrain of the South African veldt. Baker had been wounded and knew these delays meant high rates of mortality.[36] In preparation for their role, Baker helped train the FANY in cavalry drills, horse-drawn ambulance driving, signalling, stretcher bearing, first aid and camp protocol. Future FANY Commanding Officer Grace Ashley-Smith remembered Baker as a 'bluff hearty man, very large, and with a strangely pale face and large fair moustache'. Ashley-Smith writes that after his military service in the Boer War, Baker had been a policeman, although when she met him he had 'something to do with Smithfield Meat Market'.[37] It is curious that a man of his status should be in a position to establish the Corps; if Ashley-Smith's description is accurate, he could hardly have been their social equal and it is perhaps because of this that he soon disappears from FANY history. The official FANY record here is murky and details have been lost; enough to say that Baker's leadership was relatively brief once his idea took form. Historical 'facts' are always represented through culturally constructed narratives with various layers of meaning and interpretation, and, true to form, the story about the eccentric Baker is one that has a central place in FANY legend.

Although Baker's vision for the FANY as galloping ambulances was remarkable, his fantasy for women's role in battle was grounded in traditional Edwardian notions of militarism and its discourse of gallantry, glory and heroism. The FANY uniform reflected this pageantry: a scarlet tunic with high collar and white braid facings, a navy blue bell-shaped skirt with three rows of white braid at the bottom, long enough to cover the feet, and a hard-topped scarlet hat with a shiny black peak. The women wore white gauntlet gloves and carried riding crops or small canes as well as white first aid haversacks (backpacks). The mess uniform for official occasions consisted of a short scarlet jacket with pale blue facings worn over a white muslin dress with a scarlet sash. Uniform is important to all military organizations, and, in this case, alongside the uniformity created by subduing expressions of individuality into the collective and the taming of femininity through military attire, the choice of a relatively flamboyant, dashing uniform reflected these Edwardian notions of military gallantry and gave the Corps a certain identity as an adventurous and aristocratic organization. Such an identity was no doubt attractive to potential recruits. These recruits had to be at least 5ft 3in tall and between seventeen and thirty-five years of age.

A 1910 statement by Baker about the Corps in the FANY magazine *Women and War* provides insight into the ways he both relied upon and sought to change Edwardian notions of femininity. Baker's words (and his predilection for capital or upper-case emphasis) capture the curious tangle of romance and realism embedded in his vision for the Corps:

The Corps, which is the first of its kind, was established to point the way to all loyal and patriotic women who desire to work under the Red Cross Flag, and here I would like to say it is

MY FERVENT WISH

that the day is not far distant when every women in Britain will belong to one or other of the movements which work under the influence of that flag. It has no other object than the succouring of the wounded on the field of battle, and will be

THE CONNECTING LINK

between the fighting units and the base, where the work of the Field Nurses will go on as it always has done. It does not desire to take the place of any existing force, but to undergo special training so that the influence of the base will be extended. Each member of the Corps receives, besides a thorough training in First Aid work, signalling and camp work, a thorough drilling in cavalry movements, so that when the necessity arises, she and her sister nurses can ride with the skirmishing parties, take their chances with them, and, if spared to do the work for which they enlist – to attend to the wounded soldiers who otherwise might be left to a lingering death on the field of battle. It is a great work to ask of a woman, but history has shewn us that where deeds of heroism were to be done, women have ever been in the fore-front, and as one who has watched the work of women who in peace have banded themselves under our aegis, I can say confidently that should ever the horrors of war loom on our horizon

THEY SHALL NOT SHIRK

the task in front of them, but will ride forward with stout hearts and willing hands to render a great service to our country and gain fresh laurels for the brow of womanhood.[38]

If Baker's understanding of war was sentimental and essentially pre-modern, his model of femininity was at once both traditional and reflective of times to come. He was no doubt influenced by the iconography of Florence Nightingale and her devoted band of nurses: serene, efficient and offering voluntary aid to the wounded. Yet he was also before his time in offering a more dashing and efficacious vision of women aiding the wounded. Mounted on horseback (a little later modified to include the driving of horse-drawn ambulance wagons), dressed in bright scarlet tunics and voluminous skirts, his imagined Corps was involved in daring retrievals of the wounded and the deliverance of first aid to stabilize injured soldiers' condition. As such, while Baker's notion of femininity involved self-sacrifice and obeisance to military authority (he was keen not to be misunderstood and hoped to be 'cleared for all time' concerning the patriotic motives and respectability of the FANY), nonetheless, the Corps embodied a model of femininity that departed from traditional ideas of women's place in war.

This model departs from conventional notions in two interrelated ways. First, the FANY were to be present on the battlefield and must therefore be endowed with bravery and daring more associated with combatants than with any nurses hitherto envisioned by the Territorial Nursing Service and military authorities. Baker writes that the FANY can ride out on skirmishing parties and 'take their chances', and, 'if spared to do the work for which they enlist', can attend to wounded soldiers and so forth. He makes it quite clear that he envisions women within the dangerous fray of the battlefield and backs up his vision with the statement that 'wherever deeds of heroism were to be done, women have ever been in the fore-front'. In this way, women had an active military role: they were to 'enlist' and go out and seek the wounded, potentially under fire. In addition, the organization was run on paramilitary lines and was not a traditional nursing agency. Members accepted military rank and discipline, wore military style uniforms and referred to each other by their last names.

Second, FANY activities deviated from the traditional expectations of the fairer sex (and certainly from standard nursing duties) in their additional proficiencies in signalling, driving the large horse-drawn ambulance wagon, and camp preparation. Baker advocated that women take over this work in order to relieve men for combat duty. FANY recruits were taught fencing and shooting: previously masculine activities slowly opening up to economically privileged women with the time, money and motivation.[39] Indeed, an anonymous article titled 'The Training of Women to War', published in the FANY magazine a month after Baker's editorial, reports the training in rifle and revolver shooting associated with women's military service in Germany:

Every woman should be able to load and fire a revolver. In moments of danger there cannot always be one of the stronger sex at hand, and for our work especially, this would come in useful. Supposing a company of the FANY Corps were surprised while tending the wounded? Two of them with revolvers in their hands could keep the foe at bay whilst their comrades continued calmly to succour the helpless.[40]

While there is a perfunctory obeisance to the 'stronger sex' and a nod to devoted nurses calmly 'succouring' the wounded, the writer is making the case for women armed with revolvers who might 'keep the foe at bay'. Again, this is a remarkable case for women's expanded role in the military despite the profound naïveté associated with its claim.

The FANY responded to the inevitable resistance to these claims by grounding their call to service in an essentialized femininity of nurturance and a class-based rhetoric of patriotic duty. Established as a middle- and upper-class women's volunteer nursing Corps they were able to establish their credentials as a 'respectable' ladies' organization, helped by social and familial ties to various echelons of the British governing elite. Recruiting the 'right kind' of members was controlled by a potential 'trooper' (as new recruits were called) having to be introduced by an existing FANY member or patron. The FANY hoped to be at the disposal of the British government; their encroachment into masculine space, it was emphasized, was grounded in loyalty to King, country and Empire. Although patriotism was a key motive for the FANY and influenced their desire to prove their usefulness and courage, as Jennie Gould writes, at this time 'the idea that women might play roles other than those of nurse, knitter, or canteen organizer was not popular'.[41] Many found their behaviour quite inappropriate for genteel young women. Like the opponents of the Girl Guides who worried that this organization would 'deprive [girls] of every sort of maidenly modesty, and would lead to their rushing about the country with few clothes and few manners',[42] so the idea of young women in uniform performing regimental drill was to many not only absurd behaviour but morally suspect too. Maureen Healey similarly describes resistance to Austrian women volunteers whose activities were 'deeply troubling' and explains how they were accused of a 'laundry list of violations': 'they didn't display selflessness ([they were] adventure seeking); they were immoral ([like] prostitutes posing as office workers); they were frivolous ([suffered the effects of] novels and cinema); they did not dress like women ([they wore] uniforms); and they neglected key feminine duties ([they had] poor housekeeping)'.[43]

In addition, increased suffrage activity encouraged public resistance to the sight of women stepping outside normative constraints.[44] One FANY trooper remembered having stones thrown at them until their assailants realized they were not suffragettes.[45] As we shall see, while the FANY published no antagonism to the suffragettes and had much in common in terms of their desires for leadership and autonomy, like many other early women's volunteer corps, they were keen to rhetorically align their organization with the political and military elite and denied their activities might pose a political threat.[46] In this disavowal of political intent, the FANY were not alone. Groups like the Women's Emergency Corps (WEC) and the elite Women's Volunteer Reserve (WVR) also experienced resistance, and, like the FANY, denied any political motivations for their patriotic services and dissociated themselves from suffrage demands.[47] For example, as Grayzel writes: 'Differentiating the WVR from the militant suffragettes who "knocked" people down and from associations with the women's suffrage campaign, the leadership of the Reserve aligned the WVR with a different kind of politics, one based on military service.'[48] And although one might expect that demanding women's inclusion in the military might encourage suffragist thought and practice, as Anne Summers writes in her history of the British military nurse, *Angels and Citizens*, 'No matter where logical reasoning might lead, in practice there was no inevitable connection between female war service and female political equality.'[49] In this way, a careful rhetoric of patriotism and appeal to notions of genteel femininity was an important aspect of the Corps' identity and helped mould them as an organization distinct from those intent on upsetting the status quo.

Despite this careful rhetoric, a central aspect of the resistance encountered by the FANY resulted from their uniform. Even though during this early prewar period this uniform was very feminine and hardly attempted to mimic male dress, it did appropriate military style. By 1912 after the uniform was changed to a khaki tunic over divided long skirt and breeches, puttees, boots and solar topee hat (the uniform the FANY would wear throughout the war except for the later adoption of a soft gathered cap), they were looking decidedly more masculine, and initiated even more notice and criticism. Although women's wearing of uniform was sometimes written off as vanity or fashion and therefore trivialized and made the source of ridicule and jokes, it was also seen as potentially titillating to men 'by inviting them to reveal the truth about [the] body' and by the use of such gestures in the pornography of the period.[50] Grayzel writes that such anxiety about the changing social order was 'played out upon the mores and bodies of women'.[51]

Women who dared to wear khaki military-style uniform were also perceived as causing disrespect to men since khaki implied heroism and embodied male national service.[52] A *Ladies Pictorial* article, for example, explained that 'Never, surely, was there a time when we had greater reason or need to display respect to the trappings which mark men as the servants of their country, the soldiers of their king. Yet at this time when women are urging men to don this uniform, when they are rightly vaunting the glory and honour and distinction of wearing it, they themselves in many instances are rendering it ridiculous by adopting it for themselves and playing at soldiers.'[53] Indeed, a newspaper article from 1916 described the pre-war FANY as 'pariahs' struggling against ridicule whose uniform caused much disconcertion.[54] On one occasion uniformed FANY were seated behind a screen in a restaurant, made to leave the establishment by a side street, and asked to wear a real skirt if they should like to eat there again.[55] In this way a daring to appropriate the icon of male sacrifice was central in understanding early resistance to the FANY. Such opposition to 'khaki girls' highlights the relationship between military service and citizenship, especially the political rights of women in a society that still did not have universal male suffrage in these years before the war. Women's militarization as illustrated by their donning of khaki ultimately asserted their citizenship and raised the issue of female suffrage even though, as Nancy Cott has emphasized, citizenship is never an 'absolute' status but a 'compromisable' one and must be understood as a spectrum that ranges from residence to political acts.[56]

Along with the idea that their behaviour was just not respectable, critics also questioned whether women were physically able to rise to the challenges of such work. So sure was Baker of the stamina and skill of his troopers that he attempted to arrange a gruelling expedition from the south of England to Scotland 'in the month of November when the weather will not be all sunshine' on horseback and by ambulance waggon'.[57] Baker's motive included attracting potential recruits and funds as well as proving to the public the strength, resolve and endurance of the FANY should Britain be invaded. To this end in August 1910 he sent a memo to all the major London newspapers with the heading 'Are there no Florence Nightingales left?' hoping for supporters and contributions.[58] Responding to the objection that women lack the necessary strength and endurance for such missions, he explained that the weekly drills 'have given them a fine physique with which to defy fatigue; but we want to prove to the world at large, to those who sneer and smile, and sit at home by the fireside, that ours is no vain display, no idle trifling, but a great and noble movement of fit women to aid in the defence of the country; to train them in self-reliance, quickness of thought and action, endurance; to teach them to tend the sick and help the suffering'.[59]

Another point of resistance to the Corps was that it might tread on the toes of other already established military auxiliary organizations or was claiming nursing expertise comparable to professional nurses. On these points too, Baker was quick to emphasize they had no intention of infringing on HM Medical Staff or the Red Cross Society and the FANY were to be trained to administer rudimentary first aid until base hospital staff arrived.[60] In this way, as Sharon Ouditt explains in her analysis of the origins of the VAD, uniformed efforts to assert a place in any future wars were undermined by a rhetoric that claimed that women's main contribution was to serve the men who were serving the nation.[61] For example, even after war was declared and women's military services were eventually established, the WAAC would still use a recruiting poster featuring the slogan 'The girl behind the man behind the gun'.[62] Such contradictions would have important consequences for both the conditions of women's service and their opportunities once the war was over.

FANY recruitment

Although Baker made claims for the FANY as skilled defending forces of the Empire, of course in reality this was far from the truth. Most early recruits were young women with the privilege and motivation to escape the doldrums of middle- and upper-class femininity, attracted by the glamour and possible adventures of riding in uniform. Alongside the glamour of the uniform, Future Commanding Officer Grace Alexandra Ashley-Smith and fellow officer Pat Waddell explained that the term 'corps' with its connotations of mounted auxiliaries was especially appealing to them. Ashley-Smith, born into a privileged family in Aberdeenshire, Scotland, and educated at home and in Europe, was an accomplished horsewoman when she joined the Corps in January 1910 at the age of twenty-three years. 'I first read of the FANY in the *Daily Mail*', wrote Ashley-Smith. 'There was a photograph of mounted women riding in uniform. Being crazy about horses I made up my mind to become a member of this corps.'[63]

On the death of her mother soon after her birth, Waddell was raised by her father and a series of aunts. Her father was also Scottish and owned woollen mills. Waddell was educated at a local 'Dame School' and then at boarding schools, including one in Switzerland. She was a very proficient violinist, was a student of the violin master Sevcik, and worked as a student teacher at several schools. Fluent in French, she later found part-time work as a foreign correspondent in a bank until she was able to join the FANY.[64] Something of a tomboy (having been raised alongside sixteen male cousins) she recounted 'picking up the *Mirror* one day [and seeing] a snapshot of a girl astride on horseback leaping a fence . . . "That", said I, pointing out the photo to a friend, "is the sort of show I'd like to belong to . . . It would be a rag to go into camp with a lot of other girls"'.[65] Her ex-Army godfather 'aided and abetted' her dream. With several cousins in the Army and her brothers attending Yeomanry camps, Waddell was excited to be doing the same.[66]

Not all the recruits were attracted by the horsey nature of the Corps, although all seemed to have appreciated the glamour and possibilities for adventure. Muriel Thompson was one of the first women to race the early motor cars and won the 'Ladies' Bracelet' race at Brookland 'on' (driving tended to be modelled on horseback riding) an Austin motor car named 'Pobble'.[67] Thompson's brother Oscar was the founder of the Brooklands Automobile Racing Club and no doubt her interest in cars was fuelled by economic privileges and her proximity to social life at Brooklands. Other early recruits included Isabel Wicks who was among the oldest FANY at thirty-four years old. She was from Richmond, Surrey, and had joined in October 1909. A trained nurse, Wicks had worked in the Boer War. Lillian Franklin was also from Surrey and grew up in Surbiton; at twenty-six years old she also joined the Corps in February 1909. It was Franklin and Ashley-Smith who took major leadership roles in the organization. A colleague remembered the differences between these two: '[Ashley-Smith] was really the live wire. She was full of ideas and vitality, and, of course, we would never have got anywhere without her before the war ... always out for something, for some new scheme.' In contrast, Franklin was considered 'the brake on any wild ideas'.[68] Franklin became known for her calm and stoic personality that some described as imperturbable, while Ashley-Smith was more impetuous and outgoing. These traits are demonstrated in the different leadership styles and service of these two women throughout the war.

The response of FANY members to the romantic allure of serving their country and enjoying outside pursuits (what Sharon Ouditt calls 'devotional glamour'[69]) was heavily circumscribed within their identities and material status as genteel young ladies. Since the Corps was a volunteer organization, recruits had to be sufficiently well-off to be able to give their services voluntarily. There were also costs associated with FANY membership: the uniform and first aid outfit, an enrolment fee of a guinea, and a fee of 6 shillings per month to the riding school, as well as care of, or hire of, a horse. Also, since they were to be trained in first aid and home nursing, recruits had to be able to pay fees associated with these courses. A 'Ladies' Class' in first aid, for example, taught in the evenings at the Regent Street Polytechnic, cost 3 shillings.[70]

Edith Walton was one of the first recruits who signed up in February 1909, at the age of twenty. She was an exception among the FANY in her lack of independent means as well as her inability to ride, and remembered Baker not liking her very much because she was not well off and had never ridden before.[71] Walton was a member of the lower-middle class and lived in Lancaster Gate, London, where she had left school to help her mother run a small hotel. While Walton wanted to go into nursing, her mother had aspirations for her daughter and was opposed to this choice. However, it was her mother who suggested she join the Corps since they seemed a respectable choice for a daughter determined to follow this call to service. While there are no clear membership numbers and little information on new recruits in these early years, they seem to have been drawn from 'old gentry' and the *nouveaux riches* who became the 'new gentry' as a result of the industrial revolution, as well as from relatively economically privileged middle-class families in 'respectable' trades and professions.[72] Certainly working-class women and women of more modest means would have been deterred by both their own need to provide for themselves and their families as well as by the image of the Corps as an elite (and as some have said, snobbish) organization.[73]

Beryl 'Betty' Hutchinson first heard about the Corps in 1910 after she answered an advertisement in *The Times* for a girl of debutante age interested in joining a party going to Italy. She spent 'a memorable three weeks' there with this party that included Grace Ashley-Smith. When it came to actually joining the FANY, however, Hutchinson said, 'Alas, with uniform, hire of horse and so on I just could not afford it, but I watched at Marble Arch as they set off side-saddle for camp, and even passed the camp at Brookwood later, very full of envy.'[74] Hutchinson was born in 1892 in Rochdale and went to school in Harrogate. With theatre as her vocation she attended the Academy of Dramatic Arts, toured with a theatrical group and became increasingly interested in lighting and stage management as well as acting. Hutchinson's family owned woollen mills in Lancashire and was most likely a member of the *nouveaux riches*. While at least on the surface Hutchinson's family would have seemed able to support her desire to be a FANY, still she reported that she felt a need to be able to make her own living and be self-supportive.[75] Keeping in touch with Ashley-Smith, Hutchinson was eventually able to join the FANY in 1915.

For the most part, whatever their individual place in the complex class hierarchies of Edwardian Britain, FANY recruits were an economically privileged group of young women. Such privilege buffered the resistance the FANY received from society and encouraged them to believe in the unique mission and purpose of their organization. In other words, class privilege gave them the resources to keep going, despite doubts from others; it gave them the confidence to believe they could bend gendered cultural parameters as well as the means to do so. It also gave them the psychological and economic resources to be able to handle resistance to their movement. Their status in society allowed them to be more carefree, independent and flamboyant. Major Thompson, a Director of Medical Services for the British Army, declared in 1919 that the FANY had 'natural qualities of our race, which largely helped us win the war'. These qualities included their '*esprit-de-corps*, their gaiety, their discipline, their smartness and devotion'.[76] FANY volunteers were thus able to use cultural notions of genteel femininity to emphasize their good character and moral persuasion, and to underscore that they were patriotic and trustworthy, loyal, and, ultimately, non-threatening.

The inevitable collision that might occur as the FANY used traditional notions of femininity yet aspired to heights beyond its confines was headed off through their use of class privilege. For the most part, their gentility tended to render them safe and non-abrasive; notions of the psychological fitness that came from being 'well bred' and assumptions that their morality meant they would not become sexually involved with the lower ranks of soldiers, gave them a certain latitude, allowing them to perform a more adventurous role while still remaining within patriarchal confines. Constantly demonstrated in these early years of FANY history are the tensions between negotiating women's expanded role in society, the use of traditional notions of femininity in order to make this very case, and the potential for political consciousness. Ouditt makes a similar point about VAD nurses caught between the strain of their participation in militarism and their insistence that the organization would not depart from the feminine ideal.[77] The FANY too were poised in obeisance to a patriarchal social order that would ultimately give the right to serve and would in part determine the conditions of that service.

These tensions and contradictions are in many ways summed up by an advertisement on the back cover of *Women and War* for Sandow's Corset Company featuring 'A New Corset for Active Women' that is said to confer 'an essential boon on all women who are engaged in any active employment or pursuit'. The advertisement featured a photo of Grace Ashley-Smith in full FANY uniform with the following caption: 'I have worn your Corsets regularly while performing the various duties of this Corps, and am pleased to state that they preserve their shape and the outline of the figure better than any other kind I have used.'[78] In the context of this interesting jumble of compliance and resistance to social norms the FANY Corps was founded.

FANY in action

As the first women's voluntary corps in Great Britain, FANY membership numbered almost a hundred in 1909.[79] Headquarters were based at 118–122 Holborn, London, in the buildings owned by A. W. Gamage, a business that functioned as official outfitters for the FANY, selling 'uniforms, accoutrements, and all necessary accessories at [the] lowest prices'.[80] Gamage lent their van horses to the women for use with the ambulance wagon and when these horses were unavailable the women would practise regular riding drills in Regents Park and the Surrey Yeomanry Riding School. This training soon paid off: in May 1908, after receiving top marks from Colonel F. C. Ricardo of the Grenadier Guards, the Corps was invited to attend the Royal Naval and Military Tournament. Their appearance there and later at Crystal Palace where they won a silver cup for riding 'aroused the interest of the public, and applications from prospective recruits came pouring in'.[81] In 1909 the FANY performed wounded rescue races at the Territorial Forces Exhibition where Sergeant-Major Katie Baker (the Captain's daughter) also won the Gold Medal in show jumping.[82] That summer the Corps won a silver cup at the Pony Gymkhana and Ladies' Sports at Ranelagh and later in the year gave an equestrian exhibition at the Brighton Military Tournament and Torchlight Tattoo.[83] Despite these public activities, conflict was brewing within the organization. Baker had written a draft constitution in 1908 but was having problems maintaining support. In June 1909 he received a letter from a group of recruits complaining that their efforts were 'a waste of time and money'.[84] There also were complaints led by Mrs Mabel Ann St Clair Stobart about his mishandling of Corps' funds as well as against his draft constitution.[85] This issue of funds was related to a successful matinée fundraiser at St James Theatre sponsored by such wealthy patrons as Mrs Asquith the Prime Minister's wife and various high-ranking military personnel.[86] After this St Clair Stobart resigned from the Corps and took a large number of the membership with her.[87] Still, Baker's constitution was registered on 27 July and by November attorneys were determining the conditions of a split between the FANY and St Clair Stobart's group.[88] The latter went on to form the Women's Sick and Wounded Convoy Corps (officially accepted as a VAD in 1910) and to perform remarkable service during the war.[89]

Money, however, may not have been the only issue at stake. St Clair Stobart was an active suffragist at a time when women in military auxiliaries, as already discussed, tended to dissociate themselves from political demands and had ties to conservative elites (even while they claimed similar rights to leadership, respect and autonomy). According to Jenny Gould who writes about St Clair Stobart in 'Women's Military Services in World War Britain', Stobart returned to England from the Transvaal in 1907 and discovered that 'everyone was talking about two great dangers supposedly threatening England: the invasion of England by the Germans, and the possibility that parliamentary franchise might be granted to women. She believed that the juxtaposition of these two problems offered women a perfect opportunity: what better way of demonstrating women's capabilities in sharing the government of the country than by showing they could contribute to the national defence?'[90] By 1909 the Women's Social and Political Union (WSPU) campaign for the vote was becoming more radical in its increasing use of civil disobedience, alienating some people from the organization. FANY Beryl Hutchinson described the suffragettes as a 'fearsome collection of stupid people' that refused to do a good day's work. She recalled being 'seething all the time' and 'so embittered about them'.[91] As already mentioned, others recalled being mistaken for suffragettes and having stones thrown at them, pleased to be able to stop the altercation by showing the Red Cross on their uniforms.[92] St Clair Stobart was most likely an exception among FANY in being an active suffragist with aspirations for military participation and would quickly have fallen out with the more reactionary FANY members, their wealthy patrons, and with Baker himself.[93] However, that St Clair Stobart supposedly took so many members with her, speaks to the connections that some women may have made between social and political demands and military participation as well as to Stobart's flair for organization. After these conflicts and her departure, FANY membership dwindled to less than a dozen active members.

New energy arrived in the form of the aforementioned Grace Ashley-Smith, who joined the FANY in January 1910 after an interview with Baker and her payment of the guinea entrance fee. The following account of her first days with the FANY excerpted from her memoir 'Five Years with the Allies' introduces her as a confident young woman who loved a good story:

I turned up in my quaint uniform with a fast-beating heart to face the battalion of women. The riding school was not well lit. It was eight o'clock at night, and I discovered five figures clad in similar attire . . . After a few futile movements six horses came in. I was given one that the others refused. One good lady offered to give me hints on riding. We solemnly mounted, and rode round and round at a slow walk, and then at a trot. Anxious looks were cast at me. I was riding a dear little grey with a mouth like a feather and easy paces. We quickened the trot, and for some reason I could not solve, the lady who had offered me tips fell off. She did so twice. I was congratulated on riding an unmanageable horse. I left that parade in a thoughtful mood. I had been schooled by a cavalry Sergeant Major and I had been put through the tricks of an ordinary recruit. I had taken jumps without reins and stirrups, and gone over with my face to the horse's tail. I could jump on to a horse when it was cantering, and it was solely because of the title Yeomanry I had sought out this Corps. Was it Scottish reluctance to losing my guinea, was it merely Destiny that made me remain?[94]

Thrift or destiny apart, Ashley-Smith stayed with the FANY and went on to become one of its most famous Commanding Officers known for her high energy and organizational skills and sometimes difficult personality. Ashley-Smith recognized there was work to be done within the organization and wanted new troopers to avoid her own negative experiences on joining the FANY. She remembered driving a two-horse ambulance through the streets of London without any prior driving experience, anxiously finding herself in the middle of Knightsbridge and then being told to drive down Piccadilly back to Holborn. This coincided with the anxiety caused by one of the first mounted parades from Marble Arch to the Embankment with six other troopers, most of whom were not proficient riders, as well as being asked to usher at an East End factory dance, handing out programmes in full FANY uniform. After the latter experience she writes that she went down to Holborn to speak with Baker 'and expressed her dissatisfaction with the whole thing'.[95] It is interesting to note that Baker must have been in favour of recruiting for the FANY at a working-class event and even more interesting that it would be the last straw for Ashley-Smith. I assume it was the character of the event and its working-class location that irked Ashley-Smith, although this is not entirely clear from her comment. Either way, no other recruiting efforts targeted at working-class women are recorded after this one, and it is only briefly in Ashley-Smith's memoirs that this account is mentioned.

After Ashley-Smith spoke openly about organizational problems, Baker asked for her help. She agreed and proceeded to arrange drills, convincing him and other members of the Corps that the women should ride astride rather than side-saddle. 'I spent the next few months fighting for my way in the office', Ashley-Smith explained. 'Soon I had the girls in khaki astride skirts with tunics to match, and I wrote out a scheme of training based on the RAMC [Royal Army Military Corps] training manual. I laid down that we were to help the RAMC with the removal of wounded from dressing stations to clearing hospitals, and were to be mounted to save time in reaching our goals. Riding on battlefields was quietly dropped from our programme'.[96] Also dropped was the aforementioned gruelling march from London to Edinburgh.[97] Still, a few new non-traditional skills were added to the FANY repertoire, enough for trooper Muriel Moyle to record her displeasure in a letter from her solicitor: 'owing to the change which has been brought about to your Corps as originally conceived, by the introduction of such additional matter as wrestling, shooting, tilting at the ring and stirrup lifting, [Miss Moyle] feels so out of sympathy with such a movement that she is constrained to resign'.[98]

Alongside defining the Corps's objectives, training and uniforms, Ashley-Smith also took to managing the personnel: 'I hunted around for recruits and pestered all my friends to join. That was the first step. The second was to weed out the others, amongst them a songful lady with peroxide hair, very fat and hearty, who insisted on wearing white drawers with frills under her khaki skirt. She also insisted on falling off at every parade and displaying them.' 'So', Ashley-Smith writes, 'she had to go; no women's movement could have survived with those frilly drawers on parade'.[99] This Commandant knew that a women's military organization had to be stripped of obvious signs of distracting femininity that might prevent their organization from being taken seriously. It also had to be seen as entirely respectable organization. A charge of 'behaving badly in uniform' resulted in Ashley-Smith insisting that 'no member shall be allowed to sit on the box of the ambulance in the arms of a young man'.[100]

During 1910 the FANY were involved in various events that helped them receive rather better publicity and rebuild the organization: when Edward VII died in May 1910, Ashley-Smith and Katie Baker took a red and white wreath in the shape of a Maltese Cross to Buckingham Palace as representatives of the FANY and were acknowledged by Queen Alexandra.[101] And, while the London Metropolitan Police supposedly refused Baker's offer of an ambulance fully equipped with stretchers and bearers and trained nurses for the funeral, several FANY attended the lying-in-state independently and offered 'first aid to the fainting'.[102] That summer a detachment was also sent to represent the Corps at the Finchley Hospital Carnival under the supervision of Isabel Wicks and they were also in attendance at Derby Day on Epsom Downs. Although emergencies at the races were minor and included such things as ladies wilting under the summer sun, on the way home the Corps transported a man hurt in a motor accident to the hospital. The following year's Derby Day found the FANY taking the body of a policeman struck by lightning to the mortuary. Derby Day was a regular annual event for the FANY during the prewar years.[103]

In 1911 FANY headquarters moved to a residence rented by Ashley-Smith in Lexham Gardens, South Kensington, where she lived with her mother. Ashley-Smith arranged for RAMC Sergeants to give the FANY stretcher drills and teach them bandaging and for a signalling officer to give them lessons in semaphore and morse. Then she applied to the Hounslow Barracks and got permission for the Corps to ride and receive cavalry drill from the Sergeant-Major of the 19th Hussars.[104] With these preparations, the Corps was ready to take on more public appearances. Ashley-Smith recalled an exhibition at the Festival of the Empire at Crystal Palace in 1911 where she and Franklin took part. They rescued 'wounded' during the 'mimic battle', riding into the arena over a small obstacle. Ashley-Smith tells the story about this exhibition, illustrating the humour and glamour that the FANY hoped to project as well as their daring and adventurous spirit. In these examples of early FANY history, Ashley-Smith starts to create the legend of the FANY as quirky and plucky and to establish herself as an audacious leader. These rhetorical stances frame her narrative and reflect the ways she appropriated the uncertainty and 'gaps' in traditional gender conduct arising as women's traditional lives were being challenged, even while she distanced herself from the politically motivated 'New Woman' of the time. She writes:

We had [to] come in at full gallop, leap from our saddles, and gallop off amid the shouts and spears of Zulus, and to the wild applause of thousands of spectators. One admiring and rather drunken gentleman forced his way to us at the end of one performance. He hiccupped at me, 'I'm half Scotch myself', to which I tartly replied, 'and the other half soda', which had the desired effect of making him vanish.[105]

Another character who relished such performances and appears to have
been quite in sync with the budding legend of the FANY as heroic horsewomen, was Flora Sandes. Sandes later earned fame as a soldier with the Serbian Army during the First World War, passing as a man, although known as a
woman.[106] During these pre-war years she appears to have had an affiliation
with the FANY and taken part in the rescue races. About this experience it is
written that although Sandes returned with her 'wounded' soldier at least a
minute ahead of the other riders, she was disqualified from the event. 'Had the
unfortunate private really been wounded', the judge remarked, 'he would venture to observe that her precipitant haste would not only have seriously aggra-
vated his condition, but in all likelihood she would have arrived at the field
hospital with a corpse.'[107]

Between 1910 and early 1912 Baker was still listed as a titular head of the
FANY, although his influence was waning. Franklin had seniority of service
among the volunteers and was a Second Lieutenant, Ashley-Smith a Sergeant
Major, Walton a Sergeant, and Wicks was a Corporal. There were two strikes
against Baker: first, Ashley-Smith thought him an upstart (his 'Captain' rank
was honorary only) and decided the Corps needed someone with more education (most likely this decision was related to his class status);[108] second, Baker
had already shown few organizational and fiscal management skills. In November 1909 after St Clair Stobart and her group had left the FANY, Isabel Wicks
had written a letter to Baker and registered her complaints in comparatively
mild form by describing herself as a musician 'who on joining an orchestra
gets a couple of lessons on the violin (for which he is grateful) but has no
opportunity of joining in the concertos and symphonies to which he looked
forward, and which are described to him as about to take place'.[109] Almost a
year later Wicks' criticism was more direct and centered on fiscal mismanagement yet again.[110] Then several months after a meeting in July 1911 when a resolution that Colonel Ricardo replace Baker as Colonel-in-Chief had not taken
effect, Ashley-Smith went ahead and arranged for Ricardo to inspect the
troops as Officer in Charge. In addition, it seems Ashley-Smith was also keen
to remove Katie Baker from the Corps. In her logbook Ashley-Smith recorded
a meeting in January 1912 where Ricardo came to settle a dispute between
Ashley-Smith (and perhaps others) and Katie Baker. The meeting, to which
Katie Baker was supposedly invited but did not attend, was held to discuss the
ownership of a silver cup won at an equestrian event (most likely Ranelagh
Ladies' Sports or at Crystal Palace) as well as Katie Baker's absence from
Corps training. Ashley-Smith noted that the younger Baker refused 'to
acknowledge being kicked out or to deliver up the cup' and then asserted Baker
should be struck off the rolls because 'she neglected her duties for 18

months'.[111] Ashley-Smith seems to have got her way and Katie Baker no longer appears in the Corps' records. After this point in early 1912, nothing is heard again from Baker and FANY history records him one day leaving home and not returning.[112]

The change in leadership of the FANY coincided with Ashley-Smith drafting a set of regulations for the FANY, receiving Ricardo's approval, and printing these for recruiting purposes.[113] She became Secretary of the Corps and Franklin its Treasurer. Ashley-Smith's sudden rise to power was not without turmoil. She conceded that it suited her that Ricardo was rarely present to oversee the management of the Corps and wrote 'I had to win Franklin, Walton and Wicks over to work with me. They quite naturally resented a newcomer laying down the law. Franklin and Walton soon became the good comrades who were to remain life-long friends; Wicks always approved of results when they justified themselves.'[114] Ashley-Smith continued to whip the Corps into shape, consolidating regimental drills and signalling codes, and writing various orders and recruiting materials for the organization. One such order was prefaced 'Important' and read: 'Members are warned that the present habit of appearing on parade negligently dressed must stop. When in uniform each member must carry her water bottle at least half filled with water and a haversack consisting of no less than two roller and two triangular bandages, boric lint, cotton wool, a small bottle of disinfectant and a pair of scissors.'[115] In these various ways, Ashley-Smith consolidated her power and emerged as the Commanding Officer of the FANY.

FANY at camp

After the reorganization in 1910 and the consolidation of the Corps, the weekend and more extended summer camps became increasingly important as training sites and recruitment endeavours. Located in the countryside and allowing troopers to live and work in the open, the camps generally took place about three times a year with an extended summer camp. The women received instruction by RAMC staff in first aid, stretcher bearing, signalling, riding, and the driving of horse-drawn ambulance wagons, and were also given opportunities to meet male officers of their class. Comfort was at a minimum and the FANY did all the cooking, catering, pitching of tents, digging trenches, erecting latrines and so forth: perhaps fun diversions for women accustomed to servants performing personal services for them. Ashley-Smith recalled everyone loving the camps, 'we had a heavenly time, lots of real hard work and discomfort, but unfailing cheerfulness and fun and good fellowship'.[116] Pat Waddell who wrote she had always regretted that she had not been born a boy, explained how her enjoyment of camp was in part because she adored horses and 'the glorious adventure'.[117]

A typical day at camp began at 5.45 a.m. with reveille, followed by mounted parade and horse care. Breakfast was at 7 a.m. Then, after tent inspection the women had stretcher drill and bandaging, more horse care, and the preparation and enjoyment of dinner (lunch) at 1 p.m. After this they listened to lectures until late afternoon, enjoyed tea, performed mounted drill from 5 to 7 p.m. and had supper at 8 p.m. After-supper morse signalling was followed by bedtime at 10 p.m. During the later camps Ashley-Smith also arranged for a contingent of FANY to work at the Reception Hospital of the Guards Camp. In addition, such daily programmes were varied by field days often open to public spectators, and night exercises when recruits were roused from bed and sent out to carry stretchers, often over rough countryside, to locate 'wounded'. After everyone had a turn at stretcher bearing during night exercises, they would return to camp and try and get a few hours sleep before the new day began.[118] Records of these camps suggest that while the women received important training and worked hard, they also had a lot of fun together. They enjoyed the delicious freedoms of riding bareback in the early mornings, caring for and grooming their own horses, enjoying the company of other women and interacting with male officers. Present in all press accounts of the prewar camps is 'Castor' their bulldog mascot.

While the first camp took place in the summer of 1909 at a private estate in Chiddingfold, Surrey,[119] the camps after 1912 were more extensive and better attended. The weekend camp at Haslemere held in May 1912 seems to have been quite a social affair and involved entertaining Colonel Ricardo and friends at luncheon and 'masses of people came to tea, including the Marquis of Sligo, then Lord Altemont and his family'. Ashley-Smith recalled over a hundred visitors on the Sunday afternoon of this weekend camp.[120] Several months later another camp at Bourne End turned out to be a much quieter affair although very successful in terms of training. Ashley-Smith made the arrangements and wrote in her memoir how she personally helped finance this and many other camps.[121] Ashley-Smith paints herself as an important benefactor for the FANY during these early years.

Stories of camp abound with tales of the women falling or being thrown from their horses.[122] Pat Waddell recalled one of the 'rescue races' where she was chosen by Irene Wicks to be rescued. Unfortunately, Wicks' horse objected to having a passenger behind the saddle and Waddell found herself flying through the air.[123] Women from privileged homes might spend summers at their country homes developing, among other things, skills in riding and such outdoor pursuits as shooting. Ashley-Smith, for example, a very accomplished horsewoman, was not fazed when she took a very bad fall jumping a horse during one camp. She was thrown when the horse fell and injured when the horse rolled on her shoulder. Just a flesh wound and 'I was back in the saddle again the next morning', she exclaimed.[124] Such stories of uniformed women dashing about on horseback were perfect fodder for the press, who loved to cover the camps. *Tatler* reported on their camp at Norbury in May 1913, featuring an article on the FANY next to a photo exhibit of debutantes presented at Court at Buckingham Palace and suggesting they were giving up their gowns for khaki.[125] Field events in particular were covered by the press; at one camp at Pirbright several months later they received cinematic coverage and were featured on a newsreel shown in local cinemas. Ashley-Smith recalled this event in particular because it was she who almost knocked down the reporter with the horse-drawn field ambulance and was thrilled to see him on film at the New Gallery theatre seizing his camera and bolting.[126]

The success of the camps underscored the importance of communication between the FANY and the male military and political establishments. Ashley-Smith had fostered informal friendships and formal allegiances to this military establishment built from her own networks, arranging for RAMC Sergeants to give instruction, applying to the Hounslow Barracks and Surrey Yeomanry Headquarters for permission to ride and train, and receiving patronage of officers like Colonel Ricardo.[127] In the case of the summer camps it was especially important to receive the military authorities' approval in order to borrow equipment, receive instruction and enjoy opportunities for social interactions with men of their class. During the camp at Pirbright in July 1913 the Brigade of Guards took the FANY under their wing and lent equipment and the 19th Hussars residing at nearby Stoney Castle gave cavalry drill and equestrian instruction.[128] Ashley-Smith also recalled the friendship and generosity of the Royal Horse Guards (known as the 'Blues') who during a summer camp at Pirbright in 1914 had prepared the women's equipment and fixed up a marquee, bell-tents and a kitchen. When a Sergeant asked Ashley-Smith if the FANY would like a swimming pool, she thought he was joking and responded 'Rather, you fix it.' Later, she wrote they discovered a swimming pool with water in a huge tarpaulin ready for the women's bathing pleasure.[129]

Ashley-Smith recalled the social interactions between FANY and male officers during one camp when the FANY were invited as guests of the Surrey Yeomanry regiment. Attempts to overcome their mutual shyness at dinner were made more difficult by the fact that chairs were sinking in the mud and marquee poles were falling over. Things came to a head when Ashley-Smith needed to tell their host about a problem with the latrines. Her report on this delicate matter was met by the Surrey Yeomanry Captain in command with a

pregnant pause, his blurting out 'Oh, what a lovely moon', and then an agonizing silence. The awkward quiet was broken by a yell and a thud as two officers from different sides of the tent stumbled out to take care of the problem,
falling over the tent ropes and into each other.[130] Ashley-Smith seemed to
relish telling stories like this and the closer they were to a pantomime, the
better. Such stories helped construct the legend of the FANY as quirky and
vivacious and set them apart from more stodgy contemporaries. I believe these
heterosexual exploits helped the FANY avoid the accusations of being 'inverts'
or 'mannish lesbians':[131]: a notion the suffragettes also faced along with those
women who later participated in the women's armed forces.[132]

The procurement of networks and allegiances that brought the FANY
closer to the military establishment involved hard work and the active negotiation of gender and class relations. Another example of this involved a RAMC
officer with the incongruous name of Sergeant Pepper who instructed them at
camp and helped them during an important inspection. The FANY (again
through their connections) had managed to get Surgeon-General Woodhouse
to come and inspect the troops. Ashley-Smith tells the story of how when the
General was to inspect their not-yet-ready bandaging skills, they sent him to
the cookhouse where their prettiest trooper was in residence as cook. 'He was
ensnared by her blue eyes and a face as sweet as God ever made, and spent
quite twenty minutes talking to her, which made ample time for Pepper to get
himself tied up faultlessly and to coach every girl there about the whys and
wherefore's of a really intricate treatment.' After using their feminine wiles,
the FANY whisked away Pepper before he was recognized and the General
was heard to say in response to their bandaging skills: 'By gad! That's the first
time I've ever seen that done correctly.' Pepper's friendship and assistance had
important consequences: Surgeon-General Woodhouse was impressed
enough after his inspection to personally recommend Ashley-Smith for a
meeting with Sir Arthur Sloggett, Director General of Medical Services at the
War Office, to discuss how the FANY might be mobilized in case of war.[133]

The double helix

Although the FANY were very skilled at negotiating class and gendered relations to prove their credibility and viability as an auxiliary military organization, they were in no position to push beyond the space they had been given as
literal or metaphorical 'little sisters' to the military elite. Indeed, it seems that
Ashley-Smith was absolutely driven by this desire to be included in this elite.
She wrote that one of the most 'supreme moments' in her life occurred at
camp in 1914 when she was permitted to ride with various regiments:

We were attached to the Skeleton Army on manoeuvres, sixteen of us mounted and two with the waggon. We had a wonderful time, even our steeds shared the excitement . . . There was a church parade at the Guards Camp, we were the first women ever to attend that. One of the Grenadiers was our 'marker', and Franklin and I went up to salute Lord Bernard Gordon Lennox who was senior officer that day. Bishop Taylor-Smith preached, and I was thrilled and bursting with pride to be there at last with the FANY, the Grenadiers on one side, the Coldstreams opposite, the Scots Guards on our right, and the Irish Guards alongside. There are certain supreme moments in everyone's life, that was one of mine. It was worth all the labour and slogging, and self-denial and discouragement – all the ups and downs, all the jeers and the laughter – to be there at last – part of the army – yes and with the best of it.[134]

Despite the FANY skill in negotiating their role with the British military, the contradiction, of course, was that they were using traditional arguments about women's roles and ability to 'serve, succour and save' in order to make the case for moving outside the confines of these roles. This was the ambiguous cultural paradox encountered by the FANY as they attempted to both use and rework existing discourses on class and gender. Their efforts were paralleled by attempts on the part of the authorities to maintain existing gender discourses in cultural propaganda because these values would provide key foundations for the justification of British involvement in European conflicts even while, ironically, these independent women would become a central aspect of the British national defence. This situation reflects the 'double helix' or paradox implicit in the negotiation of gendered relations as discussed by Margaret and Patrice Higonnet whereby women's status is both advanced and diminished as a result of war.[135] Cultural discourses and temporary expediencies associated with the tropes of femininity allowed women forward movement at the very same time that these renegotiated notions of femininity created new kinds of constraints. In the case of the FANY, this notion of progress and regress is aptly illustrated in the following 'Ulster episode' that occurred in 1913.

Hostilities were arising in Ireland after a third Home Rule Bill was introduced and the Ulster Unionists, led by Sir Edward Carson and supported by the Conservatives, were adamantly opposed and ready to resist Home Rule by force of arms. The nation was on the edge of civil war. Ashley-Smith offered the Corps as an ambulance unit for use in case of hostilities to Sir Edward and was accepted provisionally. This is an example of the FANY formally aligning themselves with the status quo and representing themselves as non-threatening women from the right social class who could be trusted to serve and follow orders. Carson sent the Principal Medical Officer of the Ulster Army to inspect the FANY, and, once this inspection had passed successfully, Ashley-Smith and trooper Cicely Mordaunt, daughter of Lady Mordaunt of Walton Hall, Warwickshire, went over to Belfast and were interviewed by Sir George Richardson of the Ulster Ambulance. Arrangements were made and the FANY were thrilled by this opportunity to serve.[136] Describing the Corps as 'gentlewomen' willing to take a brave part, the *London Budget* newspaper exclaimed 'Will Ulster Fight? These Ladies, at Least, are Ready to Take the Field'. It emphasized their aristocratic and military connections, stating that the Corps consisted of thirty-five 'gentlewomen' and showing Ashley-Smith pictured with Lady Kilmorey, Lady Castlereigh, the Dowager Lady Smiley, and the Marchioness of Londonderry.[137]3 Unfortunately, recalled Ashley-Smith, always ready to rhetorically frame the FANY as bold and daring, the organization also had five ardent Sinn Feiners (anti-Unionists) among their recruits and these always seemed to be in the foreground of every press photo captioned 'Off to Fight for Ulster'![138]

After the Corps was invited to work with the Ulster Army, it seems Ashley-Smith was asked to have a VAD attachment with them. Ashley-Smith astutely refused this offer once she realized the VAD attachment proposed having three votes on the organizing committee and the FANY only two.[139] However, despite all this politicking, nothing came of the relationship with Ulster. This was in part a result of hostilities in Ireland being overshadowed by much larger hostilities in Europe looming on the horizon. But more impor-tant for the short term, the Unionists were anxious about the role of women in times of national security. The Secretary of the Medical Board at the Unionist Headquarters in Belfast (who had a proclivity for run-on sentences) sent Ashley-Smith a letter that contained the following:

I am keeping your Corps in rememberance [sic] but I find that the Military people here do not view with much favour the idea of ladies exposing themselves in a trav-elling ambulance. Matters at present are so exciting and people are so much employed with other work that I have had very little opportunity of having a talk with the officer in charge . . . I do not want to dishearten you but if we do have a row here the rowdy element, which is a very cowardly one, would necessitate guards being supplied to any women in the field and for that reason I think the mil-itary people are looking rather askance at the idea but as I have said before I will have another talk with them as soon as they have leisure. Your Corps is of such good material that I would love to have it over.[140]

This phrase, 'ladies exposing themselves', represents the ways women were seen to be both going beyond the boundaries of respectable behaviour and in need of protection. As Penny Summerfield has stated, the risk associ-ated with women in such masculine space was twofold: 'they were themselves sexually threatening to men [and] they incurred sexual danger from them'.[141] The valorization of the feminine undergirding the whole social order of war (what men were fighting for and hoping to return to) meant that women who claimed space in this masculine project risked being framed as gender upstarts, misfits or sexual deviants. In addition, women's entry into this masculine space of war in any role other than that of nurse, that submissive angel of mercy, threatened the foundation of wartime gender construction with its division into masculine military forces and feminine home front. Women's entrance into war, especially women in an organization bent on maintaining its independence and providing ambulance transport, provoked anxiety because it might lead to sexual immorality and the potential masculinization of women, not to mention a case for their full citizenship. The FANY of course were caught in the midst of this predicament. They presented a chivalrous genteel femininity in order for them to be accepted; the Unionists could either reject this and see the FANY as threats to the social order or accept it and protest that civil war was no place for such genteel women. It was the proverbial rock and a hard place.

Nonetheless, the history of the FANY, as we shall see, was one undaunted by the initial formal refusal on the part of the British authorities to recognize their organization. And, despite this disappointment in the spring of 1914, the summer camp took place, and, as we know, Ashley-Smith was recommended for an interview with Sir Arthur Sloggett at the War Office. With optimism Ashley-Smith set sail on the *Guildford Castle* to visit her sister in South Africa. It was aboard ship that she heard that war was declared on 4 August 1914. Back home Franklin and Walton communicated again with Sir Arthur Sloggett, although this time they found him unhelpful and immovable about the participation of women in times of war. Like his Unionist brothers, when push came to shove Sloggett and his cronies believed the battlefront was no place for women.

Notes

1 *Daily Graphic* (25 February 1908).
2 Ross McKibben, *Classes and Cultures, England 1918–1951* (New York: Oxford University Press, 1998); J. F. C. Harrison, *Late Victorian Britain, 1875–1901* (London: Fontana, 1990); Françoise Bédarida, *A Social History of England, 1851–1990* (London: Routledge, 1991).
3 John Stevenson, *British Society, 1914–1945* (London, Penguin, 1984), p. 30.
4 Harrison, *Late Victorian Britain*, p. 24.
5 Leoore Davidoff and Catherine Hall, *Family Fortunes: Men and Women of the English Middle Class, 1780–1850* (New York: Routledge, 2002); Sonya Rose, *Limited Livelihoods: Gender and Class in Nineteenth-Century England* (Berkeley: University of Cali-

fornia Press, 1992). See also Susan Kingsley Kent, *Gender and Power in Britain, 1640–1990* (New York: Routledge, 1999); and Amanda Vickery (ed.), *Women, Privilege and Power: British Politics, 1750 to the Present* (Stanford, CA: Stanford University Press, 2001).

6 Carol Dyhouse, *Girls Growing Up in Late Victorian and Edwardian England* (London: Routledge and Kegan Paul, 1981); Harry Hendrick, *Children, Childhood and English Society, 1880–1990* (Cambridge: Cambridge University Press, 1997); Sue Bruley, *Women in Britain Since 1900* (London: Macmillan, 1999); Jane Lewis, *Women in England, 1870–1950* (Brighton, Sussex: Wheatsheaf Books, 1984); Ina Zweiniger-Bargielowska (ed.), *Women in Twentieth-Century Britain* (Harlow, Essex: Longman, 2001).

7 Maureen Healey, 'Becoming Austrian: Women, the State, and Citizenship in World War I', *Central European History* 35: 1 (2002), p. 9.

8 Simon Gunn, *The Public Culture of the Victorian Middle Class: Ritual and Authority and the English Industrial City, 1840–1914* (Manchester: Manchester University Press, 2000), p. 188. See also Pierre Bordieu, *The Field of Cultural Production* (Cambridge: Polity Press, 1993); David Kidd and David Nicholls, *Gender, Civic Culture and Consumerism: Middle-Class Identity in Britain, 1800–1940* (Manchester: Manchester University Press, 1999).

9 Griselda Carr, *Pit Women: Coal Communities in Northern England in the Early Twentieth Century* (London: Merlin Press, 2001); Claire A. Cullerton, *Working-Class Culture, Women, and Britain, 1914–1922* (New York: St Martin's Press, 1999).

10 Carol Dyhouse, 'Education', in Zweiniger-Bargielowska (ed.), *Women in Twentieth-Century Britain*, pp. 119–33; Deirdre McCloskey, 'Paid Work', in Zweiniger-Bargielowska (ed.), *Women in Twentieth-Century Britain*, pp. 165–79.

11 Lewis, Women in England, p. 77; Jessica Gerard, *Country House Life: Family and Servant, 1815–1914* (Oxford: Oxford University Press, 1994), pp. 104–9.

12 Jean H. Baker, *Votes for Women: The Struggle for Suffrage* (New York: Oxford, 2002); Sandra Stanley Holton, *Feminism and Democracy: Women's Suffrage and Reform Politics in Britain, 1900–1918* (New York: Cambridge University Press, 1986).

13 Gerard, *Country House Life*, ch. 2.

14 Carol Dyhouse, *Feminism and the Family in England, 1880–1939* (New York: Basil Blackwell, 1989), pp. 28–33.

15 Dyhouse, 'Education', in Zweiniger-Bargielowska (ed.), *Women in Twentieth-Century Britain*, p. 119.

16 See Ruth Brandon, *The New Women and the Old Men: Love, Sex, and the Woman Question* (London: Secker and Warburg, 1990); Mary Louise Roberts, *Disruptive Acts: The New Woman in Fin-de-Siècle France* (Chicago: University of Chicago Press, 2002); Michele Perrot, 'The New Eve and the Old Adam: French Women's Condition at the Turn of the Century', in Margaret R. Higonnet (with Jane Jenson, Sonya Michel and Margaret C. Weitz) (eds), *Behind the Lines: Gender and the Two World Wars* (New Haven: Yale University Press, 1987), pp. 51–60.

17 Gerard, *Country House Life*, ch. 5.

18 M. Jeanne Peterson, *Family, Love, and Work in the Lives of Victorian Gentlewomen* (Bloomington: Indiana University Press, 1989); and Amanda Vickery, *The Gentleman's Daughter: Women's Lives in Georgian England* (New Haven, CT: Yale University Press, 1998) for a focus on the ways the scope of genteel female experience in the nineteenth century did not diminish. See also Martha Vicinus, *Independent Women: Work and Community for Single Women, 1850–1920* (Chicago, IL: University of Chicago Press, 1990).

19 Sean O'Connell, *The Car and British Society: Class, Gender and Motoring, 1896–1939* (Manchester: Manchester niversity Press, 1998), p. 45.

20 Janet S. K. Watson, 'Khaki Girls, VADs, and Tommy's Sisters: Gender and Class in First World War Britain', *The International Historical Review* 19: 1 (1997), 36; and 'War in the Wards: The Social Construction of Medical work in First World War Britain; *Journal of British Studies* 41 (2002), 484–510. See also the chapter in Lewis, *Women in England*, especially the section on 'Social Maternalism', pp. 92–106. See also Eileen Janes Yeo about the 'paradoxes of empowerment' associated with women's public roles in Eileen Janes Yeo (ed.), *Radical Femininity: Women's Self Representations in the Public Sphere* (Manchester: Manchester University Press, 1998). The Christian manliness movement also attempted to redefine codes of masculinity; see Graham Dawson, *Soldier Heroes: British Adventure, Empire and the Imagining of Masculinities* (London: Routledge, 1994), p. 64.

21 Margaret H. Darrow, *French Women and the First World War: War Stories of the Home Front* (New York: Oxford University Press, 2000), p. 58. See also Anna Davin, 'Imperialism and Motherhood', *History Workshop Journal* 5 (1978), 9–61.

22 Anne Summers, *Angels and Citizens: British Women as Military Nurses, 1854–1914* (London: Routledge and Kegan Paul, 1988), p. 273.

23 Anne Summers, 'Militarism in Britain Before the Great War', *History Workshop Journal* 2 (1976), 104–23; Richard A. Soloway, *Demography and Degeneration: Eugenics and the Declining Birthrate in Twentieth-Century Britain* (Chapel Hill: University of North Carolina Press, 1990).

24 John Springhill, *Youth, Empire and Society, 1883–1940* (London: Croom Helm, 1977).

25 Krisztina Robert, 'Gender, Class and Patriotism: Women's Paramilitary Units in First World War Britain', *The International History Review* 19: 1 (1997), 52–3; Watson, 'Khaki Girls, VADs and Tommy's Sisters'.

26 The Women's Transport Service *(FANY) Gazete* (Spring 1957), p. 8.

27 Allen Warren, 'Citizens of the Empire: Baden-Powell, Scouts and Guides, and an Imperial Ideal, 1900–40', in John MacKenzie (ed.), *Imperialism and Popular Culture* (Manchester: Manchester University Press, 1986), pp. 232–56.

28 Robert Baden-Powell, *Young Knights of the Empire; their Code, and Further Scout Yarns* (Philadelphia: J. B. Lippincott, 1917). See also the US experience and the history of scouting in Jeffrey P. Hantover, 'The Boy Scouts and the Validation of Masculinity', *Journal of Social Issues* 34: 1 (1978), 184–95.

29 Springhill, *Youth, Empire and Society*, p. 130.

30 Rose G. Kerr (edited by Alix Liddell), *The Story of the Girl Guides, 1908–1938* (London: Girl Guide Association, 1976), p. 25.

31 Agnes Baden-Powell, *The Handbook of the Girl Guides: How Girls Can Help to Build Up the Empire*, in collaboration with Sir Robert Baden-Powell (London: Thomas Nelson and sons, 1912). See also Juliette G. Low, *How Girls Can Help their Country, adapted from The Handbook for Girl Guides* (Savannah, GA: Press of M. S. and D. A. Byck Co., 1917).

32 Kerr, *The Story of the Girl Guides*, p. 30.

33 Summers, *Angels and Citizens*, p. 278.

34 Susan R. Grayzel, *Women's Identities at War: Gender, Motherhood, and Politics in Britain and France During the First World War* (Chapel Hill: University of North Carolina Press, 1999), p. 192.

35 At the same time that the FANY was formed, Baker also founded a group called the 'Cadet Yeomanry' for young males. This organization was a boys' preparatory school

for military service where recruits were treated as soldiers and taught, among the usual drills, such activities as wrestling on horseback. The Cadet Yeomanry shared space in the original FANY magazine *Women and War* and was 'founded to teach boys from 12 to 17 years of age horsemanship, horsemastership, cavalry drill, elementary veterinary work, ambulance drill, etc.', 'Particulars of the Cadet Yeomanry', *Women and War* (November 1910), p. 77.

36 Grace Ashley-Smith adds another insight to understanding Baker's motivation for founding the FANY. Writing about Baker's daughter Katie and his devotion to her, Ashley-Smith explained: 'I think it was probably for her that he created the corps of ambulance women': Grace McDougall (*née* Ashley-Smith), 'Prologue', red-type, loose-leaf pages, p. 1. These pages were most likely an earlier draft of the 'Prologue' in her manuscript 'Five Years with the Allies, 1914–1919: The Story of the FANY Corps'. [IWM] Perhaps the Corps was Katie Baker's idea all along.

37 McDougall, 'Prologue', p. 1.

38 Captain Edward Baker, 'A Foreword by the C.O.', *Women and War* (June 1910), pp. 3–5. *Women and War* was the official magazine of the FANY but folded in 1910 due to lack of funds and energy. The magazine began again as the *FANY Corps Gazette* in 1915.

39 Several FANY members took part in shooting competitions, among them Cristobel Nicholson who by 1910 was known as a 'well-known miniature shot', *Women and War* (November 1910), p. 75.

40 'The Training of Woman to War', *Women and War* (July 1910), p. 28.

41 Jenny Gould, 'Women's Military Services in First World War Britain', in Higonnet et al. (eds), *Behind the Lines*, pp. 116–17.

42 Kerr, *The Story of the Girl Guides*, p. 31.

43 Healey, 'Becoming Austrian: Women, the State, and Citizenship in World War I', pp. 33–4.

44 Gould, 'Women's Military Services in First World War Britain', p. 117.

45 Lecture of Corps History, lecture notes General Course – Grade II, 1961, p. 9. [FA]

46 See Grayzel, *Women's Identities at War*, pp. 195–7 for a discussion of similar strategies on the part of the Women's Volunteer Reserve (WVR).

47 Watson, 'Khaki Girls, VADs and Tommy's Sisters'.

48 Grayzel, *Women's Identities at War*, p. 196.

49 Summers, *Angels and Citizens*, p. 273. See also Sandra Stanley Holton, *Suffrage Days: Stories from the Women's Suffrage Movement* (London: Routledge, 1996). Notable exceptions to this were Mrs St Clair Stobart, discussed later in the chapter and Dr Elsie Inglis, Commandant of the Edinburgh VAD and founder of the Scottish Women's Suffrage Association. She also was involved in the First World War in Serbia.

50 Penny Summerfield, 'Gender and War in the Twentieth Century', *The International History Review* 19: 1 (1997), 7.

51 Grayzel, *Women's Identities at War*, p. 123.

52 See Gould, 'Women's Military Services in the First World War' and Watson, 'Khaki Girls, VADs, and Tommy's Sisters'.

53 *Ladies Pictorial*, 21 August 1915.

54 Unidentified and undated (*c.* 1916 and most likely the *Daily Mail*) newspaper clipping '"Yeowomen": A Triumph of Hospital Organisation' by W. Beach Thomas. [IWM]

55 Irene Ward, *FANY Invicta* (London: Hutchinson, 1955), p. 26.

56 Nancy Cott, 'Marriage and Women's Citizenship in the U.S., 1830–1934', *American*

Historical Review 103: 4 (1998), 1440–74. As Nicoletta F. Gullace explains in *'The Blood of Our Sons': Men, Women, and the Renegotiation of British Citizenship During the Great War* (New York: Palgrave Macmillan, 2002), patriotism became the essential quality for citizenship and gave women a powerful language with which to claim their space in the war.

57 'Proposed Route March', *Women and War* (September 1910), p. 44. Someone had handwritten in black ink on this edition and changed the '40 miles a day' to 30 and the journey from '10 days' to 14.

58 Baker to London newspapers (23 August 1910).

59 Ibid.

60 'First Aid Nursing Yeomanry Corps', *The Road* (October 1910), p. 39.

61 Sharon Ouditt, *Fighting Forces, Writing Women: Identity and Ideology in the First World War* (London: Routledge, 1994), pp. 7–46.

62 Grayzel, *Women's Identities at War*, p. 286–7, n. 53.

63 McDougall, 'Prologue', p. 1. Unfortunately, while McDougall wrote lucidly about the history of the FANY, she shared little in her memoirs of her own personal history.

64 Pat Beauchamp Washington (a.k.a. Waddell), typed autobiography. [LC]

65 Pat Beauchamp (a.k.a. Waddell), *Fanny Goes to War* (London: John Murray, 1919), p. 2.

66 Beauchamp Washington, autobiography.

67 'The Ladies' Bracelet Handicap at Brookland', *Illustrated London News* (11 July 1908).

68 Taped interview, Edith Colston (*née* Walton) by Peter Liddle (May 1973). [LC]

69 Ouditt, *Fighting Forces, Writing Women*, p. 34.

70 *Women and War* (September 1910), p. 45.

71 Interview, Colston.

72 Among the patrons of the FANY during these early years were the Duchess of Abercorn, the Marchioness of Londonderry, the Countess of Kilmorey, Viscountess Castlereagh, Lord Willoughby de Broke, Lord Leigh, Lord Valentia, and others: Pat Beauchamp (a.k.a. Waddell), *Fanny Went to War* (London: Routledge and Sons, 1940), p. 2; Grace McDougall, untitled, typed, loose-leafed paper fastened with leather stud, p. 4. [IWM]

73 J. D. McLachan, manuscript on FANY history (1945), pp. 1–2. [LC]

74 Beryl Hutchinson, 'My FANY Life with the Belgian Army', p. 1. [LC]

75 Taped interview, Beryl Hutchinson by Peter Liddle (June 1972). [LC]

76 Major-General H. N. Thompson, 'Introduction', in Beauchamp, *Fanny Goes to War*, p. vii.

77 Ouditt, *Fighting Forces, Writing Women*, ch. 1.

78 Inside back cover, *Women and War* (September 1910).

79 Grace McDougall, 'Brief Resumé of Corps Work', *Gazette* (August 1916), p. 7.

80 Back cover, *Women and War* (September 1910).

81 Baker, 'A Foreword by the C.O.', p. 3; Irene Ward, *FANY Invicta* (London: Hutchinson, 1955), p. 22.

82 Organisational Manager of the Territorial Forces Exhibition of Equipment and Appliances to Baker (15 April 1909). [LC]

83 Hugh Popham, *F.A.N.Y.: The Story of the Women's Transport Service, 1907–1984* (London: Leo Cooper, 1984), p. 10.

84 Eva and Muriel Greenwall and others to Baker (21 June 1909). [LC]

85 McDougall, 'Prologue', p. 1.

86 Popham, *F.A.N.Y.*, p. 5.

87 'Proceedings of the General Council' (19 July 1909). [LC]

88 M. Broderick to Baker (3 November 1909). [LC]

89 See the story of St Clair Stobart in David Mitchell, *Monstrous Regiment: The Story of the Women of the First World War* (New York: Macmillan, 1965), pp. 150–65. At the outbreak of the First World War the British Red Cross refused her services and she went to work for the Belgian Red Cross. In Brussels she was detained by the Germans as a spy and narrowly missed execution. After directing hospitals in Antwerp and Cherbourg she realized the need to help on the Eastern Front. St Clair Stobart spent the war attached to the Serbian army with a field ambulance column and 'accompanied the army in its heroic retreat': Barbara McLaren, *Women of the War* (London: Hodder and Stoughton, 1917), p. x.

90 Gould, 'Women's Military Services in the First World War', p. 116.

91 Interview, Hutchinson.

92 'Lecture of Corps History', p. 9.

93 Email correspondence with FANY ex-archivist Lynette Beardwood (17 October, 2003). In McLachan's manuscript on FANY history she writes: 'a story which is the one now repeated by Baker's family, is that the Corps was split over the question of women's suffrage', pp. 1–2.

94 Grace McDougall, 'Five Years with the Allies, 1914–1919: The Story of the FANY Corps', p. 4. [IWM]

95 McDougall, untitled manuscript [IWM], p. 1.

96 McDougall, 'Five Years with the Allies', p. 4.

97 Ashley-Smith declared the march 'wildly impractical': McDougall, untitled, p. 3.

98 W. W. Hellyar and Co. to Baker (9 January 1911). [LC]

99 McDougall, 'Five Years with the Allies', p. 5.

100 Ibid., p. 3.

101 *Women and War* (June 1910), p. 8; McDougall, 'Prologue', p. 3.

102 Popham, *F.A.N.Y.*, p. 10.

103 *Women and War* (September 1910), p. 47.

104 McDougall,'Brief Resumé of Corps Work', p. 7.

105 McDougall, 'Five Years with the Allies', pp. 4–5.

106 Flora Sandes, *An English Woman Sergeant in the Serbian Army* (London: Hodder and Stoughton, 1916); and *The Autobiography of a Woman Soldier: A Brief Record of Adventure with the Serbian Army, 1916–1919* (New York: Frederick A. Stokes Company, 1927)

107 Alan Burgess, *The Lovely Sergeant* (New York: Dutton, 1963), p. 11.

108 Interview, Colston.

109 Isabel Wicks to Baker (29 November 1909). [LC]

110 Isabel Wicks to Baker (21 September 1910). She also criticized him in a letter (19 February 1910). [LC]

111 Grace Ashley-Smith (a.k.a. McDougall), small bound logbook, entry 3 January 1912. [LC]

112 Popham, *F.A.N.Y.*, p. 1; Ward, *FANY Invicta*, p. 35.

113 McDougall, 'Prologue', p. 3.

114 McDougall, 'Five Years with the Allies', pp. 7, 5.

115 Grace Ashley-Smith (a.k.a. McDougall), undated (pre-1913) typed sheet. [IWM]

116 McDougall, 'Five Years with the Allies', p. 11.

117 Beauchamp, *Fanny Went to War*, pp. 5–6.

118 Ibid., pp. 9–10.

119 Popham, *F.A.N.Y.*, p. 9.
120 McDougall, untitled, p. 6; McDougall, 'Five Years with the Allies', p. 7. Volunteers present at camp included Ashley-Smith, Franklin, Walton, Wicks, Bennett, Moran, Archibald, O'Hea, Carson, and Ball: McDougall, 'Brief Resumé of Corps Work', p. 8.
121 McDougall, 'Five Years with the Allies', p. 7.
122 Reminiscence by Winifred Geare (*née* Mordaunt) in *The Women's Transport Service (FANY) Gazette* 21: 19 (Spring 1962), 18, is disparaging of risks and lack of safety precautions taken at camp concerning horseback riding. She described McDougall as 'abysmally ignorant about that noble animal the horse' and criticized the way she supposedly encouraged riders to wear spurs. McDougall responded to this accusation in a letter where she defended herself and her love for, and training with, horses: McDougall to Maude MacLellan (27 April 1962) (hand copied by Edith Colston). [FA]
123 Beauchamp, *Fanny Goes to War*, p. 7.
124 McDougall, 'Five Years with the Allies', p. 11.
125 'A Women's Nursing Yeomanry Corps at Work', *Tatler* (undated, *c.* 1913). [IWM]
126 McDougall, 'Five Years with the Allies', p. 10
127 McDougall, 'Brief Resumé of Corps Work', p. 7.
128 Attendees at this camp included Ashley-Smith, Franklin, Wicks, Bennett, the Morris sisters, Moran, the Mordaunt sisters, Walsh, three recruits from the O'Hea family, Cluff, Fletcher, Marshall, Jackson, Bond, Dobson, Latchford and Clementi-Smith: McDougall, 'Brief Resumé of Corps Work', p. 8.
129 McDougall, 'Five Years with the Allies', pp. 12–13. Three camps were held in 1914. The Easter camp was 17–22 April with Ashley-Smith, Franklin, Walton, Wicks, Bennett, Hall, the Morris sisters and their mother, C. Mordaunt, Cole-Hamilton, Sedgewick, Stedvisan, Moore and Harrison. The Whitsuntide camp took place from 1 to 4 June with Ashley-Smith, Franklin, Walton, Cluff, C. Mordaunt, Anderson, Stedman, Cole-Hamilton, Leatham, Hall, and Carson. The most memorable camp was the last prewar camp from 6 to 20 July. Present were Ashley-Smith, Franklin, Walton, Wicks, Cole-Hamilton, Marshall, Cluff, Lewis, C. Mordaunt, Moore, Waddell, Bond, Inglis, M. White, Lambart, Ferguson, Pace, Clementi-Smith, the Morris sisters and their mother: McDougall, 'Brief Resumé of Corps Work', pp. 8–9.
130 McDougall, 'Five Years with the Allies', pp. 9–10.
131 See, for example, Martha Vicinus, 'They Wonder to Which Sex I Belong: The Historical Roots of the Modern Lesbian Identity', *Feminist Studies* 18: 3 (1992), 467–97; and her book *Intimate Friends: Women Who Loved Women, 1778–1928* (Chicago, IL: University of Chicago Press, 2004).
132 See Roy Terry, *Women in Khaki: The Story of the British Woman Soldier* (London: Columbus Books, 1988) and Lisa Tickner, *Spectacle of Women: Imagery of the Suffrage Campaign, 1907–1914* (London: Chatto and Windus, 1987).
133 McDougall, 'Five Years with the Allies', p. 15.
134 Ibid., p. 13.
135 Margaret Higonnet and Patrice L.-R. Higonnet, 'The Double Helix', in Higonnet (ed.) *Behind the Lines*, pp. 31–47.
136 McDougall, 'Five Years with the Allies', p. 9.
137 'Will Ulster Fight? These Ladies, at Least, are Ready to Take the Field', *London Budget* (2 November 1913).
138 McDougall, 'Five Years with the Allies', p. 9.
139 Ibid., p. 45. The VAD officer, Katharine Furse, went on to form an Ulster Hospital

Corps of volunteer nurses (Summers, *Angels and Citizens*, p. 284).

140 Secretary of the Medical Board, Unionist Headquarters to Grace Ashley-Smith (21 March 1914). [IWM]

141 Summerfield, 'Gender and War in the Twentieth Century', p. 8. See also Susan R. Grayzel, 'Mothers, Marraines, and Prostitutes: Morale and Morality in First World War France', *The International History Review* 19: 1 (1997), 66–82.

2

The great adventures begin
Grace Ashley-Smith in Belgium
Autumn 1914

On the declaration of war on 4 August, 1914, Grace Ashley-Smith was aboard ship travelling to visit family in South Africa. 'We stood there speechless', wrote Ashley-Smith, 'and slowly the immensity of it pierced my heart. I was the first to speak: "Thank God it's come now." My inmost thought was that it had come *whilst I was young enough to be in it* [orig. emph.]. In my usual head-less [sic] way I did not explain this, and the captain [of the ship] turned his sombre gaze on me with a glint of anger. "God forgive you for that, my girl", he said.'[1] Ashley-Smith's response here as the first one to speak and the one to speak heedlessly illustrates her energy and impetuosity. Her near-rejoicing in the news of war also reflects her ambition and naïveté. Although she would lead the FANY in service to the Allies, the captain's words were a foreboding of what was to come in this disastrous and bloody war.

Since Ashley-Smith was desperate to return home and rejoin the FANY, on reaching Gibraltar she managed to get passage on another ship bound for England. This liner had already been commandeered into the war effort for the transportation of troops and had a naval escort. Ashley-Smith witnessed the escort attempting to sink an Austrian boat accused of laying mines. 'She was so light', recalled Ashley-Smith, 'they could not hit below the water line.' But then, 'Lo! The boat was gone' and 'we who had tarried to the end and had our reward, rushed in to dinner'.[2] This apparent lack of concern for loss of life and the rush to eat dinner once it was over illustrate the spectatorship of Edwardian war mentality, the callousness of the privileged, and the energy, excitement, and patriotism initiated by battle. This is underscored by Ashley-Smith's memory of their arrival in Portsmouth:

In one line the incoming ships were halted, and out from Portsmouth Harbour with the blood red sky behind them, came two long lines of ships. Silently, majes-tically they passed us on either side – massive dreadnoughts, torpedo boat destroy-ers, battle cruisers. We stood entranced with beating hearts and our throats too dry to speak; we could only watch in awed silence the A and B fleets put out to sea. This was our home-coming – and as the ships sailed into the silence the colours faded from the sky and all was grey and mist colour. It might almost have been a dream

– that most wonderful sight I have ever looked on; the British Fleet going out to War.[3]

These early days of August 1914 were filled with military deployments as both sides attempted to move armies and supplies. German militarism had created the Schlieffen Plan for the control of Europe: France must first be defeated, after which the armies would turn east and defeat the Russians. In order to win over the French as quickly as possible, however, the Germans required unhindered passage through Belgium. Britain was drawn in by the double obligation to defend France through the Triple Entente and to defend Belgium through the alliance for Belgian neutrality. As deployments were made, combatants received their first inkling that this war involved modern industrial technologies never before seen on the battlefield. Alongside new motorized vehicles and deadly automatic and artillery weapons, armies had field telephones for communication and aerial photography and naval calibration for mapping.

The Imperial German Army began by moving almost one and a half million troops into the Western Front, organized into seven armies under Colonel-General von Moltke. The Germans crossed into neutral Belgium on 4 August and were met by Belgian General Leman and his troops. While the Belgians fought with courage and determination, the Germans took the fortress and city of Liège and moved on to take Brussels on 20 August. The Germans burned villages and killed civilians during this advance; their plan was to terrorize the Belgian population and avoid having to leave large numbers of troops guarding rear communications. The French under General Joffré responded with a strategy of offence (a combination of *élan* [dash] and *cran* [grit]) rather than defence, and plunged forward with great disasters at Morhange and Sarrebourg and later at Lorraine and the Ardennes. By the end of August the French were in retreat. The BEF under Sir John French had been deployed to Belgium, although several divisions were held back by Lord Kitchener, Secretary of State for War, to protect Great Britain in case of invasion. The BEF also suffered great losses despite temporary victories at Mons and Le Cateau at the end of August. September came with German victory on the Western Front. In the East, the Russian allies had been severely defeated at the Battle of Tannenberg, although the Serbs had fought hard against Austrian forces with some success.[4]

This was the situation when Ashley-Smith arrived back in England on 5 September 1914. She found that many FANY had already taken VAD jobs, not believing the FANY could get into the war effort.[5] In Ashley-Smith's absence the FANY had organized sewing parties and collected equipment and FANY officer Margaret Cole-Hamilton moved to the London headquarters to pack, list and sort out their equipment in the hope that they might be sent to Belgium. Nonetheless, all had to admit that since Lillian Franklin's most recent offer of service had been refused, getting the FANY across to Belgium at this point was going to be very difficult. Indeed, the British government had already refused to authorize the Scottish Women's Hospital Units founded by Elsie Inglis, as well as Flora Murray and Louisa Garrett Anderson's Women's Hospital Corps, although all were eventually allowed to serve.[6] Such requests to help in the war effort were hampered by the fact that as soon as the war broke out, people with influence and resources but no inclination to work were able to go to the Front merely to view the war as spectators. This caused havoc for the authorities and encouraged them to be suspicious of non-affiliated volunteer groups leaving for Europe.

Most important, as already mentioned, the British War Office feared a subversion of normal gender relations if women were allowed to serve. This fear was based upon two issues: citizenship and gender anxieties. Female participation in war disturbed understandings of women's contributions to the social public or 'national' good and raised issues of gender, service and citizenship: especially troubling in the context of male suffrage and franchise grounded in both age and property qualifications. One of the major arguments concerning citizenship and suffrage was that only men should qualify since only men could fight and be sacrificed in war. Women's service to the state through work in, and exposure to, the dangers and horrors of this war (as well as, in other contexts, their role as mothers and in 'sacrificing' men they loved), precipitated debate about women's political rights. In addition, there arose the ongoing issue of women's 'nature' and sexuality. Women's place, outside of the pious nun-like role of Red Cross nurse, was supposedly at home. It was women's perceived 'nature' as irresponsible, irrational, fragile and prone to breaking down under stress, as well as female sexuality that particularly troubled the authorities. That 'problems' associated with women's sexuality (such as venereal disease and lapses in male discipline) were caused by men seems to have escaped them, enough to say that women in this masculine space not only trivialized and feminized the war effort but caused deep anxiety concerning sexuality and morality. As Susan Grayzel explains, 'the multiple debates that posited female sexuality as a threat to the fighting man point to the extent to which debates about the female body as the site of temptation and the transmitter of disease became an arena for the expression of anxiety about general social disorder'.[7] Jenny Gould sums up the resistance this way:

Some simply believed that fighting was a man's job and should remain so. Others feared that women could not cope with the reality of war at the front. Some asked, if women go off to fight and are killed in the same numbers as men, who will rebuild (repeople) society afterward? And, if men were not fighting for women and children at home, for whom were they fighting? During the First World War, people – especially women – worried about the moral consequences of allowing women to become part of the military forces and live in close proximity to men. Finally, considerable disapproval was expressed during the First World War of women who were seen as 'aping' men.[8]

The French and Belgian authorities subscribed to similar notions of women's place and held similar (if not more strict[9]) views. In the case of Belgium at this moment, however, their country was being invaded and they desperately needed the assistance any medical auxiliaries could give. The chaos and the ensuing disorganization in Belgium allowed a space for women to help in the war effort and British women's transgressions reflected on the national degeneration of Britain and thus were more easily accepted.

In the face of this resistance, Ashley-Smith hit upon a plan to go alone to Belgium as a FANY and attempt to have the rest of the Corps follow. If she could gain access to the fighting zone, she believed she could get the FANY across in due course. She visited the British Red Cross Society (BRCS) and received grudging consent to leave with the next group of nurses in the event of being able to procure a passport. Ashley-Smith told the audacious story of how she managed to get this document. She was sitting in the passport office at 3 o'clock (the office closed at 4 p.m.) when the policeman overseeing the process left the room for a moment. She jumped up, slyly looked over the passport applications in the basket and then moved hers up and placed it on the top. When the policeman returned and read the next batch of names, hers was first. 'Yours!' he said and stared at her very hard. 'Mine!' she replied, trying to look utterly innocent. Ashley-Smith got her passport. She then returned to the disgruntled Secretary at the BRCS and persisted until she received permission to leave. Within two days of this interview and dressed in FANY khaki, she was on her way to Belgium and declaring 'the great adventures begin'.[10] With her usual aplomb for mixing with the right crowd, Ashley-Smith had made friends with a Belgian Minister for the Colonies, Monsieur Louis Franck, who had also been on the ship on which she had travelled back to England.[11] He may or may not have provided official assistance in her eventual establishment in Antwerp, but he certainly helped her imagine how to get involved in the war. In addition, Ashley-Smith had connections with the League of Imperial Frontiersmen where her brothers had served and used these connections to get to Belgium.[12]

This chapter explores Ashley-Smith's work as a FANY in Belgium during September and October 1914 and highlights the second key theme in the negotiation of gender relations in war: women's participation in the dangers of battlefield and the construction of the military heroine that aligned women alongside male combatants. It explores Ashley-Smith's writing during this early part of the war and, in particular, the ways she crafted her identity as a FANY and made the case for women's place in combat.

Women writing

Despite the fact that men's writing about the war has mostly constructed the image of this period, wherever women found themselves during the First World War, they wrote about these experiences and produced a broad range of writing that included memoirs and letters, journals and diaries, political commentary and documentary, poetry, short stories, and novels.[13] While women's experiences, abilities and opportunities for writing were complicated by class differences, they wrote to have a voice: to recapture the drudgery, the adventure and the loss, and to share their emotional and political responses to this 'crippled world, the bitter day – whose striplings are no more'.[14] Mostly barred from the battle zone (British authorities did not allow women close to the Front after 1915), it was difficult for women to gain the first-hand experience of war necessary to possess the narrative authority from which to write. In addition, women were often silenced by the pity they felt for what men had suffered and encouraged to subordinate their stories to those of the combatants.[15] As Dorothy Goldman in *Women and World War I: The Written Response* explains:

It is clear that women found it difficult to identify the appropriate voice to articulate their perceptions and in this context the impact of contemporary cultural mores – that the public was reserved for men while women could exert influence in the private sphere of the home – should not be underestimated. Its literary and stylistic corollary was that argument and documentary required the voice of masculine authority whatever the sex of its author, while private perceptions were more appropriately couched in the female voice. Whose voice then should be used when a woman chose to write about the War?[16]

The war writing that has been most valued is that of the male soldier–writer or poet with the authentic voice and credibility of 'being there'. This can be compared to women's marginalized status in wartime: being a non-combatant, not being male, and being external to the zone of cultural experience of killing. Yet, as Claire Tylee writes, 'Women's literary responses to war . . . tend to be much wider and more subtle in scope than battle-tales, since they are interested in the social context of belligerence and its connection with personal relation and the quality of ordinary life.'[17] Indeed, feminine credibility in noticing and expressing the private and the domestic allowed women to understand and express the details of war's effects on society. Ashley-Smith's writing of her time as a FANY in Belgium is especially interesting because of the narrative authority granted by being so close to combat. She was in a position to resist the male monopoly of direct experience and develop a rhetoric of female heroism and war service.

Alongside these obstacles associated with narrative authority was that of official censorship.[18] Layers of social camouflage were fed by the British press, newsreels and other accounts of the war and were facilitated by the government's Bureau of Information and the Defence of the Realm Act (DORA) introduced in August 1914. All communications about the war were censored, certain activities restricted, and knowledge about the war romanticized. As a result, civilians generally, and women in particular, were shielded against the horrors of this war. In their introduction to *Women's Fiction and the Great War*, Suzanne Raitt and Trudi Tate quote Violet Hunt's haunting poem that describes the layers of propaganda and knowledge about the war as 'shiny and black. Like bombazine or taffeta,/Or the satin of my grandmother's gown, that stood alone/It was so thick.'[19]

Given these constraints, it is remarkable that women like FANY Grace Ashley-Smith were not only able to choose the path of an altered femininity and enter the masculine space of the battle zone, but also able to produce writing about it that reflected their roles as participants as well as witnesses. In this chapter I suggest the ways the sentimental, romantic genre associated with the 'Great War Rhetoric' and women's literary heritage allowed Ashley-Smith the opportunity develop a female heroism. In *The Great War and Modern Memory* Paul Fussell calls this high diction a 'feudal language' and sets out a table of equivalents in his book, where, for example, warfare is strife, to conquer is to vanquish, to be dead on the battlefield is to be fallen and the blood of young men is, as Rupert Brooke wrote, the red sweet wine of youth.[20] While this Great War Rhetoric was the sentimental way both men and women could decently write about the events of the war at its beginning, given traditional nineteenth-century literary conventions, women in particular were also encouraged to combine the sentimental with romance, the privileged voice of genteel femininity. These feminine discourses were grounded in religious and moral distinctions and involved the expression of the 'highest' feelings of tenderness and were influenced more by emotion than reason. They thrived in the relatively female-segregated spaces inhabited by middle- and upper-class women of the period and encouraged the development of emotional identity and solidarity. The language of the sentimental was abstract and heavy on pathos (the rhetoric of sympathy) and compassion.[21] Idealism (a tendency to imagine the ideal, the desired, the worthy-of-emulation, and the desirable goal, irrespective of facts that might dispute this vision) existed alongside the sentimental in these traditional perceptions of meaning. Together they created a visionary and romantic discourse that was potentially hyperbolic and impressionistic. A form well-suited to this discourse was the romantic adventure with its emphasis on the hazardous journey or quest, the ordeals involved, the emotional and psychological effects, and the truths revealed. In this way, although both men and women writers turned to the romance as a way to express the experiences of war, it was especially women who were most adept with this form.[22]

Inevitably, the heroic, inspirational and consoling sentiments of high diction were inadequate to deal with the terrible realities of a mechanized total war and these traditional styles were increasingly replaced by the more realistic and frank forms of expression associated with modernism. Bradbury and McFarlane identify key modernist tendencies as radical innovation, fragmentation, shock and despair, a move toward irony and paradox, and the rupturing of formal linguistic convention.[23] Goldman describes modernist rhetorical strategy as awareness of a 'nihilistic disorder behind the ordered surface of life and reality' and a focus on 'inward states of consciousness'.[24] While this is amply revealed in the protest poetry of such soldier poets as Owen and Sassoon and in such postwar writing as Remarque's *All Quiet on the Western Front*, it is also a component of women's writing as anyone who has read Evadne Price's novel *Not So Quiet . . . Stepdaughters of War* or Mary Borden's *The Forbidden Zone* can testify.[25] Goldman makes this point when she writes that 'both sexes were alike in their rejection of such abstractions, and alike in undergoing revolutionary experiences that brought revolutionary insight . . . women writers were like men in employing all the different modes of response available at the time – from Fussell's 'Great War Rhetoric' to modernist irony'.[26]

Most women, however, attempted to blend old romantic traditions with more modernist approaches and their writing often illustrates what Angela K. Smith has called 'accidental modernism' where there was no intentional, political desire to rupture traditional literary conventions.[27] While women writers understood the need for romantic imagery since the romance motif was still the most acceptable and familiar genre for women's writing, given the ambiguities and uncertainties of war, they also wanted to speak the truths of their lives in a more realistic or modernist voice. Smith suggests that the literary transformation occurring as a result of being faced with the inadequacies of conventional language was accidental and many women writers were 'in a traditional sense, out of place and time, inadvertently adding to the development of modernism through their anachronistic location'.[28] This describes the case of Ashley-Smith, who, unlike such writers as Borden and La Motte, had no prior exposure to avant-garde literary circles and no training in the techniques of literary innovation. Her romantic account of her experiences as a FANY in Belgium are interspersed with such an accidental modernist voice.[29] These changes represent her loss of innocence as she constructs her place as a militarized woman.

Ashley-Smith's accounts of her first months in Belgian as a FANY are recorded in *Nursing Adventures: A FANY in France* (1917), reprinted in the USA as *A Nurse at the War: Nursing Adventures in Belgium and France*.[30] Both editions are identical and anonymously written in the sense that neither include Ashley-Smith's name as author, although both are referenced under her married name (she would marry early in the war, in 1915), Grace McDougall. This false anonymity was an act of modesty: a self-effacing rhetorical strategy women used to submerge their identity as writers. Ashley-Smith also recorded these adventures in her unpublished memoir 'Five Years with the Allies, 1914–1919' and in a dispatch sent to the British Press in October 1914 that was touted as 'one of the most illuminating pieces of war correspondence ever written'.[31] 'Five Years with the Allies' is a retrospective account written after the war with the intention of recording FANY history as well as Ashley-Smith's own personal adventures and experiences. While the memoir is written in more straightforward prose than *Nursing Adventures*, it too contains elements of the traditional war rhetoric and casts Ashley-Smith as wartime heroine.

Nursing Adventures hoped to increase publicity and raise funds for the FANY and was thus essentially a patriotic text that utilized sentimental discourse, even while it is interspersed with this accidental modernist voice. It reads as romantic adventure emphasizing the hazardous epic journey or quest, distinctions between good and evil, and notions of travel into unchartered territory (part of the energizing myth of British imperialism). Along the way she revised these conventions to find more authentic self-expression, incorporating a more blunt, realist tone in many passages and producing an ambiguous text that in many ways parallels women's ambiguous gendered performances in this war. In this way, although the traditional romantic rhetoric of war underscores *Nursing Adventures* and articulates the conventional sentiments of the time, often mirroring conventional propagandist discourse, new forms are interspersed that reframe this writing in new ways. Ashley-Smith's experiences of these early years of the war encourage new stylistic innovations as well as inadvertently feminist themes associated with female action, efficacy and bravery, and, ultimately, social and political rights. The experience saw Ashley-Smith begin as bedside heroine, putting her on a footing with men in terms of the involvement with suffering, and graduates to battlefront heroine where she more actively risked the dangers of war and developed her own notion of personal heroism. Such rhetoric with its tangle of romance and realism is the first known example of a FANY attempt to write about war from the perspective of a female participant.

Frederic Jameson has suggested that romantic adventure stories are useful during such transitional moments as war since they contain within them the 'sediment' or traditional, familiar forms at the same time as they vision new cultural imaginaries.[32] And indeed, *Nursing Adventures* did vision new cultural imaginaries. It was a subversive adventure memoir in developing bold stories of female heroism on the battlefront during a period when adventure and soldiering were masculine prerogatives.[33] Ashley-Smith staked her claim to this narrative authority by framing her account in the accepted sentimental voice of femininity and, as the first FANY Corps would also do in their work with the Belgians discussed in the next chapter, by relying on nursing as the 'natural' extension of women's nurturing and domestic lives that made it not only a socially accepted route for womanly adventure but also a feminine version of national patriotic service. In addition, Ashley-Smith's adventuring relied on the accepted genre of women's travel accounts established before the turn of the century. Described as a 'lively and illuminating chronicle of a self-sacrificing and courageous woman', *Nursing Adventures* was part of a series published by the Heinemann Company on 'Soldiers' Tales of the Great War'.[34] The inclusion of this book by a woman with narrative authority to write in a series called 'Soldiers' Tales' illustrates its importance in recognizing women's place in war.

The Bedside Heroine

In late September 1914 when Ashley-Smith arrived in Ostend dressed in her FANY uniform as sole representative of the Corps, she came face to face with her first experiences of the conditions of war. The Battle of the Marne had halted the Germans temporarily and a deadlock was extending over the Western Front. While both sides entrenched with a series of slow outflanking manoeuvres later called the 'Race to the Sea', by the time the opposing armies reached the Belgian coast at Nieuport a continuous line or 'Front' stretched about 450 miles from the North Sea to Switzerland. The rapid German advance through Belgium caused the terror and dislocation of thousands of refugees who descended on such towns as Ostend and Antwerp as they fled the countryside. Ashley-Smith declared it 'a scene of desolation' with refugees crowding the streets, hungry and wretched, and soldiers amidst the chaos trying to bring some kind of order.[35] She reached the hospital in Antwerp where she was to be stationed, a Field Hospital on the Boulevard Leopold. The sanitary conditions were deplorable:

The top floor has 60 beds and no lavatory, and only one little water tap and sink which serves all purposes, dish-washing and rinsing of urinals and bedpans, surgical basins and instruments. Buckets received the filth, dirty dressings, and are emptied every few hours by Flemish servants. Towels hang together in wild confusion and are seized indiscriminately by hurried nurses to wipe cups, bedpans or basins for dressings. The next floor is the same, though there is a little corner is screened off round a commode.[36]

The head of this unit was a Dr Beavis, who agreed to consider Ashley-Smith's request to bring the FANY Corps to Belgium. In the meantime, however, the doctor desperately needed help with the nursing duties and put Ashley-Smith in charge of two wards on the third floor of the hospital. This time attending to the constant stream of wounded and dying men helped Ashley-Smith begin to understand the implications of war and her role in it. Her writing emphasizes the soldiers' bravery, gratefulness, stoicism and chivalry; her stories are filled with their pain and anguish: conditions were terrible, hospital supplies inadequate, and the wounds created by these new technologies of war caused terrible mutilations and injuries. Despite this backdrop of pain, brutality and suffering, Ashley-Smith does not subordinate her story to those of the soldiers. Instead she crafts her identity as the bedside heroine, participating in the sufferings of the soldiers and bravely facing danger as bombs drop all around. Although deferential to the suffering of the soldiers, Ashley-Smith's reports are full of agency and action and a certain amount of bravado that increases as she moves into ambulance work close to the firing line.

This narrative can be compared to the maternal and nun-like French heroines of the First World War whose service is described by Margaret Darrow in the context of war as combat to remasculinize the French nation. Their bravery, according to Darrow, came from their moral rectitude: 'the heroine's example was one of moral character and demeanor rather than of intellect or action . . . Three words most often qualified the heroine's action: calm, devotion and self-sacrifice. Commentators erased any sign of bravado from their accounts.'[37] This encouraged what Darrow describes as a suppression of the women's war. She continues:

[They] could not risk claiming an equal experience to the soldiers', an equal sacrifice to the national cause; since masculinity had to triumph, it was not a camaraderie of equals but of the nurse as acolyte to the soldier's heroism . . . Rather than commemorating a unique feminine experience, in account after account memoirists subordinated the nurse's story to the soldiers'.[38]

In contrast, as will be shown below, Ashley-Smith respected the soldiers' war but modelled an agency that circumscribed her own military experience and narrative authority.

When Ashley-Smith arrived at the hospital on the Boulevard Leopold, the medical staff were desperate for help and she quickly sprang into action and took charge of nursing tasks. One of her wards had sixteen beds and the other twelve. Ashley-Smith was at first somewhat disconcerted since she actually had little direct nursing experience. 'I was kept busy as there were a lot of dressings', she wrote, 'and I found, rather to my consternation, I was expected to do them . . . I told the Doctor I was not trained, but they counted on me to carry on, and at least I had a good idea what not to do.'[39] Indeed, Ashley-Smith with her elementary understanding of germ theory set to improving the sanitary conditions and insisted that the staff change their ways. After watching a harried nurse wipe out a cup after someone had used the same cloth to wipe a bedpan, she washed all the cloths in soda, boiling water, and disinfectant, sorted and marked the cloths, and then put up a large notice that read 'Red edges for bedpans, Plain edges for cups and plates, Blue edges for face and hands'.[40] She reports that the professional nurses were somewhat annoyed by her 'interference': an altercation that most likely involved class antagonisms, as working-class professional nurses often became irked by these mostly untrained privileged volunteers with their do-gooder mentalities.[41] Still, Ashley-Smith's ingenuity was rewarded with even more responsibility in a ward for more seriously wounded men; again she told them she was not trained, again she rose to the occasion anyway.[42] She used intellect and action born in part from her privilege and upper-class training to carve her niche in the hospital organization.

Ashley-Smith learned quickly about nursing under conditions of war. She was taught not to touch a wound but to paint it with tincture of iodine or else flush it with a saline solution. The only remedy was to dress the wound with compresses of sterilized absorbent gauze, cover with a layer of absorbent cotton, and then secure it with bandages fastened with safety pins. The nurses used both dry and wet dressings: dry for wounds that were clean and aseptic, wet if sepsis or infection was present. Wet dressings consisted of gauze soaked in a solution of corrosive sublimate or a weak solution of phenol covered by a layer of absorbent cotton. A final protective layer of 'oil silk', rubber tissue, or waxed paper was then paced on top.[43] As an American handbook for 'Sanitary Troops' dated 1917 explains, treatment of wounds of the chest consisted of 'laying the patient on the injured side and firmly bandaging the chest'. For wounds of the skull 'manifested by unconsciousness, paralysis, unequal pupils, etc., [n]o special first aid treatment is required'. As for wounds of the abdomen and stomach, they also require no special first-aid treatment except that 'the patient should be placed in such a position as may favor the escape of the contents of the intestinal tract'.[44] Treating these war wounds was indeed a grim business.

Ashley-Smith wrote about her first experiences with death, dying, and the seriously wounded and her personal resolution to cope. She provides some frank descriptions of her work with 'the cleaning, and the scrubbing, and the dying'[45] and inadvertently adopts the modernist strategy of relating to men in terms of their wounded body parts: 'a shattered thigh on the stretcher underneath; a broken arm and a shrapnel in the head opposite'.[46] She shares her first experiences with gangrene: the horrible smell by the bed and the 'ghastly green hole' that she was supposed to dress.[47] She also described wounded soldiers whose arms 'hung by a thread of flesh from the shoulder, and bled – always bled – though the tourniquet was as tight as possible; the dark blood oozed through steadily and fell with a constant drip, drip'.[48] These blunt descriptions, unconventional punctuation and the onomatopoeic 'drip drip' illustrate her more modernist voice. But then, as if to bring the narrative back in line with a conventional discourse of war, Ashley-Smith goes on to write of a soldier's last moments: 'He shouted and writhed, and at last his head fell back: then, with a mighty effort, he raised himself and opened his mouth to speak; but only a stream of blood rushed forth, and a brave soul had gone to its God!'[49] Although the last part of this quote and its description of the wounded soldier's death uses a more traditional voice, it has a shocking macabre undertone as a reader imagines blood pouring from the dying man's mouth. The ambiguity of this writing with its blending of old romantic traditions with more modernist writing formed inadvertently from the experiences of war was picked up by the *Yorkshire Observer* in its publicity for *Nursing Adventures*: 'We hear of pitiful and terrible wounds and mutilations, of heroic courage and patience among Belgians and British alike; while lighter and pleasanter topics are also touched upon and gay little dinners and teas enjoyed under all manner of unconventional and strange circumstances.'[50]

Direct nursing of war wounded required Ashley-Smith to get over the modesty of her genteel feminine socialization: 'Many of the wounds were in the thighs and buttocks' she writes, 'and at first, I felt it very trying – there were no screens in any of the wards – but the men's courtesy and consideration helped me through.' Such lamentations appear in the retrospective 'Five Years with the Allies' and are discreetly absent in *Nursing Adventures*. Romantic fiction of the period often featured volunteer nursing as redemption for fallen women at the same time as it imbued the experience with erotic implications, framing it as a means of intimate, romantic contact between privileged women and male strangers.[51] It behoved Ashley-Smith to avoid all suggestions of impropriety as she recorded her daily war service in this text.

In her role as bedside heroine tending to the wounded but sharing in their pain and suffering, Ashley-Smith sets herself apart from other women whom she believed were voyeurs of this war. This is important for Ashley-Smith because it makes the case for a distinction between militarized women like herself who are active participants in the war and those who are outsiders looking in. She describes an experience of being in the chapel in the hospital where she 'knelt to whisper a prayer for the dead' and upon leaving its outer foyer finding a group of English women 'in weird and wonderful costumes having tea, laughing and talking'.[52] She compares her service in FANY uniform to these women most likely of similar circumstances as herself in her former pre-militarized life, dressed in their civilian finery, socializing and having tea. She writes that it 'was like a tourist party attending a funeral'.[53] This reads as fragmented and disturbing narrative; one wonders where these women came from, why they were there, and imagines the surrealism of this 'party', representative of genteel femininity in the midst of the horrors of war. Ashley-Smith gives few contextual clues here and lets the juxtaposition of events speak for itself. This event serves to reinforce her credibility and heroism as participant in the war and not merely its observer.

One of the most strenuous and potentially dangerous nursing tasks performed by Ashley-Smith was the work required during evacuations. The Germans were advancing through Belgium and hospitals were constantly being evacuated. Ashley-Smith writes in *Nursing Adventures* about the terrible ordeals associated with evacuations:

An evacuation means to empty the hospital, and it was done when news came that the Germans were coming very near. The men's faces would turn white with horror and with fear, women would tremble and turn faint; and we, who had to work, would spend every ounce of our strength in dressing those poor fellows – pulling shirts over their shattered bodies, wrapping dressing gowns or coats or whatever we could round them in their weakness and suffering. And then very often, after having been taken to the station on a tramcar, the men would all be brought back and have to be carried upstairs again and put back to bed.[54]

Again Ashley-Smith dissociates herself and her colleagues from that broad class of 'women'. While the latter might tremble and faint, 'we', she asserts, had no time to tremble and faint but were workers in this war. Their experience of physical and emotional assault puts them on a par with the soldiers, actively experiencing power and autonomy and emerging as what Sandra Gilbert has (I believe over-)stated as virtual amazons rejoicing in female independence and action.[55] The soldiers in this narrative are emasculated as broken, torn and shattered; they are infantalized and dependent, dressed and undressed and 'put back to bed'. The roles are reversed: Ashley-Smith emerges as the active heroine and men who are supposed to protect women are feminized by their dependence upon them; feminized at the very moment that war is supposed to be the living embodiment of potent masculinity. Jane Marcus describes this state as living in the body of the other sex: 'each experiences war through the body of the other'.[56] She writes,

Unhoused, she must learn to operate Outside. Housed in the hole of trenches, soldiers must learn containment, self-control, and all the feminine virtues of the aware and alert Inside. Woman makes noise; man maintains silence. The entrenched and the un-trenched warfare experience profound gender traumas. The speaker becomes the listener; the listener becomes the speaker.[57]

Such gender reversals in the context of stories of female efficacy and heroism are, as Marcus points out, 'uncanny', and require considerable work, both literally in terms of the women and men involved and textually in terms of the telling of these stories, to keep 'natural' gender intact. Tangled with the seemingly paradoxical cultural scripts asserting both silence as a feminine virtue and the proclivity for gossip among the female gender, the freeing of the feminine subject to act, speak and write was both very disturbing and profoundly intriguing.

The battlefront heroine

Despite Ashley-Smith's commitment to nursing duties, she ached to get closer to the action and utilize her training in ambulance transport. Indeed, Ashley-Smith never really seems to fit the role of the self-controlled, self-sacrificing nurse – her voice is too clamouring and her desire for adventure impossible to hide. This opportunity for ambulance transport work came when she was on the street one day and a Red Cross ambulance worker asked her to help him go up to the Front lines and bring back English wounded. Ashley-Smith hardly needed to be asked twice; she wrote how she immediately got in the ambulance and 'they were off'.[58] Ashley-Smith poignantly recalled these trips to the Front among such Belgian villages as Malines, Bucherout, Lierre, and Vieux Dieu to help nurse and transport the wounded. The accounts in *Nursing Adventures* of her exploits doing ambulance work during these weeks in Belgium are somewhat fragmented and chaotic; the stories are often disjointed and loosely connected chronologically and move abruptly from one scenario to another. This form mirrors Ashley-Smith's experiences: she pieces together these disjointed adventures and attempts to record the chaos of war. They also no doubt reflect official censorship of all writing about war service. Such adventuring and tales of Ashley-Smith's courage and bravery that develop her own personal heroism and British 'pluck' are key examples of reworking gendered tropes.

Blunt descriptions of the horrors of war sprinkle the account of Ashley-Smith's romantic quest through the desolate countryside, descriptions where the tone turns to a flat and frank description as the more jocular conventional language of the traditional war rhetoric fails. One minute she is reminiscing on the adventures of war and the next describing a scene after two straight days of rain: 'the stench was terrible, thick and heavy, and too horrible for words; the soft earth was wet and heavy, and disturbed'. Her fellow workers spy human limbs protruding through the earth and she agrees that yes, indeed, '300 corpses had been hastily covered with earth after a fight a week or two before'.[59] Ashley-Smith describes the smell in one village that was 'enough to knock one down' along with charred skeletal remains and the waxen figure of a dead baby with a bayonet through its body. 'In those days, mentally and physically', she explained, 'I could endure tremendous strain',[60] emphasizing the physical and emotional assault that provides an image of her as equivalent to the trench-fighter. This passage also reflects the propagandist aspect of her writing and the need to underscore the necessity of British support for 'little Belgium' and paint the German alliance as devilish, inhuman and representative of the anti-Christ. This also underscored the combat as a holy war between good and evil.

To be successful, however, Ashley-Smith's adventure story had to incorporate traditional motifs of gender, what Jameson implied when he talked about sedimented forms or aspects of a prior generic tradition which are embedded in narrative. The forms are predictable: the lone young woman, used to the delicacies of a genteel life, suddenly thrown into the unfamiliar and inhospitable landscape; the presence of male strangers who might hurt and/or protect; and the backdrop of war: the ultimate in adventure. The sexual tension invoked by these circumstances might easily be misunderstood as promiscuity and it behoved Ashley-Smith to deny any notion of impropriety. Rhetorical devices invoking chivalry and innocence are used to remind the reader of her upper-class social status and bring safety and respectability to the experience of an unchaperoned woman in the company of strange men. In the following passage, such devices also served to remind the reader of the pastoral English countryside and the reasons for fighting this war:

When we drove back to the dressing station at Bucherout the St. John's men [St John's Ambulance workers] cheered, and one came up to me and gave me a pear. I wanted him to keep it, but he looked so hurt I took it and thanked him; then another gave me an apple, which I put in my pocket. A soldier in khaki came up to me shyly with a little bunch of mignonette; it almost brought tears to my eyes, for it suddenly made me think of a quiet garden with one corner overrun with mignonette, and my mother in a shady garden hat leaning on her stick, for it was her favourite plant.[61]

Ashley-Smith tries hard to preserve normalcy around gender relations and military combat by describing the wounded soldiers' courage and bravery as well as their chivalry and by justifying their death and suffering through the glories associated with sacrifice: heroes 'racked by the pain of their wounds, but brave as the gods of old'.[62] But still the roles are reversed as Ashley-Smith gallantly brings in the wounded men who are dependent and vulnerable, made immobile by their wounds and shell-shock. On one occasion that illustrates her agency and authoritative manner, Ashley-Smith took over a bread wagon and converted it into an ambulance, ordering a male officer to follow her command: 'A big bread wagon came along and I commandeered it; the sergeant at first demurred, but he quickly entered into the spirit of it. We spread a big blanket in a gateway and turned out all the bread. I climbed into the cart and passed the huge loaves out! Then I dragged the sergeant to an empty house, and we got mattresses and blankets and cushions, and made the bottom of that cart comfortable'.[63]

Alongside this ingenuity are examples of Ashley-Smith's disdain for Allied authority and red tape: a perspective completely at odds with the sacrificial nurse, patiently following orders and submissively dealing with authority. In *Nursing Adventures* Ashley-Smith described instances of red tape that made her gasp. 'Never had I realised', she explained, 'what victims it claims; and that evening I was witness of another distressing example of it.' This example was a staff officer demanding the demolition of a roof over an area of trench that had taken soldiers hours to build because it had wood rather than iron supports. 'The men were disheartened and furious, and many a curse fell on that staff officer's head, and personally I think he deserved them', reported Ashley-Smith.[64] This, I believe, reflects her attempt to align herself with the trench-fighters who often interpreted military authority as an obstacle. Through this allegiance she insisted she was fighting the same war.[65]

The anxieties associated with gender ruptures of war encourage Ashley-Smith to contextualize her bravery in the conventional story-line of a lone woman astray in a foreign land: 'Those were strange days when I was alone in little Belgium', she exclaimed. 'I was alone, quite alone, there was nobody English near me. At that moment I longed for an Englishman'.[66] The narrative casts her in a passive role as vulnerable heroine, in need of chivalrous intervention, and never before having seen a trench. But then, in the same passage, enemy fire puts her in danger and she jumps into a trench and finds a wounded soldier in need of medical attention. Leaping down beside him she tells the reader that 'with his hand in mine and his arm drawn round my neck, I pulled and pushed and struggled, and we got out and slowly reached the road'.[67] From this ambiguous mix of the vulnerable/powerful heroine, longing for an Englishman, Ashley-Smith emerged as the hero who saved a man's life. Another good example of this vulnerable/powerful heroine is another passage in *Nursing Adventures* where Ashley-Smith describes herself actively riding into the sunset on the footboard of an ambulance at the same time that she rejoices in her passive role as woman for whom men are fighting:

I stood on the footboard, holding on with one hand to the roof of the car. On we sped, and the sky was flaming red, and suddenly our road lay clear and straight through long lines of English blue-jackets and marines – miles of them – all marching forth with steady tramp and resolute, kindly faces. How my heart went out to them; and how their ringing friendly cheers brought the blood to my face and a great joy to my heart! No more hunger – only pride – as these lines of men – my men –went out gaily to fight for *me* and all the women of the Empire.[68]

Nursing Adventures is chock full of Ashley-Smith's adventures at the Front. To underscore these adventures she often referred to herself in the third person as 'Mademoiselle'. For example, on arriving at a collecting station for the wounded at Bucherout a mere 200 yards from the firing line, she was told to retreat and writes: 'Mademoiselle laughed and went on'.[69] Another time out on the road back to Vieux Dieu in search of casualties, Ashley-Smith was asked if she were afraid to go on: 'Mademoiselle said there was no question of fear, but of wounded; if there were wounded the car must go.'[70] Many a time she explained 'men have turned to me for strength, and dying men have held my hand in an anguished farewell to life, and women have clung to me sobbing'.[71] Ashley-Smith emerges as steadfast heroine in the face of danger and pain. This rhetoric is interesting because she consciously embraces the masculine myths of physical bravery and heroism associated with the Great War rhetoric and claims it for herself through the feminine sentimental voice. Ashley-Smith disturbed the discourse of masculine bravery by accepting its parameters and inserting herself in it. And indeed, lady readers of *Nursing Adventures* were thrilled by these tales of courage and bravery and reviews described it as a 'story illustrative of the adventurous spirit which has filled the hearts of many British women'.[72]

Much of the narrative concerning Ashley-Smith's personal heroism is conceptualized in dialogue with soldiers incredulous at finding a woman in this masculine space: '"You are not afraid?" one man asked, and seemed to wonder when I laughed. "You are very brave", said another; but I shook my head vigorously. "But you were really not frightened?" a sergeant had to ask, and when I looked up at him and said, "Yes, I was really frightened, terribly frightened for a little time", he shook his head and shrugged his shoulders.'[73] There is a chivalrous sexual tension in these details about shaking heads and shrugging shoulders; the men were curious and gave her attention, and she enjoyed being noticed. One soldier picked her a bunch of flowers; another took her to view the landscape ravaged by war. The passage ends with a re-emphasis on her mission: 'Artillery rolled past, the men all turning to salute the Englishwoman in khaki in their midst. The sun was setting, and far away the loud roar of guns cut the evening stillness. This was war!'[74] The familiarities of gender relations circumscribed by the tropes of chivalry coexist alongside gender ruptures tearing at the narrative. 'To them I was a strange being; to me they were a new revelation.'[75]

Ashley-Smith's adventures and her explicit claim to personal heroism in the military context suggest possibilities for gender transformation and provide an inadvertent feminist message. Even though she did not connect her personal ambitions with social and political struggles for women's advancement and never identified as a suffragist and certainly not a feminist, her writing about her time in Belgium inadvertently demonstrates feminist goals in providing a model of female autonomy and heroism. Such behaviour also made the case for women's collective citizenship through the logic that only men might claim this right through their participation and potential sacrifice in war. Ashley-Smith aptly showed not only the ways women could enter and work productively in the war zone, but also the necessity of such service for the war effort.

The flight from Antwerp

> The straight flagged road breaks into dust, into thin white cloud,
> About the feet of a regiment driven back league by league,
> Rifles at trail, and standards wrapped in black funeral cloths.
> Unhasting, proud in retreat,
> They smile as the Red Cross Ambulance rushes by . . .
> They go: and our shining, beckoning danger goes with them,
> And our joy in the harvests that we gathered at nightfall in the fields;
> And like an unloved hand laid on a beating heart
> Our safety weighs us down.[76]

This excerpt is from the poem 'Field Ambulance in Retreat' by novelist May Sinclair, a member of Hector Munro's ambulance unit stationed in Belgium. Ashley-Smith would come to know May Sinclair and share this 'shining, beckoning danger' when the Germans took the town of Antwerp on 9 October 1914, forcing the Allies into retreat. Despite the fierce fighting that preceded this event, the Germans were able to take over the town and push the Belgian Army down the coast to join the Allies behind the River Yser. At the same time, the Belgians opened the sluice gates and flooded this low-lying countryside as a deterrent to advancing German forces. The timing of the retreat was especially disappointing for Ashley-Smith who had just been asked by the authorities of the Field Hospital where she worked to bring over the FANY and take charge of a hospital on the Rue Maria Theresa. No sooner did she receive this request than the Belgian Red Cross also requested the FANY staff a large new hospital in Antwerp. These plans were then disrupted by the Allied retreat from Belgium and the need to evacuate the wounded.[77]

After this gruelling work, Ashley-Smith spent a sleepless night with bombs dropping all around. She tried to sleep on a bench in the hospital yard with shrapnel falling constantly and the house next door disappearing in a shower of rubble. She ended up finding some peace by sleeping on a sack of potatoes in the hospital yard: a far cry from the genteel comfort of her former life. She was evacuated with other medical workers by bus the next day, completely exhausted, driving through the night to Ghent, another Belgian town. Codes of modesty and gender etiquette are forgotten as she sleeps on a strange young man's shoulder, and, despite the irony of her romantic message, she share the modernist insight that the romance and heroism of war is a lie: 'To me in the past War had meant romance and heroic deeds, not the awful hell of agony it is.'[78]

Once in Ghent, Ashley-Smith's medical unit unloaded the wounded at several sites: the Hotel Flandria, L'Hôpital Civile and a convent. Ashley-Smith begged the reverend mother of the convent to be allowed to stay and work there and her request was permitted. Ashley-Smith wrote of the gendered arrangement of her work there:

The men themselves were worn out with the suffering of their night in the 'bus and the sleepless night of the bombardment. The doctor was very capable, and extremely clean in his methods. There was a bevy of fair lady helpers to accompany us, and they all had special duties allotted them. One very pretty girl had to hold the patients' [sic] hands and head and fondle them to take his mind off the pain of his dressings. One held the bowl of swabs, one the pail for dirty dressings, etc., etc., and not one of them was allowed to touch the dressings and bandages prepared for use. This was my work, and I had to undo all the dressings and syringe the wounds that required it.[79]

The ambulance unit working at the Hotel Flandria consisted of a group founded by Hector Munro, a doctor and psychic from the Medico-Psychology

Clinic in London, and included novelist May Sinclair, Elsie Knocker (who would become the Baroness de T'Serclaes) and Mairi Chisholm. Fatigued by Munro's eccentricity and disorganization, Knocker and Chisholm left the unit and went on to staff an advanced dressing station right behind the Front lines, becoming famous as the 'Heroines of Pervyse'.[80] May Sinclair, however, had a different story. Although she was ecstatic at the opportunity to serve with the unit, her presence was based on her financial support of the unit and she was barely tolerated once in Belgium. Aged fifty-one years and with few skills, she suffered much disappointment and humiliation at being sent back to England after two and a half weeks, ostensibly to raise more funds for the unit. She wrote a version of these experiences in *A Journal of Impressions in Belgium*.[81]

As Ghent too was evacuated, May Sinclair had communicated with Ashley-Smith and offered to have her travel with them. On arriving at Ecloo, a town between Ghent and Bruges, Sinclair was 'in great distress' about a dying British officer named Richard Foote who had been left at the Hotel Flandria.[82] Ashley-Smith decided to go back and try and find the officer and stay with him until he died. She explained that Sinclair was terribly upset and wanted to return but was deterred because she knew nothing about nursing.[83]

Later Sinclair published excerpts from *A Journal of Impressions in Belgium* in the *English Review* and referred to the dying officer Foote as 'one of her [Ashley-Smith's] four wounded', insinuating that Ashley-Smith had abandoned the officer in the first place. Ashley-Smith was offended and the *Saturday Review* wrote an editorial note in the next issue explaining her point.[84] Ashley-Smith's copy of *A Journal Of Impressions in Belgium* is full of her handwriting disputing Sinclair's 'facts' about these incidents. In particular, in response to a sentence saying that Sinclair and she spent a long time discussing who was to go back to Ghent to care for the officer, Ashley-Smith wrote in the margin '*Rot!* There was no discussion I was on my way [when] I met them [the Munro Unit]' and when Sinclair asserted that she too got on the train with Ashley-Smith, the latter wrote '*Tiens tiens*! Dear me! I never saw this happen!' She also noted 'they panicked the whole lot of them – there was no danger for a few days'.[85] These annotations show a different face to the adventure and suggest Ashley-Smith's doggedness, her keen need to maintain her identity of bravery and valour, and her hypersensitivity to accusations she might have shirked any responsibility.

Nonetheless, once back in Ghent Ashley-Smith took charge again, helped ease the dying man's pain, and arranged to have him transported to a Belgian nursing home where she stayed with him until he died. By this time the Germans had occupied Ghent and the First Battle of Ypres was being fought south-east of Antwerp. Ashley-Smith's story is full of bravado and highlights her personal heroism and British pluck as she attempted to survive behind enemy lines:

I drove to the German headquarters, having vainly appealed to the American consul and to the Spanish consul for assistance. The sentries at the gates eyed me with amazement, and the corporal of the guard came to ask my business and conducted me to the general. As he threw open the big glass doors into a sort of anteroom filled with officers, there was a dead silence for a moment. Every head turned towards me; for a moment I think they took me for a man. One or two saluted, and I saluted gravely and looked around for a likely interpreter . . . a very dapper A.D.C. asked my business. I stated it quietly:

'I am English. The officer I have been nursing is dead; I want to return to England.' A little crowd gathered around me; they all spoke perfect English. They would not permit me to go. I must indeed go to Brussels, and from thence I would be sent to Germany, and perhaps from there to England! . . . I told them if they wished me to go to Brussels they would have to send me; for myself I was going to England. So with many salutes we parted, and I swanked out through that courtyard filled with Germans as if khaki had never before been so fittingly worn![86]

This last statement of Ashley-Smith's with its assertion of her swanking out through the courtyard filled with German authorities, saluting and audaciously letting them know she would not be intimidated, provides a most glamorous story of female heroism. It is followed by other examples that also illustrate her bravado and physical courage: 'Once a man made rude remarks about the "English swine", and I told him off sharply and in execrable German threatened to report him! He took it meekly, and the Belgians round nearly embraced me. Once in a shop a German officer was buying a pencil and I a writing-block. The woman brought me one "made in Germany". I told her to take it away and see if she had English or Belgian paper, and then, as if by accident, knocked the offensive article on the floor. The officer went away without buying his pencil, and the good woman in the shop beamed with delight!'[87] Ashley-Smith enjoyed a good story and crafted her narrative to reflect the identity she wanted to present to others. Nonetheless, whether these events occurred exactly this way is less important than the fact that Ashley-Smith chose to craft it this way and took narrative authority in carving a niche for herself as a military heroine.

Ashley-Smith's escape from Belgium made riveting news in the British press (with such articles as 'British Nurse Defies the German Staff' and 'Little Sister in Khaki: Lady's Thrilling Despatch from the War Area') telling about her amazing exploits.[88] She managed to get to the border of Holland and had safe passage to England on a boat for refugees. She alighted at Folkestone and was back in London within a few hours. Exactly how she managed to secure her freedom from Belgium is not shared in *Nursing Adventures*. The censors would not have allowed it; enough for the readers to know she made a heroic escape and returned home safe and sound. This was the middle of October 1914. In 'Five Years with the Allies', Ashley-Smith explained that she escaped with the help of the Baroness de Crumbrugge who arranged to have a town councillor take her across the frontier: 'His mission was connected with the supply of food for the citizens and was not known to the Germans; if he were caught it might mean death, but if I cared to risk it, he would take me. We were frequently stopped by German sentries, but only the last two were diffi-cult to deal with. The rest all accepted, after a lot of discussion, the old Flem-ish parchments from the archives with great seals hanging from them'.[89]

Ashley-Smith's story of her ability to work and survive behind enemy lines as well as negotiate her escape illustrates an inadvertent feminism by cre-ating precedence for women's role in this masculine space of the battlefield and by constructing a brand of feminine heroism. However, while the story represents female confidence and self-possession, it also illustrates class priv-ilege. Ashley-Smith moved through the world with a strong sense of entitle-ment; she was used to having her way. She was very skilled in using the gendered expectations and prerogatives of upper-class femininity, as invoked, for example, by sacrificing her own safety and patiently tending to a dying sol-dier and waiting until his death, morally impervious as a privileged woman to accusations of waywardness or sexual impropriety. And, while her incongru-ous presence as a woman in uniform aroused interest and curiosity, it also aroused a relatively chivalrous response from the Germans. At least from their perspective at this early point in the war she was no dangerous enemy intruder, but a genteel woman and entitled to respect and chivalry. Ashley-Smith acknowledges this with her last paragraph of the chapter on her escape in *Nursing Adventures* and underscores her construction of a feminine brand of military agency:

And that was the first chapter of the war for me; and the second is, perhaps stranger still, for Providence led my comrades and myself into as strange places as ever women went before. This at least the Great War has done – it has proved to men that women can share men's dangers and privations and hardships and yet remain women.[90]

We turn now to this next chapter and meet the FANY on their way to France.

Notes

1 Grace McDougall (*née* Ashley-Smith), 'Five Years with the Allies, 1914–1919: The Story of the FANY Corps', pp. 17–18. [IWM]

2 Ibid., p. 20.
3 Ibid., p. 21.
4 John Terraine, *The Great War* (Ware, Hertfordshire: Wordsworth, 1998), pp. 56–75; Adrian Gilbert, *World War I in Photographs* (New York: Barnes and Noble, 2000), pp. 10–21.
5 McDougall, 'Five Years with the Allies', p. 22.
6 See Leah Leneman, *In the Service of Life: The Story of Elsie Inglis and the Scottish Women's Hospitals* (Edinburgh: Mercat Press, 1994).
7 Susan R. Grayzel, *Women's Identities at War: Gender, Motherhood, and Politics in Britain and France During the First World War* (Chapel Hill: University of North Carolina Press, 1999), p. 122.
8 Jenny Gould, 'Women's Military Services in First World War Britain', in Margaret R. Higonnet (with Jane Jenson, Sonya Michel and Margaret C. Weitz) (eds), *Behind the Lines: Gender and the Two World Wars* (New Haven: Yale University Press, 1987), pp. 117–18.
9 Margaret H. Darrow, 'French Volunteer Nurses and the Myth of War Experience in World War I', *American Historical Review* 101: 1 (February 1996), 80–106.
10 McDougall, 'Five Years with the Allies', p. 23.
11 Ibid., pp. 19–20.
12 Email correspondence with Lynette Beardwood (10 February 2003).
13 See such anthologies as Margaret R. Higonnet (ed.), *Lines of Fire: Women Writers of World War I* (New York: Penguin, 1999); Joyce Marlow (ed.), *Women and the Great War* (London: Virago, 1998); Suzanne Raitt and Trudi Tate (eds), *Women's Fiction and the Great War* (Oxford: Clarendon Press, 1997); Catherine Reilly (ed.), *The Virago Book of Women's War Poetry and Vers* (London: Virago, 1997); Angela K. Smith (ed.), *Women's Writing of the First World War* (Manchester: Manchester University Press, 2000); and Trudi Tate (ed.), *Women, Men, and the Great War: An Anthology of Stories* (Manchester: Manchester University Press, 1995).
14 Alice Meynell, 'Summer in England, 1914', reprinted in Reilly (ed.), *The Virago Book of Women's War Poetry and Verse*, pp. 73–4.
15 Dorothy Goldman (ed.), *Women and World War I: The Written Response* (New York: St Martin's Press, 1993), p. 8.
16 Goldman (ed.), *Women and World War I*, p. 8.
17 Claire M. Tylee (ed.), *The Great War and Women's Consciousness: Images of Militarism and Motherhood in Women's Writings, 1914–64* (London: Macmillan, 1990), p. 13.
18 Cate Haste, *Keep the Home Fires Burning: Propaganda in the First World War* (London: Allen Lane, 1977). See also Gary S. Messinger, *British Propaganda and the State in the First World War* (Manchester: Manchester University Press, 1992).
19 Raitt and Tate (eds), *Women's Fiction and the Great War*, p. 1.
20 Paul Fussell, *The Great War and Modern Memory* (New York: Oxford University Press, 1975), pp. 21–2.
21 See, for example, Suzanne Clark, *Sentimental Modernsm: Women Writers and the Revolution of the Word* (Bloomington: Indiana University Press, 1991); Mary Kelley, 'The Sentimentalists: Promise and Betrayal in the Home', *Signs: Journal of Women in Culture and Society* (Spring 1979), 434–6; and Jane Tompkins, *Sensational Designs: The Cultural Work of American Fiction, 1790–1860* (New York: Oxford University Press, 1985).
22 See, for example, Sandra M. Gilbert and Susan Gubar, *The Madwoman in the Attic: The Women Writer and the Nineteenth-Century Literary Imagination* (London: Yale University Press, 1979).

23 Malcolm Bradbury and James McFarlane, *Modernism* (Harmondsworth, Middlesex: Penguin, 1976). See also Allyson Booth, *Postcards from the Trenches: Negotiating the Space Between Modernism and the First World War* (New York: Oxford University Press, 1996); Steve Giles, *Theorizing Modernism: Essays in Critical Theory* (New York: Routledge, 1993); and Andreas Huyssen, *After the Great Divide: Modernism, Mass Culture, Postmodernism* (Bloomington, IN: Indiana University Press, 1986). For discussions of gender and modernism see Bonnie Kime Scott (ed.), *The Gender of Modernism: A Critical Anthology* (Bloomington, IN: Indiana University Press, 1990); Marianne DeKoven, *Rich and Strange: Gender, History, Modernism* (Princeton, NJ: Princeton University Press, 1991); and Alice A. Jardine, *Gynesis: Configuration of Woman and Modernity* (Ithaca, NY: Cornell University Press, 1985). Trudi Tate writes specifically about modernism and the war in *Modernism, History, and the First World War* (Manchester: Manchester University Press, 1998). *NWSA Journal* (Fall 2003) features a special issue on Gender and Modernism Between the Wars, 1918–1939.

24 Dorothy Goldman et al., *Women Writers and the Great War* (New York: Twayne, 1995), p. 79.

25 Helen Zenna Smith's (a.k.a. Evadne Price), *Not So Quiet . . . Stepdaughters of War* (New York: The Feminist Press, [1930] 1989); Mary Borden, *The Forbidden Zone* (London: Heinemann, 1929).

26 Goldman, *Women Writers and the Great War*, p. 77.

27 Angela K. Smith, *The Second Battlefield: Women, Modernism and the First World War* (Manchester: Manchester University Press, 2000), ch. 3.

28 Smith, *The Second Battlefield*, p. 7.

29 See Margaret R. Higonnet (ed.), *Nurses at the Front: Writing the Wounds of the Great War* (Boston: Northeastern University Press, 2001), and Patricia Moran, review of *The Second Battlefield*, *NWSA Journal* 15, 3 (2003), 200.

30 Grace McDougall, *Nursing Adventures: A FANY in France* (London: Heinemann, 1917); Grace McDougall, *A Nurse at the War: Nursing Adventures in Belgium and France* (New York: McBride, 1917).

31 'On the Fringe of the Storm: An Englishwoman's Experiences at the Front', *T. P.'s Weekly* (26 December 1914).

32 Frederic Jameson, 'Magical Narratives: Romance as Genre', *New Literary History* 7 (1975), 158.

33 Graham Dawson, *Soldier Heroes: British Adventure, Empire and the Imagining of Masculinities* (London: Routledge, 1994), p. 59.

34 *Liverpool Courier* (10 April 1917).

35 McDougall, 'Five Years with the Allies', p. 24.

36 Ibid., pp. 24–5.

37 Margaret H. Darrow, *French Women and the First World War: War Stories of the Home Front* (New York: Oxford University Press, 2000), pp. 109–10.

38 Ibid., p. 161.

39 McDougall, 'Five Years with the Allies', p. 25.

40 Ibid., p. 28.

41 See Irene Rathbone's semi-autobiographical novel *We That Were Young* (New York: The Feminist Press, [1932] 1989) for illustrations of the suspicions and hostilities between volunteer and professional nurses.

42 McDougall, 'Five Years with the Allies', p. 28

43 Charles Field Mason, *A Complete Handbook for the Sanitary Troops of the U.S. Army and Navy* (New York: William Wood and Co., 1917), p. 245.

44 Ibid., p. 93.
45 McDougall, *A Nurse at the War*, p. 90.
46 Ibid., p. 21.
47 McDougall, 'Five Years with the Allies', p. 29.
48 McDougall, *A Nurse at the War*, p. 14.
49 Ibid., p. 15.
50 *Yorkshire Observer* (1 August 1917). Similarly, an unidentified New York City newspaper (undated, *c.* 1917) described *A Nurse at the War* as 'telling calmly and always with a twinkle of the eye whatever was humorous of the horrors she has seen, of the endless and appalling hardships she has endured, and of the achievements of the work of mercy in which she was engaged'.
51 Darrow, *French Women and the First World War*, pp. 148–9.
52 McDougall, A *Nurse at the War*, p. 15.
53 Ibid.
54 Ibid., pp. 2–3.
55 See Sandra M. Gilbert, 'Soldier's Heart: Literary Men, Literary Women, and the Great War', *Signs: Journal of Women in Culture and Society* 8: 3 (1983), 422–50.
56 Jane Marcus, 'Afterword' in Rathbone, *We That Were Young*, p. 269.
57 Ibid.
58 McDougall, *A Nurse at the War*, p. 29.
59 Ibid., p. 19.
60 Ibid., pp. 17–18.
61 Ibid., p.27.
62 Ibid., p. 44.
63 Ibid., p. 25.
64 Ibid., pp. 35–6.
65 Darrow makes a similar point in *French Women and the First World War*, p. 160.
66 McDougall, *A Nurse at the War*, p. 4.
67 Ibid., p. 5.
68 Ibid., pp. 20–1.
69 Ibid., p. 28.
70 Ibid., p. 32.
71 Ibid., p. 29.
72 *Liverpool Courier* (10 April 1917).
73 McDougall, *A Nurse at the War*, p. 8.
74 Ibid., p. 9.
75 Ibid., p. 7.
76 May Sinclair, 'Field Ambulance in Retreat: Via Dolorosa, Via Sacra', in Reilly (ed.), *The Virago Book of Women's War Poetry and Verse*, pp. 98–9. This poem was first published in Hall Caine (ed.), *King Albert's Book* (London: Hodder and Stoughton, 1914).
77 McDougall, *A Nurse at the War*, p. 43.
78 Ibid., p. 55.
79 Ibid., p. 60.
80 See Baroness de T'Serclaes, *Flanders and Other Fields: Memoirs of the Baroness de T'Serclaes, M.M.* (London: Harrap, 1964) and G. E. Mitton (ed.), *The Cellar House of Pervyse: Tales of Uncommon Things from the Journals and Letters of the Baroness de T'Serclaes and Mairi Chisholm* (London: A. and C. Black, 1916).
81 May Sinclair, *A Journal of Impressions in Belgium* (New York: Macmillan, 1915). In this account the Baroness was referred to as Mrs Torrence and Mairi Chisholm was the

beautiful Ursula Dearmer. For biographies of Sinclair see Suzanne Raitt, *May Sinclair: A Modern Victorian* (New York: Oxford University Press, 2000); Hrisey Dimitrakis Zegger, *May Sinclair* (Boston: Twayne Publishers, 1976); and Theophilus E. M. Boll, *Miss May Sinclair, Novelist: A Biographical and Critical Introduction* (Cranbury, NJ: Associated University Presses, Inc., 1973).

82 McDougall, *A Nurse at the War*, p. 68.

83 Ibid., p. 69; McDougall, 'Five Years with the Allies', p. 37.

84 *English Review* 20 (June 1915), p. 309; *English Review* 20 (July 1915), p. 486; Grace McDougall to May Sinclair (12 June 1915), cited in Raitt, *May Sinclair*, p. 162, n. 40.

85 These writings are in Ashley-Smith's copy of Sinclair, *A Journal of Impressions in Belgium*, pp. 298, 300, 307. [IWM]

86 McDougall, *A Nurse at the War*, pp. 73–4.

87 Ibid., p. 75.

88 'British Nurse Defies the German Staff: Amazing Exploits of Mrs. McDougall in Belgium', *Weekly Welcome* (27 March 1915); 'Little Sister in Khaki: Lady's Thrilling Despatch from the War Area', *The Western Morning* (undated clipping [IWM], *c.* 1914).

89 McDougall, 'Five Years with the Allies', p. 42. Later in this account she names the councillor as Monsieur de Weert. After the Armistice she attempted to find him but discovered he was a hostage in Germany (p. 284).

90 McDougall, *A Nurse at the War*, p. 78.

3

Band of Hope
FANY with the Belgians at Lamarck Hospital
1914–15

Out of the grey mists of the past rise shadowy forms that come and go – some have deeper tints and stronger outlines than others; all are shrouded in silence. These are the women who formed what we called in jest 'The Band of Hope'. For it was no light task to take from safety to a troubled land those who had not already been there. So it was that money and friends and love itself proved no bar, and away I went light-hearted, taking with me willingly the responsibility of eleven other beings, mostly older, some younger, than I. Wise counsels of parents, the cautious teachings of friends, were listened to and lightly disregarded.

> 'Came the whisper, came the vision, came the power with the need,
> And the soul that is not man's soul was sent to us to lead.'[1]

Grace Ashley-Smith records the coming of the FANY to France with eloquent hyperbole. Members of this 'Band of Hope', leaving the safety of home for the dangers of a troubled land, embark on an ethical journey to savour the real glory of life. Although, of course, this is excerpted from *Nursing Adventures* and contains all the elements of romance and adventure necessary to enrapture the lady reader and aid in fund-raising for the Corps, it captures the vulnerability and naïveté of this 'Band of Hope' who are unprepared for the horrors they would discover through their service in the war. Still, unprepared or not, they would cope and carve out their niche on the Western Front.

Ashley-Smith's memoir 'Five Years with the Allies' takes a more practical tone: 'I had one fixed purpose', she wrote, 'to get a motor ambulance and return to the front'.[2] Ashley-Smith's brother Charlie helped her contact a firm by the name of Brown, Hughes and Strachan concerning the acquisition of a motor ambulance. Fortunately, Ashley-Smith recalled, they approved of her military service and Mr Strachan, like Ashley-Smith, was from Aberdeen and was appealed to as a fellow Aberdonian. Strachan spoke with the Unic ambulance company and persuaded them to sell her a chassis to be fitted with a van body. Ashley-Smith received money from her guardian and sold some stocks to pay for this venture.[3] In addition, the enterprising Ashley-Smith was also busy endearing herself to the echelons of the military establishment by taking a list of regimental numbers and names of British dead and wounded to the

Admiralty. She admitted that she had gone to the caretaker of the cemetery in Ghent and also visited the German Military Hospital dressed as a Belgian woman to gain this information.[4] Armed with this kudos, her experiences in Belgium under her belt, and her procurement of an ambulance, Ashley-Smith eventually received permission for the FANY to sail for France. In *Nursing Adventures* Ashley-Smith described obstacles that blocked every step of their way. '[O]fficialism, red tape, active enmity, all these had to be pushed aside.' She explained that what was needed at this point was 'infinite patience, much bluff and more blarney'.[5]

Although Ashley-Smith might have been a little short on patience, she was certainly not lacking in the bluff and blarney department. Sir Arthur Sloggett paved the way for her to meet with Mr Stanley of the BRCS requesting that the FANY be taken over to France on the next boat available. As she was waiting for this interview with Stanley, who should be there but the VAD officer who, according to Ashley-Smith, had attempted to usurp FANY authority during negotiations for their attachment with the Ulster Army. Although Ashley-Smith does not name her, it was probably Katharine Furse, VAD Commandant of the Paddington Division, London, who was given permission to leave for Boulogne after receiving orders from the War Office to set up a rest station on the Western Front.[6] Ashley-Smith describes this meeting and gives us a glimpse into the rivalries associated with women's attempts to make it to the Front:

She smiled at me now with gracious condescension, scanning my shabby khaki with a superior eye. She was very smart in a commandant's navy blue, immaculate. 'You won't see Mr Stanley, I'm afraid', she said, 'I have been waiting quite half-an-hour. I have just returned from Boulogne', she continued; 'There's a great deal going on there. No women in khaki over there though.' 'No?' I said blandly, 'Probably not, they're not fighting there are they? I've just come from Belgium. I was taken prisoner or I wouldn't be here now.' Before she had fully digested this, Mr Pennant politely informed me that Mr Stanley would see me at once. There's quite a lot of cat in all women. I departed feeling *very* happy.[7]

Alongside these preparations, Ashley-Smith had managed to make practical arrangements through her contacts in Belgium to provide nursing and ambulance support for the Belgian Army in Calais. This chapter focuses on these developments and highlights the third key theme in the negotiation of gender: the ways the FANY, mostly unprepared for the tasks at hand, were able to take opportunities and risks that stretched them and helped them cope with the labours of this war. It shares the story of these first FANY working for the Belgians at Lamarck Hospital (L'Hôpital Lamarck) from October 1914 through the end of 1915 and explores the ways they threw themselves into this service, accepting the trials and tribulations that came along with such work. The FANY were in a position to challenge the constraints of normative gender and turn the world what Nina MacDonald describes, in her poem 'Sing a Song of War-time', as 'topsy-turvy', as girls 'doing things/ They've never done before'.[8] Such coping, as I will suggest, included transforming the conditions of their lives and inventing themselves as non-traditional women under the relative safety of a respectable organization cheerfully dedicated to the war effort. For those who sought to escape (although for most this was a temporary escape) the constraints of genteel Edwardian femininity with its expectations for marriage, motherhood and charitable philanthropic duty, the FANY life brought opportunities for independence. The year 1915 was important in that it established the FANY in France and saw the development of their collective identity as courageous, competent women in the midst of this masculine space.

Working with the Belgians

Belgium neutrality had been protected since 1839 by international treaty and even during the Franco–Prussian War of 1870 the belligerents had refrained from violating it. As a result, Belgium had a small peacetime army of about 48,000 (compared to Austria's strength of 480,000). After King Albert of Belgium and his ministers refused to accept Germany's request to cross their territory and Belgium was invaded and occupied, the mobilized Belgium army increased to about 217,000 and consisted of six infantry divisions.[9] Relief efforts (led by the Commission for Relief in Belgium under the leadership of Herbert Hoover and the Red Cross) helped keep the population alive. At the eve of the war Belgium was among the most industrialized nations with sharp differences between the elite and bourgeoisie and the large mass of working people; however, unlike its neighbours, the Belgian state had not enforced social legislation to help relieve the plight of working people.

As in many industrialized societies, the Belgian elite classes subscribed to visions of genteel womanliness that were not borne out by the large numbers of women working in factories and underground in the mines.[10] Upon invasion, many privileged women escaped Belgium, although some remained to participate in the civil relief schemes for the increasingly impoverished nation.[11] This effort was epitomized by Elisabeth, Queen of the Belgians, as well as by Princess Marie de Croy, the Countess de Beughem, Countess Van den Steen, Madame Hangouvart, Countess Louise d'Urse and others,[12] as well as perhaps the baroness who aided Ashley-Smith in her escape from Ghent. The Belgians, like the French, endorsed the work of middle- and upper-class women so long as it did not violate the calm, devoted, self-sacrificing attributes of women in war; beyond this they were anxious about gender transgressions.[13] Ashley-Smith always described the Belgians as chivalrous and accommodating; she also emphasized that they were much less concerned than the British about women at the Front. This might be explained by the acute need of the Belgians and by the knowledge that the FANY were not *their* women (but still very much ladies and English gentlewomen: I believe this was very important for the Belgians). Just as it had for Ashley-Smith's service as a lone FANY in Belgium, war changed things; the *femme nouvelle* was an Anglo import and the 'English misses' running around the country unchaperoned only reflected on the uncivilized nature of the British.[14] This was the context for the FANY as they embarked on this new service.

This first FANY unit working for the Belgians consisted of twelve people: Lieutenant Ashley-Smith and her brother Bill who had been 'exchanged' from his regiment to drive the FANY ambulance, Lieutenant Lillian Franklin (who became known simply as 'Boss'), Corporal Edith Walton, Sergeant Isabel Wicks, Troopers Mary 'Molly' Marshall and Violet O'Neill-Power, and three infirmary nurses named Jordan, Dunn, and Robinson. In addition, orderlies Frank Brittain and Eric Hickson (a young medical student) came as male dressers. Pat Waddell, who had not yet passed her proficiencies in home nursing and first aid, saw this first FANY contingent off at Charing Cross Station and naively hoped that the war would not be over before she was able to join them. Along with other FANY recruits left behind, Waddell helped collect money, medical supplies and knitted garments for the soldiers, aching to prove that being a woman would not prevent her from useful overseas service.[15]

Once on the quay at Folkestone and ready to embark for work in Calais, the FANY experienced resistance first-hand. A Belgian refugee boat had been mined, postponing the FANY's travel. While they were waiting, eight wounded soldiers were evacuated and needed transport. After Ashley-Smith volunteered the FANY as stretcher-bearers, the Colonel in command condescendingly responded: 'Dear Ladies, do they think their soft white hands can carry a stretcher?' Ashley-Smith went 'white with anger' and they proceeded to carry the wounded soldiers. The FANY worked so efficiently that the Colonel was said to have conceded how invaluable their help had been and Sergeant Wicks had her photo bandaging a wounded soldier in the *Mirror* newspaper the next morning.[16]

The Corps arrived in France on 27 October 1914, a memorable day that still marks the annual FANY reunion. The First Battle of Ypres was raging and would continue until 11 November with huge casualties and loss of life. Three Army Corps of the BEF came north from the Aisne to Ypres along with a fourth Corps straight from England and a British Empire contingent of Indian

Corps, all under the command of Lieutenant-General Sir Douglas Haig. On 19 October the troops had joined the French and staged one of the last examples of open warfare on the Western Front. Trench deadlock would ensue after this with the fighting gaining and losing mere yards or a few miles, with little or nothing to show except heavy casualties. The joint Allied forces under the leadership of French General Fôche fought with strength and determination, even though the Germans had superior forces and more artillery power. The day after the first FANY contingent arrived in France, the Allies could say they had halted the German advance in front of Ypres, although this 'success' was very fragile. All along the Front line, it was touch and go as one crisis after another took the lives of thousands of men. The French held Dixmude, close to where the FANY would work, only by the 'skin of their teeth',[17] and the Belgians only saved their line by continuing to let the sea flood the low-lying land. This was the state of the war when the FANY joined the effort.

Ashley-Smith described the forlorn scene once they alighted in France: 'Calais the cruel, the pitiless; Calais swept by storms of rain and wind, cold and wet, and cheerless.'[18] Within a couple of days she communicated with the Belgian military establishment in Calais and arranged for the FANY to take charge of an empty convent school called Lamarck in the Rue de la Rivière and transform it into a hospital for Belgian wounded. The FANY unit working in this hospital became known as Unit 1 and ran the operation until Lamarck's closure in 1916. Lamarck stood next to Notre Dame Cathedral with the beautiful east window of the cathedral facing the yard. A large gateway led into the school courtyard where two long ungainly buildings lay parallel with each other; these buildings contained the classrooms that were turned into hospital wards. Unfortunately, the tranquil view of the cathedral was spoiled by a row of latrines, with a smell Cicely Mordaunt could only describe as 'indescribable'. An abundance of disinfectant and chloride of lime powder was used on a regular basis.[19] Mordaunt had been involved with the FANY before the war along with her sister Winnie and had accompanied Ashley-Smith to Ulster to make preparations for the Corps in 1913. She had since joined the VAD and worked at a French military hospital in Pourville with her friend Norma Lowson.[20] Together Mordaunt and Lowson decided to join up with the FANY at Lamarck. Mordaunt wrote about the discomfort endured by the patients who at first had to sleep either on straw *paillasses* or on wooden planks, supported on iron legs, that gave the men the most awful bedsores.[21] A majority of the first cases in the hospital were typhoid-related, since a particularly virulent pneumonic typhoid had been sweeping through the Belgian Army. As a result, one of the hospital buildings had to be devoted entirely to typhoid during the hospital's first few months.

Coping at Lamarck

Ashley-Smith threw herself into work at Lamarck, overseeing the hospital and other projects, organizing personnel and supplies, responding to administrative details, and of course the inevitable fundraising to keep a voluntary organization afloat. While the Belgians provided the buildings, meagre rations and some staff, the FANY had to finance the bulk of the endeavour, each contributing 10 shillings a week toward a common fund.[22] Back home in England the Treasurer, Secretary and Storekeeper in one, Mrs Morris, had the enormous responsibilities of the day-to-day running of the Corps: getting the FANY to France and keeping them there, ordering and delivering supplies and co-ordinating fundraising. FANY Headquarters was stationed at 192 Earls Court Road, London S.W. Morris also oversaw the publication of the *FANY Corps Gazette*. The *Gazette* had its first edition in July 1915 after the original magazine *Women and War* folded in 1910.[23] Morris would resign early in 1916 to be replaced by Secretary Janette Lean. The Reverend William Cluff became Treasurer in July 1915.

The English staff at Lamarck included Mrs Brenda Joynson, several trained nursing sisters and the FANY; the Belgian staff included two doctors, an adjutant or quartermaster, and, eventually, several Belgian male orderlies. The orderlies were interesting characters whose personae the FANY crafted to entertain readers and to highlight the poignancy and gaiety involved in the often dreary hospital work. One named Jefké was the ward clown who would lapse into bouts of melancholia and read from a prayer book. While he stole food from the kitchen, he also seemed to be in the business of stealing hearts and was said to have beautifully long eyelashes. Another character at Lamarck was the 'coffin man' who came by with the cart to pick up the corpses. He was also handsome and had been a trick cyclist before the war. One day he performed for the amusement of the FANY; shortly thereafter he came sadly to say goodbye to them having been caught taking his lady friend for a joy ride on the coffin cart. Now, '*Voila*', he exclaimed, 'I go to the trenches!'[24]

Immediately on moving into Lamarck the FANY attempted the arduous task of sanitizing the hospital and making a home out of the dirty shambles they encountered. Although such behaviour was squarely grounded in traditional notions of domesticity, the young women of the FANY would have had little experience with such tasks, most having had domestic servants at home to do such heavy scullery work. This image of the FANY as upper-class charwomen, cleaning and scrubbing, coincides with reports of the VAD who also endured much domestic manual labour and physical hardship during the war.[25] As Jane Marcus observes, 'young, healthy, well-educated women became the char-women of the battlefield, the cleaners of the worst human waste we produce, the symbolic bearers of all pollution and disease'.[26] Such work, explains Marcus, put these privileged volunteers in the awkward position of no longer being the ladies they were raised to be, nor the professionals respected for their work. This situation provided an invaluable service to the State, which relied upon their unpaid labour in order to avoid paying the wages of trained nurses.

The FANY not only set to making the hospital liveable, they also had to transform their lodgings. Although the FANY made the best of their accommodation in those early days at Lamarck, for Ashley-Smith they were a constant source of anxiety since the women had to be billeted in private homes in the town on a three-night rotation. Eventually Ashley-Smith managed to find an abandoned shop named Le Bon Génie as accommodation for the FANY. She used some flattery and coaxing, pulled a few strings here and there in her usual way, and at last they had found themselves a home. The women painted the walls, cut out pictures and put them up around the room, pasted the lower panes of the shop window with brown paper for privacy, and generally made the place liveable. Waddell recalled: 'When they first heard at home that we "slept in a shop window" they were mildly startled. We were so short of beds that the night nurses tumbled into ours as soon as they were vacated in the morning, so there was never much fear of suffering from a damp one.'[27] Along with Le Bon Génie, several FANY were also billeted over a place of entertainment called Le Bijou. The FANY especially loved to gather in these rooms and listen to the music coming from below. 'What ripping tunes they had!' remembered Pat Waddell. Once they thought to disguise themselves and join the fun, 'but unfortunately it was one of those things that is "not done" in the best circles!'[28] Again, class and gender norms worked together to inscribe appropriate public behaviour. Eventually the Lamarck staff vacated Le Bon Génie and Le Bijou and moved to lodgings in the Rue St Michel; then in turn they found a more comfortable house at 15 Rue de Richelieu overlooking the park. However, four FANY always slept on camp beds in a room on the top floor of the hospital and would join the regular night staff in case of need.

Life was hard at Lamarck. Ashley-Smith remembered these early days with their never-ending cleaning, ghastly injuries, and shortage of dressings and instruments. The place was filthy and they only had one tiny stove with a small kettle to boil water. They cut sheets in half to have enough for each bed and washed shirts and socks constantly in order to have clothes for the next day.[29] There was 'steady rain and raw cold and bad smells';[30] the food was awful and the water contaminated. As Martha Vicinus, quoting Florence Nightingale, writes in *Independent Women*, nursing was warfare and the enemy was disease, degradation and degeneration; this helped define the role of the genteel nursing volunteers as moral reform and a sort of purification that was not only physical.[31]1 Ashley-Smith in particular saw this hard physical work as a duty and sort of penance for her previous carefree life. Some of the work, such as cutting toenails and washing feet, she reported as 'quite terrible', although felt it was 'good discipline' nonetheless.[32] To confound their hardships, many FANY at Lamarck fell terribly ill with dysentery, doubling up on shifts to cover for each other as they became sick. Ashley-Smith wrote bluntly that she had 'constant dysentery' and had to spend half the day 'finding places' because of her diarrhoea. She also had an infected finger, a very common problem for nursing staff who often caught staphylococcus and other bacterial infections through a cut or a broken chilblain while dressing soldiers' septic wounds. It 'hurt like the devil', she wrote.[33]

It is important to remember that alongside such horrendous conditions, the medical staff were working without the benefit of sulphonamide drugs or antibiotics of any kind and had to perform constant amputations to prevent the ever-present sepsis and gangrene. Exploding shells caused terrible tissue damage and left shrapnel in wounds that would inevitably become infected, caused in part by the heavily manured fields of France. These infections included gas-forming organisms that caused gas gangrene as well as tetanus. Medical workers also had to deal with 'trench foot', a form of near-frostbite, as well as 'shell-shock': a psychological condition that caused disorientation, paralysis and hysteria.[34] Trying to keep water sterilized and hospitals sanitary were difficult jobs, and the sheer numbers of wounded and dying that might pass through hospital facilities during a major offensive were astronomical. While this war provided the necessity for medical research and developments in medical technologies (such as x-ray and blood transfusion), for the most part medical workers of this era fought their own losing battles against the mud, dirt, septicaemia and volume of dying. Workers at Lamarck who were dealing with typhoid patients also battled against body lice, identified as carriers of typhus fever.

Ashley-Smith described the FANY as 'gently-bred, high-spirited girls, who heard the call of misery and answered it'.[35] As a result, like most volunteer medical assistants in the war, the FANY were mostly ill-trained for this work and unprepared for the long hours, gruelling work, and horrendous tasks associated with caring for the injured and dying. However, even though they were inexperienced and relatively untrained as nurses, it is doubtful whether the acquisition of these skills would have prepared them for what they would experience in this war. Few anticipated a war that could cause so much human destruction and last so long, and the FANY were no exception in their naïveté, often vacillating between exclamations of the glamour and the horror of this war. However, precisely because this new work was not their routine everyday experience in civilian life, the ensuing 'making do' that was an inevitable part of all their service in the war seems to have been part of the adventure. Of course, as women they were expected to serve, and to hide any anger or resentment, and class codes tended to silence any critique of the war. Still, the FANY looked at their present lives and saw the stark contrast to lives lived before the war. This is illustrated in the following excerpt from a song they wrote called 'On the Road to Fontinettes' (and sung to the tune of 'On the Road to Mandalay'):

> Ship me somewhere west of Calais
> Somewhere peaceful don't forget
> Where there aint no ruddy puncture
> Nor yet, no choking jet.
> For the Bond Street shops are calling
> And it's there that I should be
> In the Piccadilly Grill Room
> Just one good friend and me
> (Just together on the spree).[36]

Although the conditions at Lamarck were terrible (what Ashley-Smith described as little more luxurious than the trenches, comfort being 'a mere detail, – a forgotten trifle belonging to a previous existence'[37]) the FANY made the best of things. Such behaviour encouraged their motto 'arduis invictus', or 'unconquered in hardships', informally known as 'I cope'. This motto was the backbone of the legend about the FANY, a legend against which personal accounts were constructed. While 'coping' was a somewhat inevitable outcome, it was an outcome that came along with risks and opportunities for change and transgressions of normative gender. For war, Ashley-Smith matter-of-factly explained, was their job:

War was work, and we looked for nothing better. We still lived on the few pounds I had brought for emergency, and we had not time to write and tell those at home of our needs. All we could spare went to our *blessés* [wounded], and overtime was never thought of. Someone was ill – that meant a night on duty to follow a day's hard work, but that was nothing. To us all war spelled work, and work spelled war; and we never looked beyond.[38]

Ashley-Smith's words represent the FANY as patriotic, loyal, thrifty, uncomplaining and hard-working: attributes tuned to fund-raising as well as to expectations of womanly behaviour and the maintenance of credibility when there was such generalized antagonism against women at the Front. Constructing themselves as self-sacrificing, loyal and devoted, they illustrated the high moral character, strength and demeanour expected of ladies of this period. All reports of these days at Lamarck represent the FANY as cheerful and stoic: whether they actually felt this way most of the time was an empirical question. Certainly it behoved them to construct themselves and the fledgling organization within the parameters of traditional genteel feminine qualities. As Jo Burr Margadant reminds us, 'no one "invents" a self apart from cultural notions available to them in a particular historical setting'.[39] Privately Ashley-Smith confessed how awful and utterly exhausting the work was, saying sometimes it was all she could do to keep back tears.[40]

An asset that helped the FANY cope during this difficult time was that they were young, and, as Ashley-Smith explained, 'tackled all the dirt and discomfort cheerily'.[41] She confessed that they were handicapped by lack of experience and training and she too longed to have someone to shoulder some of the responsibility, but was convinced that their youth and easy-going recklessness in tackling whatever had to be done carried them on.[42] Edith Walton, one of the first to join the Corps and arrive in Calais, agreed: 'We were too young really or too inexperienced to realize perhaps the seriousness of it.'[43] From these normatively feminine, dutiful and naïve responses to the misery of their work, a central aspect of FANY identity was constructed: cheerfulness in the face of adversity and an eagerness as youth to accept this war as 'their war'. This is similar to the insight from Irene Rathbone's heroine Joan in *We That Were Young*, who explains, 'We were the youth of the world, we were on the crest of life, and we were the war. No one above us counted, and no one below. Youth and the war were the same thing – youth and the war were us . . . Yes, we hated it and we loved it both . . . It was our war, you see.'[44]

Despite their enthusiasm and coping skills, the FANY invariably experienced some personal trauma and upheaval, exacerbated by the homefront resistance to women in military uniform.[45] These young women were thrown into a situation where they not only had to deal with losing their own personal privacy and the potential embarrassments that went along with crowded and insanitary living arrangements, but also with cleaning and tending to the bodies, septic wounds and excrement of male strangers. Accommodations to their new situation included such embarrassments as having to access a 'bath ticket' for a public bathhouse from male French officials or not understanding what a 'bottle' was and repeatedly giving a patient a hot water bottle instead of the urinal.

Alongside their nursing duties at Lamarck, the FANY also provided ambulance transport, accepted in part because of their success in the more domesticated role of nurse and helpmate. It was here that the FANY transgressed into less normative representations of gender. Motorized ambulances owned by the FANY in these early days consisted of two Fords (one named Flossie), the Unic and a converted Mors waggonette for walking wounded that was owned and driven by a Mr Hargreaves, known affectionately as 'Uncle'. He was past military age and had answered an advertisement for a driver and ambulance to join the FANY, not knowing it was a women's corps. He found this very amusing and volunteered himself and the car at his own expense as well as paying the salaries of two of the trained infirmary nurses.[46]

The tasks of the FANY ambulance drivers included collecting the wounded from trains arriving from the Front and transporting these wounded to the Clearing Hospitals and to the docks for transportation to 'Blighty' (England). Upon meeting the trains early in the morning, FANY drivers observed the various labels that doctors placed on patients and then took these wounded to their destinations. The drivers had to carry the stretchers and load them in the ambulances, sometimes with help from Belgian Boy Scouts or from stretcher-bearers known as *broncardiers*. On reaching their destination, drivers completed intake papers, stripped the wounded of their tunics and other mud-laden clothes and dressed them in clean nightshirts for the hospital staff to take over. When nursing staff was short-handed, drivers would help on the wards. They also had other driving and chauffeuring tasks. One such job, for example, involved four FANY driving 120 miles to Cayeux, transporting French wounded all night long, and returning to Calais the next day.[47]

After Ashley-Smith's brother Bill received a commission in the 10th King's Own (Yorkshire Light Infantry) and was transferred to the 21st Divisional Cyclists, and Frank Brittain left for Serbia to work with the First British Field Hospital,[48] more FANY came out to help work at Lamarck. Pat Waddell, who joined them in February 1915 along with Margaret Cole-Hamilton, was able to leave England after she acquired her nursing certificates and learned to drive. She reported how she had driven cars and lorries in and around London and was so keen to gain experience that she would persuade cab drivers to let her take the wheel! She came to France hoping to be a driver but found the Corps had few ambulances and a shortage of nurses, and were working in a context that expected domestic, wifely service. As a result, Waddell was immediately put to work on the hospital wards.[49] Later in July 1915, Beryl 'Betty' Hutchinson arrived at Lamarck and brought with her a motorized soup kitchen that worked at the main railway station in Calais, La Gare Centrale, providing the wounded with hot soup and other drinks. In addition, the sisters Antonia Marian and Hope 'Jimmie' Gamwell came over to France with a motorized bath. The Gamwell sisters had first worked for Dr Elsie Inglis at the Scottish Women's Hospital at Royaumont and were anxious to 'get to business and have a go at the Germans'.[50] The following year Celia Meade from St Ives, Cornwall, also joined the FANY at Lamarck after working for the Lowther-Hackett Unit.[51]

Betty Hutchinson (known to her colleagues as 'Hutch') was one FANY driver who helped out on the wards when needed, although it seems not too successfully and certainly not in the role of the demure nurse: 'I could not stand the awful syringe that was used to clean wounds and fainted five times one morning! After that I used to help Sister Wicks on the typhoid ward. There my height and strength proved useful when a delirious patient climbed the pillars up the middle of the ward, or expressed his fears in other physical ways.'[52] The typhoid wards were chaotic places:

A large proportion of our patients was delirious owing to the high temperatures and also owing to the terrible strain they had undergone and it was difficult to keep them lying in bed. At one time, we had eight wildly delirious in a row and it was seldom that they were all lying down at once. Franz, the gunner who had been through the siege of Antwerp, would go over and over his experiences, counting his ammunition and lamenting his comrades as they fell around his gun. Every now and then, he would punctuate his recital with 'boom!' If he took us for comrades it was all right, but occasionally he mistook us for Germans and then it was awkward! One day he caught Miss Hall by the throat and there might have been a tragedy had not Louis, the orderly sprung to the rescue.[53]

Hutchinson remembered 'Sister Wicks', in charge of the typhoid wards, as an impressive, hard-working individual who was so single-minded in her work that she directed her staff to simply not allow the patients to die. Ashley-Smith, who did not always see eye-to-eye with Sister Wicks, nonetheless respected her work and admired the devotion she brought to her duty. Wicks' work on the typhoid wards resulted in her developing para-typhoid and needing care. She eventually left the FANY in late 1915 citing ill-health and overwork and spent some time in a sanatorium in England before turning once more to nursing and joining the FANY again later.[54]

Although the *typhiques*, the typhoid patients, did not usually have the dreadful wounds of the regular *blessés*, the men often had such complications as pneumonia, abscesses, scurvy and haemorrhage. In addition, many soldiers during the First World War were infected with syphilis. The FANY never mention this in any of their accounts (nor do they ever mention the prostitutes who serviced the soldiers): to do so would have shown impropriety and compromised their respectability. Any mention of such things, even from the standpoint of FANY guardianship of moral virtue, alluded to women's role in the moral corruption of British manhood and raised the spectre of the dangers of unleashed female sexuality and the moral panic it caused.[55] Even though the

FANY tended to be exempt from this debate as 'respectable' middle- and upper-class women, they most likely were well aware of the profound challenges their presence as unchaperoned women made to the status quo.[56]

High mortality rates meant that the 'coffin cart' came regularly, and, as Cicely Mordaunt explained, these deaths hardened the women to their tasks. It seems that Lamarck had the only typhoid unit, and, since other hospitals would reject these patients, the wards were invariably full. Although the staff were vaccinated against typhoid, they were obliged to gargle several times a day and always had what she called a 'typy' throat.[57] There had been a new development, an antitoxin, that worked better than the serum vaccination; however, its supplies gave out quickly after the first month of the epidemic. There was always a distinctive smell hovering the wards that even disinfectant could not remove. The staff worked constantly preparing food, feeding, and 'doing mouths': swabbing patients' mouths caked with blood and sores. The most strenuous task, however, was 'blanket-bathing'. It involved sponge bathing the men with cold water to reduce fever and sooth aching limbs and resulted in serious backaches among the nursing staff. Norma Lowson who once bathed sixteen men in a row held the 'long-distance record' on blanket-bathing.[58] This image of the FANY straining to blanket-bathe umpteen men and suffering the physical strain of such challenges goes against the image of both the 'madonna nurse' and the prior experiences of these 'gently-bred' young women. By the end of April 1915 the typhoid epidemic seemed to have run its course and the hospital was again made over to the wounded.

Among these *blessés* were the severely wounded as well as those with 'trigger-finger', patients who had shot their own finger in order to keep from returning to the trenches. In addition, many of their patients were shell-shocked. Ashley-Smith recalled having to force the clothes off a man who kept trying to dress himself and leave, and another who hit out at her in his delirium. Like her descriptions of her work in Belgium in Chapter 2, Ashley-Smith often found conventional sentimental language inadequate to express her horror of the dead and the dying. She wrote of the young soldier at Lamarck with 'half his head shot off [who] lay at our feet'[59] and remembered the day 'a stretcher case was carried in unconscious, a gaping head wound healing badly – the body thin and wasted – the legs mere skin and bone'. While Ashley-Smith related to this man in terms of his wounded body parts, she continued with a more personalized account: 'I could span the ankle with my finger and thumb – yet the lad must have been twenty-four and formerly of splendid physique. His mouth was full of solid food – gone wrong; – his back already broken in a gangrenous bed sore.'[60] The repetitive use of dashes here disturbs the narrative and underscores the inadvertency, unreality and chaos of war and the poignancy of this man's predicament: solid food that he could not chew that had 'gone wrong', given to him in a rushed moment and with no one to follow his care. Nurse Jordan worked hard to keep this man alive; they never knew his name or nationality and called him 'Harry'. Eventually he was shipped out to England and they never heard of him again. However, the story goes, this was not before someone put a photo of Harry in the paper as a missing person and several hundred women claimed him as their long-lost husband.[61]

In one account Ashley-Smith recalled laying out a dead body for burial with her colleague Isabel Wicks and juxtaposed this with the consumption of cocoa, bread and jam: 'It was all Wicks and I could do to carry the body to an empty landing where we could lay him out. Then I went down and made cocoa, and we had bread and jam, and up again to the ward; this time to the other septic pneumonia, a fine boy, who said to me gently: 'If I am going to die, mademoiselle, and I feel a little frightened; do not leave me.'[62] This passage is reminiscent of the much-quoted passage from Mary Borden's *The Forbidden Zone* in the story titled 'Moonlight'. Here Borden describes drinking cocoa surrounded by the litter of war; refuse that includes legs and arms wrapped in cloths. 'The cocoa tastes very good. It is part of the routine', she writes.[63] Ashley-Smith similarly juxtaposes cocoa with death, although her account is more ambiguous as she moves back into the sentiment of war rhetoric and the poignancy of the boy's sacrifice.

St Ingilvert and Camp du Ruchard

The FANY were so successful at Lamarck that they were soon asked to run a convalescent home for recovering typhoid patients. Again, this feat was accomplished out of FANY ingenuity rather than previous experience or Belgian resources. In a discussion with the Belgian Surgeon-General less than two weeks before Christmas 1914, Ashley-Smith responded to his plea for a convalescent home with the comment, 'You shall have your convalescent home as a New Year's gift to the Belgians from the FANYs.'[64] Shocked at her own bravado, Ashley-Smith nonetheless set out with her colleagues to find an appropriate site and settled upon a church hall at St Ingilvert. Ashley-Smith's story of this acquisition is crafted to underscore her spunk and highlight the personal bravado necessary for getting her way and getting things done. Once they were moved into St Ingilvert, Ashley-Smith wrote, 'the authorities woke up to the fact of what happened, and even spoke of withdrawing passes for the cars to St Ingilvert, and vaguely protested that they had not consented to convalescents going there'. But, she exclaimed, 'possession generally ensures victory, and the convalescents remained until they were cured'.[65] St Ingilvert housed about sixteen convalescents and was run by two FANY. It was in business until March 1915 at which time the typhoid epidemic was mostly stymied.

Cicely Mordaunt was sent to work at St Ingilvert with Evelyn Laidlay. Laidlay was from Edenbridge, Kent, and was put in charge of the cooking, domestic management and accounts. The women were billeted at a local farmhouse since they were not allowed to sleep at the hall (church laws only allowed the presence of women over forty years old, and, as Ashley-Smith wryly pointed out, the joint ages of the two of them was hardly more than that). Mordaunt, used to fine living at her family home in Wellesbourne, Warwickshire, reported with good humour that their bedroom was the size of a good-sized cupboard and contained just a bed with a hay-stuffed mattress and two huge quilts, 'minus such trifles as sheets, pillows, and blankets'. It was quite comfortable though, she added, despite the 'many others' (fleas and bedbugs) that shared the bed.[66] The work at St Ingilvert might have been considered boring by those who were looking for action: it consisted mainly of cooking and cleaning, dispensing medicines and light nursing, taking the men out for walks and playing a variety of card and board games with them in the evenings. However the food was much better here than at Lamarck, so much so that Mordaunt recalled 'weeping over a boiled egg'.[67]

The final big opportunity for the FANY in 1915 was the running of a canteen for Belgian convalescents at Camp du Ruchard. Ashley-Smith had arranged this project in April 1915 after seeing the miserable conditions for Belgian troops in this area, although her absence in England through the summer of 1915 resulted in little progress for Ruchard until August. When Ashley-Smith returned, the canteen opened with Margaret Cole-Hamilton in charge, accompanied by driver Chris (Cristobel) Nicholson and Nurse Lovell. Camp du Ruchard became known as FANY Unit 2. Ruchard housed over 5,000 Belgians during 1915, including about 700 convalescents with typhoid as well as others with epilepsy and tuberculosis. Ruchard also housed a battalion of Belgian sons of Germans and Austrians whom they dared not send to the Front. The FANY hired a trained nurse to work with the consumptive patients and they also helped out on the wards. The canteen sold tea, chocolate and coffee at 5 centimes (or a halfpenny) a cup, and cake for 10 centimes. This work was quintessentially feminine and utilized the FANY skill at entertaining and hostessing. Indeed, in late 1915 the homefront FANY helped organize a 'Ruchard Cake League' with pledges to send cakes: 'home-baked all the better'.[68] It appears that FANY Secretary Janette Lean who accepted her post in early 1916, carried on this tradition with her amazing knack of 'coaxing odd hundredweights of cake from reluctant manufacturers'.[69] Cake was not the only donation to Ruchard. Lady Baird, for example, a FANY whom legend recalls as somewhat eccentric, collected all kinds of donated items for Ruchard from such voluntary organizations as the Queen Mary's Needlework Guild (through the kindness of Princess Henry of Battenberg), the Sunningdale Ladies Gold Club, the Primrose League Needlework Committee, and even from the Ladies of Pekin.[70] One story in the FANY legend about Lady Baird was that after her suggestion her maid accompany her to France was discouraged, she settled instead on travelling with her hip-flask: a quirk that seems to have brought her fame and popularity among the patients.[71] In addition, another story goes that lady Baird lost her 'kiss-curl' hairpiece in a patient's meal one morning only to find it the next day in the patient's enema![72]

Alongside the various food items, also distributed at Camp du Ruchard were newspapers, magazines and writing paper. Board games were also a central feature of entertainment there. The FANY even managed to procure a delivery of hockey sticks and soccer balls at one point and encouraged the convalescents to play. In its early months the entertainment mainstay at Ruchard consisted of a piano and a gramophone with concerts and musical evenings organized by the FANY. Australian-born Adèle Crockett who replaced Cole-Hamilton as Director of Ruchard wrote that their entertaining little orchestra (made up of a mouth organ, an accordion and someone who whistled on his fingers) was enjoyed by all despite the fact that it usually had to perform whilst the gramophone and piano were being played on either side of the room.[73]

Despite such merrymaking, Ruchard was isolated, and the work, like that at St Ingilvert, was considered boring by many; conditions were hard and the FANY sometimes found it difficult to keep staff there, although Lady Baird was one FANY who agreed to stay. Eventually it is reported that the introduction of a cinematograph at Ruchard livened the place up somewhat. It was obtained with funds raised by Ashley-Smith from the citizens of Aberdeen and a 10 centimes entrance fee was charged. The cinema was quite a hit among the patients, although it was no easy task to work and maintain. The projector had its own generator and used a lot of fuel to run, but an added advantage was that it also supplied the canteen with electric light. A competent motor mechanic was needed to run the motor and someone familiar with the projector and the workings of the cinematograph was necessary to keep things running smoothly, especially since problems included the possibility of the films catching fire and the risk of the building going up in smoke![74] Ruchard was eventually taken over by the French in June 1917 and the FANY moved to run the canteen at a Belgian Military Hospital at Soligny-la-Trappe, west of Paris.

This canteen was never very successful since casualties were low in this area and it closed in January 1918.

Firing lines

As the FANY developed their reputation for coping and competency and were seen as trustworthy, loyal and uncomplaining women willing to do traditional women's war service, they were given opportunities to extend their sphere of activity and influence with the Belgians, venturing to the Front lines where the First Battle of Ypres was raging. Having established themselves within the parameters of normative womanly behaviour, they were soon bending these parameters through a variety of risks and opportunities, aligning themselves more closely with the fighting men and developing a stronger identity as militarized women. Their presence and work here represented what Angela K. Smith called paradoxical: 'not combatant, but they are not non-combatant either; they have the best and the worst of both worlds; allied with soldiers rather than civilians, yet subordinated to them in the eyes of society, and in their own consciousness'.[75]

At this time the Allied trenches stretched for hundreds of miles from the North Sea east and south through Ypres, Arras and Albert, to Reims and Verdun and toward the Swiss border in Alsace. The Belgians held the first forty miles north of Ypres, the next ninety miles were held by the British, and the French held the rest. During the first months of the war, the FANY were in Calais and the surrounding area, relatively close to Ypres and working with the Belgian line. After the First Battle of Ypres and other fighting in Artois and Champagne through November and into the New Year, the original British Army under Field Marshall Sir John French was all but wiped out and Lord Kitchener gave his famous call for more volunteers. At the same time, according to A. J. P. Taylor, the French military had lost 'the flower of their armies – the best officers, the most eager soldiers; a loss from which they never fully recovered'.[76] German losses were also very high. Although the year ended with an informal truce held in No Man's Land (the desolate land between opposing trenches) when soldiers shared cigarettes and took photos on Christmas Day,[77] this was met with disapproval and was never allowed to happen again.

In March 1915 the British fought at the Battle of Neuve Chappelle and lost about 13,000 men. French losses were even higher. And, while the International Women's Congress met at Le Havre in April with a call for peace, the fighting continued at the Second Battle of Ypres. FANY units were consumed with the fall-out from this battle and busy transporting and nursing wounded day and night. Gains and losses continued as the battles raged at Artois and

Festubert and eventually at Loos in September. A central feature of this fighting on the Western Front was a continued deadlock and the ongoing massacre and mutilations associated with trench warfare.[78] The FANY certainly had their work cut out for them.

In the early months at Lamarck and into the New Year 1915, the FANY journeyed to the trenches to take supplies to the troops and hand out gifts of cigarettes and knitted items. The trench system was a relatively immovable system with opposing forces facing each other across No Man's Land, framed by barbed wire, and surrounded by mud. There were usually three lines of trenches: first the front-line about 50 yards to a mile from opposing enemy trenches; several hundred yards behind this was the support trench line and behind this the reserve line. Troops moved back and forth between these lines. There were also three kinds of trenches themselves: firing trenches, communication trenches that would connect the three lines, and 'saps' or trenches that protruded into No Man's Land and allowed soldiers access to observation and listening posts, machine gun positions, and posts from which to throw grenades. Trenches were usually about 6 feet deep with a high sandbagged parapet containing periscopes at intervals that allowed soldiers to look out into No Man's Land. They contained dug-outs offering various levels of comfort, usually depending upon the rank of its inhabitants, and in various condition, depending upon location and timing of an offensive. German trenches were superior to their Allied counterparts, being better built and providing more comforts.[79] Fussell describes the British trenches as 'wet, cold, smelly, and thoroughly squalid'.[80]

The FANY remembered how grateful the soldiers were when they received knitted presents and how they especially appreciated socks (even though accounts have hinted that the soldiers often used unwanted knitted items to clean their rifles[81]). Pat Waddell described in her memoir *Fanny Goes to War* how many of the knitted garments had little cards attached to them with notes for the men. Thinking of the 'kind hands that had knitted them in far-away England', Waddell nostalgically wondered if the knitters had ever imagined their things would be given out like this, 'to rows of mud-stained men standing amid shell-riddled houses on a dark and muddy road, their words of thanks half-drowned in the thunder of war'.[82] Despite the critical poignancy of these comments that encourage the reader to reflect on the wastefulness and wanton destruction imposed by military combat, *Fanny Goes to War* is generally written, like Ashley-Smith's *Nursing Adventures*, in a sentimental tone that nonetheless highlights female heroism and independence. In her first trip to the Front line Waddell delights in the 'queer thrill' associated with the 'boom boom' of the guns and enjoys a 'jolly lunch' despite the roar of the artillery.[83]

This tone is interspersed, again like Ashley-Smith's narrative, with more blunt descriptions of her experiences. Rounding a corner, for example, she saw that a recently burst shell had killed a group of soldiers. She explained that she could never forget this sight; an experience beyond words and better left to the imagination of the reader. The world seemed to tilt and appear unreal and she wondered at times if she were actually awake or if this were a very bad dream. As if to prove her presence in this field of destruction, one of the dazed surviving soldiers gave her a piece of shell and she felt it and realized it was still warm.[84]

Waddell described looking around her at the ravaged countryside and seeing dark objects sticking out of the floodwater. 'Sales Boches!' ('bad Boches/Germans') retorted one of the Belgian sergeants, bringing her back to the moment as she gazed on this horrendous scene. Ashley-Smith similarly described seeing water with 'dark things' bobbing up and down that on closer inspection were arms and legs and German uniforms.[85] She witnessed the rows of wooden crosses behind the trenches and the strangely still bodies of dead soldiers out in No Man's Land with their 'queer contorted look'.[86] She also witnessed the banalities of survival grotesquely juxtaposed against the desolation and ever-present smell of death: 'Dead cows with their legs in the air made one long for eau de cologne; beside one ungainly corpse a little party of soldiers were cheerily cooking their midday meal.'[87]

Cicely Mordaunt ventured up to the Front lines near Oostkerk and Dixmude with Lillian Franklin on 11 January 1915. She recalled the shells dropping, the terrible, terrible desolation and ravaged countryside, and the sheer enormity of war. They passed through the war-flattened village of Pervyse and had tea with Elsie Knocker and Mairi Chisholm of the Munro Ambulance Unit. Mordaunt described their house as the only one standing as well as being still equipped with a piano on which Knocker, incongruously, played and sang 'Sister Susie's Sewing Shirts for Soldiers'. The following month Mr Hargreaves took Isabel Wicks and FANY colleagues Mary Waite and Muriel Thompson in his car to the Belgian Front line armed with woollens and other knitted items, cigarettes and tobacco. The mud and squalor were terrible and the women had to wear thigh-high rubber boots. Before they left an enemy attack struck and the FANY stayed and administered first aid. Waite wrote that while a bursting shell almost stunned her, she pulled herself together and was able to crawl to the nearest wounded, who unfortunately was already dead. Together the FANY bandaged, applied impromptu splints and gave morphine to help the soldiers' pain. They tried to get the wounded to Lamarck, but the roads were impassable and they had to reroute to another hospital.[88] These FANY were decorated with the Belgian Order of Leopold II for their bravery.

For Ashley-Smith, these scenes from the firing line were also unforgettable: going up to Ypres to bring back wounded and seeing two mounted soldiers hit by a shell and dragged free from the shambles of shattered horses, observing miles and miles of railway lines broken with shell holes and zigzag trenches. The never-ending mud oozed everywhere, soaked through her buckskin breeches and caked her legs heavy and stiff, requiring her to walk with difficulty with her skirt tucked up to her knees. Waddell remembered the time she fell into the mud up to her thighs and despaired that she might never 'touch bottom'.[89] The nurses and ambulance drivers were constantly cleaning off mud from the wounds and clothes of soldiers and attempting to keep the ambulances, dressing stations, and hospitals clean from this 'invincible, inexhaustible mud of the war zone'.[90] This ever-present mud was symbolic of the desolation and despair of the front lines, captured in verse by Mary Borden:

> Mud, the disguise of the war zone;
> Mud, the mantle of battles;
> Mud, the smooth fluid grave of our soldiers:
> This is the song of the mud.[91]

In the fall of 1914 the FANY at Lamarck came close to the firing line through their work at a Regimental Aid Post associated with the battalion doctors of the 5th Division of the Belgian Army. The Regimental Aid Post, fondly referred to by Ashley-Smith as the *poste de secours*, was where regimental doctors attended to the sick and wounded immediately behind the Front line. If the wounds were severe, the *blessés* were moved to an Advanced Dressing Station and then on to the Casualty Clearing Stations. This Regimental Aid Post was located at Oostkerk, less than a mile behind the trenches between the towns of Pervyse and Dixmude close to where Mordaunt and Franklin visited Mrs Knocker and Mairi Chisholm later in January. Edith Walton, accompanied by Mary Louise Bond and Sayer, worked at Oostkerk: 'Up there', wrote Ashley-Smith, 'little Walton, with her constant smile and little, fragile face, stayed with another girl for a fortnight – sleeping on straw by night, shelled out of the *poste de secours* by day, up to the knees in mud, going to and from the trenches, shrapnel bursting everywhere'.[92] Food and supplies were scarce and Walton, Bond and Sayer lived on a steady diet of potatoes and black coffee and tinned meat called *plâtre* that resembled bully beef and was stewed, fried and boiled and combined with potatoes into a kind of mash. One time Ashley-Smith recalled a visit to Oostkerk when they had received five packets of 'Little Mary Custard Powder'. Since milk was an unheard-of luxury, they made the custard with water and all agreed it was better than anything they had ever tasted.[93]

On other visits to Oostkerk, Ashley-Smith recalled more sombre experiences. A November night in 1914 was vivid in her memory; the storm was rising and the cold keen and bitter. One after another, the wounded men were brought into the makeshift hospital. Ashley-Smith held the dying men in her arms while a doctor probed their wounds for shrapnel fragments; the dressing station had run out of anaesthetics and the men were screaming in pain: 'Each time the door opened I groaned inwardly. Would this procession of suffering never stop? The cold wind would bite through us all, the candles would flicker and sputter, big muddy men would tramp in with thick muddy boots, dump down their burden on the stone floor, and go out banging the door loudly to make it shut … and it would begin again.'[94]

There were other incidences of FANY coping with the risks and opportunities of war that pushed against the parameters of traditional normative femininity during these early months of combat. Ashley-Smith, for example, reported having to gather the body parts of a dead French soldier and put them in a blanket on a stretcher during a particularly bad air raid.[95] Equally disturbing, Edith Walton recalled a time when German prisoners were being marched along the road just before turning into their camp gates. Enemy aircraft swooped low not knowing their own soldiers were below and made a direct hit, killing nearly all and leaving others mutilated on the road. The FANY ambulances were called, wrote Walton, and 'I can never forget the stark misery of feeling my wheels skidding in the pools of blood at the entrance to the camp nor the sight of the camp doctor standing beside a table putting up emergency dressings. He was drenched in blood up to his knees and as I waited I saw him at work actually throwing a mutilated foot onto the floor. It was awful.'[96]

On 16 March 1915 there was a zeppelin raid in Calais that dropped bombs on Lamarck and its surrounding buildings. Bombs were also dropped at the railway station on a carriage inhabited by workers. All were killed instantly, 'more or less mutilated; and heads, hands, and feet were torn off. Then flames broke out on top of this carriage and in a moment the whole was one huge conflagration.'[97] Betty Hutchinson remembered: 'The casualties were dreadful, the keys of the station ambulances missing, so Chris [FANY driver Chris Nicholson] and I fetched ours and made many horrible journeys with living and dying amid a haunting smell of burnt flesh.'[98] Another bomb that same evening smashed in the roof of the cathedral chapel next door to Lamarck and took with it the beautiful gothic east window. There was glass everywhere, covering patients as they lay in their beds. The newspaper reported that all the male orderlies fled for refuge leaving the 'courageous Englishwomen' to deal with the chaos. Ashley-Smith wrote that Margaret Cole-Hamilton in particular 'was superb'. She and the other FANY on duty in the hospital (Gwendolene Strutt, Waddell, Woolgar, and the 'baby' of the FANY, Enid Porter) 'rushed around covering the men's faces with pillows, as the great sheets of plate glass shivered in fragments over the beds and floors of the typhoid wards'.[99] The FANY involved in this attack received military medals from the Belgian authorities. Unprepared and thrown into this work under fire, the FANY subverted traditional feminine war work based upon passivity and nurturance and made the case for women's active presence in the battle zone. Literal and metaphorical 'foreigners' in this zone, the FANY transgressed into this masculine project, transforming femininity as inclusive of personal and collective bravery and autonomy.

Among the stories of FANY transgressing normative femininity through taking on risks and opportunities in the face of danger, the incident of the gas attack ranks very highly. Many soldiers were affected by war gases that irritated the eyes and throat, burned the skin, and sometimes caused blindness and asphyxiation. The incident occurred in early May 1915 at the Second Battle of Ypres as the Germans attempted to break through the British lines at Ypres Salient. As already mentioned, alongside the ambulances associated with hospital transport, the FANY also had a motor kitchen or mobile canteen that could provide soup and other food for the troops. On 11 May 1915, Betty Hutchinson and Ida Lewis were ordered to leave with this motor kitchen and accompany the 7th Belgian Mounted Artillery Regiment attached to the British 5th Division headed for Ypres Salient. Here they were to help run a dressing station along with the mobile kitchen. Hutchinson remembered the long and gruelling journey that ended with their having to prepare a meal for 140 men with limited supplies and resources. Hutchinson also remembered the journey itself and the 'great deal of finesse' involved in driving a Model T Ford at horse walking pace.[100] Once at their destination at 'Hellfire Corner' on the Ypres–Menin Road, they were caught in the first gas attack of the war. The gas turned the men a livid green colour and poisoned them on contact. Lewis and Hutchinson responded by making large quantities of salt water to help the afflicted soldiers vomit the poison. They also improvised gas masks from gauze first aid dressings soaked in vinegar and gave the gasping men strong black coffee to help them breathe. The men they assisted were mostly Canadians. Sadly, the 1st Canadian Division lost a third of its infantry in this battle and aggregate losses amounted to almost 60,000 men.[101] It seems that the presence of the FANY at this gas attack caused considerable consternation from the British authorities, who were starting to object fiercely to the presence of women at the Front. Hutchinson joked that since there was so much 'red flannel' personnel involved, she thought and hoped it was too senior for a court marshal![102] Although Lewis and Hutchinson were decorated for their bravery in this incident, nonetheless, after these first months of the war, military authorities made it much more difficult for women to have access to the Front.

'Girls of the twentieth century'

Through their strategies aimed at coping with the horrors of this war, the FANY developed their reputation and credibility. They appealed to traditional feminine service but were able to bend these parameters and transgress into the masculine space of the battlefield. Pat Waddell wrote about the ways their presence at Lamarck and in the surrounding countryside turned this world 'topsy-turvy'. People asked whether they were girls or boys and 'lively arguments took place in shop and market: "They can't be young women", the villagers said, "see, that one has short hair like a man! Look how they drive these automobiles – women can't handle cars and start them up. They are men without a doubt."' Waddell reported that she overheard a chemist (pharmacist) saying to one of his clients as they left his shop: 'Truly, until one hears their voices, one would think they were boys.'[103] In addition, so the FANY legend goes, even the Germans had heard of the FANY and their transgressive activities. An illustrated German newspaper, found in a captured dugout, featured photographs of the FANY with the accompanying caption 'Eaters of Men'. On closer inspection this caption actually referred to a picture of African men said to have been hired by the British for cannibalistic purposes. The FANY were featured in conjunction with this gruesome notion; their job was to kill enemy wounded on the battlefield. The Germans had managed to procure a photograph of Lillian Franklin holding a rifle outside a dressing station as proof of their point.[104]

Although of course the FANY did not interpret their behaviour as feminist, even at this early stage in the war Ashley-Smith was aware of just how transgressive it was. The FANY were, she exclaimed, modern girls of a new century working in the midst of chaos and uncertainty and living lives never before imagined:

Up here alone, far from civilisation, very far from the homes where perhaps our people thought of us, but certainly did not imagine our surroundings – here we were, girls of the twentieth century in this atmosphere of storm and war, living what surely few women ever dreamt in their wildest fancies until this war began. This was life! My ears tingled; I breathed in long, deep breaths. Had I spoken, a sort of wild war song would have come from my lips. The Highland blood in me bubbled and frothed; I wanted to run for miles – to race, to climb – action at all costs.[105]

This image of girls living in an 'atmosphere of storm and war' is a far cry from the normative structures of Edwardian drawing rooms that only a few months earlier had kept close tabs on their behaviour and framed their activities and expectation. Ashley-Smith's exclamations of running and climbing and singing a wild war song all reflect her desire to escape such constraints. To be able to tread in this masculine space, away from family demands, and out of reach of the responsibilities placed on women, must have been an awesome change. This is the 'invigorating sense of revolution, release, reunion, and re-vision' that Sandra Gilbert suggests was felt by women during the First World War as women were empowered and men made dependent and infantilized through their wounds.[106] The photograph on p. 153 aptly illustrates this, as a wounded soldier lies in a carriage at Lamarck, reminiscent of a pram or baby carriage.

Gilbert suggests that women filled in the gaps in public life left by men with enthusiasm and competency and developed bonds of sisterhood and solidarity. They also, she emphasizes, experienced a release of female libidinal energy: the 'action at all costs' referred to by Ashley-Smith, writing of the thrill and excitement of war. Of course Gilbert is also talking about the unleashing of female sexuality as the war facilitated 'not just a liberation from the constricting trivia of parlors and petticoats but an unprecedented transcendence of the profounder constraints imposed by traditional sex roles'.[107] As we shall see, the FANY were able to provide just enough innuendo to construct themselves as heterosexually fun-loving without breaking the boundaries of appropriate sexual behaviour, although their sexuality and that of women generally in this masculine space would continue to arouse fears and anxiety. The accusation of sexual deviance was an almost inevitable consequence for women whose war service extended to non-traditional work. As Penny Summerfield reminds us, 'constructions of women's sexual morality were used to patrol the boundaries of women's changing roles at all times, but particularly in wartime'.[108] The upper-crust FANY identity whereby such women could be relied upon to not become involved with the Tommies insulated them to some extent from such accusations. Still, the FANY were keen to make sure that their service record was clean when it came to potential sexual liaisons. As will be discussed in Chapter 7, they came through the war with a reputation for having fun with the right class of men and 'fun' that did not transgress into overt sexual impropriety. They functioned with few written rules except that they were never to be in the company of men alone in the evenings without a companion. Tea alone with a male officer was also forbidden, although luncheon was allowed. Permission from a senior officer concerning various outings was always required. In addition, the FANY always had to appear in public in uniform and no public smoking was allowed.[109] While no doubt these rules were broken and problems arose (although the public record contains few such mentions and the private only the occasional infraction), the FANY were well socialized as to the limits of their behaviour and the necessity for a respectable public face for the organization.

To this end, Ashley-Smith preferred to leave her personal romantic life out of the account of her war service, even while she might use innuendo to tell a good tale in constructing her own personal heroism and FANY legend. A good example of this is the way Ashley-Smith handled her own marriage in 1915. Despite her commitment to war work, she was the first FANY to marry during the war. She did not let her status as a married woman (with new responsibilities to her husband rather than duties to the State) diminish her motivation to participate in the masculine project of war, even though these responsibilities would dictate her future in important ways. Her marriage came as a surprise to everyone, and, as Mordaunt recalled, furnished them with gossip for weeks. Ashley-Smith tells little of this important occasion in her writings and refers to it almost in passing in her memoir:

I spent 3 days in Scotland with my mother, and on my return (to England) found my brother and the man I was engaged to at the station with a special licence. It seemed absurd not to use it, so we dashed off to buy a ring and caught a train to Maidenhead in the morning. As it was the first wedding where a bride wore khaki, the parson was consumed with curiosity and rallied through the service to gasp out, 'Who are you, do tell me what your uniform is?' We had 3 wedding cakes, and everyone promised us presents when the war was over (the war has been over for some time now).[110]

This unnamed man was Ronald McDougall, an officer in the King's Own (Yorkshire Light Infantry), and from then onwards Ashley-Smith became known as Mrs McDougall or just plain 'Mac'. Not surprisingly, her husband is hardly ever mentioned in McDougall's accounts of the war; her professionalism and the belief that marital and domestic concerns had no place in military matters, associated as they were with the 'feminine' aspects of life, most likely prevented her from writing about this intimacy. In the case of *Nursing Adventures*, a realistic account of her courtship and marriage might have broken the spell concerning the brave mademoiselle adventuring in a foreign land or perhaps tainted it too much with overt romantic/sexual innunendo. Indeed, when the dispatch discussed in Chapter 2 concerning her adventures in Belgium and her escape from the Germans was released, the *Weekly Welcome* had run an article that included a section referring to her romance with Ronald McDougall. On the top of the copy that read: 'A romance in the trenches was hidden away under the brief announcement that Miss Grace

Ashley-Smith of the FANY was married in London last week', McDougall had handwritten 'rubbish!'[111]

As the publicity concerning McDougall's marriage illustrates, the British press loved to comment on this turn-of-the-century gender-bending and, in particular, comment on the moral panic and potential loss of respectability that might ensue as women sought to act like men in this most masculine of spaces. Headings like 'Amazons to the Fore' and 'Every Girl Wanted' filled British newspapers,[112] reflecting the cultural obsession with the New Woman and her challenge to the status quo that encouraged warnings that her ambitions 'would lead to sickness, freakishness, sterility, and racial degeneration'.[113] In the summer of 1915 a long correspondence occurred in the *Morning Post* concerning whether it was appropriate for women to wear khaki. Some letter-writers described the practice offensive and ridiculous, a shameful dishonouring of men in service, while others objected and supported women's patriotic call to service.[114] The intensity of such debates almost a year into the war illustrates the anxiety women like the FANY were causing at home. About the FANY in particular, the following excerpt is taken from a newspaper article whose pun in the title 'Defence of "Base" Women' prepared the reader to consider the potential scandals associated with wartime negotiations of gender:

Our own so-called Yeomanry nurses who, among other work, drive and clean and manage their own ambulance cars, are dressed in khaki. Their skirts are short, their hats, some say their feet, are large. They are accused of saluting officers as if they themselves were real soldiers; and to the French people, who are accustomed to see nurses dressed severely, almost in the guise of nuns, the spectacle is too strange to be acceptable or agreeable.[115]

While as always, the British press was consumed with images of women on the battlefield and liked to titillate their readers with stories of fair damsels doing men's work, these articles were an important part of the cultural processes associated with changing gender relations. As 1915 came to a close, alongside the alarming shortage of manpower which encouraged a new discourse on women's roles in wartime, the WSPU had thrown itself into the war effort and ceased all militant tactics against the British government. Emmeline and Christabel Pankhurst, leaders in the WSPU, were eager to support the effort and understood that by dedicating themselves to work in the national interest and playing a role in time of war, they would make their demand for the vote impossible to deny. Their position (not shared by the pacifist Pankhurst sister Sylvia) brought one aspect of feminist politics into the pro-war camp, and, as a result, the stance concerning women's expanded role in society was afforded more respectability. For example, an article in *The Wind-*

sor Magazine featured photographs of the FANY taking wounded from the trenches under heavy shellfire and bringing them into the dressing stations, and congratulated women on their expanded role in war. It commented on the 'burning eagerness with which women of all classes and stations, of all opinions, religions, social, political, and philanthropic have, in addition to giving up their loved ones, hastened to place their services, their money, their homes, their influence, their everything at the disposal of the State'.[116]

'Farewell to dear dirty old Lamarck'[117]

At the end of 1916 the hospital Lamarck was scheduled for closure by the Belgian authorities who wanted to centralize their medical service and concentrate the sick and wounded at a hospital at Gravelines. While there had been rumours circulating about its closure for many months, the FANY were very sad to see it close. A farewell concert event marked Lamarck's closure and the FANY transformed the rooms with flowers, plants and palms and erected a small stage decorated with the flags of the Allies. Several Belgian officers performed, along with Pat Waddell on violin, Ida Lewis on cello, Violet O'Neill-Power on guitar and a Miss Burnley Campbell on the flageolet. The concert closed with renderings of the national anthems of the Allied troops, which received much enthusiasm and applause. Tea in the FANY common room upstairs in the hospital followed the performance. Treats were served to the patients amidst much hearty cheering, and the men piled praise and gratitude on the departing FANY. The hospital had served over 4,000 in-patient Belgian soldiers.[118]

Lamarck had been a success. It was the first project undertaken by the FANY and five of the original staff (Isabel Wicks, Brenda Joynson, Edith Walton, Mary Marshall and Margaret Cole-Hamilton) received the Croix Civique decorations from His Majesty King Albert of the Belgians, while McDougall herself was decorated with the Ordre de Leopold, a high Belgian military honour. Medals were also won by the staff at the zeppelin raid on Lamarck as well as at the gas attack at Hell's Corner. Such success encouraged the following bold exclamation in the *Gazette* about the importance of the FANY as military personnel: 'All the old arguments against women serving at the Front have been proved invalid!'[119] Although this declaration was somewhat premature and overly optimistic, it does illustrate the success of this first FANY venture: a venture that initiated them into traditional nursing service but provided opportunities that allowed transgressions into masculine territory. The FANY were able to fashion themselves from cultural material at hand, using traditional notions of femininity and appropriating masculine space: a task Jo Burr Margadant has described as 'exploiting unsuspected fissures' and weaving new ways of performing gender.[120] The FANY were on their way!

Notes

1 Grace McDougall, *A Nurse at the War: Nursing Adventures in Belgium and France* (New York: McBride, 1917), pp. 81–2.
2 McDougall, 'Five Years with the Allies, 1914–1919: The Story of the FANY Corps', p. 43. [IWM]
3 Ibid., p. 44; McDougall, *A Nurse at the War*, p. 82.
4 McDougall, 'Five Years with the Allies', p. 44.
5 McDougall, *A Nurse at the War*, p. 82.
6 Files of the BRCS 10 2/ 9; 12 2/ 2 cited in Sharon Ouditt, *Fighting Forces, Writing Women: Identity and Ideology in the First World War* (London: Routledge, 1994), p. 13.
7 McDougall, 'Five Years with the Allies', pp. 45–6.
8 Nina MacDonald, 'Sing a Song of War-time', in Catherine Reilly (ed.), *Scars Upon My Heart: Women's Poetry and Verse of the First World War* (London: Virago, 1981), p. 69.
9 Colin Nicolson, *The First World War: Europe 1914–1918* (Harlow, Essex: Longman, 2001), p. 63.
10 Patricia Penn Hilden, *Women, Work, and Politics: Belgium, 1830–1914* (New York: Oxford University Press, 1993) and 'The Rhetoric and Iconography of Reform: Women Coal Miners in Belgium, 1840–1914', in Fiona Montgomery and Christine Collette (eds), *The European Women's History Reader* (London: Routledge, 2002), pp. 129–51.
11 Charlotte Kellog, *Women of Belgium: Turning Tragedy to Triumph* (London: Funk and Wagnalls, 1917).
12 John van Schaick, *The Little Corner Never Conquered: The Story of the American Red Cross Work for Belgium* (New York: Macmillan, 1922), p. 221. See Marie de Croy, *War Memories* (London: Macmillan, 1932).
13 Margaret H. Darrow, *French Women and the First World War: War Stories of the Home Front* (New York: Oxford University Press, 2000), pp. 74, 255.
14 Ibid., p. 239.
15 Pat Beauchamp (a.k.a. Waddell), *Fanny Went to War* (London: Routledge, 1949), p. 13.
16 Ibid.; McDougall, 'Five Years with the Allies', p. 47.
17 John Terraine, *The Great War* (Ware, Hertfordshire: Wordsworth, 1998), p. 87.
18 McDougall, 'Five Years with the Allies', p. 48.
19 Cicely Mordaunt, diary, no page numbers. [FA]
20 Ibid.
21 Ibid.
22 In a letter to the Editor of the *Daily Sketch* (26 December 1914), Ashley-Smith told of the work of the FANY for the Belgians, made the request that 'anything and everything would be helpful', and gave a list of possible donations including clothing, dressings, soap, jam and chocolate.
23 The *FANY Corps Gazette* was an important vehicle for keeping all FANY at home and abroad in touch with developments within the organization. It shared news and information concerning the FANY and printed unit reports and observations. Written and

---

edited by the FANY Secretary back in London, although often typed and printed with help from volunteers, the *Gazette* also included requests for donations of money, food, clothing and other goods. An annual subscription to the magazine cost 5 shillings in 1917.

24 Pat Beauchamp (a.k.a. Waddell), *Fanny Goes to War* (London: John Murray, 1919), p. 16.
25 See Sharon Ouditt's chapter on the VAD in *Fighting Forces, Writing Women*; and Janet K. Watson, 'Khaki Girls, VADs, and Tommy's Sisters: Gender and Class in First World War Britain', *The International History Review* 19: 1 (1997), 32–51.
26 Jane Marcus, 'Afterword: Corpus/Corps/Corpse. Writing the Body in/at War', in Helen Zenna Smith (a.k.a. Evadne Price), *Not So Quiet . . . Stepdaughters of War* (New York: The Feminist Press, [1930] 1989), p. 245.
27 Beauchamp, *Fanny Goes to War*, p. 13.
28 Ibid., p. 18.
29 McDougall, *A Nurse at the War*, pp. 90–1.
30 Ibid., p. 99.
31 Martha Vicinus, *Independent Women: Work and Community for Single Women 1850–1920* (Chicago: Chicago University Press, 1985), p. 92.
32 McDougall, 'Five Years with the Allies', p. 26.
33 Ibid., pp. 69, 70.
34 For a fascinating discussion of shell-shock and its relationship to gender anxiety, see Elaine Showalter, 'Rivers and Sassoon: The Inscription of Male Gender Anxieties', in Margaret R. Higonnet (with Jane Jenson, Sonya Michel and Margaret C. Weitz) (eds), *Behind the Lines: Gender and the Two World Wars* (New Haven: Yale University Press, 1987), pp. 61–9.
35 McDougall, *A Nurse at the War*, p. 111.
36 Anonymous (most likely Winnie Mordaunt), 'On the Road to Fontinettes', unauthored notebook, no page numbers. [FA]
37 McDougall, *A Nurse at the War*, pp. 99–100.
38 Ibid., p. 100.
39 Jo Burr Margadant (ed.), *The New Biography: Performing Femininity in Nineteenth-Century France* (Berkeley: University of California Press, 2000), p. 2.
40 McDougall, 'Five Years with the Allies', p. 55.
41 Ibid., p. 60.
42 Ibid., p. 62.
43 Taped interview, Edith Colston (*neé* Walton) by Peter Liddle (May 1973). [LC]
44 Irene Rathbone, *We That Were Young* (New York: The Feminist Press, [1932] 1989), pp. 464–5.
45 See Jenny Gould, 'Women's Military Services in First World War Britain', in Higonnet et al. (eds), *Behnd the Lines*, pp. 114–25.
46 Beauchamp, *Fanny Went to War*, p. 17.
47 Grace McDougall, 'Brief Resumé of Corps' Work', *Gazette* (August 1916), p. 12.
48 Brittain was over the age for active service. He later died of cholera in 1916 while tending the sick and wounded in Mesopotamia. He had been driving a hospital boat on the River Tigris: McDougall, 'Five Years with the Allies', p. 94; *Gazette* (August 1916), p. 2.
49 Beauchamp, *Fanny Went to War*, p. 14
50 Eileen Crofton, *The Women of Royaumont: A Scottish Women's Hospital on the Western Front* (East Linton, Scotland: Tuckwell Press, 1997), p. 305.
51 This unit was founded by Toupie Lowther, a brilliant fencer, musician, sportswoman

and motorcyclist. Meade's papers are in the Imperial War Museum Department of Documents.

52 Beryl Hutchinson, 'My FANY Life with the Belgian Army', p. 2. [LC]

53 *Gazette* (June 1916), p. 9.

54 McDougall, 'Five Years with the Allies', p. 93.

55 Penny Summerfield, 'Gender and War in the Twentieth Century', *The International History Review* 19: 1 (1997), 8–9.

56 See Susan Grayzel, *Women's Identities at War: Gender, Motherhood, and Politics in Britain and France During the First World War* (Chapel Hill: University of North Carolina Press, 1999), ch. 4.

57 Beauchamp, *Fanny Goes to War*, p. 44.

58 Mordaunt, diary.

59   McDougall, *A Nurse at the War*, p. 90.

60 Ibid., pp. 109–10.

61 Mordaunt, diary.

62 McDougall, *A Nurse at the War*, pp. 106–7.

63 Mary Borden, *The Forbidden Zone* (London: Heinemann, 1929), p. 55.

64 McDougall, *A Nurse at the War*, p. 117.

65 Ibid., pp. 120–1.

66 *Gazette* (May 1916), p. 6.

67 Mordaunt, diary.

68 *Gazette* (October 1915), p. 5.

69 *Gazette* (February 1917), p. 3.

70 *Gazette* (May 1917), p. 5.

71 Hugh Popham, *F.A.N.Y.: The Story of the Women's Transport Service, 1907–1984* (London: Leo Cooper, 1984), p. 24.

72 McDougall, 'Five Years with the Allies', pp. 92–3.

73 *Gazette* (October 1916), p. 3.

74 Popham, *F.A.N.Y.*, pp. 24–5.

75 Angela K. Smith, *The Second Battlefield: Women, Modernism and the First World War* (Manchester: Manchester University Press, 2000), p. 40.

76 A. J. P. Taylor, *The First World War* (Ware, Hertfordshire: Wordsworth, 1998), p. 25.

77 Terraine, *The Great War*, p. 119–20. See also Stanley Weintraub, *Silent Night: The Story of the World War I Christmas Truce* (London: Penguin, 2001).

78 John Keegan, *The First World War* (New York: Alfred Knopf, 1999), pp. 192–203.

79 Paul Fussell, *The Great War and Modern Memory* (Oxford: Oxford University Press, 1975), pp. 36, 41.

80 Ibid., p. 43.

81 Lynn Knight, 'Introduction' to Rathbone, *We That Were Young*, p. x.

82 Beauchamp, *Fanny Goes to War*, pp. 33–4.

83 Ibid., p. 23.

84 Ibid., p. 24.

85 McDougall, *A Nurse at the War*, p. 94.

86 McDougall, 'Five Years with the Allies', p. 66.

87 McDougall, *A Nurse at the War*, p. 97.

88 *Gazette* (October 1917), pp. 6–7.

89 Beauchamp, *Fanny Goes to War*, p. 32.

90 Mary Borden, 'The Song of the Mud', in Margaret R. Higonnet (ed.), *Lines of Fire: Women Writers of World War I* (New York: Penguin, 1999), p. 506.

91 Ibid., p. 507.
92 McDougall, *A Nurse at the War*, pp. 91–2.
93 Ibid., p. 92.
94 McDougall, 'Five Years with the Allies', pp. 72–3.
95 Ibid., pp. 241–2.
96 Edith Colston (*neé* Walton), untitled, handwritten account. [LC]
97 Beauchamp, *Fanny Goes to War*, p. 57.
98 *Women's Transport Service (FANY) Gazette* (Autumn 1972), p. 26.
99 McDougall, 'Five Years with the Allies', p. 75.
100 Hutchinson, 'My FANY Life with the Belgian Army', p. 7.
101 Terraine, *The Great War*, pp. 137–8.
102 Hutchinson, 'My FANY Life with the Belgian Army', p. 11.
103 Beauchamp, *Fanny Went to War*, p. 43.
104 Ibid., p. 57.
105 McDougall, *A Nurse at the War*, p. 132.
106 Sandra M. Gilbert, 'Soldier's Heart: Literary Men, Literary Women, and the Great War', *Signs: Journal of Women in Culture and Society* 8: 3 (1983), 422–50.
107 Gilbert, 'Soldier's Heart', pp. 440–1.
108 Summerfield, 'Gender and War in the Twentieth Century', p. 9.
109 Notes of the FANY Board Meeting (9 November 1915). [FA]
110 McDougall, 'Five Years with the Allies', p. 59.
111 'British Nurse Defies the German Staff: Amazing Exploits of Mrs. McDougall in Belgium', *Weekly Welcome* (27 March 1915).
112 'Amazons to the Fore', *Ladies Pictorial* (20 February 1915); 'Every Girl is Wanted', *Sunday Pictorial* (7 November 1915).
113 Elaine Showalter, *Sexual Anarchy: Gender and Culture at the Fin de Siècle* (New York: Penguin Books, 1990), p. 39.
114 Letters to the Editor, *The Morning Post*, 16 July, 19 July, 21 July 1915.
115 W. Beach Thomas, 'Defence of "Base" Women: Their Work in France', unidentified newspaper clipping (undated, *c.* 1915, probably *Daily Mail*). [IWM] Mr Beach Thomas would often visit and have tea with the FANY at Lamarck (Beauchamp, *Fanny Went to War*, p. 91).
116 Beatrice Harraden, 'British Women and the War', *The Windsor Magazine* (November 1915), p. 193.
117 *Gazette* ('Xmas Issue' November/December 1916), p. 5.
118 Ibid.
119 *Gazette* (July 1915), p. 2.
120 Margadant (ed.), *The New Biography*, p. 3.

4

Not a woman, but a FANY
Working for the British in Calais
1916

One day during her travels to inspect the various FANY projects in the area around Calais, Grace McDougall tried to persuade the Railway Transport Office to give her a service order to travel by one of the trains reserved for troops. On being told no woman was ever allowed on such troop trains, McDougall exclaimed she 'wasn't a woman but a FANY!' and proceeded to board amidst the cheers of the men.[1] On another occasion she defied a similar ban barring women from troop ships and pretended to command a company of Belgian soldiers en route to Calais. It was only through some fast talking and use of feminine wiles that she managed to escape the wrath of the Military Landing Officer.[2] Through such stories McDougall constructed herself as audacious, flaunting her femininity while acting in 'masculine' ways, using class privilege and renegotiating gender. This 'performance' was a disruptive act in the sense that McDougall was challenging the regulatory norms of gender and the very meaning of 'woman'; in the words of Mary Louise Roberts, McDougall was in effect 'making herself new'.[3] This chapter explores such gender renegotiations by the FANY as they threw themselves into the manly tasks of driving and mechanics. Although they might consider themselves FANY first and women second, they never positioned themselves outside of this latter construct and indeed relied upon it to establish their own quirky version of transformative femininity. This version successfully combined all things 'feminine' with 'masculine' competencies associated with driving and mechanics, thus defusing the potentially subversive impact of such an identity through the familiarities of the 'fairer sex'.

Despite the resistance and red tape put up by the British War Office, still it was always the FANY's greatest hope that they might be attached to the British Army and provide ambulance and other transport for British troops. The authorities had considered the FANY to run a military hospital at Bramshott back in England and had kept McDougall at headquarters for several months during the summer of 1915 working on details of the project. However at the last minute it was cancelled when they decided not to use this hospital for war wounded. Still, even if Bramshott had become a reality, it did not fulfil McDougall's dream of working with the British wounded in France, nor did it fit the bill as a way for the FANY to work in ambulance transport. Although she had been told repeatedly by the authorities that women had no place in such work, as we know, McDougall was not easily dissuaded by such rhetoric: they were FANY, not women. In August 1915 McDougall and Lillian Franklin visited the War Office and offered a proposal that the FANY take over hospital and driving tasks currently performed by male orderlies and chauffeurs in Calais, as well as in Boulogne, Rouen and Le Havre, thus releasing men for other service. The proposal is interesting in presenting a women's perspective on the gender anxieties associated with women and war, since it articulates their perceptions of the Army's objections to women and rebutts these with detailed explanation. The proposal that survives is handwritten and signed by McDougall; it is not clear how much input Franklin had in the crafting of the document.

The Army's objections as the FANY (or McDougall) saw them were threefold: one, such a scheme was a 'novelty' and had no precedent; two, employing women might cause a possible 'scandal'; and three, women were not as 'amenable to discipline' as men. In response to the first item, the FANY explained they had already been doing this work and doing it well: the role was hardly a novelty and they had already proved their competency through service at Lamarck and other work in Calais. The second item was a little more tricky since it required crafting an argument that relied on both traditional essentialized notions of womanhood as well as a claim for a different kind of service by women. The FANY presented their argument in the third person: 'They are educated women whose self-respect guards them from insult. They have lived alone [orig. emph.] in the midst of the Belgian army in the foremost line of trenches, have worked for one year amongst soldiers, were unprotected save by their uniform, and their mission [and . . .] have never met with anything but the utmost chivalry and courtesy . . . They also speak French.' The subtext to McDougall's reference to 'educated women whose self-respect guards them from insult' was of course their claim to class status and defence against sexual impropriety. Language proficiency was another way of claiming elite status as well as stating the practical advantages of such a skill: French was the language learned by cultured wives and proficient hostesses. In addition, the proposal explained that women are 'better suited' as orderlies and chauffeurs. Unlike the 'old RAMC men with years of training [who] learned gentleness', the 'new [orig. emph.] RAMC with two or three months instruction are very rough; women with the same amount of training are more fitted for such work'. These arguments used traditional discourses of class and gender to make their case. At the same time, however, an argument was made based on the ways the FANY were different from ordinary women: '[they] are all trained and accustomed to lifting wounded in and out of ambulances, carrying them into wards, etc. . . . Having been themselves in the firing-line and having witnessed the horrors of warfare, the FANY do not ask the War Office to send them into the line of fire; but they do most earnestly urge that they be extensively employed at Base Towns' [orig. emph.].

The proposal responded to the third objection concerning women's lack of discipline by again making a case for the FANY outside traditional gender relations. They were a disciplined body, McDougall explained, accustomed to obedience and military life. 'For five years previous to the outbreak of war the FANY have been trained under military supervision following the lines of the Royal Army Medical Corps training. Every member is selected by the Organizing Officer, and no member is enrolled until the Organizing Officer is thoroughly satisfied as to the applicant's character, ability, and power of physical endurance.' In this way the proposal addressed the arrogant, intolerable attitude of the British War Office with grace and diplomacy, articulating arguments that, although somewhat contradictory, certainly made the case for women's service. The last sentence of the proposal sent an important message: if the British would not incorporate their services, the FANY would work elsewhere: '[The FANY] would like the assurance of the War Office that their services cannot be utilized by British wounded or by British authorities before offering their personnel elsewhere.'[4]

The official response to the proposal was not encouraging. In essence, it declared the scheme a totally impractical idea and stated that women would never drive for the British Army.[5] This refusal, reiterated in a formal letter declining McDougall's offer of a convoy for the British, had its roots in both the British authorities' desire to maintain the gender status quo as well as in their response to the fiercely independent nature of the FANY itself. If McDougall had agreed to submerge the FANY into the BRCS, no doubt a place would have been found for them. It was the requirement that the FANY stay an independent organization that caused added friction with British authorities.

With her usual dogged persistence, McDougall would not take no for an answer to her proposal; any opposition to the enterprising 'Mac' merely acted like a 'delayed time-fuse'.[6] In her favour was the fact that the FANY had been asked to help the BRCS temporarily in June 1915 when the British were using Calais harbour as a base for all hospital ships and a converted casino as a Base Hospital. The BRCS ambulances met the troop trains and brought wounded to this hospital as well as providing general transport between the various medical facilities in the region. In May 1915 the French had been fighting at Artois and the British were still battling at Ypres. British troops had attempted a disastrous offensive at Aubers Ridge and another offensive at Festubert. The latter created a deceptively small gain although thousands of casualties too. This was the 'rush' after Festubert that temporarily employed the FANY when there was a shortage of BRCS ambulances. This important service, performed in exemplary style, was an important aspect of McDougall's argument. She refused to internalize humiliation or allow failure to silence her personal ambition or vision for the Corps. She accepted the chauvinism of the British authorities and put her energy into using her connections to plan the next strategy. Franklin was better known than McDougall for her stoic patience and for her calmness under stress. Together no doubt their knack for single-minded purpose allowed them to persist when others might have given up.

They decided to wait a few months and again visited Army General Headquarters and the BRCS in Boulogne. McDougall used her connections with various military personnel (Colonel Alexander, a former Director of Army Medical Services, Major Smallman, and Surgeon General Woodhouse, as well as her old fencing master, a gentleman named Colonel Dodson) to help woo the authorities into submission. In December 1915 the official sanction was given and on 1 January 1916 the FANY did indeed become the first women's ambulance convoy to work with the British Army. A compromise of sorts concerning the Corps' independence had been worked out with the Joint War Committee of the BRCS and the Order of St John of Jerusalem (the male ambulance driver's organization). The Corps was to be employed or commissioned by the BRCS to provide transport for the British sick and wounded at Calais. The FANY would provide the drivers and the BRCS would furnish ambulances, stores and so forth; the FANY would keep their name and uniform and receive the same privileges as other BRCS members. Lillian Franklin was the Commandant of this Calais convoy, FANY Unit 3, and ran it until the Armistice in 1918.

The FANY had to fight to keep their name and uniform during these contract negotiations. Despite this, a group of FANY on their way to join the convoy in France were refused certificates of passage because they were not attired in VAD uniform. Of course this made McDougall furious: after being denied an interview with Furse, Commandant of the VAD, she reported she told the second-in-command that her orders were clear and she would let Sir Arthur Lawley (who had signed the contract on behalf of the BRCS) know that 'his signature had no value in England'. She then went to Sir Arthur Stanley at BRCS headquarters in England and made sure the FANY got their passes that very afternoon.[7] McDougall had a way of working the system, using her connections and getting her way. She understood the importance of the FANY uniform and name as a symbol of their independence and morale, wound up as it was with her own personal ego and ambition.

This success and commitment to FANY growth and independence, however, had serious consequences for McDougall's health. Under great strain and emotional stress, she was exhausted from the demanding schedule she had given herself and the poor conditions under which she lived and worked. In addition, there were family demands that caused McDougall grief and anxiety. After enduring the death of her brother Charlie in May 1915, she heard in January 1916 that her brother Bill (who had crossed with the original FANY unit in October 1914) had been killed in action and recommended for the Victoria Cross after attempting to rescue a wounded comrade.[8] Her mother and Bill's wife were in shock and the family was in turmoil. McDougall had been close to Bill and was understandably shattered by the news. Indeed, First World War memoirs and novels are full of women grieving for brothers (one thinks of Vera Brittain, Katherine Mansfield, Virginia Woolf and Irene Rathbone), identifying with them and professing great love and affection. Jane Marcus comments on this seemingly incestuous theme but recognizes the shared grief of youth and the desire for women to be their brothers: 'The repressed wish to be the brother or an androgynous approximation of him works behind the safety curtain of women's war dramas.'[9]

The weight of responsibility on McDougall's shoulders left her little time to grieve. She explained the predicament with words that are as relevant today as they were in 1916: 'Again, duty [had] torn me in two directions. It was the old struggle women always have, families versus work.'[10] She complained of being completely exhausted from the strain of managing both her personal and professional life, and had two or three fainting spells and repeated attacks of pain. In early February 1916 when her sister arrived from South Africa to care for her mother, McDougall attempted to go back to France. Unfortunately, during the journey she had several bouts of fainting and such severe attacks of pain that she was given a diagnosis of appendicitis, which required three months' rest and recovery in England. Remarking on McDougall's condition in a letter to Violet Cole-Hamilton, Franklin wrote that 'naturally all this trouble has completely unhinged her, and she cannot see things as clearly as she would under different circumstances'.[11] After encouragement from Franklin, McDougall took a few months' rest away from the responsibilities of the Corps. During this period she received treatment for a burst eardrum that had been affected by a shell blast in Antwerp. It was during these months of respite in early 1916 that McDougall wrote *Nursing Adventures*.

The success on the part of the FANY as the first women to officially drive the British wounded and thus venture into non-traditional women's work cannot be overestimated: not only was it an incredible feat in and of itself but it also set a precedent allowing VAD and others to drive for the British. Even though their argument for service was contradictory and reflected the conflicting identities associated with the organization as it attempted to use and rework traditional gender, still their behaviour was disruptive in providing new horizons for women in the field of driving, mechanics and ambulance transport. An article in a popular British daily newspaper summed up their achievements as 'one of a series of victories for women workers and organisations', calling it a striking but by no means unique example of 'the complete triumph of women workers during the past few months'.[12] Even though this 'Special Correspondent in France' might have been a little carried away in seeing FANY accomplishments as evidence of the 'complete triumph' of women in this masculine terrain, nonetheless, the Corps' success was symbolic of the changes afoot in the British formal response to women's involvement in the war. Not only women's proficiencies, but also the sheer need for aid, challenged resistance to women at the Front. During Christmas 1916, the War Office identified some 12,000 jobs of non-combatant male soldiers in France as suitable for women.[13] As the war dragged into the New Year 1916, Allied forces met with constant challenges amidst failed campaigns. The British disaster at Gallipoli (where many Australians and New Zealanders in particular lost their lives) was especially poignant and marked, in effect, the end of British imperial supremacy. It became increasingly clear that no help could be refused, even that from women. This chapter focuses on 1916 and features the story of FANY Unit 3 driving for the British Army. It records their activities and experiences and in particular examines their work in transport and mechanics that subverted traditional mythologies about femininity.

'First anywhere'

Although the FANY were delighted to overhear a British soldier telling his friend that the acronym 'FANY' stood for 'first anywhere', this trailblazing was not pursued entirely without some trepidation.[14] Working for the British came as quite a responsibility to the FANY, who could compare the relative security of the hospital at Lamarck with this new arrangement: initially a camp of flapping tents amidst sand dunes overlooking the sea, and increased responsibility for driving and ambulance transport at a time when war casualties were increasing and resources being stretched. Work for the convoy involved meeting trains and barges from the Front and transporting the wounded to various hospitals and to the docks and ships bound for England. They also drove supplies and personnel to and from various destinations around Calais.

The convoy included twenty-two personnel with a considerable number of seasoned FANY who were released from Lamarck to establish this new unit: 'Boss' Franklin, Marian and Hope 'Jimmie' Gamwell, Beryl 'Betty' or 'Hutch' Hutchinson, Chris Nicholson, Norma Lowson, Mary 'Dicky'. Richardson, Winnie Mordaunt, Muriel Thompson and Pat Waddell.[15] As already mentioned, Franklin was the Commandant and Sergeant Thompson would become its Section Leader.

Despite the careful contractual agreements with the BRCS, there were organizational problems and Franklin feared the convoy might have to draw on FANY funds for its support. She spoke of a 'fresh agreement' with the BRCS whereby the latter would pay for all repairs on the vehicles 'in exactly the same way they do for their own people' and that the British Army authorities would supply rations.[16] Eventually a new agreement was drawn up between the FANY and the BRCS whereby the former was relieved of financial responsibility in connection with the vehicles and the latter would provide stores, as well as grant to the FANY all facilities given to the VAD. At the same time, the FANY maintained complete control over personnel and their uniform. 'This new agreement is rather a great achievement', Franklin explained in her report in the *Gazette*, especially 'when one remembers the old one and the very great monetary responsibility under which the Corps was placed'.[17] In actuality, the FANY were saving the British authorities considerable money since they were volunteers and the Red Cross men they replaced had earned 42 shillings a week. The FANY also saved them 25 per cent of the costs of repairs on the vehicles.[18] Not only was the BRCS willing to quibble about the conditions of these women's free labour, but they also had initially suggested having a male BRCS officer to oversee the women and relate directly to the military authorities. Still suspicious that women could work and organize themselves, this was a common arrangement where female leadership was involved. Fortunately, wrote Franklin: 'everything is working so smoothly here, it [the question of male supervision and go-between] has been declared unnecessary'. She had spoken with Lord Donnaghmore, the Commissioner of the BRCS, who said he was so very satisfied with their work that he had quite given up the idea of appointing a male officer.[19] While we may feel some astonishment that the FANY would be willing to accept such arrogance and ingratiate themselves under these conditions, it is important to remember that the FANY as an organization had always aligned itself with these military authorities towards whom they had strong class allegiances. In addition, given the resistance towards women and the misogyny and chauvinism of the War Office, the FANY had little choice if they wanted to survive as an organization and be a part of the war effort.

During the month of January, as the FANY were first settling into their work in Unit 3, the British were facing a new conscription law passed under the Military Service Act to provide more manpower to the various Fronts. Conscription imposed service on unmarried men without exemption certificates and was extended in May to all men between eighteen and forty-one years old. Sir Douglas Haig (whose cousin Henrietta Fraser was a member of the FANY) had replaced Sir John French as commander of the British forces in December 1915, although all Allied forces were under the command of French General Joffré. Haig's inflexible approach only exacerbated the entrenchment between the combatants, unfortunately, and as each continued to gain or lose mere yards of the Front line, thousands of men were gassed, injured and killed in action. At this point the war had reached global proportions as Allied troops fought against the Turks and struggled to take over German colonial territories in New Guinea, Western Samoa, China and Africa.

Work began in earnest for the new FANY convoy as offensives and skirmishes along the line brought in the wounded to Calais by barge and trainload. The FANY moved most of these men to the British Army hospital at the casino in Calais and evacuated others to ships waiting to take them to England. Convoy Commandant Franklin reported moving almost a thousand cases between barges, casino and ships as well as about 160 convalescents to Boulogne in the first two weeks of their work there. In addition, they transported many local sick and accident cases and the lorries were at work all the time fetching supplies for hospital trains and barges.[20] In February they moved about 2,000 cases.[21] East of Calais, the Germans under General von Falkenhayn had attacked the French at the fortress of Verdun and this battle would rage from February through the rest of the year. Under the leadership of General Philippe Pétain, the French fought doggedly against the Germans at Verdun until a French counter-offensive later in the year won back previously lost ground. These offensives stretched medical resources immeasurably and resulted in the French loss of about 3,500 men.[22]

At the end of May the FANY were shaken by news of the Battle of Jutland that toppled British naval superiority and inflicted heavy casualties on the British fleet. Waddell said the news of Jutland 'fell like a bombshell in the camp',[23] made worse a few days later by Kitchener's drowning when HMS *Hampshire* was sunk. This plunged 'the whole of the BEF into mourning. Everyone in khaki wore black crêpe armlets, and the French showed their sympathy in many touching ways.'[24] Muriel Thompson was very moved by her experience of seeing the remains of a bombed British destroyer, a part of which had sunk to the bottom of the sea. Most likely this was the British destroyer

Zulu which had been blown apart by a mine. With startling modernist clarity Thompson described the experience:

Black darkness again, and a blue-white fierce light biting into the blackness – above a towering shape, and now, where the light strikes, a twisted, distorted mass – tubes, wheels, cogs – blades – incredible, misshapen remains of what was but a few hours back, a living destroyer . . . her dazed, battered crew already working to prepare her for the repair gang. A sad sight, a broken ship. Next day – two gun-carriages, two coffins. Bare-headed survivors on either side. French blue-jackets bringing up the rear of the sad procession, and two more English boys 'go West'.[25]

Close to home for the FANY was the Somme offensive that began in late June 1916 and lasted until November, taking the lives of thousands of British soldiers. The Battle of the Somme started after artillery fire was supposed to knock out German defences; instead, rigid line after line of British soldiers went 'over the top' and were mowed down by German guns. There were approximately 57,000 British casualties on the very first day of the offensive, the highest the British had ever faced. A brief mention allowed by the censors in the July 1916 report of the convoy published in the *Gazette* hinted at the situation for the British forces: 'The work of the convoy has been a good deal brisker the last few weeks, the whole convoy of 20 ambulances, one bus and lorry having turned out constantly.'[26] It carried almost 5,000 cases that month. And again in August Franklin wrote that the work of the convoy 'has been much brisker lately and there are times when one feels one could do with at least another ten ambulances'.[27] Haig's charge at the Somme was to break through the German line allowing the cavalry to pass through and defeat the Germans further north while the French simultaneously battled German forces at Verdun. This new strategy hoped to time Allied advances to prevent the Germans transporting reserves from one source of fighting to another. Lasting until late autumn, when it was stopped by conditions of freezing mud, this battle had far-reaching effects on British morale. Losses were very high and the battle came to symbolize the hopelessness of war. This sense of despair and a new-found realism can be compared to the jubilance and traditional rhetoric that framed the war at its onset. While many casualties from the Battle of the Somme were sent by rail to Boulogne, this battle and the huge number of wounded would also define 1916 for FANY Unit 3.

As the convoy for the British was up and running and schemes for FANY expansion in the works, back in London personnel at FANY Headquarters were concerned with the issue of uniforms and consternation over the frequent FANY inattention to the formalities associated with military dress. Eventually Secretary Janette Lean wrote in the *Gazette* that 'for some months members have been more or less pleasing themselves, and a result that can hardly be called successful, one costume in particular can only, with a stretch of the imagination, be called "uniform" at all'. Regulations, she emphasized, must include a 'khaki jacket with four pockets, FANY buttons and badges with plain sleeves, a Red Cross circle on each sleeve, and the centre of the cross to be seven inches from the shoulder; bottom of khaki skirt to be 10 inches from the ground; and khaki puttees and brown shoes or boots, or long boots to be worn'.[28] A long navy blue coat with red piping was worn as an overcoat, although drivers also managed to get fur coats to help keep out the biting cold and wind in their windshield-less ambulances. While these coats were practical, they also added a certain pizzazz to FANY identity. The mechanics also wore breeches and blue smocks when working on the cars. Finally, another important innovation was the soft FANY beret designed by driver Chris Nicholson in collaboration with a millinery outfitters in the Rue Royale, Calais, made of cotton cloth, quartered and gathered on top with a band around and the FANY emblem on the front. This emblem was the Maltese cross, a symbol of sacrifice, within a circle. To the FANY this implied duty as unified sacrifice in service.

Despite the complaints and creativity associated with the uniforms, the FANY were very proud to wear khaki and rebuffed accusations that such dress was inappropriate for women. They had developed a group identity and their uniform was worn proudly to identify them as competent, disciplined and independent women whose individual identities were submerged into the larger identity of the FANY. Generally the FANY thought the civilian obsession with women and uniform a waste of time and energy and defended their right to wear it. These thoughts are reflected in the following poem 'An Apology for What We Wear', author unknown. This mocking verse with its reference to 'this stinking war' as well as the inclusion of such biting statements as 'oh you criticize the clothes' and 'we do not like your smile' illustrate FANY defence of their service in face of resistance to their war work.

> Oh you criticize the clothes
> or lack of them, as worn
> By members of the female sex
> who rise at early dawn
> And carry on throughout the day
> to help this stinking war
> Just try to think, a thing I feel
> you've never done before
>
> We're sorry if our garb offends
> we do not like your smile

When you observe a skirt that reaches
to the knee only of our breeches
We do not wear for choice you see
these clothes utilitarian
We hate our nails to be unkept
our hair like a barbarian

So do not blame us overmuch
we're useful we believe
And for a precedent we show
the costume worn by Eve;
For when engaged in useful work
after 'the fall' they say
The clothing worn by Eve was not
what people wear today.[29]

Camp for Unit 3 consisted of various tents, a canvas hut, and bathing chalets on a hill in the sand dunes overlooking the British Channel. The camp was outside the town of Calais and was halfway between town and the casino that had been taken over by the BRCS.[30] The *Gazette* emphasized that the tents were of course a temporary arrangement and future plans involved building a wooden barracks of twenty-four cubicles and two bathrooms, heated by hot pipes.[31] In the meantime, however, they lived in these tents and made do, getting up in the night to secure ropes, enduring collapsed tents, and trying not to freeze to death. The tents were ex-Indian army supply and better suited to that climate than the windy, northern French coast. Several of the FANY converted bathing machines (tiny wooden structures for changing and privacy when bathing on the beach) into living quarters and the little chalets also served as storerooms for the cookhouse, pharmacy and tool shop. Most of the FANY slept in 'flea-bags', army sleeping bags on cots, and tried to keep warm in the draughty and chilly tents. In this endeavour they were helped by oil stoves that Waddell remembered giving a wonderful 'fug' inside the tent.[32] Hutchinson counted herself lucky when Boss asked her to share her little canvas hut. Hutchinson explained that it was on a frame and more 'luxurious' than the flapping canvas with guy ropes that had to be adjusted for the different hazards imposed by wind and storms.[33]

All cooking for the camp was done on a small primus stove and the cookhouse, a shed of corrugated iron under the protection of a group of trees, was one of the few warm spots in the camp. Working for the BRCS gave the FANY the advantage of a laundry allowance of 10 shillings a week which enabled the cookhouse to make a small levy to buy fresh fruit, vegetables and real milk and butter: a welcome addition to the army rations.[34] Much to her chagrin, Waddell (who hoped that at last she might be allowed to drive, having spent her Christmas leave in a garage learning about engines) was sent to help in the cookhouse. Always willing to make the best of things, she recalled the temperamental primus stove and the difficulties associated with lighting and keeping it going. The first time she attempted the former, filling the little cup with methylated spirits and priming the pump, she was met with a huge roar and a sheet of flame roaring up to the roof of the tent. The regular kitchen staff had to hurl the stove out onto the sand to prevent the whole place going up in flames! Waddell also had to endure the perilous journey carrying trays of food between the cookhouse and the mess tent where the women would eat. Unfortunately the tents had not been placed next to each other and she would lose food and utensils blown away by constant winds or lost when she tripped over the tent ropes. Eventually the mess tent was moved closer to the cookhouse; Waddell said it was a preventive measure to save what few eating utensils they had left. She named the camp the 'abomination of desolation'.[35]

Ironically, the new huts were ready in April just when the weather was getting to the point that the women could endure the tents. Each FANY driver was now given a small cubicle laid out on each side of a central passage that formed a horseshoe arrangement complete with a communal bathroom at one end. Since each cubicle only had a bed and shelves, the women improvised by making 'furniture' out of anything on which they could get their hands. The builder had agreed to paint the inside of the huts at no cost, although all were surprised to see the brilliant green colour that appeared. And, despite the many problems associated with tents, it seems the women missed the communal 'fug', and the huts turned out to be rather cold and draughty and started to warp when the weather turned bad the following winter. This problem was remedied by the installation of asbestos in the cubicles to help insulate against the damp and cold. Given what is now known about asbestos as a toxic material, they would have been better off enduring the cold and keeping their old tents. While they now had a bathhouse that added considerably to their comforts, the FANY were loath to rip down the old tents that had been their home for the past four months. Waddell had brought a little fox terrier dog from home that she named Tuppence. He was quite the convoy pet and anchored her flea-bag at night and helped keep her warm. He did not approve of the move to the huts either and preferred to be able to chase the mice that nested under the tents. Unfortunately Tuppence disappeared sometime after the move and Waddell was distressed to never see him again.[36] Dicky Richardson also had a special dog named Peter of whom she was very fond. Sadly, she left him in the care of a British officer when she was away on assignment and the officer was killed in a German attack. After many days the little dog returned 'from the Boche trenches',[37] but had to be euthanized since it was starved, miserable and covered in sores. The FANY always attempted to make a 'home' out of the accommodation they were given, and home often included a variety of pets that became camp mascots.

Living in camp meant that the women always had 'fatigues' or chores alongside their various professional duties. These included the many housekeeping tasks associated with keeping the camp clean, tidy and in good shape, and folding the overnight coverings from the cars' bonnets or hoods and leaving them by the mess hut (a feature not originally built with the cubicles but constructed later, and then greeted with great cheer by the women at a 'warming party' complete with tea and music). Other tasks included 'doing the stoke hole' (keeping the boiler or furnace functioning), chopping and transporting wood, and weeding the little garden. It seems that Thompson 'fired with patriotism' had 'turned her attention most valiantly to the land' and dug a small vegetable garden.[38] There were also inspections when there was a lull in the fighting and there was the cleaning and greasing and general upkeep of the various vehicles to keep the drivers busy. In addition, as the hosing of the cars was constrained by the bad water supply at the camp, often the women had to drive the ambulances into a depot in Calais to have them thoroughly washed.

As their reputation grew as a Corps who could tackle anything and tackle it well, Unit 3 was asked to assist with local canteens to serve British soldiers. The first was an emergency canteen at Fontinettes, arranged by Franklin. Here the FANY helped feed two divisions of the British Army: again the reports of their work emphasize their hard work and commitment to duty.[39] The second involved a longer stay and more commitment on the part of the FANY. In December 1916 the YMCA requested help to run a 'Dundee Hut' (donated by Mr Brown of Dundee): a canteen providing refreshments for British troops as they passed south from Ypres. Margaret Cole-Hamilton and Ida Lewis, nicknamed 'the Sergeant' and 'the fair Corporal' respectively, jumped to the task and found themselves serving refreshments to about 4,000 men on a regular basis. They helped organize performances of touring troops' entertainer Lena Ashwell and arranged lectures, as well as collecting books, magazines and games for the hut.[40] Another task included helping censor the letters written by the soldiers[41]: a task that illustrates the class allegiances between the FANY and military officials who trusted the women as honorary officers to oversee regulations associated with the ordinary soldier. Of all war work (and especially compared to driving), canteen duty was coded feminine and encountered the least resistance from a doubting public concerned about women's encroachment into masculine space. As one British newspaper article explained, 'when all is said the best opening for women's work is in the canteen and the semi-domestic work of war . . . women still know more than men of the essential facts of domestic economy'.[42] The bitterly cold winter of 1916 made food hard to come by and the hut was eventually closed. Ida Lewis wrote the final report for the FANY as their work at the Dundee Hut ended, claiming it 'a drear and desolate spot' but one always to be remembered, if for nothing else, for the immense gratitude the men showed for the women's kindnesses.[43]

Driving for the British

Driving in Edwardian society was a glamorous activity, coded as it was for women as both elite, and, owing to its masculine connotations, quite subversive. By 1914, however, new production methods allowed firms to standardize the production system and cars became somewhat more affordable, even though the British automobile industry's pride in making a 'better class' of vehicle than American manufacturers kept the industry from mass-producing cheap small cars.[44] This extension of car ownership beyond an affluent elite opened up driving to more women as middle-class families might be able to afford an automobile. While Muriel Thompson was the only known early FANY to be publicly renowned as a driver, many FANY who joined after 1914 were familiar with driving and readily accepted the driving courses they had to take and pass in order to drive for the organization. Still, driving was such a masculine endeavour that the idea of women hand-cranking a large vehicle or mending a tyre was quite scandalous. It goes without saying that in their development of skills in mechanics, driving and ambulance transport, FANY drivers were breaking new ground and venturing into masculine space. This work as driver-mechanics helped forge the identity of the FANY as women on the audacious cutting edge of appropriate gendered behaviour.

I believe the FANY took to driving not only because of prior opportunity to partake in this elite and glamorous activity, but also because it was an extension of their relationship to horses. The FANY had originally been founded as a yeomanry organization with 'galloping ambulances'; its identity was based upon a transport function. They trained on horseback, most grew up around horses, and, as discussed in Chapter 1, it was the horsey identity of the Corps that attracted many women to the FANY in the first place. Since motor vehicles were replacing horses in this war, it made sense that the women would transfer their relationship and orientation towards horses to these motorized vehicles and certainly they tended to treat their cars in the affectionate way they might have treated horses. Indeed, even though these early temperamental vehicles were for the most part a huge pain, reading reports and stories about FANY service in France, one is struck by how much these FANY really seemed to love their cars and how they cared for them as if they were animate beings. Just as they might be amused and feel affection for an unpredictable though amiable horse who never failed to surprise when out on a ride, the women treated the quirks and idiosyncrasies of the cars with similar affectionate patience. Even the Siddley-Deasy (a common make of the day), so temperamental given its revolving gearbox that Hutchinson named it the 'Sizzley Beasty' – even this was referred to with affection. The FANY named the cars, tended to them, and generally treated them as they would a horse. In the manner of the day all FANY referred to being 'on' the car and not 'in' it as we do today. Hutchinson used equine analogies in describing a car as 'a little lame in body', and when she shared her story of the near-miss with the train, explained it just missed the car's 'tail'. Other vehicles were described as 'most gentle' and one as a special 'breed' of car in being so 'pleasant and willing'.[45] Indeed, Thompson recalled letting a car run and remarking how lively it was, just as you might let a horse move into faster gaits when out in the country on a flat stretch of land.[46]

Although some might have lamented the relative demise of horses for ambulance transport, it is hardly possible to overestimate the effects of the development of the internal combustion engine on military transport and communications. Buses and lorries, cars, and motorcycles as well as armoured cars and later tanks all changed the face of battle during this war. Many of these vehicles (such as the Mors waggonette owned by 'Uncle' that resided at Lamarck) had once been private cars donated to the BRCS before becoming converted to ambulances. At its inception, Unit 3 consisted of twelve ambulances (that would soon be increased), several lorries and a motorcycle, and included such makes as Mors, Argylls, Napiers, Siddely-Deaseys and Crossleys. All the glass windscreens had been removed to avoid reflecting light and attracting enemy fire or splintering and causing injury to the driver, and the passenger seats had been replaced by fittings for stretchers, with a wooden seat in front for the driver. A waterproof canvas roof covered the car but provided little protection to the driver against wind, rain and snow that would blow over the low dashboard. The absence of headlights also made the frequent nighttime driving over muddy and snowy shell-pocked roads very treacherous. Drivers were only able to use small oil sidelights to avoid enemy detection. During that bitterly cold winter of 1916–17 the snow froze so hard that it was difficult driving up the hills even with chains. Nonetheless, as one male officer remarked about the FANY, 'when the cars are full of wounded no one could be more patient, considerate and gentle than the FANY, but if the car be empty they drive like bats out of hell'.[47]

The driving difficulties were of course confounded by the fact that none of the vehicles were self-starters and all had to be hand-cranked. This was a gruelling task and required much strength as well as dexterity to avoid a back-fire that could break a limb. Marian Gamwell, for example, broke her arm when an ambulance backfired in the summer of 1916. Waddell remembered the cars 'groaning, back-firing, spitting, refusing at all costs to start, and the girls winding, winding, winding, their cheeks whipped pink by their exertions, their backs on the point of breaking'. This process, explained Waddell, was known as 'getting her loose': an apt term since it usually resulted in the women lying winded across the cars.[48]

After Lamarck closed, the famous motor-bath brought over to France by the Gamwell sisters was transferred to Unit 3. This Brown, Hughes and Stra-chan motor-bath, affectionately named 'James', was a converted 1907 Daimler engine containing ten collapsible canvas baths, a cold water tank, a disinfect-ing cupboard and two huge Primus stoves for heating the water. Waddell, ever the mechanic, described the bath with the following technical details: 'he had both low and high-tension ignition, a governor and a curious bicycle-pump stowed away under the steering-box, the function of which was to produce pressure for the oil and petrol systems. Other of his peculiarities were: two gear-levers, a hand-brake which moved in a vertical line, and the absence of an accelerator.'[49] The women started the motor bath by hand: a mammoth task in itself. It is interesting to note that this vehicle was referred to as masculine, whereas the other ambulances were invariably 'shes'. Perhaps this is related to its bulk and large size or perhaps it is a reflection of its job bathing male bodies: a 'feminine' vehicle would most likely have been quite inappropriate for this task. Nonetheless, James could give 250 baths in one day and also disinfected mud and lice-infected clothes. The FANY drove and tended the Primus that kept the water hot and male orderlies helped the bathers.[50]

As already mentioned, driving for the FANY in Unit 3 included meeting trains and barges from the Front, transporting the wounded to hospitals and to ships en route for England, and driving supplies and personnel to and from various destinations around Calais. The most tedious aspect of the cars involved night duty drivers having to go out in the freezing cold and hand-crank the engines, warming up the cars at hourly intervals during the night to avoid the engine freezing. Anti-freeze was useless and draining the radiators and carburettors did not help.[51] A special system was used to decide who should take individual driving cases that were requested on an *ad hoc* basis. The driver whose name came first in alphabetical order always took the job and told the woman who was next that she was now placed first. This would con-tinue down the alphabet so that no one was able to dodge unpopular jobs and all had a fair chance at whatever came along. At first orderlies came from the casino hospital and other sites and notified the FANY when ambulances were needed. After huts replaced the tents, the FANY acquired a telephone and eventually they had a Secretary who co-ordinated the drivers. As Franklin explained, the Secretary's position was a difficult one and required much tact and diplomacy since 'there are many people who seem to forget an ambulance Convoy is not a cab rank, and demands for cars have to be firmly but gently refused'.[52]

The FANY undertook all ambulance duties for the outlying camps and their vehicles were regularly scheduled for such special duties as transporting German wounded to the hospital in Boulogne and driving the Army Nursing Sisters from their lodgings in town to the hospital or to the docks, where a Sister would supervise nurses taking and coming off from leave. Hutchinson had the job of transporting the Sisters to and from their billets through the winter and was given a silver cigarette box inscribed 'From the Sisters to their driver, Christmas 1916' in gratitude for her work.[53] She made these trips in an Army vehicle – a Wolesley car that the Army was not using. It seems she caused a bit of a stir, as no woman had ever driven such a vehicle before. Hutchinson reported that for the next month a procession of 'Geraniums' or 'Red Flannel' (senior British military officers) came to Calais to see the extraordinary sight of a woman driving such an Army vehicle.[54]

Through their work the FANY became very proficient mechanics. In some ways they had no other choice since some of the BRCS men were displeased enough on vacating their posts to leave the ambulances in poor condition and these huge, temperamental vehicles were always breaking down under the rough conditions of wartime service. The drivers completed all regular maintenance, which by modern standards was quite elaborate. Hutchinson, for example, explained how they de-coked an engine:

The complete cylinder block had to be hoisted up clear of the pistons. Valves, piston rings and all surfaces were thoroughly cleaned and the cylinder block gently lowered while the mechanic squeezed the three rings around each piston back into place. We had raised the block with the help of a rope over the bough of a tree; to lower I had a foot on the chassis each side where the wing joined on and kept the block in its place as it went down over the three levels of rings. The end of the rope was most easily regulated by keeping it under one foot and paying out as needed.[55]

Hutchinson's desire to be seen as competent and not negligent when it came to car maintenance was also illustrated by her response to the time she reported for duty and found two male officers clad in overalls inspecting her car. To her horror she saw they were ripping up the floorboards and looking at places she never knew existed and, according to Hutchinson, certainly never greased. She played for time and told the inspectors she feared that she might be late for her duties. She pleaded with them to substitute another car for hers, saying she would bring back her car for them in the morning, and made mental note of all the parts the inspectors had disclosed as potential problems. Hutchinson went to work that night and cleaned and greased for hours. 'By the time she was ready next morning', said Hutchinson, 'the Sergeant and I had found 92 oiling or greasing points.' Needless to say the car passed its inspection.[56]

In these maintenance endeavours, Hutchinson liked to explain that she had special help. Her friend Major Shaw-Paige had given her a cat ('a tabby in a rather loud grey suiting') that she named Pussica Shaw-Paige. Hutchinson explained that Pussica was a great help at engine cleaning: 'When I slipped a long rag or mutton cloth through his collar he would go in by the floor boards, under the dash and out by the engine which gave me a chance to get the engine fly-wheel casing etc. really clean. Pussica had his little basket in a space between the right hand brake and the side of the cab and often came out with me for the run. Just a whistle to let him know I was starting and he pleased himself.'[57]

While most of FANY Unit 3 were drivers, several (such as Evelyn and Madge Laidlay and Cicely Mordaunt) worked as orderlies and cooks and had little contact with the vehicles. These women knew little about driving, as Pat Waddell was keen to emphasize. One day she overheard a conversation between a non-driving FANY and a friend: the friend made the comment that her companion must really have picked up a lot about cars from working with the convoy. 'Rather', the non-driving FANY replied, 'one constantly hears people exclaiming, "I've mislaid my big end and can't think where I've put the carburettor!"' The big-end story, said Waddell, really 'went the rounds', highlighting as it did how FANY drivers relished their non-traditional identity that set them apart from ordinary women, who understood little about the workings of the internal combustion engine.[58] This is also illustrated in the following poem with its light-hearted parody of Rudyard Kipling and its nod to the previous existence of most FANY as gentle-bred girls who 'used to be in Society once':

> I wish my mother could see me now with a grease gun under my car
> Filling my universal, 'ere I start for the sea afar
> On top of the sheet of frozen iron in a cold that would make you cry
> 'Why do we do it?' you ask. 'Why? We're the F.A.N.Y.'
>> I used to be in Society once
>> Danced, hunted, and flirted once
>> Had white hands and complexion once
>> Now I'm a F.A.N.Y.![59]

Longing to be given a reprieve from kitchen duties, Waddell was at last able to drive one of the lorries or trucks for the convoy and show her driving and mechanical skills. They had two of these large vehicles: a Vulcan lorry used to transport medical supplies during evacuations and a smaller Mors lorry that was a general transport vehicle. Waddell jumped at the chance to drive the Mors when its regular driver, Mary Baxter-Ellis, had to return home to England because of illness. Perched on the box seat on top of a cushion, Waddell said she felt like a regular race-car driver, and enjoyed picking up rations and stores for the convoy and several Army hospitals.[60] Eventually the little Mors lorry was removed from the convoy due to fuel shortages and Waddell drove a new vehicle instead: a 4-cylinder Napier she called 'Susan' that had been donated to the war effort and converted to an ambulance.

Soon Waddell advanced to driving the ambulances, meeting the barges and transporting the wounded to various hospital facilities. Barges were used to carry the most seriously wounded men from the Front who could not have endured the jolting of the trains. This was similar to the tasks of the drivers at Lamarck, except that these soldiers were coming from the British lines, not the Belgian, and were going to British Army hospitals. The wounded were placed on lifts and brought up from inside the barge into the ambulances parked on the canal side. These cases were handled as tenderly as possible and the FANY drove as carefully as they could. It was not easy to start up the slope from the canal without jerking or stalling the ambulances given the clutches in these vehicles and the bumps and hazards along the way. Waddell recalled that after she drove her first lot of wounded, her back and knees were aching from the strain and the physical exertions of driving under such conditions. She had, she said, complete 'stretcher face', the ragged look she had seen in others who were doing this work. The call for 'barges' brought the whole convoy to duty.[61] Waddell wrote that when the war was over, one of the FANY drivers named Hilda Moore who became an actress was rumoured to have paused mid-curtain-call with Gerald du Maurier and almost left the stage when she heard 'barges' being shouted from somewhere in the gallery.[62] For all the cheerful face the FANY legend put on this task of driving to and from the barges, it must have been excruciating work that exposed them again and again to the horrors of the technology of this war.

While nursing had become a relatively routine task for women in war, it was the FANY emphasis on mechanics and ambulance transport that confounded the public and facilitated much discursive anxiety. Such issues were being debated in the British press on a regular basis. One article from a British daily focused specifically on the negative unforeseen consequences of driving for women. 'The uncongenial atmosphere of the garage, yard, and workshops', it read, as well as the 'alien companionship of mechanics and chauffeurs' are likely to cause serious damage to a woman in terms of her 'mental outlook' and will not only rob her of feminine charm, but, worse still, will 'instil into her mind bitterness that will eat from her heart all capacity for joy, steal away her youth, and deprive her of the colour and sunlight of life'. When the convoy got hold of this newspaper cutting, Waddell explained, they found it 'especially pleasing'. Actually, she wrote, it was met with uproarious jeering and exclamation. She said they accepted none of it and found the line especially hilarious where the author explained that for some women it may be too late to counter-act the ultimate effects and all will be lost. Waddell, at least in the telling of the story, constructs the FANY as women who were conscious of wartime gender renegotiations and who enjoyed their placement outside of the norm.[63]

The FANY were most likely more approving of an article in the *Daily Mail* making the case for women's expanded role beyond nursing. It asked two simple questions: are women ready to undertake this work and can they do it? Its author, novelist Elizabeth Robins, explained that there are women who are unfit or prefer to avoid the drudgery of nursing and want to do other service. There have always been women, she wrote, who have done exceptional work in tasks requiring physical strength, steady nerve and endurance. Girls today, she continued, have 'lived much in good air, on generous food where they have played tennis, cricket, golf; hunted, rowed, climbed mountains. Many a girl, obliged to admit she has no gift for nursing feels she has little more, or indeed, little less, to offer to her country than have the young men whom the posters implore her to coax and charm into going to the front.' So much for the posters of 'Is Your Best Boy in Khaki?' Women, the article exclaimed, are no longer begging men to go, but asking them to come. This is an audacious reversal that illustrates how the war encouraged negotiations of gender in public discourse.

In response to a question posed concerning whether women can perform the work, Robins was equally affirmative. 'We are told', she wrote, that 'these horrors [of war] are not for women. No – nor for men – who not infrequently go to pieces under the strain. These horrors are our common burden. Why should the specially qualified woman, who knows herself capable of bearing a share, not be allowed to? . . . Why should a woman be compelled to live on in weary safety instead of following the brave spirit by means of a dedication like [man's] own?' This remarkable discourse of equality of opportunity is followed by proof of the necessity to substitute women for men in ambulance work.[64] Whether the press lauded FANY efforts or saw it as proof of degeneracy, their articles and reports about them were almost always romanticized and illustrated the public imagination's fears of sexual anarchy.[65]

Indeed, several years later in 1918, a book was published by motor enthusiast Gladys de Havilland titled *The Woman's Motor Manual* that aimed at educating women on the intricacies of the combustion engine and encouraging them to pursue work in driving-related activities. Complete with advertisements for both spark plugs and driving corsets, the manual also included a section titled 'Women Doing Noble Work' and featured the service of the FANY in France, warning the reader about the specific character traits associated with FANY who perform these roles. De Havilland emphasized the personal bravery and physical stamina required of FANY drivers and juxtaposed this against what she called 'butterfly chauffeuses': girls out for new experiences and a good time who find out quickly that driving an ambulance in France is 'not so thrilling and enjoyable as some inexperienced girls imagine it to be'.[66] She shares the story of one woman who, unprepared and unwilling to work and finding she could not 'stick it out', soon returns home to England. Although de Havilland does not identify this 'butterfly chauffeuse', most likely she is still writing about the FANY. And, while such a story would most likely have been 'flattened'[67] and not included in the annals of FANY legend, it is instructive in giving another glimpse into the public construction of women's war service:

I am thinking with longing of those glorious days in England, for that is, in fact, what they were when compared with the time I am having in this bleak Spartan spot . . . The tragedies here are colossal! Just picture me at this moment, sitting on my wardrobe-dressing-table-washstand-combined (in other words my packing case), a smelly oil stove filling the hut with black fumes, and every part of my body absolutely frozen. I am asked daily how I like being here. In reply I can only stare and say, 'Don't be so silly!' Somehow, I never discover that there is any work to be done until the convoy has started and got well away, and I and my ambulance are left to ponder over the super-ghastliness of life in khaki. 'It's an experience', you say. Yes; and so would be being tossed by a bull. I am all for a quiet 'comfy' life now – a sofa, a large fire, and a book. And oh! To be able to wear a crêpe de Chine blouse instead of this everlasting manly uniform.[68]

This story was meant as a 'warning' to other butterfly chauffeuses. Ambulance driving, wrote de Havilland, 'is very strenuous work indeed, and generally entails an extremely Spartan mode of living'. She explained that nothing substantiates this statement so decisively as the fact that many women ambulance drivers in France have cut their hair quite short, finding 'they have not sufficient time to attend to long hair properly, and, in some places, they have even found difficulty in keeping it clean'.[69] For women in non-traditional roles short hair was a symbol of freedom from the constraints of femininity; it also stood for lack of vanity. With this as proof, de Havilland wrote, 'it will be readily understood that the butterfly woman is absolutely out of her element in such a position.[70]

'Experts at the geography of hell'

In the 'Afterword' to Evadne Price's *Not So Quiet . . . Stepdaughters of War*, Jane Marcus likens the volunteer women ambulance drivers to Wagnerian Valkyries who guarded the borders between life and death as they transported the slain and dying. With their ambulances like the mythical horses of the Valkyries, the drivers, writes Marcus, 'had to be superhuman, driving for weeks on three hours of sleep a night, eating spoiled food, and very little of that (no decent Army rations for volunteers). They became experts at the geography of hell, driving at night with their lights off in the freezing cold and snow . . . with their loads of screaming and moaning wounded.'[71]

Of all the FANY writings, the few accounts penned by Unit 3's Second-in-Command Muriel Thompson provide the bluntest descriptions of this geography of hell. The following is from her private recollection 'Base Notes' and describes transporting severely wounded soldiers to the docks en route for England:

Black darkness all around, the smell of the sea and the rain – just in front a semi-circle of light thrown by the ship's lamps, showing up the wet rails on the quay, and shining on the deck space below. Twinkling in the distance other lights, and at regular intervals ambulances arriving and stopping by the gangway, while slowly – carefully, four limp forms on stretchers are drawn out one after the other, lowered for a moment to the ground, then raised, and carried on board. The light shines on the Medical Officer's face; his clerk steps to the stretcher, cuts a white label from the patient's coat and calls briskly, 'gunshot wound, left thigh, sir' – 'Ward B' says the Medical Officer and the bearers carry on. Not even the darkness hides the next stretcher, it shows up startlingly as the lamp light strikes it – no particles of human face is seen – only holes, in a white mask, 'Severe burns sir', intones the orderly – 'Ward A' is the reply – and another load of bitter human suffering, heroically endured, goes silently away.[72]

Thompson's writing is unique. Generally, informal and formal censorship constrained FANY representations and encouraged stories in sync with the cheerful, flamboyant and quirky legend of FANY history. However, I also believe that a distinct practicality circumscribed their work, flattened exclamations of despair and encouraged the 'I cope' motto. This is illustrated in their attitude toward 'doing corpses'. This was a task the FANY hated since it dirtied their ambulances as well as caused emotional strain. 'Doing corpses' meant transporting bloated, dead bodies to the mortuary. On one occasion

FANY driver 'Bobs' Baillie was called to give evidence concerning a body, and, after being asked how she could be sure it was retrieved at 4.30 p.m. she replied that, well, it was like this: 'When I heard it was a corpse, I thought I'd have my tea first!'[73] Despite the tragedies associated with this duty, it was readily accepted as a practical fact that doing corpses was the only job that was not allowed to interfere with meals since the emergency had already passed and the person was in fact already dead.

However their work was represented, the FANY did indeed drive, and drive well, under the most horrendous conditions of war. Often woken in the middle of the night, the drivers would set off, 'giant shapes, one after the other through the silent streets, to bring in their ghastly loads'.[74] Arriving at the railway sidings, they might have to wait several more hours in the cold night air until the train eventually arrived. Sometimes a canteen would be open and they might be able to warm themselves. The trains usually carried between 300 and 450 wounded and took many hours to empty. The 'sitters' (less badly wounded) would alight first and then the ambulances reversed to the doors of the railway carriages and brought out the stretcher cases that were slid along runners into the waiting ambulances. Each car could take four stretchers. Sometimes an ambulance would get what they called an extension case or very severely wounded man whose limbs were attached to splints and an overhead frame. These each had an orderly in attendance and would take up the whole space in the FANY ambulance. Such cases needed to be driven with great care to avoid jolting; a journey that usually took about fifteen minutes could take up to an hour under these conditions. These journeys transporting injured men gave Waddell her 'stretcher face' and the inevitable eyestrain caused by driving in darkness with no headlights and peering constantly into the gloom.[75]

In July 1916 FANY Secretary Janette Lean visited the convoy and wrote a report for the *Gazette*. A version of this was also published in *The Englishwoman*. Lean accompanied the drivers on one of these duties to meet the trains and described what she saw and felt. The Battle of the Somme was underway and the wounded were pouring in. These men, wrote Lean, were such 'quiet unobtrusive burdens wrapped in brown blankets, with a small brown pillow on a brown stretcher. How much agony and suffering', she asked, 'do those blankets hide and what tales of heroism could be unfolded, were each man to tell his tale?'[76] Indeed, Waddell wrote in her memoir about her conversations with wounded and the awful strain associated with driving and listening to their pain. Her usually cheerful tone subsided in describing these poignant conversations and the insufferable conditions and chilling experiences of the wounded men. They talked about 'going over the top' until they were hit, the retreats under enemy fire, and the overpowering enemy advances. One evening

Waddell had to transport a severely injured young soldier who was crying in agony for his mother. She told him she would come and see him in the morning, but he died in the night, 'somebody's son and only nineteen'.[77] Waddell also remembered a young man who had been blinded. 'Was the war worth even one boy's eyesight?' she asked, looking out at the glare on the horizon where battles were raging and more and more men were being 'smashed to pieces'.[78]

During the Somme offensives in the summer and autumn of 1916 the whole convoy would often turn out with twenty-five cars weaving their way to meet the trains or barges. Waddell remembered throngs of French inhabitants watching these processions, showing surprise that English *mademoiselles* drove under fire during air raids, and exclaiming how 'Le Bon Dieu protège les FANY' (God protects the FANY).[79] Many bombs were dropped from aeroplanes and zeppelins on Calais during 1916 but, amazingly, the FANY suffered no serious casualties. The zeppelins had been difficult to shoot down at first, although by this time, in 1916, the Allies had a defensive system of anti-aircraft guns and night-fighters, searchlights, and barrage balloons in their fight against these huge airborne crafts. One night a 4 foot torpedo bomb fell in the camp and lay buried, unexploded. It was disinterred and immobilized after an astute FANY driver noticed a slight disturbance in the sand. The bomb ended up proudly displayed in their mess hut.[80] Hutchinson found the memory of these air raids unforgettable. Since her cubicle was near the telephone, she acted as the runner between the office and the air-raid shelter, alerting drivers to duty. The air-raid shelter was a dugout in the side of the hill: a 'long tunnel like place with a row of benches each side all dimly lit by the odd hurricane lamp'. She would run across the yard and its two lanes of parked cars and enter the shelter through the double curtained doorway, then call out the job and the number of ambulances needed. The drivers would rise, two to each job where possible, adjusting their tin hats, and running to their vehicles in the moonlight. Hutchinson explained that it was 'difficult to convey the drama of those moments of summons, partly the lighting, partly the ordinariness of the duty call, but our luck held and they all returned in due course'.[81]

Early one morning the FANY woke to loud crashes and explosions filling the sky and heard that the enemy had bombed a nearby ammunition dump at Audruicq. 'When the cars arrived', recalled Waddell, the whole dump was one seething mass of smoke and flames, and shells of every description were hurtling through the air at short intervals, several narrowly missing the cars. The roads were littered with live shells and it was with great difficulty that the wheels were steered clear of them. Many shells were found later at a distance of five miles, one even travelling ten before it buried itself in a peaceful garden.'[82] Despite these explosions that caused a crater 'big enough to bury a village' and many burn casualties, there were only five deaths. Dicky Richardson drove the ambulance with these severely burned men. She recalled that one, a Scotsman, was making a terrible noise and she asked if perhaps he could be just a little quieter to help out the others. He responded by asking if she would like him to sing a song instead and proceeded to sing 'Stop Your Tickling Jock' all the way to the hospital. Once they got there Richardson said she found he was dead. 'They all died', she added simply.[83]

'Boss' Franklin was remembered for her bravery on this occasion as well as her reputation for calmness under most chaotic conditions. An officer at Audruicq called Franklin 'the bravest woman I ever met'. She just stood there, he recalled, 'out in the open, helping to load the ambulances, and standing by between vehicles quietly smoking; she had a cheery word for everyone. The bombs were continuous, and the shrapnel was raining down, but she never went for shelter, and never flinched.'[84] A few days after the explosion Waddell had to go up to Audruicq on business and saw the huge crater and the remains of the inferno:

There were fires still burning and shells popping in some parts and the scenes of wreckage were almost indescribable. Trucks had been blown bodily into adjacent fields by concussion. We walked up a 'hill' formed of 9.2's [bomb remains] and found ourselves on the lip of an enormous crater eighty feet across, already half full of water. It was incredible that it had formed in a minute; no wonder the earth had trembled.[85]

This experience was another reminder of the technologies of this war that were unlike anything modern civilization had seen prior to 1914. Such technologies changed the face of the war and participants' experiences of it by making human qualities associated with combat irrelevant. Even Lord Kitchener himself was said to have exclaimed 'This isn't war!' after seeing the destruction wrought by these new technologies.[86]

Keeping the interior of the ambulances relatively clean and sanitized must have been another absolutely agonizing task given the cold, icy weather, the lack of water at the camp, and the often gruesome contents of the ambulances. For the most part, adherence to the FANY legend and identity of cheerful flamboyance (and most likely organizational censorship) seemed to have prevented the FANY sharing such details. In contrast, the novel *Not So Quiet . . . Stepdaughters of War* that chronicles the experiences of English volunteer drivers performing very similar tasks to the FANY, is raw and blunt and harrowing in its details of this work. Based on the (now lost) diaries of a driver named Winifred Young who was most likely a VAD, the book throbs with the chaos and deafening roar of the war and presents a critical class critique. With

reference to the cleaning of ambulances, for example, Evadne Price's protago-
nist Helen Smith, known as 'Smithy', explains:

Cleaning an ambulance is the foulest and most disgusting job it is possible to imagine . . . The stench that comes as we open the doors each morning nearly knocks
us down. Pools of vomit from the poor wretches we have carried the night before,
corners the sitters have turned into temporary lavatories for all purposes, blood
and mud and vermin and the stale stench of stinking trench feet and gangrenous
wounds . . . How we dread the morning clean-out of the insides of our cars, we
gently-bred, educated women they insist on so rigidly for this work that apparently cannot be done by women incapable of speaking English with a public school
accent! . . . I wonder afresh as I don my overalls and rubber boots. I know what to
expect this morning, remembering that poor wretched soul I carried on my last
trek to Number Thirteen, who will be buried by one of us to-day. I am nearly sick
on the spot at the sight greeting me, but I have no time for squeamishness.[87]

Price's brilliant modernist representation of the war from women's experiences underscores the silences in the FANY texts. Between the censored
reports in the *Gazette*, the mostly cheerful accounts by such FANY as Pat
Waddell and Betty Hutchinson, the matter-of-fact recollections in the various
oral histories, and the heroic adventures of Grace McDougall there are gaps
and silences that reflect the horrors of this war. The one description of the
unpleasantness of cleaning ambulance interiors is given by Hutchinson in the
context of the nasty job of driving soldiers who had drowned in the quay at
Calais to the mortuary. She writes in the understated tone to be expected of
FANY who had internalized both the improprieties of speaking too bluntly of
bodily fluids and the unwritten expectations associated with the FANY
legend. Still, disgust and grief at the spectacle and a half-hearted critique of
the war comes through in her writing nonetheless: 'Though the blanket hid
the poor, swollen figure, no blanket could hide the smell or the liquid that
oozed from him. The journey to the mortuary took only a few minutes, but
getting the interior of the car clean and sweet before the "lea" journey was no
easy task. It all seemed such a tragic waste.'[88]

Among one of the worst aspects of navigating the geography of hell was
driving on the infamous Calais quay. It was dangerously narrow: one false
move and they would be in the water. Reversing the ambulance for the return
journey was especially tricky and there was a rule that empty cars took the sea-
side of the quay. One day FANY driver Eva Money skidded and dived straight
into the sea. Luckily, reported Hutchinson, the driver had the canvas rolled up
behind her and so she was pulled right up through the ambulance to safety.[89]
Another hazard associated with driving to the quay was the presence of the
enterprising but very inexperienced local women who had started driving the

trams in Calais. Although the French were desperately short of manpower and needed to turn to women, they wanted to avoid women's militarization since it might lead to women's full citizenship and thereby suffrage. Instead they hired women as private civilians.[90] The inexperience of these women caused some 'near-misses' according to the FANY, although most likely the latter enjoyed comparing themselves as accomplished drivers (and *British* drivers) to these inexperienced Frenchwomen as a way to dissociate themselves from these 'non-professionals'.

The French had also employed women as crossing keepers on the railways and they also earned some derision from the FANY. Hutchinson, for example, told the story about a journey to the Calais quay with her ambulance loaded with four stretcher cases and two walking wounded. Just as she was crossing the railway lines her engine petered out. 'To restart it was impossible', explained Hutchinson, since '"Madame" level crossing keeper had thought that I should just have time and the train was bearing down on us.' The two walking wounded quickly jumped out of the ambulance and together helped Hutchinson push the vehicle clear as the train skimmed by.[91]

Driving in the vicinity of the railway tracks was always a hazard for the women. Jimmie Gamwell told a story where she was 'chased in her lorry by a train', explaining that she had been caught inside the crossing gates and had to turn her wheels to the track and try and outpace the train in order to avoid a collision. Fortunately the train was going slow enough and the engine driver could hardly avoid seeing her racing alongside the tracks.[92] A more sobering story was told by Pat Waddell who had an accident on the tracks and was so severely injured she had to have her leg amputated. Her passenger was killed. The accident occurred during an air raid when the French sentries that normally monitored a particularly dangerous tunnel, where ammunition and hospital trains sped to and from the port, had been removed. She was crossing the tracks with a lorry full of stretchers and recalled:

[T]here to my horror was a train coming full speed out of the tunnel. I had to make up my mind either to reverse (I was already on the lines), or go on. It (the lorry) was a brute to drive and the reverse gear difficult to get into at the best of times. I decided to press on. But the train caught the rear of the lorry, swung it round, threw me onto the line and dragged me along. I remained conscious and French soldiers from an anti-aircraft battery rushed to drag me free. One of them took off his bootlaces to make a tourniquet as I was in the numb condition one is in when bleeding to death. They stopped an ambulance train and a Dr. gave me a merciful injection. I asked the men if both legs were broken and they said, yes, and did not tell me that my left leg was practically severed.[93]

Waddell also wrote about her accident in a chapter of *Fanny Goes to War* titled 'The Last Ride'. She described being hurled from the car into the air and being swept along for some distance with her face rubbed in the ground. She did not know until she was recovering several days later that one leg had been amputated below the knee. She described the anguish of the French soldiers who helped her and the intense pain she endured despite the morphine. 'So this is what the men go through every day' she wrote, reflecting whether the world would really be any better for all this suffering or if it would be forgotten as soon as the war was over.[94] Waddell was at first in denial about her injury: 'It was merely someone else I was hearing about. "Jolly bad luck on them", I thought, "rotten not being able to run about any more".'[95] But recurrent twitching from the severed nerve reminded her of her fate and caused her to spend several long nights in despair over her loss. It took inspiration from men who had learned to walk and dance with artificial limbs to lift her spirits. Once in this frame of mind she presented optimism and humour over her situation in a manner consistent with the FANY persona and legend. Surrounded by the love and support of her colleagues, the staff of the hospital in Calais, and masses of soldiers and medical personnel, Waddell's recovery continued until she learned to walk, drive and even ride a horse again. Although she had originally been sent to the hospital in Calais, she was removed to England soon thereafter.

There was some conflict about the accident because the British Command were the ones to make the decision not to have a sentry in the tunnel. Since King George V was coming to Calais to visit the hospital, it was thought best to remove Waddell to England and avoid embarrassing questions about injured ladies and British negligence. Waddell herself was exonerated from all blame.[96] Waddell's accident shook the Corps; many expressed sympathies in the *Gazette* and sent their concern and best wishes. These accounts emphasize that the 'brave little comrade' was not to blame for the accident and highlight her courage in face of adversity. 'Sorrow is only equalled', wrote Violet O'Neill-Power, 'by our pride in the great pluck and courage she has displayed.'[97] Waddell's accident was framed as a microcosm of FANY identity generally: courage, cheerfulness, self-sacrifice, and, of course, British pluck. She was decorated for her bravery by the Governor of Calais, General Ditte, with the Croix de Guerre (silver star).

Finally, the hazards of driving this geography of hell were illustrated by the work done by the little-known FANY Unit 4 established in the summer of 1916 in aid of a Belgian Field Hospital at Hoogstadt very close to the Front. At a time when women were no longer allowed so close to the firing lines, the personnel at Hoogstadt (who included Norah Cluff, Doris Russell Allen and

'Bobs' Baillie) had their work cut out for them. This work involved driving camouflaged vehicles and retrieving food and hospital supplies from Dunkirk, Adinkerke and La Panne. Hoogstadt was constantly in the line of fire and the women endured almost nightly raids with the coffin cart bringing its horrors on a regular basis.[98] However things did not run entirely smoothly at Hoogstadt and by August 1916 it seems that two of their drivers had applied for a transfer. McDougall was very upset about this because the authorities had shown their displeasure over the inconvenience of first agreeing to have women so near the Front and then having to replace them. The Commandant of the hospital at Hoogstadt was, according to McDougall, 'a most disagreeable man, and was rude and unpleasant to the girls' (whom he most likely resented in this masculine space). She went on to explain that 'They (FANY drivers) felt they were not wanted and thought I was riding roughshod over them in expecting them to stay.' McDougall recalled that this barrier against getting a convoy with the Army near the Front was a 'bitter blow' to her.[99] In December the FANY were withdrawn from Hoogstadt or perhaps the hospital was evacuated, and Russell Allen returned to England to take a motor certificate, while Cluff was transferred back to the British convoy. No doubt since all articles in the *Gazette* were submitted to the Press Bureau for censoring, little could be said about a field hospital so close to the firing lines. What was reported, however, was that Cluff and Russell Allen showed 'true FANY spirit' by sticking to an often very trying post, living in wet, cold and rat-infested tents, and being constantly on duty.[100]

As the war dragged on, poet Siegfried Sassoon wrote in his diary just before Christmas, 1916: 'The year is dying of atrophy as far as I am concerned, bed-fast in its December fogs. And the War is settling down on everyone – a hopeless, never-shifting burden.'[101] At this time French General Robert Nivelle had become the new Commander-in-Chief (although he would soon be replaced by General Pétain in 1917) and the British Prime Minister Asquith was replaced by David Lloyd George. Everyone was in shock at the sheer scale of military confrontation, the enormous numbers of lives lost, and the apparent deadlock once again. The cold winter that year exacerbated the miseries of the troops and the difficult conditions under which the FANY worked. Their bathing water and sponges froze solid inside their rooms and had to be melted in basins over an oil stove and the vehicles slipped and skidded on the icy roads. The year 1917 brought few reasons for cheer, as Chapter 5 will show; the work continued steadily for the British convoy and kept them busy through to the end of the war.

Notes

1 Grace McDougall, 'Five Years with the Allies, 1914–1919: The Story of the FANY Corps', p. 105. [IWM]
2 Ibid., pp. 121–2.
3 Mary Louise Roberts, *Disruptive Acts: The New Woman in Fin-de-Siècle France* (Chicago: University of Chicago Press, 2002), p. 8.
4 Organising Officer to Director General, Medical Service, War Office (August 1915). [LC]
5 McDougall, 'Five Years with the Allies', p. 103.
6 Pat Beauchamp (a.k.a. Waddell), *Fanny Went to War* (London: Routledge, 1940), p. 97.
7 McDougall, 'Five Years with the Allies', p. 110.
8 Lieutenant W. G. Smith obituary, *The Times* (4 February 1916). It is interesting to note that ingenuity and a penchant for schemes was a central aspect of Bill Smith's persona as well as of his sister's. His obituary explains that he was due for leave but had postponed it to carry through a 'scheme'. It reports that he said: 'Every one says I'm a fool to put off my leave, but what's the good of leave if you haven't done something worth while? If I come through this it may mean a Military Cross.' Smith was 26-years-old when he died, married with two young children.
9 Jane Marcus, 'Afterword: Corpus/Corps/Corpse. Writing the Body in/at War', Helen Zenna Smith (a.k.a. Evadne Price), *Not So Quiet . . . Stepdaughters of War* (New York: The Feminist Press, [1930] 1989), pp. 490–1.
10 McDougall, 'Five Years with the Allies', p. 112.
11 Franklin to Cole-Hamilton (11 February 1916).
12 W. Beach Thomas, '"Yeowomen": A Triumph of Hospital Organisation', unidentified newspaper clipping (undated, *c.* 1916 and probably *Daily Mail*). [IWM]
13 Doron Lamm, 'Emily Goes to War: Explaining the Recruitment to the Women's Auxiliary Corps in World War I', in Billie Melman (ed.), *Borderlines: Genders and Identities in War and Peace, 1870–1930* (New York: Routledge, 1998), p. 377.
14 Beauchamp, *Fanny Went to War*, p. 90.
15 Also included in the British convoy were Mary Baxter-Ellis, Dinah Heasman, Evelyn and Madge Laidlay, D. Reynolds, G. Quin, O. and P. Mudie-Cook and M. Lean.
16 *Gazette* (February 1916), p. 7.
17 *Gazette* (September 1916), p. 5.
18 Beauchamp, *Fanny Went to War*, pp. 103, 114.
19 *Gazette* (August 1916), p. 5; *Gazette* (September 1916), p. 5.
20 *Gazette* (February 1916), p. 7.
21 *Gazette* (April 1916), p. 6.
22 Ian Ousby, *The Road to Verdun* (New York: Anchor/Doubleday, 2002).
23 Pat Beauchamp (a.k.a. Waddell), *Fanny Goes to War* (London: John Murray, 1919), p. 135.
24 Beauchamp, *Fanny Goes to War*, p. 136.
25 Muriel Thompson, diary, 'Base Notes', undated. [LC]. Thompson left two handwritten diaries, both small black notebooks with lined pages and no page numbers. One begins 1 January and ends with a note saying she went on leave on 3 February 1918. After these diary entries are several pages of writing titled 'Base Notes', 'Backwash of the Retreat', 'A Raid', 'T.A.T.s', and 'Calais Quay', perhaps written while she was on leave. The second diary begins 24 March and ends 29 August 1918. At the very back of the second diary, upside down and going the other way, is some writing from 1919 concerning the unit's work after the Armistice.

26 *Gazette* (August 1916), p. 4.
27 *Gazette* (September 1916), p. 5.
28 *Gazette* (October 1916), pp. 1–2.
29 Signed 'Paynter', 'An Apology for What We Wear', unauthored notebook, no page numbers. [FA]
30 Beryl Hutchinson, 'Work with the British: The Calais Convoy', p. 1. [LC]
31 *Gazette* (February 1916), pp. 6–7.
32 Beauchamp, *Fanny Goes to War*, p. 130.
33 Hutchinson, 'Work with the British', p. 1.
34 Ibid., pp. 1–2.
35 Beauchamp, *Fanny Goes to War*, pp. 117–20.
36 Ibid., p. 138.
37 *Gazette* (April 1920), p. 5.
38 *Gazette* (April 1917), p. 4.
39 Grace McDougall, 'Brief Resumé of Corps' Work', *Gazette* (August 1916), p. 12.
40 *Gazette* (February 1917), pp. 6–7.
41 Beauchamp, *Fanny Went to War*, p. 90.
42 W. Beach Thomas, 'Defence of "Base" Women: Their Work in France', unidentified newspaper clipping (undated, *c.* 1915, probably *Daily Mail*). [IWM]
43 *Gazette* (March 1917), pp. 6–7.
44 Sean O'Connell, *The Car and British Society: Class, Gender and Motoring, 1896–1939* (Manchester: Manchester University Press, 1998), pp. 15–16. Virginia Scharff writes about the gendered nature of the US automobile industry in *Taking the Wheel: Women and the Coming of the Motor Age* (New York: The Free Press, 1991).
45 Hutchinson, 'Work with the British', pp. 2, 3.
46 Thompson, diary (11 January 1918).
47 *Gazette* (September 1916), p. 8.
48 Beauchamp, *Fanny Goes to War*, p. 191.
49 Beauchamp, *Fanny Went to War*, pp. 91–2.
50 Irene Ward, *FANY Invicta* (London: Hutchinson, 1955), p. 48.
51 *Gazette* (February 1917), p. 1.
52 *Gazette* (August–September Supplement, 1918), p. 2.
53 Hutchinson, 'Work with the British', p. 7.
54 Ibid., p. 8.
55 Ibid., p. 4.
56 Ibid., pp. 8–9.
57 Ibid.
58 Beauchamp, *Fanny Went to War*, p. 135.
59 Anonymous (most likely Winnie Mordaunt), 'With Apologies to Kipling', unauthored notebook.
60 Beauchamp, *Fanny Went to War*, pp. 110, 116.
61 Beauchamp, *Fanny Goes to War*, pp. 131–2.
62 Beauchamp, *Fanny Went to War*, p. 117.
63 Beauchamp, *Fanny Goes to War*, pp. 156–7.
64 Elizabeth Robins, 'Stretcher-Bearing for Women', *Daily Mail* (18 August 1915).
65 See, for example, Rev. A. W. Anderson's article, 'The FANY Girls: Indominatables in the Battle Area', *War Budget* (30 March 1916).
66 Gladys de Havilland, 'The "Fannys"', in Agnès Cardinal, Dorothy Goldman and Judith Hattaway (eds), *Women's Writing on the First World War* (Oxford: Oxford Uni-

versity Press, 1999), p. 193. This is an excerpt from Gladys de Havilland, *The Woman's Motor Manual* (London: Temple, 1918).

67 Alistair Thomson uses this concept in his book *ANZAC Memories: Living with the Legend* (Oxford: Oxford University Press, 1994), p. 12.

68 De Havilland, 'The "Fannys"', p. 193.

69 Ibid., pp. 193–4. As in Evadne Price's novel *Not So Quiet* (pp. 13–18) when Tosh, an upper-class volunteer ambulance driver, cuts her beautiful red locks in rebellion against traditional Edwardian femininity, hair is an important signifier for femininity and acts associated with hair are often represented as indicators of gender anxiety and emancipation. See Rose Weitz, 'Women and their Hair: Seeking Power through Resistance and Accommodation', in Rose Weitz (ed.), *The Politics of Women's Bodies: Sexuality, Appearance, and Behavior* (New York: Oxford University Press, 2003), pp. 135–51.

70 De Havilland, 'The "Fannys"', p. 194.

71 Marcus, 'Afterword', pp. 244–5.

72 Thompson, 'Base Notes'.

73 Beauchamp, *Fanny Goes to War*, p. 188.

74 Beauchamp, *Fanny Went to War*, p. 129.

75 Beauchamp, *Fanny Goes to War*, p. 133.

76 *Gazette* (September 1916), p. 8.

77 Beauchamp, *Fanny Goes to War*, p. 190.

78 Ibid., p. 175; Beauchamp, *Fanny Went to War*, p. 131.

79 Beauchamp, *Fanny Went to War*, p. 127.

80 Pat Beauchamp Washington (a.k.a. Waddell), typed autobiography, p. 4. [LC]

81 Hutchinson, 'Work with the British', p. 5.

82 Beauchamp, *Fanny Went to War*, p. 124.

83 Taped interview, Mary Runciman (*née* Richardson) by Peter Liddle (June 1973). [LC]

84 Irene Ward, *FANY Invicta*, p. 80.

85 Beauchamp, *Fanny Went to War*, p. 126.

86 Robert L. O'Connell, *Of Arms and Men: A History of War, Weapons, and Aggression* (New York: Oxford University Press, 1990).

87 Smith, *Not So Quiet*, pp. 59–60.

88 Hutchinson, 'Work with the British', p. 11.

89 Ibid., pp. 2–3.

90 Margaret H. Darrow, *French Women and the First World War: War Stories of the Home Front* (New York: Oxford University Press, 2000), ch. 7.

91 Hutchinson, 'Work with the British', p. 3.

92 Edith Colston (*née* Walton), handwritten account, 'A Railway Crossing Episode (Hope Gamwell's adventures)'. [LC]

93 Beauchamp Washington, autobiography, p. 5.

94 Beauchamp, *Fanny Goes to War*, pp. 227, 232.

95 Ibid., p. 233.

96 Beauchamp Washington, autobiography, p. 5.

97 *Gazette* (May 1917), p. 6.

98 *Gazette* (November–December 1916), p. 9.

99 McDougall, 'Five Years with the Allies,' pp. 125–6.

100 *Gazette* (February 1917), p. 5. Also, *Gazette* (August 1916), p. 4; (January 1917), p. 16.

101 Siegfied Sassoon, Diary, 22 December, 1916, quoted in Samuel Hynes, *A War Imagined: The First World War and English Culture* (New York: Collier, 1990), p. 97.

FANY in their swimming pool

FANY callisthenics

Grace Ashley-Smith

'Boss' Lillian Franklin

The staff at Lamarck Hospital

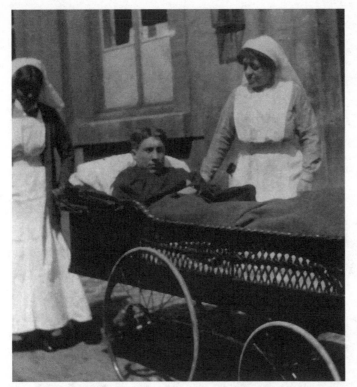

Wounded soldiers were often represented as infantalized and passive
(Molly Marshall with Brenda Joynson on right)

FANY in their fur coats (from left: M. Lean, Dinah Heasman, E. Money, Gertrude Cant, Norma Lowson)

The FANY at work

Pat Waddell

Grace McDougall

Ready to roll (Marguerite Moseley Williams is at left holding the oil can and Grace McDougall is seated bottom left. Between them is Violet O'Neill-Power. Mary Baxter-Ellis is middle row, far right and Gladys Marples is middle row, fourth in from right.)

The Belgian convoy

Christmas at Port à Binson Priory Hospital, 1917

FANY drivers for the French (Henrietta Fraser is sitting, bottom left)

Repairs on cars at St Omer

FANY Unit 12 washing ambulances

Grace McDougall after the war

FANY at summer camp in 1928

5

Progression is our watchword
The Belgian convoy and Port à Binson Priory Hospital 1917

During 1917, as the war dragged on and women's role in this masculine space became increasingly integrated and essential, the FANY saw organizational expansion and consolidation. Grace McDougall was the driving force behind the FANY momentum, fired as she was with personal ambition and a keen desire to maintain organizational growth. She had written an article for the FANY *Gazette* back in the summer of 1916 summarizing their work to date and emphasizing the necessity for them to expand the organization and their influence. 'As progression is our watchword', she explained, 'new developments must be looked for'.[1] McDougall was anticipating the closure of Lamarck and felt strongly that this service should be replaced by other work proving FANY skill and commitment. As a result, 1917 saw two new FANY projects come to fruition.

The first project was the establishment of an ambulance convoy in Calais (distinct from the British convoy Unit 3) for the Belgians, known as the Corps de Transport Militaire Belge, FANY Unit 5. It worked out of the Calais railway station, *Gare Centrale*, with a base camp at L'Hôpital de Passage. McDougall transferred eight drivers from Lamarck to this site and by early 1917 the unit was consolidated and up and running. The second project was a new hospital for the French at Port à Binson that became known as L'Hôpital Auxiliaire 76 and took over the old Lamark name FANY Unit 1. After Lamarck Hospital finally closed, the rest of the staff was officially transferred and relocated to Port à Binson in March 1917. This chapter features FANY service with these two new projects as well as their plans for new expansion. It also explores the concept of authority in terms of both power within the organization and the relationship of women to masculine authority in the context of war. This is theme five in the negotiation of gender relations. Although McDougall led the FANY in altering relationships with men as authority figures and modelled autonomy and independence for women in war work, she had her own problems with issues of power within the organization.

A convoy for the Belgians

McDougall enjoyed the Belgians because, as already discussed, they were willing to invite and respect the work the FANY could do for their armies. She compared this to the attitude of the British authorities who on the whole tended to see women as nuisances. To illustrate this difference McDougall shared a story about a trip to the Front in 1917, when her lunch with Belgian officers was interrupted by a report of the arrival of an English General. McDougall and colleague Gladys Marples hid under trench coats hanging on the wall and only came out when it was discovered that the General (who was subsequently invited in to tea) was actually Australian and not British. 'English Generals are apt to send reports when they meet a woman at the Front', explained McDougall.[2]

Although it was very true that the BRCS and the British Army wanted to consolidate power and were uncomfortable with British subjects (especially women) working outside their auspices, it was especially the FANY who piqued British authorities. There were several reasons for their discomfort. First, the FANY had a monopoly driving in Calais and performed almost all official military-related driving. Such a monopoly by an independent organization able to negotiate on its own behalf with the BRCS and the Anglo-French Hospital Committee in Calais (a British-controlled area), was problematic for them.[3] Second, FANY allegiance to non-British allies most likely irked the British authorities in the sense that it raised concern over ownership and potential improprieties. Third, the chauvinism of these authorities was not only offended by official claims to independence on the part of the FANY but also by their ongoing quirky ingenuity that often defied authority and official rules of conduct. Unsure enough about women generally, they found the FANY, who did not consider themselves bounded by the constraints imposed on women, to be especially problematic. No doubt they would have liked to 'liquidate' the FANY – as well as the Corps' energetic Commanding Officer who had recently been decorated by the Belgians with the prestigious Order of Leopold II. Both McDougall and Franklin, however, made it their business not to let the FANY lose their independence.

The BRCS were concerned enough in their motivation to maintain control that they created a ruling that any new units for any army in the British area of Calais had to be sanctioned by the British Adjutant-General.[4] Irene Ward, long-time friend of the FANY, shared a story about how McDougall avoided this sanction that would have potentially prevented any agreement to work for the Belgians. It is a story uncorroborated by other reports and whether it actually happened this way is unclear; nonetheless, it is a story that illustrates the FANY legend and the representation of FANY personnel as independent, incorrigible and undaunted in the face of authority. It highlights the constructed identity of this organization and its members with their pluck and flair for standing up to male military power and avoiding or manipulating control. It also illustrates the antagonisms mentioned above between the FANY and various military and medical authorities who feared women's independence and felt a strong need to consolidate power. Ultimately, they wanted to close down all FANY activity except the British convoy Unit 3 over which they had direct authority. Ward explained that when McDougall heard that the BRCS was sending a representative to shut down the newly formed Unit 5 working for the Belgians, she went to the Belgian military command and requested their assistance:

That very afternoon the whole of the Convoy were paraded at the État Majeur and there, in the presence of the Base Commandant and Colonel Dieu-Donne, his first chief of staff, the FANY members were all weighed, measured, photographed and finger-printed, and sworn in as *Soldats* of the Corps de Transport de Calais (Belge). Blue gorgets, the insignia of the Belgian Corps de Transport, and silver rank badges were issued to the members, and overnight, the FANY Unit V became a fully-fledged unit of the Belgian Army.

The next day the BRCS party arrived and stormed down to the *Gare* to liquidate the unit. It was a dramatic moment. They entered the FANY mess in a belligerent mood, to find themselves confronted by the Belgian Base-Commandant and his Staff officers, who, very politely, asked to what did they owe the pleasure of this visit? The BRCS party replied that they had come to inform the FANY that their services were no longer required. The Belgian General drew himself up, and quietly but firmly reminded the British representatives that they were, at that moment, 'standing on Belgian soil', and that the ladies to whom he referred were Soldats de L'Armée Belge and therefore, no concern of the BRCS. Never, I think, was any delegation so completely stunned. It was checkmate to any future designs to prevent the use of FANY by allied armies. And it was for this reason that all subsequent French and Belgian convoys worked under army auspices, and not under the Red Cross.[5]

This new convoy Unit 5 was based at L'Hôpital de Passage in Calais and attached to the Belgian Army. There was no shortage of work for FANY Unit 5 as the convoy served seven hospitals for Belgian wounded. Drivers met trains coming from the Front, carried casualties to the various facilities, and chauffeured doctors and nurses to and from the hospitals in Calais and the surrounding area. In addition the FANY undertook medical transport for all French military hospitals in the area and handled transport for air raids and bombardments for both civil and military French and Belgian authorities. At this point the French had started incorporating their women into the war effort, but as already explained, they preferred to avoid their militarization and utilized women as Red Cross nurses or hired them as civilian employees of the Army. The need for women's labour was great however, and, as before, the French aversion to women performing non-traditional work gave way to the necessity of the job at hand especially when the women performing the task were not 'theirs'.

Huts, sleeping cubicles and mess room were erected next to L'Hôpital de Passage, although their completion was delayed by the terrible winter weather. The mess hut was a much more comfortable and attractive space than other FANY accommodations to date. It was painted cream with oak-coloured beams and the cubicles were double-lined and furnished with spring iron bed-steads and good mattresses as well as equipped with basin, jug and hanging cupboard. There was a recreation room and state-of-the-art garage complete with hose for washing cars, and a pit for car maintenance. As a gift from the City of Aberdeen, the convoy had received a beautiful Bon Accord ambulance 'made on the latest model' which ran very smoothly.[6] They were also lent an ambulance from the Women's Volunteer Reserve in Birmingham and another from the BRCS at Boulogne. Personnel in Unit 5 included Violet O'Neill-Power, Margaret Hoole, Gladys Marples, Celia Meade, Ida Lewis, Marguerite Moseley Williams, Evelyn Mackenzie, Mrs Marcia de Belleroche, Marion Bowles and Lilian Crossland.[7] Mary Baxter-Ellis, who had been convalescing in England, joined Unit 5 in April 1917 as Corporal-Mechanic, bringing with her an Armstrong Whitworth ambulance. McDougall was Commandant of this unit, seeing it as 'her' convoy and using it as her base as she travelled to inspect FANY units and negotiate with authorities. When she was away, as she frequently was on various inspections, meetings with allied officials and on fundraising excursions, she relied upon Second-in-Command Violet O'Neill Power as Commandant.

On top of terrible conditions associated with the coldest winter on record since 1870, a damaged grain ship closed the harbour at Boulogne and increased the workload for the FANY in Calais. There was also a series of hospital evacuations at the Front with increasing numbers of patients passing through the Clearing Hospitals. This work was conducted under almost constant air raids, and in addition, in February, Calais was shelled by submarines. Working during this raid, McDougall was almost electrocuted by falling wires. She leaped out of the ambulance: 'a queer serpent-like thing coiled up all round me, and a flash of flame wrapt [sic] round me', she wrote. Luckily, she was wearing rubber boots and a leather coat.[8] Eight cars (two were in the shop) carried almost 4,000 cases during this month, with even higher numbers in March and April. To add to McDougall's worries, about this time a young soldier had deserted from the British troops and was found by three FANY who befriended him instead of reporting the matter to the authorities. McDougall had to send the main FANY 'culprit' home to save her from worse penalties.[9] Finally, to compound everything, a measles epidemic spread through Calais in the Spring and one by one the FANY caught the disease:

> Ten little FANY girls, feeling fit and fine
> One got the measles and then there were nine
> . . . Seven little FANY girls, one in a fix,
> Swallowed the thermometer, and then there were six.[10]

The timing of the measles epidemic was particularly problematic because increased casualties were coming from the Front daily. The Belgians' twenty miles of Front line started at Ramscappelle until it gave way to the British line at Ypres. Increased casualties, however, were related to French General Nivelle's ill-fated offensive in Champagne, conceived as the plan to win the war. Although he hoped to crush the German lines along the Chemins des Dames overlooking the Aisne River, the Germans retreated to the 'Hindenburg Line', their heavily fortified defensive system, once they heard of the plan. French troops advanced on April 16 nonetheless, secured some forward momentum and captured some German prisoners, but did not succeed in the grand manner anticipated. German machine guns decimated the advancing French troops who went over the top with the tragic French *élan*. Medical services prepared for 15,000 cases and were faced with 90,000. After Champagne and other related offensives along the line, the ensuing number of dead and wounded caused a serious lack of confidence and low morale among the French troops. Mutinies broke out and the French army was in chaos. Pétain replaced Nivelle and instigated court marshalling and executions; he also responded to the grievances of the troops concerning the poor conditions in the trenches. Order was eventually restored and the French Army was mobilized and able to mount an offensive at Verdun by late August.[11] Although censorship prevented formal discussion of the mutinies and the *Gazette* is silent about such events, the FANY were aware of these frightening developments among the French troops. Writing after the war, McDougall recalled a trip to Fismes when they were held up by mutineers with machine guns and had to hide a French doctor in the back of the car under sacks and rugs for his own protection. 'The French troops were very restless at that time,' she explained, 'defeatist propaganda was widely spread, and some regiments had locked up their officers. The disaster at Chemin des Dames had a lot to do with this.'[12] The casualties created by these doomed French offensives fell to the great medical auxiliary forces who attempted to cope with such incredible loss of life.

The Belgian convoy reported dealing with 2,000 wounded in one week during the summer of 1917;[13] work was also increasing for Unit 3 working for the British. Despite the pessimism of Prime Minister Lloyd George who doubted Nivelle's assertions for success in Champagne, British forces participated in a diversionary offensive at Arras to be staged before Nivelle's plan. This offensive began in April and dragged into the end of May and saw the Canadian Corps successfully taking the Vimy Ridge. At this point the United States had entered the fight, provoked by the German policy of unrestricted submarine warfare against neutral ships. Ethnically linked to all combatants and isolated by distance and self-sufficiency, the US had managed to stay neutral. Public opinion in the US changed after the sinking of the *Lusitania* in May 1915, the continued loss of American lives by German submarine warfare, and because of Allied propaganda. In addition, President Woodrow Wilson found his position of neutrality politically weakening. As a result, the US declared war on Germany on 6 April 1917. The American Expeditionary Force (essentially an army of riflemen: artillery, tanks, aircraft and so forth were supplied by the Allies) moved slowly into France under the guidance of General John Joseph Pershing who wanted to form them into a separate army rather than see them deployed as Allied divisions. It would be 1918 before they would make a difference in this war.

At the same time that fighting on the ground (and to some extent in the air) shook Allied confidence in their ability to win the war, British naval prowess was also being challenged. The naval battles of 1916 (especially the Battle of Jutland in May) featured German advancements in gunnery and artillery as well as strategy through the widespread employment of U-boat submarines. These battles resulted in the loss of British naval forces and merchant ships and challenged British naval dominance. In response, the British offensive focused on the U-boat bases at Ostend and Zeebrugge as well as the railway communications to these ports at Ypres. The first action in June 1917 was an attempt to capture the Messines Ridge south of Ypres and attack through the detonation of mines under the Ridge. For once the element of surprise held and General Sir Herbert Plumer and the British Second Army were successful. While there was an unsuccessful attempt to take Ostend from the sea that was abandoned in July, by September Plumer kept advancing with a series of offensives known as the Third Battle of Ypres, commonly known as Passchendaele.[14] FANY Unit 3 affiliated with the British forces in Calais helped with the endless British casualties from these offensives as Unit 5 dealt with the Belgian and the French.

Passchendaele evolved in three stages. The first stage occurred in July and August at Picken Ridge, Gheluvelt Plateau and Langemarck, resulting in some gained ground and some 67,000 British soldiers dead (yet only about 10,000 men more than the number lost on the first day of the Battle of the Somme). The second stage along the Menin Road Ridge in late September and early November was more successful and battles were fought (with important contributions made by Australian and New Zealand forces) that pushed the Germans back. Then, unfortunately, the weather changed and torrential rains turned the battlefield into mud, stopping the advance. The water table in Flanders was less than a foot below ground level and resulted in low-lying marshy ground. The surface drainage system had also been destroyed by continual bombardments such that any amount of rain turned the land into an impassable quagmire. In these conditions, the third stage commenced and the Battles of Poelcappelle and Passchendaele I and II were fought in October. Eventually the battle ended on October 26 as the Canadian forces captured the village of Passchendaele. This battle claimed the lives of thousands of men who were killed or literally drowned in the 'bottomless mud'.[15] Fussell quotes Wyndham Lewis who remembered Passchendaele as an all-but-inevitable collision between two relatively complementary forces: the 'German fondness for war' and the 'British doggedness', two forces that 'found their most perfect expression on the battlefield, or battle-bog, of Passchendaele'.[16]

As the rush continued through the summer with fighting at Verdun and this onslaught at Passchendaele, the number of casualties carried by the FANY increased.[17] Air raids were continuous and a FANY was always there at the station unloading casualties for the hospital. One raid was so bad that the whole of the staff at the L'Hôpital de Passage retreated and the FANY were left to receive incoming casualties.[18] Injury from shrapnel was a constant fear for the FANY, piercing their ambulances and blowing holes in their huts. The ambulances were so primitively equipped by contemporary standards that a glance at the 'Rules for Ambulance Drivers' illustrates the courage and poignancy of their task. Each car had to carry one can each of water, paraffin and oil, plus two bags each labelled 'A' and 'B' that were to be kept in a locked box. Bag 'A' contained towel and soap, matches and tobacco or cigarettes, three field dressings, 'Oxo' (broth mix), boric powder and a nailbrush. Bag 'B' contained three iodine ampoules, four bandages, five safety pins, two packets of compressed gauze, one packet each of adhesive plaster, cyanide gauze and absorbent cotton gauze, one yard of jaconet, a duster, two slings and a pair of scissors.[19] Very often their meagre supplies (and tools) would be stolen and some FANY themselves resorted to 'borrowing'. Ultimately, the most the FANY could provide to injured soldiers was a car in running order for speedy transportation, some basic antiseptic followed by voluminous bandaging, moral support, and the inevitable offer of a cigarette.

By the autumn of 1917 the FANY in Unit 5 were carrying over 6,000 casualty cases a month, although at last they had the luxury of dug-outs (built with 'poetic justice', according to McDougall, by German soldiers[20]) where they could retreat when air raids were exceptionally bad.[21] By this time new innovations in the German air force had moved its role from reconnaissance and surveying to incorporating fighter tactics and bombing missions. As a result, these almost nightly raids on Calais were an example of the advancements in German aerial power as Gotha and Giant long-range bombers provided strategic air offensives directed against both military installations and the civilian population. The raids were always dangerous affairs for the FANY who often drove under fire. Just like the drivers in the British convoy, the drivers for the Belgians not only had to dodge bullets but also had their own series of driving near-misses, underscored of course by the tragedy of Pat Waddell. Luckier than Waddell, FANY driver Calder was driving the Unic ambulance along the railway line during the rush in the summer of 1917. A train switched from one rail to another in front of her, making her climb the heaps of coal by the side to get clear. After smashing the front seat of her car and sending the orderly leaping out of the vehicle, the train caught the hub of the Unic's front wheel and dragged the car along for about a hundred yards. According to McDougall, 'Calder held tightly to her steering wheel and saved the situation.'[22]

During October FANY Unit 5 was also asked to assist in a military funeral, with three cars converted as hearses and each carrying three coffins. Moseley Williams, White and Mason were chosen, driving so expertly that they never once outstripped the walking mourners nor stalled their engines.[23] Women were rarely allowed to participate in such a way on official occasions. They also took part in a touching ceremony on All Saints' Day (1 November) in honour of the Allied war dead and presented a beautiful wreath of autumn leaves. Several senior FANY went to the Belgian, French and British cemeteries where the wreaths were presented, poignant speeches made, and the Last Post sounded.[24] McDougall in particular relished these military rituals, seeing the participation of the FANY as official indication of their acceptance as militarized women. As we have already seen, it was always her greatest wish that the FANY be officially attached to military forces, and these shows of pageantry that included the FANY as *soldats* were particularly rewarding to her. She told stories of the French 'who thought there was nothing the FANY could not do' and of British officers coming to her with tears in their eyes to say how proud they were that the FANY were Englishwomen.[25] McDougall treasured these shows of support, the many thanks from military authorities, and the letters, cards and bouquets of flowers sent in appreciation of outstanding service. As she liked to say, 'The name FANY had come to stand for unselfish devotion to duty.'[26]

McDougall especially seemed to relish meetings with important civil and military dignitaries where she could alter women's traditional subservient relationship in war.[27] She met with British Prime Minister Lloyd George in February 1917, for example, and was also invited to attend the inspection by the King and the Prince of Wales of a French military hospital in Calais. The Director of the hospital wished to present McDougall and other senior FANY to the King in recognition of the work they had done for the French.[28] Ironically, while McDougall was the driving force behind the alteration of patterns of communication with masculine authority, once granted authority for herself and the organization – or, in other words, once the FANY were recognized as military personnel – McDougall was willing to play by rules of military organization. The Inspector General from Le Havre, for example, told the FANY they were the only organization that did not inundate him with complaints and requests.[29] In this way, although the FANY were keen to keep their independence and refused to be integrated as military auxiliaries under the auspices of such agencies as the BRCS, once granted that leeway they worked well within the system, knew their place and never wavered in their class allegiance. They were willing to be seen as a nuisance by military officials in their demand for a place at the table; once given a place, they understood the need to make themselves indispensable and keep their demands limited.

This 'place at the table' for McDougall meant that they would be treated as military personnel rather than as women. For example, the Belgian authorities became alarmed by the severity of the air raids in Calais at one point and wanted to curb the scope of the Unit 5's work by decreeing that only men might work on night duty. McDougall received a note from the Belgian Base-Commandant forbidding their night service marked 'seen and approved'. McDougall, unintimidated by such authority, returned the note and sent it back with 'seen and not approved' scrawled across the top. The Belgians backed down.[30] This was also around the time McDougall flouted military authority by dressing up as a French aviator and testing the authenticity of her costume by spending several hours undetected in a British aviators' mess.[31] This last prank was an especially fine gender performance that underscored McDougall's claim to the instability of gender identity. Despite such performances, however, ultimately McDougall and the FANY were women and military authorities in the war always saw female service personnel as women first and foremost. Sharon Ouditt's work on VAD nurses illustrates this perfectly, highlighting the problems associated with these women's organizations that fashioned new gendered behaviours at the same time that they developed a 'sororial' identity deeply rooted in the traditional tropes of gendered class relations.[32] The FANY aspirations of militarization were predicated upon these conservative pressures of class and gender that constrained their behaviour even while they battled (often very successfully) against them.

The fighting and the killing continued through the autumn of 1917 as the French had some success at the Battle of Aisne and the Italians suffered crushing losses at Caporetto. The Russians were in total defeat and could no longer be relied upon; in addition other forces in Russia were mounting as the October Revolution saw the Bolsheviks taking power and Trotsky negotiating peace with Germany a few months later at Brest-Litovsk. The final Allied offensive of this tragic year was in November at the Battle of Cambrai where British troops under General Sir Julian Byng used tanks to successfully crush the German lines. Working for the British Convoy, Pat Waddell remembered these outrageous machines resembling anything in size from 'a hippopotamus to Buckingham Palace'.[33] Still, the Germans revived after this onslaught and gained back much ground. The battle ended on 5 December, bringing a gloomy year to a close. Despite this gloom and mounting casualties, for the public record the FANY rallied on with the usual cheerful British pluck. The following excerpt from a letter to Margaret Cole-Hamilton from McDougall written during this period illustrates this steely nerve and understated bravado in its description of the barracks 'going on fire':

We had a bad go here the other day – baths and kitchen gone and Robertson had a very narrow shave. She was washing in her cu [cubicle] and a piece of bomb came through the wall passed across her head and tore her skirt to ribbons and is now firmly embedded in her door. She was undrest [sic] and took a few minutes to pull her things on. Cadell got her wall pierced and a bit of bomb under her bed. Moses was thrown down on the ground, and I got a bit of bomb on my coat and saved myself falling by catching the gate post. Our cook was thrown down and got splinters in her sleeve – ditto Van C. the aviator who was having tea with us that day . . . It wasn't a bit nice.

Coley dear I am afraid we are in for bad luck! I was interrupted by the barracks going on fire. It started in the mess hut and ran up the ceiling – the electric wires short-circuited – Mason and Moses climbed up the rafters like cats and now we are a messy smoky swamp. I got a fire hatchet and a ladder and luckily a hospital man came and took these from me and I ran down to the drs.' rooms and told them to cut off the main thing – the three of them sat and stared like idiots and I didn't know where it was 'till at last — grasped it and turned off the thing. I feel quite shaky still![34]

Despite her bravado, McDougall worried for the safety of her colleagues. She loved the FANY and she loved the young women who worked so hard and were so loyal. Once during a Surgeon-General's inspection of the unit when Belgian officials spoke eloquently of FANY devotion and courage, Mc Dougall wrote that she

looked at the girls as he talked. They were so young and pretty and I felt how utterly selfless they were. Speeches like these embarrassed and bored them. To them the danger was all in a day's work. It was not that they were unafraid, but they would not let the Corps down. I don't think ever girls like them have been before. They are so loyal to each other, to me, and to the Corps.[35]

Anxiously looking at these young women, McDougall remembered how she feared for their safety. 'I was haunted day and night', she wrote, 'by the thought of any of the girls getting killed. I felt terribly the burden of responsibility.'[36]

Frictions among the troops

With her usual industrious opportunism and desire to increase the scope of work for the FANY, Grace McDougall managed to overcome French resistance to militarized women like the FANY and was asked to run a military hospital officially known as L' Hôpital Auxiliaire 76 at Port à Binson with the recycled unit name of Unit 1. McDougall responded to the intimidating task of holding her end of the bargain by launching a fund-raising extravaganza that sent her and Mary Baxter-Ellis to the north of England and to Scotland. With amazing resolve and skill in representing the FANY and their mission as central to the war effort, as well as knowing the right people to ask, McDougall and Baxter-Ellis came through with enough money, beds, medical instruments and supplies, and vehicles to get Binson up and running. McDougall explained how her request to the Newcastle Workmen's War Relief Committee had resulted in 'a most generous grant of hospital supplies and surgical instruments, mattresses and sterilising drums' as well as promises of soap and bandages and a present of a dozen pairs of scissors. Baxter-Ellis personally appealed to HRH Princess Louise, Queen Victoria's daughter, and received a donation of 5 guineas. Lady Allendale and Lady Londonderry also sent money. In Scotland McDougall secured a Buick ambulance, supplies of pillowcases, slippers, bandages and towels. Mrs Bernard Allen, a long-time benefactress of the FANY who had donated an ambulance to the Belgian Convoy, also promised to help fund the new hospital.[37] In addition, they inherited the inventory from the now–closed Lamarck hospital.[38]

Despite this success, there was turmoil at FANY Headquarters concerning McDougall's decision to take over the hospital. This altercation illustrates not only McDougall's relationship to authority generally but her disrespect for non-militarized FANY personnel on the home front with no experience and therefore little credibility when it came to making orders about FANY service in militarized zones.[39] Relations had been strained for quite some time between Secretary Janette Lean and McDougall and both Lean and Treasurer William Cluff were defensive about accusations of mismanagement. After threatening to resign unless they received the 'support and absolute confidence of all the officers of the Corps and each of its members', Lean and Cluff attempted to consolidate their authority with a handwritten document titled 'Suggestions for the Future Government of the FANY Corps'.[40] Included in this document was a stipulation that any new schemes of work must ideally be brought before the Board or at least before the Treasurer and two other officers, including 'at least one of the Senior Lieutenants' (Franklin and McDougall). This stipulation ensured Franklin's equal position with McDougall and aimed to control McDougall's authority. Cluff was also given authority to have complete control of funds and to forbid the use of funds for new schemes if he felt so inclined. After these suggestions Franklin had written a short paragraph thanking Lean and Cluff for their 'strenuous work' and stating that Lean and Cluff both rank as a Honorary Lieutenants with full control of headquarters and finances, respectively. McDougall's and Franklin's signatures then follow.[41]

Minutes of a Board Meeting several months later (where McDougall was absent) again show conflict between her and Headquarters and suggest that McDougall might have threatened to fire Lean. Motions were passed that no one officer had the authority to dismiss another officer on her own responsibility and also (with direct reference to the initiation of the hospital at Binson) no new FANY unit may be formed without previous consultation with Headquarters.[42] Aimed as a way to stem McDougall's impetuosity, the timing of these rulings in November 1916 coincide with McDougall's preparations for the hospital at Binson. She ignored Headquarters' decision and went ahead with her plans for the hospital. Indeed, McDougall had also irked FANY Headquarters during her negotiations for the Belgian convoy Unit 5. Cluff and Lean had resisted McDougall's supposed request for new members of the Belgian convoy to sign a contract in her name rather than use the standard FANY application form and they saw this violation of standard procedures as further evidence that McDougall took authority from no one but herself.[43]

There was also trouble during this period concerning McDougall's decision to send FANY up the line to work at the YMCA canteen at St Pierre

Brouck. In a distinct show of lack of solidarity within the organization, Lean went so far as to write to the YMCA and tell them it was a breach of the Geneva Convention for FANY to work in these military canteens. 'Mr Cluff and I', wrote Lean in a letter to Franklin, 'are quite determined that unless Mrs McDougall conforms to the rules of the Corps, she will forfeit all right to the name, money, stores, and personnel of the Corps, and, if necessary, steps will be taken to enforce the decision'.[44] Money was always an issue and Lean and Cluff were the ones who had to handle the administrative and financial issues associated with running the Corps and keeping them out of the red. This was particularly difficult for a volunteer organization that relied totally on the philanthropy of others. In addition, McDougall's way of doing things: risk-taking, disdain for authority and bureaucracy when they did not agree with her plans, and her independent decision-making without consultation with Headquarters staff were especially irritating to Lean and Cluff. This friction arose in effect because of the home team's need for structure and limits, and their repeated requests for inclusion in decision-making concerning FANY development, which conflicted with McDougall's independence, lack of respect for red tape and disdain for non-militarized, homefront personnel. McDougall danced to the beat of her own drum, so to speak, and Lean and Cluff were tired of being surprised by new developments they felt stretched the resources of the organization beyond its capacities. They feared potentially negative consequences associated with taking on additional responsibilities and were anxious about subverting male military authority. FANY Headquarters was preparing to register the organization under the War Charities Act and did not want to jeopardize a process that included meeting a series of conditions and stipulations.[45]

It is interesting to read about Lillian Franklin's role in the turmoil, although she left few known personal accounts of these years. As a Senior Officer and soon to be official Co-Commandant, Franklin's style was very different from McDougall's. She appears to have worked as liaison between McDougall and Headquarters, supporting Lean and Cluff, yet not completely putting the brakes on McDougall's schemes. In a letter Franklin offered her support and sympathy to Lean and suggested that the annoyance felt at McDougall's impetuosity extended to other FANY senior personnel. At this point Franklin was willing to put a stop to McDougall acting alone. 'Dear Miss Lean', it began,

I am sincerely sorry to find that Mrs Mac is taking up this impossible attitude, but of course the resolutions passed at our meeting must be upheld. There is no question of anyone of us wishing to cramp any forward movement of the Corps but as anything undertaken by any unit of it concerns all the others it is absolutely imperative that Hdqrts be fully informed of any fresh responsibilities undertaken. There has been heaps of time for some little outline of the scheme to have been forwarded . . . I am writing to Mr Cluff and suggesting that he as chairman representing the committee should write and inform Mrs Mac that she must either conform or her unit must be considered no longer a part of the FANY and no help be appealed for it under that name . . . If we are not loyal to each other we are bound to go under. Joynson, Thompson and Wicks are quite of the same opinion. I have just had a letter from Wicks on this point, a quite straightforward and sensible letter. Why did not Mrs Mac put in even half an hour at the meeting to give us some idea of her scheme? No one wants to interfere with it only to ensure if possible its complete success. She cannot work everything herself therefore she must trust others to help her.[46]

The minutes of a Board Meeting in February 1917 report even stronger words against McDougall, and all members present (McDougall and Franklin were both absent) expressed disapproval at the way McDougall had violated their resolution about no unit being formed without approval from FANY Headquarters. The minutes reported that McDougall had entered into an arrangement for the management, control and staffing of the hospital at Port à Binson without approval of the Board of Officers and had declined to give any information in spite of repeated requests. If details of McDougall's plans were not submitted to FANY Headquarters within fourteen days, the officers unanimously agreed that the FANY would renounce all liability or responsibility for any agreement McDougall might make. In addition, Lean lobbied hard for a request that McDougall withdraw immediately from the Corps 'since she had been repeatedly warned as to the folly of her actions'. The other officers declined to support the last resolution and the minutes read that they were not in favour of 'any step which might land the Corps in legal difficulties'.[47]

For McDougall's part, she recalled that Lean 'bombarded' her with letters and disavowed her, most notably through a letter sent to the French Red Cross official in England speaking against McDougall's plans for the hospital at Binson. According to McDougall, Mr Illingsworth of the London Committee of French Red Cross responded by affirming McDougall and promising his help: 'Tell them to go to blazes, only don't tell them I said so. I'll get your people out for you', he is reported as saying.[48] Despite tough words against McDougall from FANY headquarters, the furore over Binson was resolved by McDougall raising funds for the hospital and Janette Lean resigning her post as Secretary.[49] Lean went on to work for the BRCS in London coordinating visitations for prisoners of war. Irene Cowlin replaced Lean at FANY General Headquarters, although as we shall see in the next chapter, Lean returned to her post with the FANY at a later date.[50]

In terms of public face, the *Gazette* was keen to condone the expansion and militarization of the FANY and therefore in the same edition that published Lean's resignation there was an account sanctioning the transfer of Unit 1 to Binson. 'Mrs McDougall', it read, 'must be congratulated on this achievement as it is particularly difficult for women to get into this area and the French Red Cross own that it is a very important piece of work.'[51] The next month McDougall was careful to report that the Board had not actually sanctioned Binson since it had not met, but that Treasurer Cluff was 'quite satisfied with the arrangements'.[52] McDougall with her usual high energy and ambition and disdain for authority had her way and FANY war service was expanded once more.

Port à Binson Priory hospital

The hospital at Port à Binson was an old Cistercian monastery located near Rheims on the River Marne, quite close to the Front. Although the Priory had functioned as a French divisional hospital since 1915, it was still occupied by the strict Order of the White Fathers. McDougall reported a conversation with the Father Superior where he admitted to not having spoken to a woman in thirty years. She exclaimed how she and Cole–Hamilton had felt guilty ever since lest he had had to do penance for talking to them: he had supposedly walked up and down the stone cloister outside, barefoot, saying prayers in the snow.[53] For the most part however, it seems the Fathers and the FANY got along quite well. Other than shock on the part of the Fathers at seeing one of the nurses sleeping outside and an incident when the FANY had tea in the cloisters, the arrangement seemed to work fine.[54]

The Priory housed 200 beds and two operating theatres, and was in need of much work. When the advance party arrived at Port à Binson in January 1917 after travelling through a snowstorm and having numerous car problems along the way, they found the place filthy and in much disrepair. Some of the mattresses had never been turned in years and had dirty bandages wrapped in 1914 newspapers under them.[55] The stone floors of the cells had not felt the warmth of a fire in a long time; the cold was intense and the large sewer that crossed the ground outside Binson was one mass of icicles.[56] As usual the women set to work and rigged up braziers out of petrol tins and lit fires on the floors of rooms with chimneys. Despite these endeavours, they had to break the ice with hammers before they could wash in the morning and McDougall recalled sleeping in three pairs of pyjamas and two coats under fourteen blankets and still shivering. Nonetheless, despite the harsh conditions and disarray, when the doctors arrived and witnessed the new–found cleanliness, chintz bedspreads and coloured screens around the beds, they were impressed with the changes and put it down to the natural womanliness of the FANY. 'Women were like fairies', the doctors were said to have declared, 'they brought home with them.'[57] Still, almost worse than the cold and general disorder was the discovery that the French hospital director affiliated with the French Société de Secours aux Blessés Militaires (SSBM) was a 'thoroughly unpleasant little man'. With her British superiority and class-consciousness McDougall declared him 'underbred, and made as only a French of that class can be, detestably narrow-minded'.[58] He did not last long and was soon replaced.

The hospital was formally opened in March 1917. The second floor of the main building housed the FANY staff and the mess hall – and, good news – rations were very good, laundry was included, and the staff received free first-class rail passes.[59] McDougall negotiated with the SSBM in Paris and agreed to provide staff for nursing and transport, medical equipment and beds if the SSBM would supply doctors, heating, rations and so forth. Margaret Cole-Hamilton was put in charge. She left her work at the YMCA hut at St Pierre Brouck to move to Binson and was soon joined by her colleague, 'the fair Corporal' Ida Lewis. Other staff included the matron Miss Bullock and drivers Doris Russell Allen, Margaret 'Molly' Marshall and Mrs Wybrants. Nurses included the Misses Mansel, Hunter, Pounds, Robinson, Marjorie McDougall, Sidebottom, Russell Allen (Doris's sister 'Gerry') and Mrs Montagu 'Monty' Brown. The Quartermaster at Binson was FANY Sergeant Grace Anderson whose tenure with the Corps went back to its prewar days.

The Priory was situated on a hill and stood in its own wooded grounds with formal gardens surrounding the buildings. Despite the fact that it was within twenty miles of the firing lines, the views were lovely and many of the wards opened onto grassy terraces. When Spring finally burst forth and thawed the chills of that terrible winter, Binson was described as being at its very best: 'long windows wide open, and every ward filled with sunshine, fresh air, and contented patients. The grounds are a mass of flowers – lilacs, lilies of the valley, laburnums, acacias, syringa, banks of purple iris scarcely faded before plots of scarlet poppies have succeeded them, and on every side wooded hills, sloping into the distance, and the Marne winding through the picture.'[60] This tranquil portrait is described as one of the best places for 'sick soldiers who can sit out in the air and grow strong';[61] it was, as one visitor explained 'difficult to believe that just over the hill yonder men were killing and being killed. At first the incessant roar of the cannons was unpleasant, but after a short time one became accustomed to it, and only remarked it when a specially loud burst came.'[62]

Although Binson Priory looked out on beautiful countryside not yet spoiled by the ravages of war, the land between the Priory and the Front in the opposite direction was one of utter desolation. McDougall had a harrowing journey bringing the ambulances to Binson as bombs dropped all around them and a loose scared horse kicked in their windshield. On her arrival at the hospital she was feeling terrible and suffering from a very bad cold and cough, found a burst pipe had flooded the cubicles and 'a lot of worry to straighten out'.[63]3 Eventually her cold developed into pleurisy and the French doctors removed blood from her lungs. McDougall's constant travelling and responsibility were always hard on her health, even though these travels were sprinkled with accounts of dining with a Comte or supper with such and such General. On one trip she spent a night in a farmhouse and felt something on her neck in the night. In the morning, she recalled, 'I sat up and felt a pain in my throat and [when] I got out my little hand mirror, there were teeth marks on my throat and the sleeve of my red silk pyjamas was bitten through, and there were teeth marks and blood on my arm. Rats! Ugh!'[64] That McDougall was still wearing her red silk pyjamas in a farmhouse in the midst of the chaos of the First World War is testimony to her sense of class and style.

Although no patients arrived at the hospital until the end of March, they arrived then in full force: over a hundred at two in the morning and almost seventy several days later. Cole-Hamilton wrote that the work began in earnest and kept the operating theatres busy. The hospital was almost full and they were often short-staffed. Patients with acute needs were treated here; those with tuberculosis or ailments that needed long-term care were evacuated and sent elsewhere. The FANY had managed to procure 'spinal chairs' for men too badly injured to be moved otherwise and a 'fracture apparatus' for healing fracture wounds.[65] By May there had been over thirty operations performed and only four patients had died. Many of the operations of course were amputations: a consequence of artillery that blew bodies apart and caused terrible tissue damage.[66]

In June 1917 McDougall wrote about a dangerous journey to deliver stores from Binson to a French depot. Driving with Doris and Gerry Russell Allen through the French countryside in their 'joy-ride' bus (one of the faster vehicles at Binson), they arrived at a region close to the Front ravaged by fighting. Nine people had been killed in an attack that morning and houses were blown apart. As darkness approached, the women lost their way, and since headlights were forbidden, they took it in turns to hold a flashlight in front of the car. Progress continued with the help of illumination thrown up by artillery rockets, but was then stymied by a burst tyre. The jack was too high and the pump broken so they drove on the rim of the wheel away from the firing and found themselves on the edge of a deep drain by a shell–shattered mill with only two narrow footpaths as outlets. Driver Doris Russell Allen reversed back up the hill 'trusting to luck and the feeble light of the torch'. Once on firmer ground McDougall went in search of water to mend the tyre and bumped into a soldier with head wounds who had been wandering with his injury since that morning, looking for the railhead. 'His bandages', explained McDougall, 'were soaked through with blood so we slung him aboard, and as we were too much weary, and thought him too ill to look for the railhead, we took him back with us.'[67] Doris Russell Allen managed to mend the tyre 'kneeling in the mud with hell raging all around'.[68] This notion of kneeling in the mud with hell raging is a poignant reminder of women's claim to strengths beyond the traditional notions of women's moral strength and superiority.

Also during June the FANY were asked to take over a *Foyer du Soldat* or canteen near the Front at Fismes for four weeks while the Directrice, a Miss Joseph, was on leave. McDougall described Fismes as previously being subject to much shellfire, although now about fourteen miles behind the Front line and 'protected by Craonne which the French took so gallantly some months ago'.[69] This assignment was led by FANY Grace Anderson with help from Wybrants, Doris Russell Allen and Mrs Crisfield. The women were said to work so gallantly under almost continuous machine–gun fire that the French named them *les petits soldats*.[70] Although this was another reminder of their militarization and claim to masculine space, the diminution of their status as 'little' soldiers highlights the conflicting identities performed by the FANY.

Anderson wrote a report about their time at Fismes in an article for the *Gazette*. She explained that the canteen or *foyer* was a series of buildings separated across a dusty yard where the men would sit at tables when the weather allowed. On their arrival the FANY acted as they almost always did on relocation to a new place: they cleaned. After bribing local children to help them haul water, they set to work giving the place a good scrub down and worked until the concrete became visible again and the tables were washed thoroughly. The children brought them wild flowers to brighten up the place and soon Fismes was transformed. They also took to adapting the menu and alongside the usual tea, coffee and chocolate, they added fresh lemonade, as the weather was so hot, and a drink concocted from condensed milk mixed with cold water and sugar that the French colonial troops particularly enjoyed. Biscuits could be purchased, and, if the soldiers brought them eggs, the FANY would make omelettes for them. After a few days the soldiers arrived in droves, especially in the evenings, and they found themselves trying to serve about 800 men all wanting drinks at once. As a result, the mugs got only a 'lick and a promise of a wash, if that'.[71] Hours of work were 9.30 a.m. until 12.30 and 2.30 until 8 p.m., although it was invariably nearer 9 o'clock when the women were able to leave and return to their billets, usually to spend the night in the cellar because of constant bombardments. Often the men would spend the night in the recreation room and would tidy it up and leave a note of thanks for the FANY in the morning.[72] The increase in business at the canteen was related to the fact that the FANY found a soldier who had once been a master painter who painted them a sign and notice board; it was also related no doubt to the general cleaning and brightening up of the place, as well as the FANY attitude. Miss Joseph came back from leave in July and the FANY returned to Binson.[73]

The FANY were running this French hospital and the canteen at Fismes during the period when the French Army was in chaos and mutiny and executions were occurring. Again, while the FANY at Binson were prevented from writing about it, they were well aware of the problems and even cared for a traumatized French doctor who had to attend the execution of six men of his own regiment.[74] This chaos among the French troops in early summer caused a lull in casualties and no big convoys of troops arrived at Binson until a very large contingent arrived from Verdun in August. Then the drivers were kept busy carrying wounded as well as fetching supplies and driving administrators and other officials. The hospitals at Boursault, Troissy and Verneuil also relied on the Binson ambulances.[75] In addition, FANY drivers had to respond to emergency calls within their vicinity. Alongside numerous railway accidents, there were drownings, as the River Marne near Binson Priory was especially treacherous at this time of the year. Despite all this the FANY had to undergo repeated inspections by authorities, which also taxed their resources and energy. They made do, it was reported, because they were very good at playing 'the old FANY game of turning up at every corner' so that no shortage of staff would be noticed.[76]

By all accounts the hospital was a great success. By the end of the year the SSBM decided to make the hospital a Triage Centre for the whole French Army in that District and met with McDougall and Cole-Hamilton to make arrangements for more FANY nursing staff to be sent from England.[77] However, ten days later the FANY received a curt letter from the head of the SSBM stating that they would like the FANY to turn over the hospital to French nurses. This was a major blow to the FANY, given that they had spent much time, money, and energy at Binson, had the hospital running so smoothly, and were enjoying such excellent relations with the French doctors and orderlies.[78] Cole-Hamilton resigned from active service with the FANY at this time and called their dismissal from Binson 'a distinct slur' against the FANY.[79] She explained that although an inquiry was made, this kind of thing was constantly happening because the French preferred to use their own nurses.[80] In reality, the French were anxious about any women being involved in war and perhaps when it came to nurses, their own nun-like Red Cross nurses were preferable to the more militarized FANY.[81] The doctors and patients at the hospital gave the FANY a silver tea service and Cole-Hamilton and McDougall were presented with silver medals and diplomas from the SSBM.[82]

More expansion and consolidation

As the hospital at Binson was coming to a close, McDougall had been negotiating more work with the French. In June 1917 she had taken a trip to Paris to see the Ministry of War about a scheme for a convoy for the French and followed up this visit with a formal offer to provide a convoy along similar lines to the Belgian convoy in Calais where the French Army would provide board, lodgings, laundry and free travelling facilities for the drivers. In her favour was the dire need for drivers as well as the exemplary service of the FANY driving French wounded under the auspices of the Belgian Army. In early July McDougall received formal acceptance of her plan and by August had been asked to increase the offered number of fifteen drivers to twenty and proceed immediately to Amiens, a central hospital hub for French wounded quite close to the Front.[83]

Even more anxious than the British authorities about *la femme-soldat*, as already mentioned, the French were employing civilian women for auxiliary military work but were still slow to recruit women in the masculine role of driver. The French were more comfortable with the FANY running their hospitals and more cautious about employing them in convoy work. Indeed, Margaret Darrow in her discussion of the French response to women driving reports that Commander Doumenc, the Director of the Army Automobile Service (the Direction de Service Automobile or DSA), repeatedly dismissed offers from women volunteers like the FANY, refusing to acknowledge that the British Army was already using FANY drivers effectively in the war zone.[84] Still Darrow writes that some French units were using women drivers (both Frenchwomen and 'foreign' help) despite the official resistance. By the spring and early summer of 1917 the shortage of men and the British example, which included the establishment of the WAAC, allowed the employment of French women drivers.

The first FANY convoy to officially drive for the French Army was Unit 6, up and running at Amiens in August 1917 and led by Joan Bowles. Three months later Unit 7 was established at Epernay, headed by Doris Russell Allen. At this time the French authorities wanted to consolidate any units working for them into a series of organizations or Sections Sanitaires (SS) with a French Lieutenant and a FANY officer at their head. One large consolidated section of about forty drivers became known as SSY2 and eventually included Unit 7 and two new units: Unit 9 (formed in December 1917 at Chalôns-sur-Marne) and Unit 11 (stationed at Vitry-le-François in August 1918). Unit 6 was eventually joined by the new Unit 10 (formed during summer 1918 and stationed at St Dizier) and together these formed SSY4. Suffice to say, the constant naming and renaming and consolidation of the various units working for the French is quite confusing and difficult to keep straight. Unit 12 (known as SSY5) was formed in London amidst great fanfare in October 1918. It was devised as a Mobile Unit complete with trailer kitchen presented by the British Committee of the French Red Cross and consisting of twenty-two ambulances, a staff car, workshop car and lorry, and staffed by twenty-three drivers, two cooks and two mechanics. The unit also had a Renault ambulance bought with funds raised by the FANY. Ida Lewis transferred from her position as Commanding Officer of Unit 9 to head this unit having high hopes of entering Germany with the victorious Allies.[85] But although it was inspected by the French Ambassador in Hyde Park on 5 October and left London three days later, SSY5 did not began work in Nancy, France, until after the Armistice on 28 November. The last two units, 13 and 14, were also late in their conception: Unit 13, led by Gladys Marples, was attached to the Belgian Army in November 1918 and drove in the Brussels region; Unit 14 was a short-lived unit attached to a large French hospital at Pointoise during November and December 1918. The head of each of these ambulance units held an officer rank in the French Army.[86]

When the French authorities wanted to consolidate the various units at the end of 1917, McDougall and Franklin were asked to nominate a FANY officer to represent all French convoys. At this point McDougall was 'sorely tempted' to consider vacating her position in the Belgian Army and taking up this post with the French. It would have provided a wider scope of work and she believed she would receive a warm welcome from the French. 'I was playing a lone hand with the Belgians', wrote McDougall in her memoir 'Five Years with the Allies'. But it was the Belgians, she explained, that had given her that first chance to work in 1914 and she felt a strong allegiance to them: 'I had shared their retreat and their struggles, and I longed to be with them in the hour of their triumph. They had laden me with kindness, and I knew their gratitude was warm and sincere.' In addition McDougall believed that if she left, the whole unit would want to go with her and this, she wrote, was 'unthinkable'.[87] While McDougall reported Doris Russell Allen as saying only she (McDougall) was 'up to the task' of heading up these French units,

McDougall decided to stay with the Belgians and it was Russell Allen herself who became the new Commanding Officer. It is difficult to know whether McDougall had an over-inflated opinion in terms of popular support for herself as potential Commandant of the French units; certainly as a Senior Officer she would have had the opportunity to take this position.[88] The French officer working with Russell Allen was Lieutenant Ibarnegaray.[89]

By the New Year 1918 there had been further administrative reshuffling and consolidation among and between the FANY and Allied armies. The Commissioners of the British Red Cross Society desired that there should be one person nominated as the representative of all the units working with the British and with whom they could deal directly. A subcommittee consisting of Marian Gamwell, Beryl Hutchinson and Muriel Thompson elected Lillian Franklin (who had long commanded the British convoy in Calais) as the official representative of FANY (British Sections).[90] She would eventually receive the honour of an MBE in 1923 for her outstanding work. The units working for the French and Belgians were then organized into the FANY (Allied Sections) with the obvious leader, Grace McDougall, at the head. At this point Franklin and McDougall officially served as Co-Commandants of the organization. The two Sections each had their own Secretaries: Janette Lean returned to FANY headquarters in January as Secretary of the British Sections, knowing, no doubt, that McDougall's affiliation with the Allied Section would mean she might have few dealings with her old nemesis. Grace 'Andy' Anderson returned to England and became Secretary of the Allied Section. Each Section put out its version of the *Gazette*, with the reports of the Allied units appearing in the regular *Gazette* and the British Section publishing its own 'Supplement' in the same format. Headquarters also moved from the Earls Court office to 34 Wilton Place in Knightsbridge. The old office at 192 Earls Court Road became a clubroom and welcomed all FANY members, new and old.[91]

At the end of 1917 as the units driving for the French were established and consolidated, McDougall and Franklin were working on plans to start yet another new convoy driving for the British. After the military losses of 1917 the need was there and of course McDougall was always willing to expand the influence and service of the Corps and exercise her personal ambition. Successes with the British unit in Calais as well as FANY accomplishments with the French and the Belgians brought renewed credibility to this new scheme. Despite the haranguing and red tape that always seemed to accompany work for the British, the FANY were always wildly enthusiastic to be serving their own men. And so after some negotiation, in January 1918 the new FANY Unit 8 was established at St Omer, south east of Calais. Muriel Thompson was in charge with Betty Hutchinson as master mechanic. Other familiar names included Section Sergeants Norma Lowson and Winnie Mordaunt (who had returned from a driving assignment at Lady Michelam's Convalescent Hospital for British Officers on the Côte d'Azur at Cap Martin), Nora Cluff, and Mrs Marcia de Belleroche. Mary 'Dicky' Richardson was the workshop sergeant. Twelve VAD drivers were also attached to the convoy in addition to VAD housekeeping personnel, serving under the Joint War Committee of the BRCS and the Order of St John.[92] The symbol for this unit, a red herring with its tail elevated, adorned the dashboard of all cars in the convoy. This symbol was chosen as a result of a remark attributed to Surgeon-General Woodhouse about the identity of the FANY. On reflecting that they were neither Red Cross nor Army but worked for the Red Cross and were attached to the Army, he is said to have responded, 'Upon my soul! You are neither fish, flesh nor fowl, but if I may so say, you are thundering good red herring!'[93]

Although 1917 saw the expansion of the FANY into these new units and a broadening of its organizational influence among the Allies, it was a tumultuous year that reflected issues of power both within the organization and between the FANY and military authorities. This transgression of women into new territory and its accompanying renegotiation of the cultural terrain was never an easy process. Still, the organization expanded, as also did the right of the FANY to fashion a feminine identity in masculine space.

Notes

1 *Gazette* (April 1916), p. 3.
2 Grace McDougall, 'Five Years with the Allies, 1914–1919: The Story of the FANY Corps', p. 128. [IWM]
3 According to Hugh Popham's account in *FANY: The Story of the Women's Transport Service, 1907–1984* (London: Leo Cooper, 1984), p. 33, FANY Treasurer Rev. William Cluff is said to have said : 'I cannot make her understand that the British Military Authorities as well as the British Red Cross Society are very jealous indeed of British women working outside the area of the BEF', adding that at this point they were prohibiting all new units even within this area.
4 *Gazette* (December 1917), p. 3.
5 Irene Ward, *FANY Invicta* (London: Hutchinson, 1955), p. 56. Although this FANY victory may not have occurred in quite this way, McDougall does write of an event that happened in June 1918 which might have been the basis for Ward's story. McDougall explained that the British were still trying to get control of the Belgian convoy even then and the BRCS had ruled that any new units for any army in the British zone of Calais were not only to be sanctioned by the British Adjutant-General but were not allowed to wear 'foreign' military badges: *Gazette* (December 1917), p. 3. When McDougall attempted to return to Calais from England she found she was denied a permit and told that in order to receive permission to travel she must put the Belgian convoy unreservedly in the hands of the BRCS. 'I felt', wrote McDougall, 'the most

dreadful feeling of helplessness before injustice'. Fortunately such feelings were temporary and McDougall remembered that even though a British zone may inhabit a French area, still a French Governor can give a *sauf-conduit* or permit to travel. She contacted her great friend General Ditte, Governor of Calais, who helped her overrule the authorities and return to France: McDougall, 'Five Years with the Allies', p. 203.

6 *Gazette* (November–December 1916), p. 6.
7 Ibid., p. 7; *Gazette* (January 1917), p. 11.
8 McDougall, 'Five Years with the Allies', p. 145.
9 Ibid., p. 144.
10 Cicely Mordaunt, 'Ten Little FANY Girls', unauthored notebook, no page numbers. [FA]
11 See Martin Gilbert, *The First World War: A Complete History* (New York: Henry Holt, 1994).
12 McDougall, 'Five Years with the Allies', p. 154; see also Beryl Hutchinson, Questionnaire, no. 12. [LC]
13 McDougall, 'Five Years with the Allies', p. 164.
14 John Keegan, *The First World War* (New York: Alfred Knopf, 1999), pp. 360–7.
15 Siegfried Sassoon quoted in John Terraine, *The Great War* (Ware, Hertfordshire: Wordsworth, 1998), p. 308.
16 Paul Fussell, *The Great War and Modern Memory* (London: Oxford University Press, 1975), p. 16.
17 *Gazette* (October 1917), p. 5.
18 Ward, *FANY Invicta*, pp. 56–7.
19 *Gazette* (January 1918), p. 2.
20 *Gazette* (October 1917), p. 5.
21 *Gazette* (August–September 1917), p. 5; (November 1917), p. 3.
22 McDougall, 'Five Years with the Allies', pp. 164–5.
23 *Gazette* (October 1917), p. 5.
24 *Gazette* (December 1917), p. 1.
25 McDougall, 'Five Years with the Allies', p. 246.
26 Ibid.
27 *Gazette* (February 1917), p. 10; (February–March 1918), p. 5.
28 McDougall, 'Five Years with the Allies', p. 164.
29 *Gazette* (January 1918), p. 5.
30 McDougall, 'Five Years with the Allies', p. 177.
31 Ibid., p. 209.
32 Sharon Ouditt, *Fighting Forces, Writing Women: Identity and Ideology in the First World War* (London: Routledge, 1994), p. 7.
33 Pat Beauchamp (a.k.a. Waddell), *Fanny Goes to War* (London: John Murray, 1919), p. 165.
34 McDougall to Margaret Cole-Hamilton (20 December, *c.* 1917). Quoted in Barbara W. Gordon, 'A History of the FANY from its Foundations to the End of the First World War', Diploma of Education thesis, Sunderland Polytechnic (April 1974), p. 18.
35 McDougall, 'Five Years with the Allies', p. 198.
36 Ibid., p. 251.
37 *Gazette* (March 1917), pp. 1–2.
38 *Gazette* (February 1917), p. 5.
39 McDougall, 'Five Years with the Allies', p. 142.

40 Janette Lean and William Cluff, typed statement on FANY letterhead, pp. 2–3; 'Suggestions for the Future Government of the FANY Corps' (stamped 21 July 1916). [FA]
41 Lean and Cluff, 'Suggestions for the Future Government', p. 3.
42 Minutes of FANY Board Meeting (17 November 1916). [FA]
43 Ibid.
44 Lean to Franklin (16 December 1916). [FA]
45 *Gazette* (January 1917), p. 1. The registration occurred in March 1917. It went smoothly, except that they were investigated as to whether the canteen at Camp du Richard was 'truly Red Cross'. Adèle Crockett, Commanding Officer at Ruchard, stuck to the guidelines of the Geneva Convention and the camp passed the test.
46 Franklin to Lean (11 December 1916). [FA]
47 Minutes of FANY Board Meeting (1 February 1917). [FA]
48 McDougall, 'Five Years with the Allies', p. 143.
49 *Gazette* (February 1917), p. 8.
50 *Gazette* (March 1917), p. 2.
51 *Gazette* (February 1917), p. 1.
52 *Gazette* (March 1917), p. 2.
53 McDougall, 'Five Years with the Allies', p. 140.
54 Ibid., p. 152; Popham, *F.A.N.Y.*, p. 35.
55 Report, 'Work of FANY for French Wounded Only. During the War 1914–1918', Section II: FANY Hospital Auxiliaire 76, undated, no page numbers. [LC]
56 McDougall, 'Five Years with the Allies', p. 140.
57 Ibid.
58 Ibid., p. 141.
59 *Gazette* (February 1917), p. 5.
60 *Gazette* (June 1917), p. 1.
61 *Gazette* (May 1917), p. 4.
62 Rose Allen, 'The FANY Hospital at Binson', *The Inquirer* (19 May 1917).
63 McDougall, 'Five Years with the Allies', p. 144.
64 Ibid., p. 123.
65 Report, 'Work of FANY for French Wounded Only', Section II.
66 McDougall, 'Five Years with the Allies', p. 159.
67 *Gazette* (June 1917), pp. 4–5.
68 McDougall, 'Five Years with the Allies', p. 152.
69 *Gazette* (July 1917), pp. 1, 3.
70 Popham, *F.A.N.Y.*, p. 36.
71 *Gazette* (July 1917), p. 3.
72 Report, 'Work of FANY for French Wounded Only. During the War 1914–1918', Section III: Work of FANY for French Canteen at Fismes, undated, no page numbers. [LC]
73 Ibid.
74 McDougall, 'Five Years with the Allies', p. 158.
75 Report, 'Work of FANY for French Wounded Only', Section II.
76 McDougall, 'Five Years with the Allies', p. 160.
77 Report, 'Work of FANY for French Wounded Only', Section II.
78 Ibid.
79 *Gazette* (February–March 1918), p. 4.
80 Ibid., p. 3.

81 See Margaret H. Darrow, *French Women and the First World War: War Stories of the Home Front* (New York: Oxford University Press, 2000).
82 Report, 'Work of FANY for French Wounded Only', Section II.
83 McDougall, 'Five Years with the Allies', p. 154; Report, 'Work of FANY for French Wounded Only. During the War 1914–1918', Section IV: FANY Work for French Amiens Convoy, undated, no page numbers. [LC]
84 Darrow, *French Women and the First World War*, p. 255.
85 *Gazette* (August–September Supplement 1918), p. 2.
86 Ibid., p. 6.
87 Grace McDougall, 'Five Years with the Allies', pp. 244–5.
88 In a letter home to her family, FANY Phyllis Puckle described McDougall as the most prestigious of all the FANY. She called her 'the Great Panjandrum of all Fannies' and wrote about her in the context of the unit's preparations for McDougall's inspection. She also added: 'Mrs Mac is a most blown-about looking person, not in the least bit smart, and as we had spent a lot of spit and polish on our badges and belts and things we were rather annoyed at the waste of time': Phyllis Puckle to 'Dear Moll' (Puckle's sister), 27 August 1918. [LC]
89 *Gazette* (February–March 1918), p. 3.
90 *Gazette* (March Supplement 1918), no page numbers.
91 *Gazette* (April–May 1918), p. 3.
92 R. Josephine Pennell was a VAD who served as an ambulance driver at St Omer. She kept extensive log books of driving and mechanic duties that are in the Department of Documents, Imperial War Museum.
93 Lecture on Corps History, lecture notes General Course – Grade II (1961), p. 8; www.fany.org.uk (1 February 2003).

6

Petticoat warriors
The French units and the convoy at St Omer
1917–18

The winter of 1917–18, like the one before it, was one of the coldest on record and sorely tried the FANY knack for coping with whatever came their way. Doris Russell Allen, newly promoted Commanding Officer of the French FANY units, reported on these horrendous conditions. The roads were cut up and pitted with shells and the never-ending mud had frozen into huge, often impassable ruts. However she reported that true to their motto, the drivers were not deterred, and, indeed, one ingenious FANY in particular, was both unfazed and creative. On a journey to bring in wounded her car became stuck on the high part of the road where the going was very bad and ice and snow had piled up. 'So', Russell Allen explained, 'having nothing else to use, she took off her petticoat (which she always persists in wearing, presumably for some such occasion) and put it under the wheel, which was then able to get a grip of the road, and she triumphantly finished her journey and brought the *blessé* safely to Hospital'. 'I am afraid', added Russell Allen, 'no amount of attention will restore the petticoat to its wearer'.[1] As always, ingenuity and flair as the basic staples of FANY service carried the day and framed another story central to the FANY legend.

This story is interesting in its illustrations of the ways women might construct self and personal bravery through the appropriation of femininity and its accoutrements. 'Petticoats' (a signifier of genteel feminine domesticity, passivity and dependency and usually considered a constraint against women's claim to masculine terrain) win the day in this most masculine of all public spaces, the battle zone. As Roberts explains in *Disruptive Acts*, 'by reiterating domestic ideals in unlikely contexts, [women] defamiliarized their appearance as absolute, and marked them with their own history'.[2] Refusing to subordinate their experiences to the masculine stories of war, the FANY created narratives from the feminine fabric of their lives and became petticoat warriors: fully militarized women whose experiences were represented through the prism of traditional femininity.

In accordance with such history-making, FANY accomplishments peaked in late 1917 through 1918 and consolidated their organization's reputation and authority. This chapter explores these accomplishments of the FANY driving for the French and those working in the new British convoy at St Omer. It focuses on the sixth theme associated with the renegotiation of gender: the competence and indispensability of the FANY finally as fully militarized women operating independently with authority in masculine space.

Driving for the French

After FANY Unit 6 started work at Amiens on 21 August 1917, they had three weeks of very strenuous work. The full staff of twenty had not yet arrived and they often drove day and night, with over thirty hours of consecutive duty not unusual. The French doctors were laying bets as to when they would give in: a sure way to keep the women at their posts.[3] Driving was difficult since the cars they were given were old and in very poor shape and the hospitals around Amiens had very narrow entrances set at impossible angles that confounded their work, especially at night. Some French male drivers and mechanics (this was true of some British and Belgians also) so resented women taking over their jobs that they tried to sabotage their work by leaving cars in poor shape or refusing to maintain them properly. The men's obstreperous attitude was exacerbated by comments from a male officer who publicly rebuked a male chauffeur, telling him to take a lesson from *ces dames*.[4] Despite these altercations, FANY commitment and competency won respect from the French who were surprised at the way the women maintained the cars, and eventually these successes encouraged the French authorities to replace the ageing vehicles.[5] Daily, Joan Bowles explained, the FANY in Unit 6 were expecting more drivers out from England and were also pleased to receive help from Rachel Gertrude Moseley, Gladys Marples and Muriel Thompson. Despite their being so short-staffed, 'we never failed to send a car the moment the call came in', she said.[6] Their lodgings were also less than comfortable: 'a very large box erected with great triumph and trouble at the end of the long shed'.[7]

The stint at Amiens lasted only six weeks. On 20 September Bowles telephoned McDougall to come at once as trouble was brewing. The problem was that Amiens was located in a region governed by the British General Headquarters, and although the British could not stop the FANY working with the French, they could require they move to a region under French governance. The British needed to give permission for British subjects to enter certain zones and this, apparently, they were unwilling to do.[8] Again we see another example of British antagonism to FANY independence, the consequences of red tape, and perhaps tensions between the Allies. So Unit 6 packed up on 24 September and headed for Villers Cotterets where they hoped to reconstitute and continue work. The journey, like their work in Amiens, was gruelling and relieved only by the compassion of the Scottish Women's Hospital staff who were 'kindness itself', taking in the FANY for several days and helping them rest until they got settled into new lodgings.[9] Unfortunately these lodgings turned out to be a vacant pork butcher's shop: a version of 'settled' not quite what they had in mind. A FANY in Unit 6 described the accommodations:

We really were intensely uncomfortable. Chiefly owing to an entire lack of furniture, an overpowering smell, and the presence of a ghost who groaned and played the violin 'cello all night, he sometimes mysteriously hung a sack over an attic window; it really was a very eerie spot particularly one horrible loft with German writing on the door, the remains of three ropes with slip knots hanging from a beam and some old clothes huddled in a corner.[10]

Although these descriptions of the infamous pork butcher's shop read like figments of an over-zealous imagination, official FANY reports also describe their lodgings as 'unspeakable'. In addition they lament the lack of work for the FANY in this town.[11] In the meantime McDougall was running around dealing with French officials and the London Committee of the French Red Cross, and Irene Cowlin, working with the organizational details at FANY headquarters, was worried out of her mind about the situation. She had to work with a Mrs Watson, Chief Matron of the Anglo–French Hospital committee whom she described as the most disagreeable person she had ever met and who kept putting the brakes on any FANY leaving England.[12] More red tape.

Once all this was sorted out and the FANY drivers were given permission to leave for France, Unit 6 was transferred on to Château-Thierry with seven cars attached to a clearing hospital. McDougall had been prevented from leaving Calais on account of the air raids, but she did manage to arrive in Château-Thierry in time to insist that the new lodgings (two small empty rooms with a little straw in one corner) again would just not do, especially give their experiences at Villers Cotterets. In the usual McDougall way, she insisted until a large, well-furnished house complete with a garden was 'discovered'.[13] Not surprisingly, again the cars provided by the French were in poor shape: some refused to start and those that did were prone to fall apart soon thereafter.[14] However the FANY received a mess and washing allowance in addition to their rations and the French Army issued a goatskin fur coat to each driver.[15]

In contrast, the next new convoy unit, Unit 7, attached to L' Hôpital d'E-vacuation at Epernay and beginning work in late November 1917, was welcomed by the French staff there with champagne, cakes, and bouquets of mimosa and carnations.[16] The accommodations were good: the mess hut and

FANY sleeping cubicles were part of the clearing hospital, there was an out-side kitchen, and the women also had a dug-out as shelter from ongoing raids.[17] Russell Allen described the mess hut as 'very pretty' and lined with white paper over cardboard. They stained and polished the floor and tables and found coloured rugs, 'charming chintz curtains' and a homemade sofa. They even boasted electric lights, greatly adding to their comfort.[18] The original members of Unit 7 were Second Lieutenant Doris Russell Allen and her second-in-command Gwendolyn Peyton-Jones (who eventually took over leadership of the unit upon Russell Allen's promotion), Rachel Moseley, O'Conor, Blacker, Cousins and Shaw. The first two months of work were very hard, again exacerbated by that very bitter winter of 1917–18.

Christmas Day 1917 was so freezing cold that the women of Unit 7 were unable to travel to Port à Binson and take part in the festivities there. They had little time, however, to consider their disappointment, as work came in heavy in January and all their energies were needed to cope with driving in such seri-ously hazardous conditions. The weather was unrelenting with snow and ice covering the inside as well as the outside of their billets. Russell Allen reported that the poor drivers endured many hardships as stoves refused to burn, snow came in through the walls, and the women were frozen through day and night.[19] Joan Bowles of Unit 6 also looked back on the freezing weather and described January as a 'black and bitter month'. The roads were like glass and since they had no chains for the cars, their progress driving was always dan-gerous and erratic. 'It is rather distressing to find oneself unable to mount a hill owing to the icy surface while the wheels whirl round, the engine makes a noise like an aeroplane and a wretched man lies on a stretcher inside the car.'[20] Despite this, she reported, the women did not complain nor grumble.[21] These patriotic values of self-denial and obedience, seen as crucial for maintaining 'King, country and Empire', were heavily inscribed in FANY legend.

As the snow and ice were beginning to thaw in April 1918, the next French convoy unit, Unit 9, was formed. It resided at Châlons-sur-Marne with fifteen cars and drivers under the leadership of Ida Lewis, with FANY Moody (at first recovering from appendicitis at Binson Priory Hospital) as second-in-com-mand. Lewis reported that this unit had none of the welcome nor the cham-pagne given to Unit 7. Our entry, she said, 'was about as humble as theirs was conspicuous. The welcome we received was not even doubtful.'[22] The first sur-prise for Lewis arriving ahead of the other drivers at the end of March was finding the whole convoy either evacuated at night or else underground with the cars moved some distance from the site. These underground night accom-modations for those on duty were in champagne cellars that the women named 'the cave'. Down in the dimness of the cellar were doctors, orderlies, a telephonist and many French families who nightly bundled their valuables into wheelbarrows and went underground out of danger. Lewis wrote that although it was sometimes difficult to sleep and report for duty amidst the wailing of the children from neighbouring cellars, she found it an honour to share the discomforts of these poor French families.[23]

One of the biggest challenges for Unit 9 was dealing with ongoing prejudices against 'lady drivers'. These beliefs were exacerbated by the previous French women drivers who had had minimal training and were required to drive ancient cars that confounded the few skills they had. As a result, these drivers had been the 'terror of the town'. Like the cars in Unit 6, the cars in Unit 9 were in terrible shape and the FANY were appalled. Lewis said the transmission either bounced out of gear or was stuck in neutral: 'Quite a lot of coaxing had to be done with the knee whilst changing speed, whilst as for going into first from neutral it could not be done without rousing the whole neighbourhood!' It was so bad, joked Lewis, that she decided then and there to write to FANY Headquarters and tell them to screen drivers and send her only those accustomed to playing full-sized organs with the foot pedals and stops thoroughly out of order! Despite this, the experienced FANY drivers were soon able to change public opinion and were rewarded with two new cars as well as the responsibility of taking over the garage.[24] When Lewis was transferred to head the new SSY5 mobilizing in London, O'Conor took over as Commanding Officer of Unit 9.

'Strenuous' described work for all French units during the Spring of 1918, as drivers evacuated hospitals, dealt with civilian casualties and endured nightly air raids. Although driving was relieved by better weather, it was complicated by a huge increase in traffic on the shell-pitted muddy roads and many drivers reported witnessing accidents since no lights were allowed at night and men driving reinforcements to the Front worked so incessantly that they would fall asleep at the wheel. A German Gotha plane was gunned down and fell within a half mile of Unit 6's mess, bombs exploding on impact as the plane fell.[25] Unit 7 was similarly engaged with evacuations and carried thousands of wounded from hospitals to waiting trains. Sadly, the women reported, many of these wounded were 'gas cases' where the victims were not only blinded but had their faces paralysed.[26] Much of the FANY's work was done under fire: 'we always have a hail storm of shrapnel all over the hut and garage, as the guns are all round us', explained Russell Allen, adding sardonically that 'a miss is as good as a mile' and 'so the work goes on'.[27]

A FANY in Unit 7 was always on night duty in case of air raids and would drive that shift with three French male orderlies. They all slept in the cellar of a house when not called out and the FANY driver had to deal with the embarrassments and potential improprieties of sleeping in the same room with three men. Irene Ward tells a story about this in *FANY Invicta*; a report on FANY Unit 7 corroborates the incident and names the FANY in question as Rachel Moseley. With her femininity coded through the pink pyjamas peeping through her uniform and having to endure the chivalrous attention of her room-mates, it was a most gendered incident: 'The driver (Moseley) was waved with true French courtesy to the fourth bed, and was told it was really the surgeon's but as he had not turned up she had better have it; she had still not grasped what she was to do if he did turn up! The orderlies in the meantime began to make their preparations for bed, modestly watched by the fascinated driver, sitting bolt upright on the bed until she realized that the top of her boots did not meet her skirt, disclosing the fact that she was wearing her pink pyjamas which in her hurry she had forgotten to cover.'[28] Along with being severely bitten by bedbugs through the night and almost freezing to death, she also had to endure the snoring of the orderlies. The report explains that it was with great relief that Moseley saw dawn break.

This incident is a reminder of the gender transgressions experienced by the FANY as they navigated their service in France. As intimate work with male strangers encouraged encounters considered inappropriate by the standards of the day and the upbringing of the women, war facilitated the breaking of these gendered conduct norms, normalized their experiences, and reprioritized their behaviour. Those at home, however, not exposed to the daily encounters of war but still experiencing this anxiety caused by shifting gender performances were still unsure about women taking on masculine roles and men coming home shell-shocked from their experiences at the Front. As women's role in the war expanded and they were officially incorporated into the armed forces with the establishment of the WAAC, WRNS and WRAF, the public became increasingly curious about these gendered adaptations and reversals and eagerly consumed stories about them. The Women's War Work Committee held an exhibition at the Whitechapel Art Gallery and FANY activities were well-represented in this display with photographs, buttons and badges, and medals and decorations, as well as fragments of shells and the famous aerial torpedo that fell in the camp of the British convoy in Calais.[29]

At the beginning of 1918 the Germans had signed an armistice with the Bolshevik powers in Russia, and the Central Powers under General Ludendorff moved their forces from the Eastern Front to bolster the Western Front. The Allies were suffering from a serious shortage of manpower, especially the French divisions, and British forces were stretched fighting on the Italian Front as well as against the Turks in the Middle East. In addition, US forces were slow to mobilize. However, the German Army was weakened too: the U-

boat campaign had not been as successful as hoped and blockades were causing much suffering among the civilian population. In response, the Central
Powers staged an all-out offensive that began on 21 March and took Bapaume,
Albert and other surrounding towns, extending the German line and causing
the British troops to retreat. Haig, who had been promoted to Field Marshall
in 1917, issued his famous 'Backs to the Wall' Order of the Day that demanded
every position be held to the last man with no retirement and a fight to the end.
French General Foch took over command of the Allied forces and US General
Pershing agreed that US troops, whom he had previously insisted would fight
as an independent army, would be brought into the British and French armies
as reinforcements. During April the Germans won advances along the River
Lys, and in May an advance along the Marne that included a diversionary
attack against the French known as the Third Battle of the Aisne. However,
even though the dearly won Passchendaele Ridge was lost, the British army
was able to repulse an attack against Arras and the centre of Amiens was still
outside German reach. In addition, the German line now had a bulge that
required additional troops to hold its new length.

During May, Unit 7 was faced with the terrible casualties resulting from
this German advance on the Marne and evacuated hundreds of wounded.
Russell Allen almost had her car overturned by stampeding horses terrified by
the noise and violence of the bombing.[30] In one day they worked straight
through from 4 o'clock in the morning until 8.30 at night, carried 500 patients
and filled two trains. Seventeen thousand 'cases' passed through this area in
five days.[31] In addition, one of their more distressing tasks was to take the dead
to the mortuary: a building that was full to overflowing with corpses. There
was a shortage of coffins and some bodies would lie unburied for many days.[32]
Unit 7 also made dangerous runs with medical supplies and personnel to the
Front lines and Russell Allen and Moseley were sent briefly to help at a Field
Dressing Station about three miles behind the line at Chânteuil-La-Fosse.[33]

The evacuations during this very difficult period of the German advance
on the Marne were hindered by the crowds of refugees on the roads as well as
convoys hurrying by with reinforcements and stragglers coming back from the
line after their armies were sent in retreat. FANY drivers wanted to stop and
help refugees or pick up wounded who begged for help: 'It was a ghastly sight
to see them and be able to take so few' wrote Russell Allen. She also wrote
about an attack that wounded scores of soldiers and required their working
constantly around the clock.[34] The next day she continued this report of the
situation at Epernay, hurriedly writing in the short staccato phrases that char-
acterize such rushed narrative about the ghastliness of war. The fighting coincided with the German diversionary attack on 27 May at the Third Battle of

the Aisne which took the French by surprise. 'The wounded', Russell Allen wrote, 'are simply pouring in, in all sorts of conveyances. Hundreds waiting to be received, situation appalling, not enough staff to deal with them . . . wounded lying all over the ground, nothing being able to be done for them until we kept going around and finding the worst cases and trying to get someone to attend to them. It was simply ghastly . . . Several men were absolutely dying unattended – too late to do anything for them . . . There were so many ambulances waiting to be unloaded –sometimes fifty at a time' [orig. ellipses].[35] FANY drivers had no definite hours of duty; they just worked for as long as they could possibly stand and then took brief periods of rest and started all over again. Thousands of wounded passed through in several days.

When the Germans broke through the Allied line in late May and early June 1918, they advanced about ten miles (the greatest advance during the war since trench warfare had begun) and arrived near Château-Thierry, the site already evacuated by the FANY Unit 6 who had moved on to Bar-le-Duc. Unit 7 at Epernay got the order to move out on 1 June. While the staff of the Evacuation Hospital had already left on foot, half the FANY convoy decided to stay until the following morning in order to evacuate any further wounded who might come in during the night. The unit then had about two weeks' rest at Connautre, a small town to the south, away from the fighting and housed in a German prisoners' hut (complete with guards and barbed wire entanglements which the FANY said gave the place 'an air of great distinction'). Here they managed to spend some quality time with the FANY from L' Hôpital Auxiliaire, 76 (Binson) as well as with McDougall and other friends. But in June Unit 7 received marching orders again and travelled on to Sézanne. This evacuation coincided with the new (unsuccessful) German offensive halted by French and US troops at the Battle of the Matz and again the next month at the Second Battle of the Marne.

Once again accommodations at Sézanne were poor and the FANY arrived to find an inhospitable and thoroughly insanitary cowshed that kept them sleeping in their cars until the place had been cleaned and whitewashed. They reported the picnics in their cars with good humour but were glad to see the new shed once the weather turned rainy. With the help of a few straw mats it seemed the mess hut looked most attractive: 'the cross beams and sand floor giving quite the farmhouse touch'.[36] Unfortunately one of the cars parked on a hill above the hut was left without its brake on and came charging down the hill and smashed through the wall of the new mess hut. Other than this, the main problem the FANY encountered was insubordination from French mechanics who refused to work in the open air, neglected the cars and most likely resented working for women. A visit of inspection in July did improve matters in this respect and work continued more smoothly for this FANY unit.[37] In its seven months of existence Unit 7 had carried over 15,000 cases.

Although Unit 9 at Châlons was also very busy during the German advance on the Marne, it was during the French offensive near Rheims in July that the brunt of the work fell on them. They evacuated hospitals, transported patients to hospitals further away from the fighting, and endured incessant night raids. The women longed for a rainy night which might prevent the raids and allow them to have a good night's sleep. One of the unit's drivers, Henrietta Fraser, was driving an ambulance when a torpedo hit in front of the car, killing the orderly beside her and severely wounding her. It is reported she crawled over 200 yards to a hospital to bring help to the wounded men in the car and refused to have her own injuries attended to until the men had been brought in and their wounds dressed.[38] She received the Legion d'Honneur and the Croix de Guerre with palm leaf for her bravery. In addition, her photograph was shown in the cinema and was met with great applause.[39] Corporal Moody and driver Bennett also received the Croix de Guerre for their bravery during this period, as did Peyton-Jones, in charge of Unit 7. They stood in line with French soldiers who were also being decorated and took part in the March Past ahead of the French troops. They were intensely proud of being treated as real *soldats* but nervous as to whether they would be able to keep in step and do 'Eyes Right' at the proper moment.[40] Again these examples of female heroism make a case for a 'women's war' that bends normative gender relations and represents new performances of women's independence and autonomy.

Buoyed by US reinforcements, the Allies decided on a series of counter-offensives and won victories at Albert and Scarpe in August. The Central Powers were losing ground and the morale of the German forces beginning to wane; General Ludendorff looked back on this fighting as the 'black day of the German Army'.[41] Despite this new cause for celebration among the Allies, from the point of view of medical personnel August was a very difficult month. Thousands of gas cases arrived daily; Peyton-Jones described ambulances streaming in all day long and doctors begging the FANY drivers to help them dress wounds and perform other nursing tasks. The situation was most distressing as the wounded were in terrible condition and the building that was accommodating these hundreds of patients reeked of gas. One day alone, 15 August, saw the arrival of 1,400 gassed soldiers. The FANY nursed these wounded through the night even though they had been up since 4 o'clock in the morning driving the ambulances.[42]

McDougall was appalled by the experiences endured by French FANY units. She would leave the Belgian convoy and try to visit them as often as possible to inspect their work and give help and moral support, although often these journeys themselves were fraught with danger. On one occasion on a trip to Châlons, McDougall and 'Moses' (Marguerite Moseley Williams) drove by mistake too close to the Front and were only three kilometres from enemy lines. The Germans saw them and were puzzled by the sight of the women; McDougall and Moseley Williams only barely escaped with shells thundering all around. 'Oh, Mrs Mac', Moseley Williams was said to have exclaimed, 'if I'd gone into the German lines with the Renault what would the Belgians have said?'[43] Another time McDougall and Gladys Marples were on their way to visit the French units when they were attacked by two men, a civilian and one in a Belgian soldier's uniform. Marples shoved a tyre lever into McDougall's hand and watched as McDougall whacked one of the men on the head, stalling the attackers long enough to allow for the women's getaway.[44] Such anecdotes about grave dangers were often reported with humour and helped the women cope with the anxieties of the war; they also invariably served as 'anchors' or 'punchlines' that helped organize the collective history of the FANY.

It was during this intense summer of 1918 that Eveline Shaw, a FANY in Unit 7 at Sézanne, became sick with dysentery. Shaw kept working while she was not feeling well but soon collapsed and was returned to the mess hut in a rapidly worsening condition. Many of the women in the unit were ill at this time too. Phyllis Puckle, newly arrived in Unit 7 in August, recalled many years later that sanitation there was non-existent, thus increasing the possibilities of water-borne infectious diseases: 'There was a raised platform and underneath were enormous tubs and these tubs got maggoty and the smell was awful. This was what we used you see', Puckle said, 'and I suppose they were taken away and emptied from time to time . . . but this was how I should think [Shaw] caught dysentery.'[45] The doctors moved Shaw to the hospital and although she was very weak, she seemed to hold her own. Unfortunately, on 24 August she died. She was buried two days later at the cemetery at Sézanne with full military honours.[46] She was the only FANY who died on active service during the First World War.

The tide was turning for the Allies. US forces under General Pershing were successful at St Mihiel in early September and Allied forces had found victory against the Turks in the Middle East. The climax of the Allied offensive occurred in late September as the British attacked the Hindenburg Line while French and US forces began a new offensive in the Argonne and a mixed offensive of French, Belgian and British units attacked in Flanders. On 29 September the British Fourth Army had broken through the Hindenburg Line and the end of the war was in sight. Despite these victories, September was a dreary month for the FANY working for the French. Bad storms almost blew over Unit 7's mess hut and the cold rain seeped through the walls. Many FANY were ill with influenza and all were tired of being continually cold and wet. After three of their ambulances broke down, the women were relieved to receive orders to return to Epernay. However the old Evacuation Hospital where they used to work was almost completely demolished and they were saddened to find the town destroyed and their housing arrangements in disarray.[47] They were also saddened by the near-constant news of a brother, friend or relative killed in the fighting. Although the FANY were surrounded by suffering and dying and one might think that they would have been prepared for these inevitable deaths in a war that took the lives of so many young men, of course when it did happen they were just as numbed and shocked as if they had never witnessed the horrors of their work in France. When Captain John Allen, Doris and Gerry Russell Allen's brother and Moseley's nephew, died of wounds in a hospital in Rouen, the shock hit the whole unit. Allen had been a frequent visitor to the FANY convoys in Calais and his death was mourned by many.[48]

Casualties also abounded due to the influenza epidemic that raged through the troops. Called the 'Spanish flu' (although locally the FANY called it the 'Flanders grippe') it emerged in the Spring of 1918, peaked in June and July, and was followed by another wave in October and November. Mortality associated with this pandemic was enormous, killing thousands of people around the globe. India was especially hard hit and children and vulnerable adults were particularly susceptible. While some believed this 'plague' was divine retribution against the human actions in this war, the pandemic was fuelled by the aetiology of a virus that stymied scientific pursuit of a vaccine and by the consequences of the war itself: all populations of affected countries were weakened by the effects of displacement, rationing and blockades. On the military front, the squalor and insanitary nature of trench life helped spread the pandemic. Worldwide it has been estimated that at least 20 million people died from influenza.[49]

During October as the Allied advance progressed, the hospitals scattered throughout the southern regions moved up and the FANY driving routes extended in a northward direction to places they had worked during the May retreat and over which there had been fighting during the summer. At the beginning of November a railway connection had been established with Rheims as the railhead and all the French FANY sections drove there. Villages were deserted and the roads still camouflaged, and the FANY found themselves driving long distances across the largely demolished countryside thinking about the toll the war had taken on families and communities. Phyllis Puckle recalled a village named Maurupt which had been taken and retaken by the Germans seven times in 1914 alone and was now being rebuilt. The church spire was broken and houses lay in rubble. Scores of German and French soldiers were buried by the church, still within sound of the guns after four years.[50] This long distance driving took its toll on the FANY ambulances as well as on the drivers. And, through all this, the influenza continued to spread. By the end of October drivers from SSY2 were sent with reinforcements to St Dizier to support several FANY who were already there. Even though the war was almost over, the medical facility at St Dizier was overflowing with influenza patients. Sick soldiers also lined the floors of an adjacent building, dark and streaming with damp. With few resources the overworked staff tried to make do while the men lay mostly fully-clothed (including their boots) on stretchers on the floor.[51]

The end of the war came none too soon for Unit 9, who had been severely tested in October when German bombs struck a cinema being used as a hospital. FANY Crisfield, reporting on the activities of Unit 9, described the ghastly scene. The place was in total darkness and when the FANY attempted to enter the building they were met by screams and groans and found themselves walking over the dead and the wounded who were lying in heaps everywhere. More than sixty men were killed outright and about the same number wounded. Many of the wounded died the next day. It was, explained Crisfield, an absolutely gruesome night.[52] The French units serving during 1917 and 1918 saw some of the heaviest casualties of the war and performed exemplary service under the most dire conditions: making the case again for their place as women and official militarized personnel in the combatants' war. They continued their service through 1918 and into 1919 helping collect prisoners of war and undertaking various kinds of driving duty. We will meet these units again in the next chapter in their work after the Armistice.

A convoy for the British at St Omer

Just as the FANY working for the French endured that terrible winter of 1917–18, so too the FANY in the new convoy for the British at St Omer, established in January 1918, were also negotiating the influx of casualties amidst snow, ice and terrible driving conditions. Roads were often impassable with huge lumps of snow and frozen slush lining the narrow streets.[53] Winnie Mordaunt recalled the differences between her work at Cap Martin in the south of France with its sunshine, flowers, and spectacular ocean views and the dreariness of conditions at St Omer (a cold and dirty camp 'pleasantly situated on a mud-swamp'[54]). Camp consisted of Nissen huts cubicled off into four units with an adjoining mess room with kitchen, office, and bath and toilets beyond.

All rooms formed three sides of a square and across the road was a large parade ground that included a large workshop shed and parking for the rows of ambulances.[55] As already mentioned, there were a number of VAD attached to Unit 8 who worked alongside the FANY.

By April 1918, Unit 8 was officially attached to the British Second Army and by May they were swamped with work associated with the German advance. Commanding Officer Muriel Thompson began her unit report for the *Gazette* with the following words: 'This month's report is a difficult one to write, as most of what one would like to say has to be left unsaid.'[56] She refers here not only to the incessant censoring that removed the details of war from their reports but also to the poignancy and banality of war and the threat of their defeat at the hands of the advancing German Armies. The town was full of refugees 'and men, dead and dying'.[57] During this month the convoy at St Omer worked around the clock evacuating hospitals, driving wounded and military personnel, and, as was commonplace by this point, enduring nightly raids. They worked through various Casualty Clearing Stations, meeting Temporary Ambulance Trains known as 'TATs' and unloading the wounded men who often had to sit with severe wounds in the ordinary train compartments before being transported to the Stations. The men would then receive treatment and be operated on if necessary with orders given for the next stage of their transportation. Some would need to be driven to barges or to properly equipped ambulance trains for transportation to permanent hospitals away from the line or to Calais or Boulogne for a trip home to Blighty. As very little notice was ever given for the arrival of these trains, twenty ambulances were always on duty after 5 p.m. to handle the rush. All their cars were in constant use almost all the time.

Muriel Thompson's diary allowed her to write the unspoken emotional impact of this service. The matter-of-fact logged entries in early 1918 give way to poignant recollections written as essays about misery, suffering and death. Unlike McDougall, and to some extent Waddell, whose narratives tended to be grounded in the sentimental high diction of the Great War rhetoric, Thompson writes with the modernist edge of despair and critique; her narrative almost never contains examples of female heroism and bravery and her descriptions of male bravery involve poignant references to the wastefulness and brutalities of war. This illustrates how literary modernism, successful in subverting and destabilizing the sentimental nonsense of imperialism and the discourse of masculine honour and courage through a focus on death, desolation and destruction, also to some extent closed off women's claim to their own stories in this war, at least stories that utilized their traditional literary heritage. Still, even though a primary focus was on men killed in the context of a world gone mad, women like Mary Borden and Ellen La Motte were able to write of a feminine experience, and Muriel Thompson to some extent does this too. In an essay titled 'T.A.T.s' Thompson wrote about the charade associated with the home front that helped hide the ghastly realities of war during this period in early 1918:

There are thousands of Londoners who have seen wounded arrive at Charing Cross. The police on guard, the arrival platform swept and garnished, the rows of beautiful cars, each with its driver and orderly, the wounded men, all nicely band-aged, each with his little bag, his cleanly, well-cared for look. It used to come back to my mind, when I saw a T.A.T. come in, the contrast – the torn ragged blood-stained uniforms, and utter, utter dead-beat appearance of the wounded men – the makeshift trucks in which they travelled, their blood-stained bandages, sometimes their bare shoulders. . . Many of the wounded are still under anaesthetics, and will be well on their journey before they are fully conscious . . . We looked to the future and thought: 'how long?' How much longer must the procession of pain endure, how much longer must men be mangled, day in, day out – – –. [orig. ellipses][58]

Raids continued through the spring and the drivers at St Omer worked under almost constant bombardment with rumours of an advancing German Army within easy shelling distance of the town. Troops came into town for a couple of days' rest before being sent back to the Front and refugees contin-ued to pour into the area. 'The town is full of refugees', wrote Thompson, 'the most pathetic sight on earth – and the women often wear their best clothes, to save them I suppose. The old grannies sit perched up on carts with fixed mis-erable faces, I pity them most of all. Caterpillars pulling heavy howitzers shake the earth as they thunder along. Umpteen barges arrive, loaded to crisis strength . . . Ambulances passing the camp: dead men in them, and were drip-ping with blood, one with no foot, and one with the bone of his leg sticking out in three places. The men [drivers] were done in absolutely and could hardly sit up to drive and had to go time after time again tonight.'[59] The morning after this report was written the FANY took the remains of the last night's victims to the mortuary, a particularly difficult task because the corpses were not cov-ered. In the meantime, 'Boss' Franklin called up from Calais to see if they were still alive.[60]

By the end of May, Thompson reported that Unit 8 had had one of the most hectic months she could remember. Temperatures were soaring and the night raids (that increased in good weather) almost constant. Although they had days of continuous duty and slept on stretchers in one of the ambulances waiting for the trains to come in, this arduous work was tempered by a won-derful cookhouse staff who set up a buffet camp between the hospital and the train and as the mechanics checked the ambulances, the drivers were fed and sent off armed with a bacon sandwich in case of an emergency.[61] Fortunately, just as their workload reached its peak, the Casualty Clearing Station was moved and the FANY enjoyed some respite in a new camp (with an especially spacious mess hut) in the garden of an old monastery outside of town. The garden was tended by old monks, confused and disconcerted by the noise and activities of war, not to mention the sight of women in uniform camping in their garden and driving and fixing strange machines. One old Brother, reported Thompson, died of shock during one particularly noisy raid. 'He just "went out" with no sign of injury or illness on him.' Shortly after this move, their Nissen huts at the original camp were severely bombed, although later rebuilt. The unit returned to this rebuilt camp in the autumn when the cooler weather and the dampness of the monastery garden made the latter a less desirable place to live.[62]

On the night of 18 May there was a particularly severe raid. Thompson reported that three French officers came to their dug-out and asked the FANY to help with civilian wounded. Bombs were falling everywhere and there was much broken glass, falling bricks, debris and general confusion. The sky was lit up bright as day and the noise from the guns terrifically loud. They helped transport a group of women and children who were severely injured from shrapnel, bleeding profusely and in severe shock. Then they received the order to go to a boulevard where a bomb had caused serious havoc. Thompson's comment, 'This was a sad sight', was understated. One woman had been wounded and her baby killed in her arms and there were many other casualties. And still the night was not yet over. Their next duty was the most dangerous: an arms depot along the Arques Road had been hit. As they approached on the long, straight road to the dump, all that was left was a huge hole accompanied by explosions and flares going up all the time. There had been Chinese workers tending the place and those that were not dead or injured were terrified and in shock.[63]

Sixteen military medals and three Croix de Guerre decorations were given to the drivers of Unit 8 in response to their bravery that evening. These medals were awarded by General Sir Herbert Plumer at his headquarters with the Second Army. They even had tea with the General ('not at all a war-tea', it was reported), proudly accepting his thanks and congratulations.[64] Almost as treasured as these medals were the responses of the ordinary soldiers, who were not only proud of the women's work but were also starting to see women generally in a new light. The FANY functioned as impressive role models, demonstrating that womanhood had no fixed horizon but could be imagined in new (practical and patriotic) ways. One man was said to have retorted that he 'didn't 'old with women [driving]', but since the raid, if any man says anything about the drivers, ''e's for the guard room'.[65] Thompson congratulated the 'senior FANY', the old-timers from Calais who already had three or more years of 'grinding hard work behind them', especially Hutchinson who handled the mechanical work, and Lowson, Mordaunt, Richardson, Freeth and Cant for their stamina and leadership.[66]

Also in May, a large hospital in town was struck and destroyed by bombing. Two of their members, Miss Snyder, a FANY, and Miss Rose, a VAD, were in the Sick Sisters' Ward of the hospital at the time. The floor collapsed within two feet of their beds and in the confusion of the darkness, smoke and fumes that followed the attack, they barely avoided falling into a chasm three stories deep. They managed to find a way to get down and ended up in the mortuary: another shock, no doubt. Rescue parties dug furiously for survivors and the hospital was evacuated.[67] Thompson reported that through the end of May they had no peace and constant bombardments. She was tired, busy and sad. A Belgian Officer offered to take her to Paris and she exclaimed what she would give to go. 'It seems a year since I came off leave – and it's only 2 months', Thompson mused, 'but what a two months!'[68]

When summer arrived, Unit 8 could report that while 'April was a month of rush [and] May was a month of bombs', June had risen to the 'paltry anticlimax of being a month of "flu"' (the same 'Flanders' Grippe that floored the French convoys).[69] Alongside those FANY lying in bed were many pathetic cases staggering around the camp attempting to work while their eyes were streaming and their bodies racked with coughing. Beryl Hutchinson was on leave during this time, and since Thompson was sick with influenza a lot of work fell on Norma Lowson, who instantly became first, second and third in command at the same time. It was suggested that the lull in the fighting during June was because the Germans were down with the 'flu too.

The St Omer unit were recovered enough in August to host and enjoy a visit from HRH King George V who alighted from a Rolls Royce and dazzled them all as he strolled the monastery garden, flashes of gold and scarlet being seen through the trees as he walked. Accompanied by General Plumer, the King met and shook hands with the senior FANY (Thompson, Hutchinson, Lowson and Mordaunt), inspected their mess and offices, and inquired about their work, its dangers and their comforts. FANY legend reports that the King spied a caricature of General Plumer on Hutchinson's office wall and exclaimed 'Plum, Plum, come here. Look how these girls have your picture.'[70]

The day before the King's visit the FANY took part in an impressive service held by the Second Army in commemoration of the outbreak of the war. Several drivers were asked to escort personnel and lots were drawn as to who would be allowed to attend. The service took place in a huge aeroplane hangar with hundreds of troops packed inside. Among those present were about thirty women, with the FANY sitting in the third row. Thompson found the service and the singing in particular very poignant: 'never again', she wrote, 'shall we hear the "recessional" sung by such a congregation, and under such conditions'. And then with blunt honesty that showed her tiredness of this war and its human toil, Thompson described how they went out after the service to watch the troops march past. She recalled watching a review of troops in peace time when 'scarlet and gold shone in the sun, lances flashed, and everything was gorgeousness, and cheers, and colour'. Now here, she reported, there was 'nothing but khaki, no colour, no cheering, no show, just the real thing, tired soldiers just out of real trenches'.[71] As if to illustrate the last gasps of Empire, the King in his shining uniform was the only semblance of colour left.

Later the King visited again and attended another service led by Army chaplains in a large marquée. This time in the quiet of the prayers the distinct sound of a German plane was heard overhead. 'The big congregation seemed to hold its breath, the Padré's voice continued the prayer he was speaking and we all pretended we had not noticed anything', said Hutchinson, adding that perhaps their 'fervent prayers united into an umbrella of protection for the plane flew on its way never knowing that one bomb would have wiped out the King and nearly all his Generals.'[72]

Mechanics under fire

By 1918 almost all the work of the FANY was associated with driving. However in addition to driving expertise, the women also had to be interested in and proficient enough in mechanics to maintain their own ambulances. Born in 1888 in Kew, Surrey, Sara 'Sadie' Bonnell was a dentist's daughter who loved fast motor cars. At 5ft 11in tall she was athletic and especially enjoyed playing cricket and swimming and diving. She had the good fortune to attend Bedales, one of the first progressive co-educational boarding schools in Britain, and excelled in sports. After school she returned home, learned to drive and got her own motor car. She enrolled in the training at the Red Cross depot at Devonshire House in Piccadilly and passed that test in preparation for joining the Canadian Army Service Corps in the summer of 1917. She transferred to the FANY in December 1917 and started work with Unit 8 at St Omer. Even though she was an accomplished driver with a sound understanding of mechanics, all drivers at St Omer were also required to work in the workshop and acquire practical expertise in overhauling and repairing engines before they were allotted an ambulance.

Similarly, Phyllis Puckle who joined the French ambulance Unit 7 in August 1918 after a short stint at a VAD hospital in Shrewsbury, also had considerable experience with automobiles, having spent the first few years of the war as her father's chauffeur and mechanic at their home in Bishop's Castle, Shropshire. The family had two vehicles: a Belsize and a Model T Ford. Unlike Bonnell, Puckle was educated by a succession of governesses, but still had a passion for driving. Despite the fact that her father was opposed to this passion and believed it was no job for a woman, eventually Puckle was able to go to London for a six-week course in driving and car maintenance and pass her driving test. In June 1918 she had seen an advertisement for the FANY and then took two more weeks' training at Devonshire House and passed another test before she was accepted. Puckle described this training as extensive, thorough and practical: 'we were taught to change a tyre, and the knack of swinging a heavy engine without risking a broken wrist by a backfire, also the correct way to lift a stretcher with a wounded man on it and to load it into an ambulance'. This training can be compared to the less extensive expectations in mechanics and driving for FANY at the beginning of the war and reflects their status as fully authorized, militarized personnel.

By the time Puckle arrived in France in August she considered herself an experienced driver, accustomed to bad country roads and difficult wartime conditions. As well as being able to change a tyre, she could also vulcanize an inner tube, decarbonize an engine, and generally cope with the basic ongoing mechanical problems (that often included spontaneous combustions!) associated with these early vehicles.[73] It is difficult to exaggerate just how awkward and monstrous these vehicles were by contemporary standards. As the war progressed, the use of converted private cars as ambulances decreased and the new ambulances were usually large enough for two stretchers with a little passage down the middle and a seat for the orderly at the back. Fortunately, according to Hutchinson, even though they still had to drain the radiators during the cold weather when layers of paper and rugs were insufficient to keep them from freezing, the cars had gentle clutches and most started reasonably well if the driver had the know-how.[74]

Still, despite the relatively extensive training and advanced skills in driving and mechanics expected of the FANY, sometimes new drivers still found they had much to learn on the job. For example, some time after the St Omer unit was first organized, a brand-new FANY was confronted with a car standing in running water with four flat tyres. On being told to get it ready the young woman responded in a timid voice: 'Will I give it a wee sweep out?' The newcomer was taught how to handle this emergency, although the 'wee sweep out' story entertained on its rounds of the units for quite some time.[75] Like the 'big end' story in the early convoy driving for the British, this story illustrates the pride and status the women enjoyed in their knowledge of driving and mechanics. It also demonstrates a realignment of social territory that occurred in their lives and underscores their consciousness as women transgressing gender boundaries who set themselves apart from other women without these skills or intentions.

FANY mechanical expertise by this point also extended to salvaging or 'rescuing' abandoned vehicles for parts or for use. This was how the St Omer unit acquired their Model T Ford. On noticing it stranded down an embankment by the road, the FANY managed to haul it out, pump up its tyres, and tow it home. They salvaged it for parts before reporting its 'rescue' and were relieved to hear its ownership was cause for a bitter debate and their rescue had settled the score. They added new parts, got it running, and added an invaluable second van to the convoy.[76] Their resourcefulness concerning these invaluable spare parts extended to emergency situations too. On one particularly severe raid a FANY and VAD co-conspirator found an Army vehicle that had just been hit, although the part of the car that contained the spare wheel was still intact. They not only safely transferred the stretchers from the remains of the Army vehicle but ever after had an extra spare tyre, invaluable for long runs when a burst tyre was almost guaranteed.[77] While these drivers were recommended for Military Medals for their work that night, their colleagues joked that the citation was incorrect and was really for the theft of a spare wheel.

A key component of the skills of these driver-mechanics was the ability to be unfazed by constant attention to their 'abnormalities' as females who liked machines. Puckle, for example, remembered arriving to relieve other FANY at the French ambulance unit at St Dizier and seeing a FANY wearing ancient gumboots and overalls with a red hanky tied about her head, changing a wheel with an admiring crowd of French soldiers gathered around the car.[78] Since the FANY almost always seemed to draw a crowd, a prerequisite alongside mechanical skills was confidence and self-assurance in the face of doubt and a certain ability to enjoy the quirkiness of the moment. As middle- and upper-class women, they were not only given the opportunity to drive but were also given the confidence to believe it was their birthright.

Yet despite their confidence and competence in working in masculine jobs and their official role as driver-mechanics for the Allies, the women were still painfully aware of the opinions of some of their male colleagues concerning their work. Captain Goff, in charge of the workshops at St Omer, for example, had been 'horrified almost to mutiny' at the idea of women drivers not to mention mechanics.[79] When the FANY had their first engine casualty, they made sure that the car was in impeccable shape before they took it to him: 'We took it into our workshop first and cleaned it until one could almost go underneath in evening dress without mishap', explained Hutchinson. The receiving officer could hardly believe his eyes, their job was completed at once, and the women became 'the spoilt pets of Captain Goff and all his men'.[80] Such an incident illustrates how women had to go the extra mile (as they still do today) compared to men in order to be taken seriously.

Another illustration of the ongoing battle fought by the FANY for respect and credibility occurred in the Spring of 1918 when the British authorities were concerned about the safety of women in light of the threat of a German takeover. Just as the chivalrous British authorities back in 1913 prevented FANY service in Ulster in part because the FANY were seen as vulnerable and in need of protection, so too five years later and with much fine service under the FANY belt, the issue was raised again. Ironically it was genteel intervention and not the evidence of FANY competencies that settled this problem. Hutchinson wrote that they had help from the Duchess of Sutherland, who had moved her Officers' Hospital from Calais to St Omer. 'With her usual skill she fed, soothed and reassured them that both she and the FANY would be capable of evacuating themselves should the need arise, but we were all far too busy to go now.'[81] The FANY still submitted schemes for their evacuation as necessary, reporting one serious panic when the plans included 'Wisque and Wizerne', two piglets that Hutchinson and Lowson had procured to eat the swill left over from rations. The young Staff Officer reviewing the plans had an anxiety attack until it was revealed that Wisque and Wizerne were piglets and not French villages.[82]

In September 1918 the *Gazette* announced the surprising news that Muriel Thompson had resigned. Franklin as Commanding Officer of the British Section of the FANY explained that Thompson's health had suffered from this long sojourn in France and that the new Commanding Officer was to be Beryl Hutchinson. She wrote the formal report of the unit for September and also explained that the call of home affairs was implicit in Thompson's decision to leave, as well as the fact that she was just 'worn out' from her service.[83] It is difficult to glean the personal nuances involved in such a decision from official reports, and, of course, health and home duty were commonplace explanations for personal leaves, transfers and resignations. Thompson had written in her diary back in July that her right arm was very painful after a kick-back starting one of the big ambulances, her left first finger had a splinter festering in it and was very sore, and, on top of everything, she had 'Calais fever and am rotten and hate everyone'.[84] No doubt she was not alone in such private recollections of misery, and within the next day or two (since she was writing about having fun dancing at parties and other amusements) things were probably looking a little less bleak. Nonetheless, the accumulated stress and work took its toll on Thompson's health and spirits and she, more than any other FANY, wrote with the most critical edge about the war and her experiences in it. Thompson would return to help the FANY after the Armistice.

As Allied victories mounted, an agreement was offered to US President Woodrow Wilson that included an end to unrestricted submarine warfare and the German withdrawal from occupied territory. At the 'eleventh hour' (at 11 a.m. on the eleventh day of the eleventh month), the Armistice was signed. Official reports counted Allied dead at about 5 million and the loss of lives among the Central Powers at over 3.5 million. The British FANY Section recorded the end of the war in the *Gazette* graciously, honouring the sacrifice of men and in this public moment deferring to the story of the soldiers' war and its imperial subtext:

November 11 will remain in the memory of all as one of the most wonderful days of our age. From the long, long burden and horror of war it seemed almost impossible that there could be an end: yet all knew, and knew confidently that in spite of everything a victorious end would come, and none were more sure or more hopeful than the members of the Corps who had been privileged to work among the British and Allied troops from October, 1914, throughout these last years.

. . . We FANY would like to take this opportunity to put on record the deep gratitude we feel to the men who have suffered and endured so much that we may live and be free of the unspeakable horrors inflicted on the civilian populations of other less fortunate nations.[85]

The war was over.

Notes

1 *Gazette* (February–March 1918), p. 6.
2 Mary Louise Roberts, *Disruptive Acts: The New Woman in Fin-de-Siècle France* (Chicago: University of Chicago Press, 2002), p. 14.
3 *Gazette* (October 1917), pp. 5, 6.
4 Grace McDougall, loose papers in McDougall collection, undated, no page numbers. [IWM]
5 *Gazette* (October 1917), p. 5; Lawrence Binyon, *For Dauntless France: An Account of Britain's Aid to the French Wounded and Victims of War* (London: Hodder and Stoughton, 1918), p. 110.
6 *Gazette* (October 1917), p. 5.
7 Quoted in Irene Ward, *FANY Invicta* (London: Hutchinson, 1955), p. 65.
8 Report, 'Work of FANY for French Wounded Only'. [FA]
9 *Gazette* (October 1917), p. 6.
10 Ibid.

11 Report, 'Work of FANY for French Wounded Only'.
12 Irene Cowlin to Grace McDougall (27 September 1917); Cowlin to McDougall (3 October 1917). [FA]
13 Report, 'Work of FANY for French Wounded Only'.
14 *Gazette* (October 1917), p. 6.
15 *Gazette* (December 1917), p. 3.
16 Ward, *FANY Invicta*, p. 65.
17 *Gazette* (December 1917), p. 3.
18 *Gazette* (February–March 1918), p. 6.
19 Ibid.
20 Ibid., p. 5.
21 Ibid., p. 6.
22 *Gazette* (June–July–August 1918), p. 6.
23 Ibid.
24 Ibid.
25 *Gazette* (April–May 1918), pp. 3–4.
26 Ibid., p. 4.
27 Ibid.
28 Ward, *FANY Invicta*, p. 66.
29 *Gazette* (August–September Supplement 1918), no page numbers; (September–October 1918), p. 2.
30 Report, 'French Units: First Aid Nursing Yeomanry Corps', p. 4. [LC]
31 *Gazette* (June–July–August 1918), p. 9.
32 Ibid.
33 Ibid., p. 8.
34 Doris Russell Allen, 'Extracts from the Official Diary of Unit 7, 1917', pp. 5–6. [LC]
35 Russell Allen, 'Extracts', p. 6.
36 *Gazette* (June–July–August 1918), p. 5.
37 Ibid., pp. 5–6.
38 Ibid., p. 7.
39 Report, 'French Units', p. 3.
40 Ibid., p. 4.
41 Colin Nicolson, *The First World War: Europe 1914–1918* (Harlow, Essex: Longman, 2001), p. 105.
42 Report, 'French Units', p. 4.
43 McDougall, 'Five Years with the Allies, 1914–1919: The Story of the FANY Corps', p. 232. [IWM]
44 Ibid., p. 274.
45 Transcribed interview, Phyllis Puckle by Peter Liddle (May 1973), p. 9. [LC]
46 *Gazette* (November–December 1918), p. 5.
47 Ibid., p. 6.
48 *Gazette* (June–July–August 1918), p. 7.
49 J. M. Winter, *The Experience of World War I* (New York: Oxford University Press, 1989), p. 195.
50 Phyllis Puckle to 'Dearest Mother' (20 October 1918). [LC]
51 Phyllis Puckle to 'Dearest Daddy' (5 October 1918); *Gazette* (September–October 1918), p. 6.
52 *Gazette* (November–December 1918), p. 7.
53 Muriel Thompson, diary (5 January 1918). [LC]. See ch. 4 n. 25 for Thompson's diary.

54 Thompson, diary (5 January 1918); *Gazette* (March Supplement 1918), no page numbers.
55 Beryl Hutchinson, 'St Omer Convoy', p. 19. [IWM]
56 *Gazette* (June Supplement 1918), no page numbers.
57 Thompson, diary, 'Backwash of the Retreat', undated.
58 Thompson, diary, 'T.A.T.s', undated.
59 Thompson, diary (12 April 1918).
60 Thompson, diary (13 April 1918).
61 Ibid.
62 *Gazette* (June Supplement 1918), no page numbers; (August–September Supplement), no page numbers.
63 *Gazette* (July Supplement 1918), no page numbers.
64 Ibid.
65 Ibid.
66 Ibid.
67 *Gazette* (June Supplement 1918), no page numbers.
68 Thompson, diary (26, 28 May 1918).
69 *Gazette* (July Supplement 1918), no page numbers.
70 Beryl Hutchinson, 'My FANY Life with the Belgian Army', p. 26. [LC]
71 *Gazette* (August–September Supplement 1918), no page numbers.
72 Hutchinson, 'St Omer Convoy', p. 28.
73 Bonnell's service is described in a *Times* article (9 September 1993); 'Recollections of Phyllis H. Puckle', undated, p. 3. [LC] 'The car was getting nice and hot and there was quite a blaze under the bonnet' exclaimed Puckle when her car caught fire unexpectedly: Puckle to 'Dearest Daddy' (5 October 1918).
74 Hutchinson, 'St Omer Convoy', p. 19.
75 Ibid., p. 17.
76 Ibid., p. 20.
77 Ibid., p. 22.
78 'Recollections of Phyllis H. Puckle', undated, p. 3.
79 Hutchinson, 'My FANY Life with the Belgian Army', p. 17.
80 Ibid., pp. 17–18.
81 Ibid., p. 25.
82 Hutchinson, 'St Omer Convoy', p. 24.
83 *Gazette* (August–September Supplement 1918), no page numbers; Hutchinson, 'St Omer Convoy', p. 27.
84 Thompson, diary (8 July 1918).
85 *Gazette* (October–November–December Supplement 1918), p. 1.

7

Esprit de corps
FANY service after the Armistice
1918–19

A central aspect of the motivation to work under gruelling conditions was the thought, however fleeting, that life at some point would return to 'normal' and those things once taken for granted would soon be enjoyed again. However, many FANY found that when this actually happened, their lives had been so changed in the process that things would never quite be 'normal' again. When the Armistice was declared and the FANY really could look forward to enjoying past pleasures knowing their service in France would soon be over, the strong commitments of the women to their work and to each other meant that most FANY reflected on this ending with mixed emotions. Unit 6 Commandant Joan Bowles, for example, expressed her feelings of loss associated with the end of the war: 'It seemed strange at first, never to hear the guns nor the humming of the Boche avions, to go down roads which were no longer under shell fire; life has lost some of its salt and there is a certain flatness in the runs now; no more orders for "*casques* and *masques*", no more being told not to loiter at certain places, but also, mercifully, no more heavy trains of suffering men.'[1]

Many FANY treasured their months or years in the Corps and were happy to return to civilian life: the *Gazette* in late 1918 is full of news of weddings and engagements. But many also felt the loss and recognition of the ending of something most treasured by them: friendship and solidarity as well as fun, independence and adventure. Lillian Franklin spoke for many when she said that 'although all are thankful that this terrible war is over, yet there is a feeling of sadness when one realises how many great friendships will be broken up'.[2]

In this way, although most common was this joy implicit in the end of such a bloody war that had disrupted and taken the lives of thousands of people, many FANY knew they would miss the fun and friendship shared by living and loving together and feared their loss of independence. This is illustrated by the fact that when most of the units were demobilized in 1919 and many FANY returned to England, a substantial number of FANY volunteers stayed in Europe, reconstituted into new units to help with various Civil Relief schemes. These units worked under the auspices of organizations like the Belgian and French Military Automobile Services in Brussels and Paris; the Imperial War Graves' Commission at St Omer; the Service des Blessées et Refugies of the French Red Cross at St Quentin, Maignelay, Mourmelon-le-Grand, and Vitry-en-Artois; the Regions Liberées of the French Army at Versailles and Commercy; and the Leave Club at Cologne. These members were still FANY but did not wear FANY buttons and badges. By 1920 the last of these units was dissolved, though some individual FANY like Phyllis Puckle of the French Unit 7 stayed independently and worked for the American Committee for the Devastated Regions of France until 1922.

When the fighting ceased, a huge area of Europe was left ravaged and desolated, littered with the remains of war. In terms of human trauma it meant homes destroyed by war, hundreds of refugees returning to villages and desiring repatriation, and prisoners released from across the occupied territories. It also meant removing the debris of war that clogged the roads and countryside and bringing some semblance of normality back to the landscape. Not surprisingly, women were very active in these clean-up activities or Civil Relief schemes (referred to by Hutchinson as the 'Great Tidy') and the FANY responded with traditional vigour and enthusiasm to the request to participate. Many FANY saw this opportunity as a way to experience first-hand a crucial moment in European politics: they understood on some level that memories, senses and glimpses of this time were fading and life would soon be transformed. Hutchinson in particular was aware of this and had a keen sense that the FANY were a part of a transitional moment in history. 'We are indeed fortunate', she wrote, 'to be stationed in such a historic spot, and to have had the opportunity of working in one of the most famous areas so soon after it had been evacuated by the enemy'.[3]

Hutchinson also saw this as a unique opportunity for women: 'To the other girls in England who have worked just as much, but who cannot see these things, and who must envy us, I would say the only thing that may reconcile them to someone else having what they want, is for us to appreciate our luck – we do.'[4] Since cleaning up after the activities of war meant picking up the clutter and detritus created by men, it is ironic that women would lend their 'domestic natures' to such societal-level cleaning and be the ones to shoulder a heavy burden of the work and a double irony that they should see this as a privilege. Although through contemporary eyes we hardly see women being allowed into masculine spaces to cater to men's demands as 'good luck', for most women in military service at this historical moment, the perspective was different. The FANY, like other women who had fought to create a space for themselves in the public world, were eager to play their part and do what they needed to do to maintain their role within the constraints of the system. For many it was the opportunity to extend their time in uniform and postpone the inevitable return to civilian life and all its gendered expectations. This return was implicit in the conditions of their service since all along the FANY had made it clear that they were serving to release men for combat duty; when that duty was no longer required of men, inevitably they would be expected to vacate these positions and return to the prewar gendered social order. This was the progress and regress associated with their relationship to the masculine project of war. It was especially poignant for the FANY because, unlike many other female auxiliaries, they were militarized and saw themselves as *femmes soldats* with a history of service alongside male combatants. Ultimately, however, their claim to this service was grounded in essentialized understandings on the part of male authorities of their class and gender as devoted, self-sacrificing women willing to transform the public world according to the moral yardstick of domesticity. Because the FANY colluded in the appeal to femininity and class in their negotiation of this service, it should be no surprise that these very same structures limited their options after the war ended. These ideological structures that ensured these women their trip out to war, as Sharon Ouditt reminds us, 'equally ensured that they made the round trip'.[5]

For the moment, however, the year following the end of the war allowed a brief period when the FANY were still able to enjoy the autonomy granted to them by their role as war workers, yet without the constraints of the war itself to limit their movement and behaviour. Coupled with the release and euphoria associated with the Armistice, this relatively chaotic transitional period allowed them some unparalleled freedoms. And while freedoms would be curtailed as life settled down, still these experiences allowing women to imagine alternative ways of living and working in environments where they were not subject to the naturalized limits imposed on the feminine would have important implications for gender negotiations during the interwar years. This final chapter highlights the experiences of these FANY in the year following the Armistice and focuses on the last theme of the book: the development of solidarity and friendship that encouraged a shared feminine identity. Alongside the exploration of FANY fun and friendships in this transitional time between war and peace, it also looks back at the various FANY units in service during the war and discusses the ways the FANY constructed and enjoyed the *esprit de corps* for which they are remembered.

Although some women (like the 'butterfly chauffeuses' perhaps) must have been disappointed with their FANY lives and returned to England, their stories do not subvert the collective history of the organization. This collective history of solidarity was especially important since it was believed that one of the greatest obstacles for women working in military auxiliaries doing traditionally male work was the inability of women to get along together. A *Vogue* article featuring 'these sturdy girls' of the FANY not only told stories of their heroism and how they worked 'up to their knees in blood, amputating, tying up, bandaging, without rest or relief' but also that their success has 'killed the irritating masculine "gag" that women cannot work together'. It is now 'generally accepted', explained the author, that 'not only can women work with men, but they can work together with remarkable harmony'.[6]

As a result, seldom are there any public reports of FANY misbehaviour, although Muriel Thompson wrote about a couple in her personal diary. One was a FANY defying Thompson 'to her face' that required Hutchinson to see her off for England. Other incidents included FANY drivers taking out the cars for joy riding and a FANY travelling on Army transport against the rules. All were swiftly dealt with.[7] One of Thompson's tasks as Commanding Officer of Unit 8 was censoring for the War Office letters written by the drivers. Reading and censoring their personal letters must have created a most difficult ethical situation for Thompson, and, of course, for a staff that would have been constrained from writing honestly about their experiences.[8] Such censorship provides more insight into the creation of FANY legend.

Despite the flattening of contradictory stories that occurred in order to maintain organizational legends, FANY writing (both public and private) is full of exclamations of friendship and support. Such solidarity established within the FANY was central for coping with the difficulties of their work and helped counter the stress of death at such close quarters. Although cultural myths tended to represent women as competitive and divisive, the FANY reworked these gendered scripts through the reality of their shared lives and by constructing themselves as good comrades. These friendships were facilitated in two ways: first, by their close living accommodations and by the shared aspects of their everyday material lives; and second, by the opportunities the women took to having fun and creating sources of entertainment for themselves and the troops.

A foundation for FANY identity and success was the camaraderie of the women as they lived, worked and played together. No doubt many FANY were attracted to the opportunity of living in the company of other women and to establishing friendships and close intimacies with each other. As middle- and upper-class women they would have been familiar with the gender-segregated spaces of the home, educational establishments and social service organizations, even while these spheres were beginning to be eroded by the early twentieth century.[9] The FANY would also have been able (at least temporarily) to avoid the constraints of marriage and domestic responsibility: some experienced the war as a freedom that postponed marriage; some would have preferred romantic partnerships with women. As already discussed, given the high need for FANY 'respectability' this question of lesbianism is of course completely silent in all FANY accounts of their war service, although one assumes that there were romantic relationships among them.[10] The trial of Oscar Wilde and the negative reception after the war to novels like Radclyffe Hall's *The Well of Loneliness* that had lesbian characters in them would have discouraged this aspect of their public record. The innocence associated with the golden age of romantic relationships between women was being displaced throughout the first few decades of the twentieth century as a result of the work of various sexologists and a push toward the 'modern' companionate marriage, which saw lesbianism or 'inversion' as abnormal and pathological. It behoved the FANY to construct the narratives of their lives and experiences together with great care to avoid censorship and disapproval. Indeed, the heterosexually oriented stories of FANY fun, as already mentioned, were most likely constructed in part to avoid accusations of their being 'mannish lesbians'.[11]

The FANY reputation as fun-loving and glamorous rather than stodgy and prudish had class roots. As an elite organization, they wanted an identity that reflected the privileges of travel, outings, parties and other social occasions of middle- and upper-class women's lives to set them apart from other (perhaps more dreary) women war workers. 'They were such a normal, happy, high-spirited, friendly team', wrote Irene Ward in *FANY Invicta*, adding that their ability to be 'good mixers' made them stand out. 'To be able to "mix"', Ward emphasizes, was 'essential when working in a foreign country.'[12] As an '"art" not easily acquired', Ward is referring to class: their 'good breeding' that taught them certain kinds of social skills and public behaviours as well as fluency in French. These 'skills' of the FANY to organize parties and act as accomplished hostesses familiar with social niceties, and their gaiety and light-heartedness, no doubt had their roots in the parlours, drawing rooms and ballrooms of privileged British families.

In addition, the FANY focus on fun and entertainment was connected to their desire to distance themselves from the subversive New Woman whom Mary Louise Roberts has described as 'bespectacled, bookish, and austere in dress' with a 'Jane Eyre-like plainness'.[13] The FANY had no desire to be associated with the New Woman in the public imagination. Their fun-loving heterosexuality-oriented identity was at odds with the 'cultural weight' of the New Woman. Of course the sexual anxieties associated with the New Woman meant that she might just as easily acquire a sexually promiscuous, smoking-in-public type of identity as a frigid one, although the FANY were more at risk of being accused of the latter than the former.[14] Beryl Hutchinson, for exam-

ple, once exclaimed that the FANY had proved gentlewomen could do pro-
ductive work without being seen as a 'convent school'.[15] Still, such gender
instabilities meant they had to tread carefully as they fashioned themselves in
unconventional ways. This negotiation was a skilled gendered performance,
shaped from cultural material at hand.

The British units

The FANY working for the British in Calais with Unit 3 celebrated the
Armistice early as word ran through Calais on 10 November that peace had
been signed. Ships sounded their sirens, trains whistled and cars honked and
'everyone went mad'. Several bands turned out and the FANY helped light a
huge bonfire in the park, dancing around the flames.[16] Lillian Franklin
described the merriment:

British, French and Belgians, attracted by the glare, all came and sang the national
anthem, cheering wildly, while Mrs MacDougall [sic] and one or two of her girls
came up and joined us. A little later a deputation of French people arrived, bearing a case of excellent port, which they explained our French landlord had
instructed them to bring round to us, should Peace be declared while he was away.
Of course, we invited them in, and toasts were drunk with much singing of the
National Anthem. Altogether it was a very merry evening, and when we learnt the
next morning that it had been a little premature, we felt that we did not much care,
as we had all been thoroughly cheered up, after the strain of the last four years. Yesterday, of course, the Armistice really was signed, and although everyone again
rejoiced, somehow it was not like that first night.[17]

The FANY drivers at St Omer also rejoiced with much merrymaking.
Before they had too long to contemplate peace however, they were asked to
send two cars and three drivers to an outpost at Poperinghe and their workload actually increased. Tasks included transporting medical personnel to various sites, evacuating sick to regional hospitals and helping clean up devastated
areas. Another outpost at Hazebruche was also established. Here Hutchinson
described the discovery of dud shells, bombs, packets of cordite and yards of
wire that lay in the rubble alongside field telephones and other artifacts. The
roads, as always, were terrible: 'On a dry day with an ordinary shell hole',
explained Hutchinson, 'it is possible to go on the slope, get into first gear, and
drive out of it'. On a wet day, however, this was impossible and the car would
sink in, its wheels burrowed into the soft earth. 'Then a jack would be out of
the question and the only alternative involved digging and planks on a tow
rope.'[18] Hutchinson wrote about a typical journey from the outpost to St Omer
that illustrated the conditions of their work:

The first twelve miles passes quite quietly, it is a really good cobble road, then you climb the long hill into Cassel and always there is either fog along the road and you climb in to the star light, or vice versa, you creep through the town with its head-quarters flags fluttering from every window and its big staff cars with their lamps lit, all ready and waiting . . . then comes as twisting and greasy a bit of road as you can find anywhere. You play with your front wheels and proceed the whole way with your heart in your mouth, and a prayer that you shall not meet any lorries, here in their one haunt there are strings of them, often one or two ditched and the others waltzing about in the slightly drunk way as yourself. At the seventh mile from home, you pass over a bleak and windswept bit of moorland, and after that you meet no more traffic. On your right the road is nicely sheltered by camouflage, if you have any imagination you think of the Boche shelling it, and drive extra quick past the entrance to the fields – if you are a practical person you are thank-ful for the shelter from the wind.[19]

Their work at the outposts was described as strenuous but interesting. Overall, while the Armistice of course changed the conditions of work for the St Omer unit (as Hutchinson wrote, 'the Boche has gone for good this time so everything is worth while'[20]), the workload itself continued and they were as busy as ever. In addition, Hutchinson reported that one of their new tasks was to provide transportation for nurses who were touring the battlefields in the Boulogne area. This tour hoped to show nurses the conditions under which their patients had lived and fought. Lowson and Hutchinson were part of the excursion to map out the tour and Hutchinson recalled with much sadness the way old battles were reworked over picnic lunches. Arguments would break out between Infantry and Staff on reaching a spot where the Infantry had lost countless men and the Staff Officer might say: 'You were told to make X yards and you did not wait', or 'Why did you . . . when the orders were for . . .'. And so on. Hutchinson explained that they were supposed to go on to the Somme but she personally decided against it: 'it was just mud ploughed by a giant's plough which had run amok'; there was 'no central point one could show'.[21] Death and desolation were everywhere. Nonetheless, after a guidebook was written for a route starting at Ypres and the Menin Road and on south to the Somme, the 'avalanche' of Sisters began. These nurses usually started the day in jovial good spirits as befitted a day's outing; they tended to return in a much more sombre and wiser.[22]

Muriel Thompson, ex-Commanding Officer of Unit 8 who had resigned in September 1918, returned to the convoy briefly after the Armistice. She recalled seeing the desolation of the countryside along the Menin Road and through Hell Fire and Shrapnel Corners and was very moved by the pain and sorrow associated with this area: 'It is quite impossible for me to describe the desolation of the scene. The poor trees hurt very much; their heads gone and all looking indescribable wrecks, or else, just stumps. On the Menin Road we found a whole herd of abandoned tanks. They were on each side and were sinking slowly into the morass which is caused by immeasurable shell holes filled with water. This makes regular lakes in places.'[23] Hutchinson made these runs across the French countryside too, although her take was a little more optimistic as she saw the stumps of trees in No Man's Land starting to sprout leaves again. Driving away from the Front line, the trees increased: 'How hopeful the world seemed to be with the young greenery and the fruit trees which lined so many miles of the road, in full blossom. Surely', she wrote, 'all the sacrifice and effort and ugliness must have been worthwhile'.[24]

As Hutchinson reflected back on her service she wrote that her account of her FANY life failed to portray the most important aspect of all: 'the pure comradeship' between all personnel 'with whom one shared the conditions, the life of dedication. We may have been naïve, lived with illusion; we did not say the actual words, but we all had the feeling that we really were keeping the world fit to live in, that our many sacrifices had been worthwhile.' This sense of solidarity, comradeship and service to the Empire is broadened here to include 'every man and woman, senior General, to FANY Bugler, to aged and wobbly men Base Detail stretcher bearers'. With them all she reported a sense of shared commitment and sacrifice, buoyed still by the patriotism implicit in such service.[25] The real comradeship for Hutchinson however, as for most FANY, was with each other. They stuck together and they lived, loved and laughed together. A shared identity of being unique and special developed from these experiences as well as from the shared class privileges that had shaped the organization from its inception. This comradeship rivalled the experiences of male combatants and facilitated the development of a parallel war experience for women. While as Graham Dawson reminds us, scenarios of male camaraderie tend to be set apart from the imagined world of domestic femininity,[26] the FANY used the tradition of women's middle- and upper-class domestic communities to build a collective feminine identity. Ironically, however, as Hutchinson goes on to make the case for male comradeship across class lines (and establishes once more the FANY privileged identity) in describing 'the butcher's boy and our own brothers' going through this war together,[27] she does not comment on the lack of feminine solidarity across such class boundaries for the very reason that it was the exclusive traditions of women's middle- and upper-class communities that helped found that solidarity in the first place.

The St Omer FANY working at the outposts had comfortable billets and were also greatly appreciated by the local personnel. Indeed, it seems that no women had been stationed in the Poperinghe area for a very long time and so they were quite a novelty, especially since they used their rations carefully and possessed such signs of civilization as silverware and a tablecloth. They had frequent invitations to dinner with 'bring your knives and plates and tablecloth (it was the *tablecloth* [orig. emph.] that was really wanted!)' explained Hutchinson. They each took turns 'in being the "Martha" and [did] all the housework and cooking for the day'. Since they drew rations and did the best they could with them, they got 'more or less a variety as each girl in turn fancied herself in some special branch of cooking'.[28] Back at St Omer the mess had had been updated with heavy green curtains dividing various spaces and the addition of a brick fireplace on which they burned logs stolen from their various travels.[29] They congregated here or in their tiny cubicles drinking coffee, smoking cigarettes and listening to the gramophone, and attended the cinema whenever they could.[30] Although smoking cigarettes in public (a sign of feminine rebellion and degeneracy) was against Corps rules, many smoked like chimneys in private. They also had acquired six new baths all with running hot water supplied by a new boiler. This was their biggest treat and 'only those who have had to carry every drop of water from a field boiler to a bath can realise our joy'.[31] In this way, the everyday living and working together helped bring the women together and encouraged them to appreciate each other.

Back in November 1916 the FANY of Unit 3 had acted on their appreciation of each other's small material pleasures by holding an 'auction' to help a fund-raising effort for the prisoners of war fund. As was common among women's local voluntary corps in Britain, the FANY had 'adopted' several Belgian prisoners of war and were always requesting donations to be able to send them parcels and so forth. As Norma Lowson explained to readers of the *Gazette*, everyone took the keenest pleasure in breaking the tenth commandment, 'thou shalt not covet thy neighbour's goods'. 'We all decided', she said, 'that there was nothing we wanted so much as so and so's china vase, and that old bird's silk handkerchief.' Small personal possessions were auctioned off and the women tried to outbid each other in acquiring a series of dubious trinkets and items.[32] Such amusements helped build solidarity among the women and raised funds.

Christmas was an important time for the FANY and they always planned something special with a tea or dinner and dance alongside church services. For the FANY of Unit 3, Christmas 1916 included a fancy dress party that resulted in various odd costumes, reflecting no doubt their desire to wear something other than khaki. Waddell went to this Christmas event as a model from a *Vie Parisienne* cover, complete with the bodice of her dress made of crinkly yellow paper and a chrysanthemum in her slicked back hair 'in the latest door-knob fashion'. Someone went as a magpie with a white towel draped over black garments and another as a 'charming two-year old'.[33] This is reminiscent of another fancy dress party in 1917 when McDougall borrowed a French officer's uniform and gave one of the doctor's assistants, a nun, a terrible shock at seeing a rakish officer emerge from McDougall's room. 'I do not blame her', exclaimed McDougall, 'my moustache was a *tour-de-force!*'[34]

The FANY at St Omer also enjoyed many opportunities for parties, dances and other social engagements during the war. Muriel Thompson wrote about the 'hops' or dances in her diary and the poignancy of dancing with officers about to go back to the Front: 'one wanted to laugh and cry all at once'.[35] Everyone, it appears, was crazy to dance and relieve the misery and tensions of this war. Thompson recalled dinners at a local hotel where the service was vile and the lights kept going out but where they would desperately laugh their way through dinner and cope with matches stuck in bits of bread. We have seen that community for the FANY in Unit 8 included a number of VAD attached to the convoy. Even though the FANY set themselves apart from, and often above, the VAD, they integrated fairly well and friendships developed between the women. On April Fool's Day, for example, the drivers decided to play a joke on Thompson and came to roll call dressed in each others' uniforms (the FANY wearing VAD uniforms and vice versa). Despite the fact that Thompson called their bluff by responding in a very serious tone that personnel would be shot at dawn as spies if found wearing uniforms not their own, the women used such incidents to build community and solidarity.[36] When the VAD were forbidden to dance at the local YWCA hut, the FANY got around it by allowing the VAD to dance in their (the FANY) mess right next door.[37] And when news came down that Miss Crowdy, 'Queen of the VAD', wrote to Thompson proposing the VAD be moved from the convoy, the reaction was tears and a series of petitions initiated by the VAD that they be allowed to stay.[38]

Entertainment for the St Omer FANY included sports races that helped build solidarity among them. The competitive FANY tug-of-war team won a 'glorious' victory over a team of New Zealand nurses who had offered the FANY a challenge. The FANY were fastidiously coached for this event by a Sergeant from the Australian division who probably had his own rivalries going with his fellow mates from New Zealand. An Australian Advance Hospital had arrived at St Omer and the New Zealanders had a Base Hospital about five miles outside the town. In turn the FANY challenged these and other local women personnel to a sports meeting and there were some exciting moments with various high-ranking British military personnel judging events like the high jump. The unit also enjoyed a 'charming bathing pool' that gave much respite during the hot late summer weather. Rafts and a rope were provided as safety precautions for those women who could not swim. Finally, riding was another activity always seized upon by many FANY volunteers. They worked with the French Cavalry and arranged to borrow their horses at the large indoor riding school at St Omer four afternoons a week as duty allowed. It seems that the VADs were not allowed this equestrian opportunity until Hutchinson requested that the invitation (just like the dancing opportunities) be extended to them too.[39]

A key aspect of the FANY *esprit de corps* was the 'social outreach' or entertaining they fulfilled in the places where they worked and lived. Even at the outposts after the end of the war, for example, the FANY of Unit 8 made a speciality of afternoon tea and soon got quite a reputation in the neighbourhood, entertaining visitors and providing some fun in the town.[40] Back at the bases in Calais and St Omer the FANY of Units 3 and 8 were well known for their entertaining, both the teas and other get-togethers, as well as the more formal entertainment for the troops and fund-raising concerts.[41] 'Formal' was perhaps a misnomer since they had little time for rehearsals, and performances tended to be impromptu events that were constantly interrupted by the arrival of casualties. Rehearsals usually took place in the back of an ambulance and the shows were performed in draughty tents.[42]

Despite this, Unit 3 called themselves 'The Fantastiks', wore a black and yellowy-orange pirouette costume with bobbles, and were in great demand both during the war and after the Armistice. Pat Waddell was a member of the Fantastiks before her accident and played the violin for the group. She also played in church services for the troops. Edith Walton remembered the Fantastiks as a rather amateur production that soon passed the awkward stage and developed 'a degree of slickness neither expected nor imagined possible'.[43] A big part of the act was the parody of popular songs of the time with new words substituted. Mordaunt and Quin wrote new words for Unity More's 'Clock Strikes Thirteen' referring to their endless work hand-cranking the cars: 'Wind, wind, Oh what a grind! / I could weep, I could swear, I could scream, / Both my arms ache, and my back seems to break / But she'll go when the clock strikes thirteen'.[44] This always got a laugh.

A typical evening performance by the Fantastiks would begin with a chorus of original words to the opening music of the 'Bing Boys' that went like this: 'We're the Fantastiks, and we rise at six and don't get much time to rehearse, so if songs don't go, and the show is slow, well, we hope you'll say it might have been worse.' The opening act was often violin solos by Waddell, followed by a humorous recitation by Norma Lowson or Betty Hutchinson, and then a chorus song of 'Picadilly' performed by the Fantastiks. Then Dicky Richardson might read several stories again followed by the Fantastiks performing 'China Town', sung in the dark with lighted Chinese lanterns. The 'Clock Strikes Thirteen' duet would inevitably be next, perhaps another violin solo, and then the show would close with Winnie Mordaunt singing 'Au Revoir', all the Fantastiks doing the 'Kangaroo Hop' wearing fur coats and various animal masks, and then the singing of the national anthem. Refreshments would be served after each performance.[45]

These shows were usually performed in front of a large white linen sheet upon which the women had appliquéd big black butterflies fluttering down to a large sunflower in the corner, whose petals matched the bobbles on their costumes. Waddell recalled that one of the best shows they ever did was for the Motor Transport Department, when they included a ventriloquist stunt in the performance. Despite the fact that it was rather impromptu and barely rehearsed, Waddell appeared clad in bowler hat and Charlie Chaplin moustache with Dicky Richardson as the doll. Richardson managed the glassy stare, had round shiny patches of red on her cheeks, and wore a hospital gown. The skit was improvised from a concert party put on by Lena Ashwell. The funniest part, said Waddell, was that Richardson spun around on her stool and showed the audience Waddell's lines taped to her (Richardson's) back and said, 'the bloke's got all the words on my back!' This seemed to have brought the house down, helped by the fact that the audience had seen the 'real thing' several weeks earlier at Lena Ashwell's performance.[46]

The FANY of Unit 8 were also performers. They called themselves the 'Kippers' (a play on their symbol the red herring) and wore the old FANY pierrot concert costume of the Fantastiks but with a touch of red and the company sign of the red herring on the front of their hat complete with red pompoms. They claimed to be the first 'entirely girls' concerts ever given in a Casualty Clearing Station.[47] On one occasion after the Armistice, Unit 8 was graced with a visit by HRH Princess Mary. Norma Lowson, who was scheduled to meet her, had not had time to change out of her 'Kipper kit', and, the story goes, to everyone's amusement (including the Princess's), the reception occurred with Lowson in costume.[48] This story about Lowson in the Kipper costume quickly became a FANY staple retold in both private and public accounts. Its popularity is based upon several key aspects of FANY identity crucial to the FANY legend: spontaneity, flair and confidence in the face of authority. The subtext of the latter of course is social class: 'confidence' is synonymous with the comfort and familiarity these privileged young women felt during a visit with a member of the royal family; a comfort that even extended to being able to handle it dressed in Kipper kit. As late as January 1920 the *Gazette* reported that the Kippers were still in good form and provided entertainment over the New Year giving a public show and raising some funds.[49]

These concerts were central for constructing a narrative about the FANY that underscored their flair and pizzazz.

When not performing, the FANY were often invited to troops' shows where they would sit in the front rows with the officers and other military officials. Walton remembered these shows as quite hilarious with a choice of programme depending upon whether 'ladies' were present or not. All versions of this entertainment included nostalgia and sentiment with 'roses around the door and songs about home and Mother'.[50] Such outings allowed opportunities to meet officers and by all accounts, quite a few FANY met their future husbands at these various venues and were married during or right after the war. The FANY called these men their 'pursuitors'. 'No one by the way', insisted Pat Waddell, 'ever got involved sexually – we were put on our honour not to let the Corps down and were extremely innocent about most ordinary sex matters. A kiss was as far as anyone went!'[51] As already mentioned, there were few written rules for the FANY but these rules could not be broken. If not on duty and if granted permission, they could leave camp and dine out in pairs one a week, but had to be home by 10 p.m. An unwritten rule associated with their class standing was that they would only accept invitations from officers and not become too friendly with ordinary soldiers.

The FANY created a semblance of 'Society': used to entertaining and being entertained, they asserted their class position through a focus on social pleasures. Given their class connections, the FANY were also in demand by British authorities to play hostess to visiting VIP guests. Hutchinson recalled one such event when she and Chris Nicholson were asked to facilitate a dinner for an important guest at a fancy hotel in Calais. Things did not go quite as planned since Hutchinson had been on duty, had had car trouble and found herself late, and the room at the hotel where they were to dine also contained a huge double bed. As usual, the story crafted by Hutchinson about this event highlights FANY spontaneity and their ability to remain unfazed under any circumstances.[52] No doubt these skills were exactly those that the authorities sought when choosing the FANY for such tasks: social graces, 'good breeding', and an ability to meet any occasion unperturbed.

As the FANY were relied upon for certain duties, they in turn made use of their close connections to military authorities to facilitate travel and entertainments when off-duty or on leave. For example, many FANY took advantage of their one day of leave a month and in true yeomanry fashion went in search of horses to borrow, enjoying many a glorious gallop along the Calais strand. There were veterinary camps along the coast at Peupelinge and the women appreciated the opportunity to exercise the horses there. McDougall recalled one such ride that was 'the best day in the war' on a jumping course specially designed by the Belgian Cavalry. The Colonel in charge had to take along twenty-five men from his own troop as an excuse for the 'training' ride. 'I kept my place the whole afternoon', exclaimed McDougall, thrilled that the Adjutant ('a real woman-hater') told the Colonel he had never seen a woman ride so well.[53] During the late autumn of 1916 when the 'push' associated with the Somme was slowing down and weather prevented major fighting, the Rifle Brigade who were resting at Calais before going back up the line organized a series of beach horse-races, including of course, a 'Ladies' Race' just for the FANY. Some British officers had their polo ponies with them and lent these horses to the FANY to race. There was much betting and hundreds turned out as spectators. Dinah 'Heasy' Heasman, a very accomplished rider who had won many events before the war, was the winner, with McDougall second, and Waddell and Mordaunt tied for third place.[54]

During other relatively slow periods for the FANY working with the British, several women had taken up fencing and went once a week to a local fencing hall where lessons were taught by famous Belgian and French fencers who were stationed nearby. Jimmie Gamwell was an especially accomplished fencer and always gave the masters a good run for their money. Waddell also tackled one of these fencers at boxing and sent him reeling against the wall, winded. Waddell said he came up laughing and always fled from her in mock terror when he saw her in the street.[55] McDougall wrote of one trip to the Front where she was able to shoot into the German lines and enjoy a fencing round or *assaut* with the Comte de Meeus. 'It was great fun', she declared, 'with the guns booming all round and shaking the doors and windows.'[56] In this way the FANY loved constructing themselves outside of the box of ordinary expectations for women. These comparisons helped found their identity and helped build solidarity and comradeship.

After the Armistice, despite the continued work for the St Omer unit through the winter of 1919 and the creation of a new outpost at Marquise with the Royal Air Force in January headed by Mary 'Molly' Marshall, Unit 8 prepared for demobilization as Spring approached. At about this same time the British convoy Unit 3 in Calais was disbanded too. Franklin shared the numerous letters of thanks and regrets this unit received on their departure from Calais and explained in her closing report that the skills and high regard of the FANY drivers had resulted in many requests for their continued service in France. Hutchinson and Lowson from St Omer went to Cologne to make arrangements for the disposal of supplies and equipment and there had dinner with General Plumer in a beautiful home overlooking gardens and a glimpse of the Rhine.[57] But Hutchinson's work was not yet over. She worked with Franklin to supply drivers from the demobilized British convoys to take over work of the Touring Car Section at Boulogne under the auspices of the British Red Cross, and begin service with the Imperial War Graves Commission taking relatives to gravesites and battlefields. By the end of June 1919 this work was mostly finished and the drivers' active service was over.[58] Lillian Franklin again spoke for many when she wrote the following in 1920: 'there are many among us to whom this order is a welcome relief, yet there is a great spirit of sadness in the thought that we shall soon be leaving for good the little camp that has been our home for the last three years, and also the comrades whom we have learnt to know so well and to appreciate so much. However, it had to be, and as it means the fighting is over, all is well.'[59]

The French Units

A few days after the Armistice the much-lauded and well-equipped Unit 12 (SSY5) arrived from London and made its way via Paris to Nancy. These FANY arrived in Nancy on a cold wet evening only to discover they were to be billeted in a German concentrated soup factory. Unfazed, it is reported they managed to attain 'a fair measure of comfort' even though some had their beds among the machinery. Work involved taking influenza patients and supplies to the various hospitals and depots as well as driving around former German territory with personnel who were assessing the damage to devastated villages and roads. They also helped with repatriation and the task of dealing with refugees pouring into town by train and by foot.[60] The numbers of refugees increased over the New Year and by January 1919 this unit had ten cars on duty every night to meet the refugee trains and would move 700 to 900 people in one shift. Very often, explained Rachel Moseley, the refugees came with all manner of belongings, and animals as well as small children. 'A sheep, big dogs, animals and birds of all descriptions' arrived; 'one began to wonder', she said, 'if one were helping to repatriate a zoological garden as well as a Babies' Home'. Many refugees arrived with tiny babies; once Moseley was shocked to hear that a driver had been handed a bundle and was about to throw it down onto the pavement when a tiny squeak revealed a baby inside. 'This sort of thing rather upsets one's nerves', she said.[61] In February 1919 SSY5 was demobilized and the cars driven to Compiegne where eight drivers stayed to help with Civil Relief work. These drivers kept their identity as FANY Unit 12 and their Civil Relief efforts were led by FANY officer Lee-Barber.

November 1918 found Unit 7 leaving for Châlons-sur-Marne. After a couple of days with all the personnel of the combined FANY units SSY2 and their kit living together in a mess hut at Châlons, and several more 'nightmare' days packing all the consolidated supplies, bedding, furniture and personal

belongings, they left Châlons and headed for Nancy on their way to Strasbourg. Their role here was driving for the various hospitals and helping mobilize the return of hundreds of prisoners crossing the Rhine from Germany.
Work included retrieving prisoners from various camps and transporting
them to area hospitals. Very often the Germans just opened the prison camps
and let the prisoners go, and, as a result, former prisoners walked miles, sick
and starving with few clothes and inadequate or no footwear. Many died along
the way because no provision was made for them.[62] The FANY's job was to collect these prisoners or intercept them on their journey to Strasbourg. The
prison camps were terrible places and shocked the FANY beyond belief, even
though they were hardened to the horrors of war by this point. McDougall
shared the following description of a Russian camp visited right before the
Armistice:

There were jobs to take doctors to the camps of Russian prisoners left behind by
the Germans, but dear God! That was hell let loose on earth. These starved, ema-
ciated, wolfish creatures were animals, not human beings, and their cries and gestures and bestial ways made the girls turn sick. The climax came when one girl
thoughtlessly tossed them a packet of sandwiches, which she could not eat in front
of these tortured, hungry eyes. The whole mob was on the food and almost on *her*
with claws that dug feverishly for crumbs – with lips that shrilled for more.[63]

Phyllis Puckle (who, as we have seen, had joined Unit 7 in August 1918)
wrote home to her family about the departure of SSY2 from Châlons and the
journey to Strasbourg. She described the long stream of cars laden with lug-
gage, furniture and supplies that managed the winding winter roads relatively
well but slipped and stalled on some of the hills causing cars to back into each
other. They continued on to Strasbourg, driving through beautiful hilly country dotted with pinewoods and castles; then, by contrast, they passed into No
Man's Land with its characteristic war-ravaged desolation and despair. The
landscape was littered with anti-tank barricades, camouflaged roads and
trenches in every direction they looked. As they continued on their way they
saw signs for villages written in German and it must have finally sunk in that
this war was over. Puckle wrote about the blackened trees, remains of villages
and huge shell holes, as well as the sensations of picnicking in a place where
only two weeks earlier a German gun had been firing. Her descriptions of
these experiences carry the naïve genteel air of 'jolly good fun' and 'topping
adventures', recorded in letters home that are meant to entertain and amuse as
well as connect with family. Puckle missed the agonies of war experienced by
more veteran FANY and perhaps because of this her uncensored accounts
come across as more naïve and often quite flippant.[64]

Puckle reported that since the FANY and their attachments were the first British to go into this region, their reception was cool and in one instance small boys hurled stones at them. However, while the unit needed to be guarded by sentries at night, Puckle said that most people were considerate and allowed them to do their work. She found it 'horrid' to hear German spoken everywhere in Strasbourg and described the local children as 'horribly Hun-like in their manners'.[65] Of course the children, like the whole town, were starving since almost no food had been able to get to the area in over a year. The FANY tried to bring back supplies of food whenever they could on their trips to retrieve prisoners; sardines were a common item and Puckle recalled never again being able to look a sardine in the face after this stint at Strasbourg. She felt sure the sardines she had eaten stretched easily from Dover to Calais. Other than sardines, the women lived on bad coffee and hard army bread that was inclined to be mouldy.[66]

During their journeys retrieving prisoners, the FANY drivers were also able to witness celebrations associated with the reunion of Alsace-Lorraine with France, and, on one such occasion involving high-ranking British military personnel, the women watched from a window and cheered at troops going by. Puckle recalled they were quite hoarse by the time General Douglas Haig passed through and made such a noise that he looked up and gave them an enormous salute. As a result, the rest of the procession thought the FANY were VIPs and gave them salutes and recognitions too. Puckle exclaimed that one officer was so thrilled to see the FANY he almost fell out of his carriage.[67] That very same afternoon they saw the Grand Review of Troops in the Place de la Republique that had formerly been called Kaiser Platz and declared it a most magnificent sight with the Alsatians parading by in their beautifully decorated costumes and head-dresses.[68]

In Strasbourg, SSY2, now consisting of thirty women, inhabited a large, comfortable villa complete with double windows, central heating, a grand piano and two bathrooms, whch had been the headquarters of General von Falkenstayn.[69] One wonders what the intrepid Sister Wicks would have thought of the FANY living in this luxury. But still the women had to cope with the perennial problem of 'unwanted guests' and Puckle hastily ended one of her letters declaring she had to catch one such pesky flea that had been jumping around on her bed for several days. Some of the women were also tired of wearing khaki, especially when it had been worn for months without cleaning and was stained and dirty. Puckle described evening engagements when she managed to borrow one clean item from each of her friends to put together a uniform that was presentable.[70] The women often shared clothes with each other. Many evenings off-duty were spent with colleagues in their pyjamas so that a friend on a date might wear the few clothes they had.

Puckle spent that first Christmas after the Armistice both missing her mother's cooking and the festivities of home and relishing in her new-found freedom and friends. Some days before Christmas her unit hosted a fancy dress party and Puckle's friends Davidson and Smith had her stand on a chair while they arranged a curtain around her, deciding whether she should be 'Aladdin' or 'Rebecca at the Well'. Eventually they hit upon her transformation into a 'High Caste Balocchi' complete with baggy trousers, rubber boots, red cummerbund, and a rug on her head. It was, she announced 'très chic' and stood out against the rest of the FANY whom she described as dressed either as tissue paper ballet dancers or Arab sheiks. However, the costume turned out to be a little hot for dancing in, especially, Puckle explained, around the head and feet! Puckle wrote to her father that this fancy dress dance had been quite a success despite the fact that the guests had tended to sit together in a bunch and let their hostesses (the FANY) dance with each other. But dinner had been good, she explained, with *pâté de foie gras* and iced cakes and tarts.[71]

Puckle enjoyed Christmas Day even more and reported it as another terribly jolly evening of innocent good fun:

We had 3 English officers in . . . played snapdragon, musical chairs, and twos and threes, and Captain Reid (one of the English officers) kept us in one wild screech of laughter the whole time . . . We sang choruses conducted by him, and danced round the room in a long line, all holding on to each others' shoulders, Toy Town style. We finished up with Auld Lang Syne (sung quite wrong) and got to bed at 3 a.m. It was an awfull [sic] jolly evening, and a great treat to have some Englishmen to play with again.[72]

The *Gazette* announced that SSY2 'danced the New Year in at a magnificent ball given by the Army to celebrate joyously the commencement of the New Year and the coming Peace'. National costumes and military dress were worn and it was quite a splendid affair, with national anthems and the Marseillaise sung by the crowd. But the New Year brought bad weather and Puckle's letters home were soon filled with complaints about the cold, the food she described as tasting of grease and old washcloths, and how her radiator had frozen and overflowed.[73] Despite such hardships it seemed the FANY were still enjoying parties and teas with various officers and local gentry and had quite a reputation for dancing. Puckle's letters are full of such amusements that were written most likely to shock and entertain her family; they also illustrate changing notions of gender and underscore women's comparative freedoms during this transitional period. She illustrates this in a letter written to her mother about meeting several British naval officers in Strasbourg. These officers were most likely associated with the British Flotilla sent out to patrol the Rhine:

Four of us were tea-ing in a café when in walked a commander, lieutenant and mid-shipman, and we nearly fainted with the shock. We wondered how we were going to get into conversation with them without their thinking we were forward minxes, but the commander solved the problem by coming up and asking us to go to tea on board next day. We fell on his neck with tears of joy and asked them to come up to Schutzenbergen Villa [where the FANY were lodging] and dance that evening, as there were 20 of us all a'growing and a'blowing and never a man. Ten of them came, and we had a perfect evening – danced, played musical chairs and twos and threes, and cat and mouse, and bumps . . . They enjoyed themselves immensely, as they'd seen no English girls since they left Dover, and did not know we were here . . . They gave us a topping tea, and that evening we had a proper dance, with supper and a band and they all came, also 2 Americans and some French officers. We danced till the gunpowder ran out of the heels of our boots, which was 4 a.m.[74]

By early February 1919, SSY2 heard they were to be demobilized at the end of the month. 'SSY2 broke up with the greatest regret. All had worked together with the greatest happiness throughout many vicissitudes and dis-comforts';[75] they were going to miss each other a lot. However, like Unit 12, some drivers from this section were invited to work in the Civil Relief scheme. After the section was demobilized the personnel reorganized again as FANY Unit 9, headed by Henrietta Fraser, and went on to join Lee-Barber and Unit 12 at Compiegne. In addition, some drivers from the disbanded SSY2 reformed as Unit 7 under Blacker and started work at Commercy attached to the French First Army.

Phyllis Puckle was invited to join the group going to Compiegne and decided to go since her expenses would be paid and it gave her an opportunity to see a new part of the country.[76] Puckle and FANY colleagues Knight and Crisfield took the train to Châlons and picked up the Red Cross cars they were to use. Then they drove to Compiegne via Rheims: 'a most extraordinary sight, street after street of hopelessly ruined houses, and the shell of the cathe-dral standing up in the middle with the French flag on one of the towers'. Puckle wrote that she never saw a single house in one piece even though this had once been a city of over 100,000 people. The countryside beyond Rheims was similarly destroyed and desolate with shell holes, barbed wire, dug-outs and trenches. They went to Fismes where Crisfield had once worked in the canteen temporarily run by the FANY Unit 1 at Port à Binson. They took her photo standing by a pile of rubble that was once her house.[77]

During the summer of 1919 Puckle and her colleagues moved to Mourmelon-le-Grand where the work involved chauffeuring various personnel around the region: not always an easy task since the roads were still terrible and their cars not always well equipped.[78] At Mourmelon they still enjoyed the rounds of dancing and entertainment and made do as best they could to create some fun when things became dull. For example, Puckle wrote about one dance in late September 1919 when guests consisted of a General and his family and six officers, most of whom she declared 'duds' who did not know how to dance anything but the polka and who were not even completely shaved. Still the women danced among themselves and played a lot of musical chairs. The General, Puckle explained, was 'a fat vulgar old thing', but since he lent them horses and provided German prisoners as help, 'he has to be encouraged'. In addition, he had a very nice wife whose company the FANY appreciated.[79] Puckle and her good friend Davidson ended the year 1919 managing to escape the mud and relative desolation of Mourmelon and enjoying a few weeks working in Cologne attached to the British Army of the Rhine.

They found it strange to be in the heart of Germany and surrounded by British and even felt sorry for the occupied German officials 'wilting' before them with so much courtesy.[80] Throughout the war the FANY learned to hate the Germans and saw them as a different 'race' from the English. These culturally constructed notions of race were part of the imperial mandate that saw differences between nations and then essentialized these differences and used them as justification for social policy. Still for Puckle, like many FANY, her experiences in France exposed her to more cultural and ethnic diversity than she had ever before encountered even while her interpretation of these experiences was often (in keeping with the manner of the time among the privileged classes) quite racist. She wrote in one letter about the Anamites (Vietnamese) who worked as orderlies for the Allies: 'funny little yellow men – they walk just like ducks and quack'. Later in the same letter she reported driving a 'nigger' who had been severely wounded, was in a lot of pain and was as 'white as he ever will be'.[81] Other FANY writings also demonstrate the racist-imperialist attitudes of the period, especially against the Chinese whom Hutchinson publicly called 'chinks' in her *Gazette* report.[82] These derogatory descriptions and statements reflect the superiority of white British in their understanding of the Empire and their arrogant ethnocentrism when confronted with people different from themselves. After the war when the armies went forward and left miles and miles of devastation to be cleared up, much of this labour was left to Chinese workmen, who often suffered severe casualties from encountering unexploded bombs and other munitions.

SSY4 (which at this point included Units 6 and 10) was stationed at Bar-le-Duc when the Armistice was declared. Bar-le-Duc was a dreary spot and when the weather could not have got any worse the women were pleased to be relocated to the more glittering town of Metz. Joan Bowles, Commanding Officer of Unit 6, wrote in the *Gazette* that they were billeted in comfortable German houses in Metz and their work consisted of driving long distances to such places as Strasbourg, Nancy, Brussels and Karlsruhe, transporting supplies and personnel. She reported that while work was steady, they had lots of opportunities for play. 'Life here', wrote Bowles in March 1919, 'is very gay and dances and dinners are of almost nightly occurrence'. It seems they were routinely receiving invitations from 'exalted personages' and many were difficult to refuse. Bowles wanted it to be known that despite these distractions, Unit 6 always put work before play and 'quite often I have to beg them to turn out to come to some gaiety which cannot be avoided'.[83] Eventually Unit 6 was sent on to Chantilly, Charleville and the Ardennes, and later formally demobilized, some of their members joining other units and continuing service in the various Civil Relief schemes.

The writer Enid Bagnold, one of the most famous FANY (although Bagnold herself appeared to have a relatively loose association with the organization and did not even mention her time with them in her autobiography), joined Unit 6 at Bar-le-Duc right after the Armistice in November 1918. Bagnold was 29-years-old when she began her FANY service, had lived a privileged life with opportunities for education and travel, and was relatively well known in the literary circles of London as witty, sociable and opulent. Bagnold is remembered for her novels and plays, most notably the book *National Velvet* published in 1935. During the war, however, Bagnold wrote *A Diary Without Dates* about her experiences as a VAD at the Royal Herbert Hospital in Woolwich near her home. It was a compelling critical account of life and death in the hospital, written in a raw style that exposed the hypocrisy of the system and the desperation and desolation of war. Its publication in 1918 caused her to lose her job at the hospital and gain critical acclaim as an innovative writer.[84] The motivation for *A Diary Without Dates* had come from Prince Antoine Bibesco, first secretary of the Roumanian Legion and her former lover. It was he who also encouraged her to apply to the FANY and receive an appointment with a convoy driving for the French, saying it would be 'so "chique" to go'.[85] These experiences with Unit 6 were recorded in letters home (carefully numbered and typed by her mother) that provided the basis for her semi-autobiographical novel *The Happy Foreigner*. The reader is never told that this is a FANY unit although the heroine of the novel is aptly named Fanny.[86]

Grace McDougall recalled first seeing Bagnold at a hotel in Brussels when Bagnold walked into the room with two French officers. McDougall, never one to miss an opportunity to wax eloquent on fine aesthetic virtues, especially when it coincided with nationalist rhetoric, described Bagnold as 'one of the loveliest girls I have ever seen, and in our FANY uniform. Tall and graceful with a wonderful roseleaf complexion, fair hair rippling under her cap, perfect eyes and a crimson mouth, she looked like a young godess [sic]. She was the type incarnate of traditional English beauty; a vision of radiant loveliness.'[87]

After the war when McDougall asked Bagnold (who in 1920 married Sir Roderick Jones, President of Reuters News Agency, and became known as Lady Jones) to contribute to her 'Five Year with the Allies', she was told *The Happy Foreigner* was all she could offer. Bagnold did not like to write directly about the war (she barely mentions either the First or Second World Wars in her autobiography) and was a well-published author at this time, having just written *National Velvet*. Perhaps she found it a chore to dig up old memories for a memoir that might never be published. Whatever her motivation, this was Bagnold's response, according to McDougall:

I don't know that I could contribute anything except *Happy Foreigner*. Everything that I put into *Happy Foreigner* has in a way obscured the happenings as they occurred. A book is such a queer thing. It feeds on what it will, and it takes its nourishment here and there, when it has finished it means there is nothing left. I wish I could help you, but I remember so little that did not affect me directly. Would it be possible to form a chapter by picking fragments from the Book?

So, wrote, McDougall, 'that is what I have done, for it is all that we can get'.[88] Over forty years later Bagnold was interviewed and was again loath to talk about the experience. After briskly chastizing the chivalrous interviewer and asking him to 'drop the Miss [Bagnold] all the time. Omit the Miss. Just say Enid Bagnold saying', she rebuked him for asking questions about her child-hood. She explained they were spelled out in her autobiography and told him outright that he should have read it. 'Everything is in my book', she said. The only information she shared when asked why she wanted to join the FANY was the response: 'Well everybody wanted to go, I suppose. I mean we all wanted experience of this great bloody new war. You know we didn't imagine that war was going to happen at all ever again.'[89]

The Happy Foreigner rightly describes Bar-le-Duc as a most depressing place: 'liquid in mud, soaked in eternal rain'.[90] In real life within two weeks of starting work with the FANY Bagnold wrote home to her parents saying, 'I don't believe I can stick it out . . . I can't think how the others stick to it. Of course I can't think or write or get any impressions at all.'[91] She found the loca-tion desolate and the work hard. In the novel she describes the war-ravaged countryside and its reconstruction and gives meticulous descriptions of the French landscape and its destruction and rejuvenation. She provides a docu-mentary account of this period when villagers returned to piles of rubble, lived in shell holes and managed to get water siphoned from car radiators. She writes of young American soldiers, pink and good-looking, acting like generous children and standing out against the stark, war-weary maturity of the local people. The novel presents a transitional narrative poised between the ravages of the past and the hopes of the future and sets the heroine, the ambulance driver named Fanny, in the centre of this landscape as an independent woman.

At first Fanny feels anything but empowered by the dismal work under these equally dismal conditions. She is to drive officers on their rounds of inspections, claim assessments and damage evaluations, and describes the accommodation at Bar-le-Duc as utterly depressing: 'It was built upon simple lines. A narrow corridor ran down the centre of it, and on either hand were four square cells divided one from the other by grey paper stretched upon laths of wood – making eight in all. At one end was a small hall filled with mackintoshes. At the other a sitting room.'[92] A 'bright-eyed rat' shared her cubicle, tore up the walls and left droppings on her bed, and all around the rain continued to fall. Her character Fanny was miserable and lonely. This description of FANY life flies in the face of cheery accounts in memoirs and unit reports; instead Fanny reports a lack of camaraderie at Bar-le-Duc and focuses on the difficult solitary work and the ways the women scurried back to their cubicles after eating the terrible rations of food. There is little glamour and fun here. McDougall included this excerpt in 'Five Years with the Allies' without comment.[93] Just as the FANY wanted to create a legend of camaraderie and cheerfulness, no doubt Bagnold needed a physical and emotional backdrop for the unfolding of her narrative:

The early start at dawn, the flying miles, the winter dusk, the long hours of travel by the faint light of the acetylene lamps filled day after day; the unsavoury meal eaten alone by the stove, the book read alone in the cubicle, the fitful sleep upon the stretcher, filled night after night. A loneliness beyond anything she had ever known settled upon Fanny.[94]

Fanny's loneliness lifts when the unit is transferred to Metz, a glittering city where the women are billeted in comfortable quarters, food is relatively plentiful, and dances and other social engagements frequent. Bagnold writes that in 'this happy summer, Fanny turning her vain ear to spoken flattery, her vain eye to mute, danced like a golden gnat in fine weather'.[95] It is here that Fanny experiences the freedom of this period and here that she meets a handsome French artillery captain named Julien Chatel with whom she falls in love. The narrative unfolds as a romance with a twist. While it is moved forward by Fanny's relationship with Julien, the love story is described in such an impressionistic style that the reader learns very little about Julien except Fanny's attraction to him and a series of romantic exchanges. Eventually Fanny is sent to Charleville close to where Julien, now demobilized, lives and works. She transforms a house there and waits for him, and, although he does not come until it is too late and Fanny is ready to return home, the experience of living alone and realizing that her love affair was a fantasy grounded in the myth of war and its aftermath is very empowering for her. When Julien does eventually come to her, she does not tell him of her plans and moves on with her life, rejoicing in her independence and strong sense of self-worth: 'she was invincible, inattentive to the voice of absent man, a hard, hollow goddess, a flute for the piping of heaven'.[96] She realizes her love was part of the romantic fantasy of war; understandings of this and the possibilities of her own freedom are fuelled by seeing Julien in civilian clothers: 'This is Julien as he will be, not as I have known him . . . here beside her in the darkness stood the civilian, the Julien-to-come, the solid man, the builder, plotting to capture the future.'[97] In the introduction to the Virago edition of *The Happy Foreigner*, Anne Sebba writes that Bagnold had told her parents about her disappointment with Bebesco when she saw how his civilian clothes and departure from army rations had increased his bulk.[98] By the time she wrote *The Happy Foreigner*, Bebesco had married someone else and Bagnold could write that her character Fanny was 'half out of reach of pain'.[99]

The Happy Foreigner of course is no ordinary love story: the message is feminist and captures women's autonomy and strength at this particular historical moment. The romance is conceptualized in the independence and authority of Fanny's everyday life as a FANY: she drives expertly, manages vehicles, and transports men unchaperoned all over the French countryside. She approaches her work with confidence, assurance and a strong sense of purpose and soon is happy even though she is a 'foreigner' or outsider in this masculine sphere. On one occasion in the novel, Fanny's colleague 'Stewart' was told by a French officer that she was not strong enough to handle her car. Stewart understood the enormity of the situation as all the women assembled in the garage waited with bated breath and Fanny imagined the men saying, 'March out again, Englishwomen, ridiculous and eager and defeated!'[100] Despite the fact that Stewart injures her wrist when the car backfires, she starts it and the women are accepted. Fanny mends countless punctures along equally countless dreary and often snow-filled roads and survives accidents and a robbery, fashioning the handle of a wheel jack as a weapon (just as McDougall had done when she was ambushed during one of her trips). Fanny responds to many questions and comments about the inappropriateness of Englishwomen doing such work and on one occasion explains that a certain independent masculine woman mentioned in conversation as being English was actually French: an illustration of what such women might do 'when they are free'.[101]

In the novel Fanny is sexually empowered. It is she who picks out Julien and asks for him to join her and some friends for dinner. She risks a journey across a frozen river to spend time with Julien and revels in the excitement of it. She also drives a Russian officer unchaperoned to Verdun and spends the night in this fortress unfazed although surrounded by men who have not seen a woman in a long time. As Angela Smith notes in her discussion of *The Happy Foreigner*, Bagnold here illustrates Sandra Gilbert's thesis of the empower-ment experienced by women who entered such masculine terrain during this period.[102] Nonetheless, Bagnold finishes the novel with Fanny's observation that toward the end of her time in France people are reminding her that times are changing again: 'It is time mademoiselle bought her dress for the summer!' since already 'khaki seems as old-fashioned as crinoline'.[103] As Smith notes, Bagnold seems to engage Margaret and Patrice Higonnet's 'double-helix' argument that 'Although the women drivers have enjoyed a privileged status as members of the forces, as civilian life once more takes precedence over the military so they are moved "backward" as they recognise that the time to return home is approaching.'[104] In this way Bagnold's novel mirrors the situa-tion of the FANY in real life. They are empowered and they have autonomy, especially during this transitional period between war and civilian life; they are also faced with a future where khaki will seem old-fashioned and a return to normal gender relations imminent. Still, as Bagnold emphasizes, Fanny has been transformed and will never be the same again.

The Belgian units

Grace McDougall's Corps de Transport attached to the Belgian Army, was the first to cross back into Belgium when the Germans left Bruges in October 1918. McDougall was overjoyed that Unit 5 could be a part of this. 'We are all under orders to move at an hour's notice', explained McDougall. 'I went up (with Marples and the old Unic) to see the lie of the land. It was a wonderful experience . . . What a run that was and what wild excitement to feel Belgian soil under our wheels!'[105] And then upon entering Bruges, McDougall was overcome by their reception. According to her report, hundreds of people sur-rounded their car, clinging to them, kissing and patting their cheeks; the *Gazette* more soberly described the response as one of welcome and celebra-tion.[106] The FANY were also displayed as curiosities; the Belgians had been in exile for four years and were not used to seeing women driving: 'women drivers were a strange and uncanny sight, they were aghast, amazed, almost horrified to think we did a man's work, and wore uniform'.[107] When peace was first declared in November, McDougall wrote that there was little rejoicing and only startled disbelief. The women stared into each others' faces and were unable to visualize the meaning of it. Slowly it seems to have sunk in and McDougall and several colleagues headed for Ghent, waxing eloquently on the liberation of Belgium and the heroism of its people coming home in victory. Even after all this time and her participation in, and witness of, the stark realism of war, McDougall's writing still reflects the traditional rhetoric of glory, heroism and the jubilant homecoming. Such writing, while it reified the imperialist story of the war, still gave women like McDougall a narrative authority to voice the women's war and the role of the FANY in this struggle:

Sturdy war-worn little Belgians going back to your own country, to your own home. Your exile is ended, your torment of separation is ended. Why, look! *Chasseurs-a-pied* surely, and the second regiment! By all the gods we are going into Belgium with the 5th Division, with whose doctors we served in 1914 at Oostkirk, at Caeskirk, Loo and Fortheim! People used to scoff at the idea of women in the trenches, but these Belgians, soldiers, officers and doctors, know – their smiles are different, they are the smiles of the comrades who trusted us, smiles of gratitude for the binding of their wounds, smiles of good-fellowship for the discomforts and dangers we shared. They will not forget nor shall we, that we stood beside their dying and their dead in the battle of the Yser.[108]

McDougall's memories of the Armistice in Ghent bring her adventures full circle, finishing in Ghent where for her it had all begun.

Within the next few weeks McDougall was invited to Germany to meet with authorities and decide whether to have her unit attached to the Army of Occupation there or stay with the Belgian Ministry of War. She decided upon the latter and spring 1919 found Unit 5 working in Brussels. In the *Gazette* McDougall explained that the 'unpleasantness of working among a hostile population' made her choose Brussels, a choice, she added that nobody regretted since it was an interesting and comfortable city and there was much work for the FANY to do. This work consisted mainly of driving personnel associated with the War Office rather than driving ambulances, a change for them; McDougall reported the work as different but interesting with cars in good shape.[109] She explained that 'the girls were given the best cars in the Army to drive and their work was to drive the higher command, to places like Paris, Arras, Lille, Luxembourg, etc.'.[110] No doubt FANY were chosen for this work with the military elite not only because they were accomplished drivers but also because of their social class and the reputation of their organization. In

March 1919 the unit numbered twenty-two FANY with the possibility of work for more and extended invitations for visitors.[111]

These FANY were also excited to find themselves living in a house once owned by the Germans that boasted electricity and central heating and came complete with large mess and dining rooms. These rooms encouraged all sorts of get-togethers that included Sunday soirées and parties that stretched into the night after evenings on the town. They also had been given German prisoners to work as servants, who, according to McDougall, became quite attached to the FANY and wanted to return to England with them. Despite being on such friendly terms with these prisoners, it still fell to Mary Baxter-Ellis to take a revolver and march the prisoners to their attic quarters and lock them in every night.[112]

The FANY working for the Belgians had many opportunities for fun and friendship in this wonderful city of Brussels; it was only the necessity of work that kept them from dancing day and night, explained McDougall. They enjoyed the opera and frequented the nightclubs. McDougall wrote that they went often to such nightclubs as The Continental and were able to do so as long as they did not go alone.[113] The Commandant of the Cavalry School also lent them horses to ride when they had free time during the day. 'Life was an endless round of fun', reported McDougall: 'Invitations poured in on us, luncheons, receptions, dinners, dances, nobody thought ahead. We all revelled in the present, in the freedom from strain, the knowledge that the dance of death was ended. We were perhaps a little unbalanced', admitted McDougall, 'a trifle distraught, after years of exhaustion, years of living on nerves, and on willpower.' But who was to blame them, she added 'for snatching at life and love? At all the things of which war had deprived us?'[114] This brief transitional period between their service during the war and their demobilization provided a time of relative freedom for the FANY. Never known to shy away from a good time, still the women's fun and adventure was always contextualized in devotion and service. After the Armistice this service was still their guiding force and the work was still intense; now, however, it was patterned with knowable parameters and without the surprises and spontaneous casualties of war. This is the release from pressure and stress that McDougall says encouraged their 'endless round of fun'.

Indeed, the Belgian FANY had already developed quite a reputation for being outgoing and fun-loving. This was due in part to their Commandant McDougall who was frequently described as the mixer *par excellence*. Back in April 1915 there are stories of McDougall and Chris Nicholson going up to Pervyse to help collect the wounded and on to Ramscappelle to help with casualties there, dining with the artillery officers of the 6th Division, eating asparagus and drinking champagne. After dinner they went to a shelled house that had a piano and sang and played music: 'Wonderful up there, with guns booming close by and all windows blocked up, to stand round Chris playing the piano and singing – a topping crowd.'[115] While visiting troops 'up the line', McDougall commented on this poignancy of merrymaking in the midst of war: 'We had champagne and sing-song, and a badly wounded man was carried in; we fixed him up, and another arrived; then we resumed the sing-song. It sounds heartless, but it's war, everyone good-humoured and trying to be happy, and the tragic moments come and go.'[116] It was understood that they had to take their fun as they could and that to do otherwise would not help them succeed in their work.

McDougall had spent a large proportion of her time during the war organizing and inspecting the various FANY projects, hatching plots for new work for them, and entertaining influential people on whom the FANY might rely for financial or moral support. As a result, she was often found, for example, taking important guests to the opera and to concerts, enjoying an invitation to dine aboard a Royal Admiralty yacht and journeying across the Channel to Dover, spending an afternoon with the novelist Elizabeth Robins and the doctors Flora Murray and Elizabeth Garrett Anderson and entertaining the Duke and Duchess of Lisander.[117] McDougall always had her eye toward fundraising and did raise a lot of money. For example, a benefit concert at the Carlton Hotel in London under the patronage of HIH Princess Clementine Napoleon (to whom McDougall had the honour of serving tea) and presided over by Sir George Reid, the High Commissioner for the Australian Commonwealth, was quite a success. Miss Lillian Braithwaite recited and several well-known Belgian performers sang and played. Muriel Thompson, a very accomplished speaker, gave a talk about the brave deeds of the FANY and their work to date and they all 'gathered in the shekels splendidly'.[118] Edith Walton was not exaggerating when she remembered McDougall as a live-wire always looking for some new scheme and the one without whom the FANY would never have got anywhere during the war.[119]

The first FANY Unit 1 working for the Belgians at Lamarck had been well known for its *esprit de corps* and fond friendships among the women. This was in part because they lived, ate and slept together at Le Bon Génie and Le Bijou and these places became quite a gathering place for the FANY to meet and socialize after work as well as a place to sleep. The room on the top floor of the hospital where on-call FANY would sleep also became a special place for the FANY to congregate and enjoy the camaraderie of colleagues. 'It was in this room', recalled Waddell, 'a big untidy, but an oh so jolly, sitting room', that the FANY gathered at 10 o'clock every morning 'for twenty precious minutes during which we had tea and biscuits, read our letters, swanked to other wards about the bad cases we had got in, and generally talked shop and gossiped.'[120]

Waddell told many stories about their fun and friendships at Lamark. She recalled, for example, how she had been hoarding a large case that arrived from her godfather's wine-merchants in London. It had fortunately been misidentified as a case of hospital stores and she had managed to keep it undetected and let it function as a bedside table. Before she was to go on her first leave to Paris in the spring of 1915, she opened the case and discovered champagne, sherry, port and whisky. The women decided to throw a party 'in their pyjamas' and mixed the various alcohols together. They invited Sister Wicks, who was said to have remarked, 'It's very good. I think I'll have another glass. There's nothing in it, I suppose?', and Waddell and friends, sipping happily, are said to have replied, 'Oh, no.'[121] Nursing a headache the next morning on the train to Paris, Waddell recalled her godfather's wise words about not mixing 'the hops and the vine'. Waddell also remembered this first leave in Paris with fondness, having met a group of young American men from Yale and Harvard 'who had come over to see what the war was really like'. Waddell recalled one saying to her, 'Quit this war, Princess, and marry me.' 'I couldn't quit', she said. 'Leave was up and we said good-bye.'[122]

One summer early in the war five of the FANY working for the Belgians went in together and rented a bathing chalet on the beach at Calais, lending it to friends when any of them had leave. The chalet was a great source of fun although the sea that year was plagued with jellyfish and the women had to use hot vinegar compresses to relieve the stings if they dared go into the sea (which of course they did). Occasionally they would also be invited by officers of the Belgian cavalry to ride on the beach and in the sand dunes.[123] Waddell remembered one officer who would go streaking up the side of a dune to its highest point with the sand slipping and crumbling behind him and then fly down the other side. Accomplished riders like Waddell would follow him, lying almost flat on their horses' backs on the descent in order not to fall off: 'we felt', explained Waddell, that 'English honour was at stake'.[124] There was also a cavalry camp at Fort Neuilly, outside Calais near Peuplinghe where the women would sometimes ride, enjoying what they remembered as glorious half-days off duty.[125]

Like the FANY in the other units, not only did their *esprit de corps* develop from shared living conditions, they were also facilitated by various forms of public entertainment taken on by them. A series of open-air concerts, for example, featuring recitations, songs at the piano, and solo voice and instrumental performances were very popular. Pat Waddell was a very accomplished concert violinist and Betty Hutchinson an actress, while Ida Lewis played the cello and Chris Nicholson not only had a beautiful voice but was an accomplished pianist. Although it was considered an important asset for women of their class to have a smattering of talents in art and music in order to be proficient wives, mothers and hostesses, several FANY were actually very accomplished performers. The concerts were first held in the hospital yard for the men at Lamarck. After this the FANY were invited to perform at the YMCA concerts for the troops, were given passes to go 'up the line', and rehearsals began. As already mentioned in the context of the performances by FANY units working with the British, rehearsals and performances were very impromptu, since the women would be on duty in the wards or driving ambulances up to the very last minute. Waddell shared poignant memories of these concerts given against the backdrop of booming guns and the knowledge that most of these men were going off to the Front line the next day.[126] Finally, occasionally the FANY would perform with professional performers at bigger events in Calais. Waddell remembered one such event where a Parisian opera singer in Paris was ready to go on stage. She wore a gorgeous long red velvet dress and 'swept up and down the boards snorting like a war-horse' and brushing everyone out of her way. She would suddenly burst into scales 'with the utmost abandon' and then would beat her chest and cry 'Mon Dieu, que j'ai le trac', which could be loosely interpreted as 'My God, I've got the wind up'. Waddell declared she too had *le trac* but was too nervous to say so.[127] When the Lamarck staff was transferred on the closure of the hospital, many kept up their skills by joining the Fantastiks.

McDougall always encouraged the concerts and public performances. She understood that it was good for the morale of the FANY as well as the soldiers, and it helped create notoriety and publicity for the Corps. McDougall defended these entertainments, even though the French in particular were disturbed by the dancing and merriment that often occurred during the months of 1917 when casualties were so high and much of their country was under enemy occupation.[128] From the FANY perspective, gloom and heavy casualties should not prevent them organizing concerts and celebrating holidays; instead, depressed times underscored the need of such celebrations for boosting morale. Christmas in particular was a time for celebration. McDougall explained, 'Everyone enjoyed their Christmas, and if sad thoughts would come of other Christmasses with those who had passed to Christ's own company, we smothered them as best we might for the sake of the living.'[129] On Christmas day 1917, for example, the FANY of Unit 5 filled a car with presents, cakes and apples, and brought in children from the poor areas around Calais that had been recently bombed. In the afternoon there were British and Belgian tea parties for those off-duty and in the evening a mess dinner and games. Luckily, McDougall recalled, it was a stormy night and they did not have to finish dinner in the dug-out. Then, as part of the New Year celebrations, they held a big concert with over thirty guests present. McDougall reported that they borrowed a Belgian canteen for the occasion and had 'a rattling good pro-gramme'.[130] And, horsey as ever, the FANY had a special event to themselves with nineteen entries at a big horse show in Calais.[131]

Just like their sisters in the British convoy, the FANY of Unit 5 were keen to liven up their days as best they could. McDougall certainly enjoyed her own share of merriment and her memoir records the fun times she had during the war. Even as a married woman McDougall wrote about innocent flirtations at parties as well as one incident when an American officer filled her taxi with red roses.[132] McDougall understood that the fun and flair surrounding the Corps and their almost-saucy-but-still-respectable reputation was a key aspect of FANY identity. 'The gramophone was in constant use and dancing went on at any spare moment', wrote McDougall. 'We read surprisingly little. An outdoor community does not lend itself to literary pursuits. Tea time was the signal for the arrival of numerous airmen, generals, doctors, staff officers, a Belgian Prince, an Italian aviator, an American driver, an artillery man from Verdun, a naval commandant from the Dover patrol . . . occasionally a woman' [orig. ellipses].[133] These ellipses emphasize the unlikelihood of women visitors and highlight the unconventional placement of the FANY as women in male com-pany. But then, as if to emphasize that such merriment never came before duty, McDougall followed her description of their fun with the following: 'the laughter and shouting would cease abruptly. A train was in. The Fannies would melt away to their cars, the visitors would pause a moment to watch the wounded being lifted into the cars.'[134]

Even though McDougall wrote that an outdoor life did not lend itself to intellectual pursuits, she kept a book of Rupert Brooke's poetry with her. Brooke wrote in ways that nostalgically glorified British pastoral life and the heroic aspects of battle (although his later poems before he died in 1915 were starting to take a more critical stance).[135] McDougall's copy of Brooke's poetry was heavily inscribed in her hand with other published verse, poems written in the 'Great War Rhetoric' that valorized fallen soldiers and spoke of the heroism of those who gave their lives.[136] McDougall also acknowledged Rud-yard Kipling as an important influence and one that kept her going when her spirits were low. She explained that she said the following lines from Kipling's poem 'If' over and over mechanically when the going got tough: 'If you can force your heart and nerve and sinew / To serve your turn long after they are gone / And so hold on when there is nothing in you;/Except the will that says to them – hold on [sic]'.[137] Kipling of course exhibited a keen stoicism and was a strong supporter of British imperialism with a virulent hatred of the Germans. McDougall's penchant for Kipling highlights her conflicting identity as someone who stretched the limits of the female self but in the name of nationalism, patriotism and class allegiance.

In the intervening months between the Armistice and the New Year 1919 when important issues were being raised about the demobilization of FANY units and the future of the Corps, McDougall's mother fell ill again, and died the following April. As McDougall explained it, 'fate intervened' and she was torn once more between her duties to family and to the FANY.[138] McDougall received the telegram about her mother's impending death after an evening described as a particularly 'wonderful night'. The Coldstream Guards had given a dinner and dance for the FANY and they had 'danced the soles off [their] shoes' until 5 a.m.[139] The telegram about her mother's condition shook McDougall to the core and precipitated her departure from the FANY.

In McDougall's absence, Mary Baxter-Ellis, adjutant and second-in-command with the Belgian convoy, wrote the final demobilization report for the Belgian FANY. She explained that in May 1919 the convoy themselves decided it their duty to demobilize despite the fact that they had been dreading this for a long time. 'All loved the FANY life and were very loth to *rentre en civile*' (go back to civilian life); they especially hated leaving behind their 'comfortable khaki for the trials of mufti'. The final straw was this: 'when the FANY, whose job had been to release men for the fighting line, saw demobilized soldiers and returned civilian prisoners back from Germany and out of work, applying for jobs at the Cinquentennaire garage and being turned away because there was no room, they determined that the thirty places filled by FANY could and should be opened to some of the needy ones'.[140] Despite their accomplishments, skills and ambition, ultimately they were women doing men's work and pressure to return to 'normal' gendered relations was strong. Their work would cease in the middle of June.[141]

A couple of days before their mobilization, the whole Belgian convoy had the distinct pleasure of being visited and inspected by the Queen of the Belgians. There was intense excitement in preparation for such an honour, preparations that included dipping grubby uniforms into petrol and hanging them out to dry in the sun in the vain hope that they would dry. The mascot dog Bobby was bedecked with ribbons and the FANY, reeking of gasoline, went forward to be received by the Queen. She was unperturbed and fortunately ignored the fire hazard; instead she invited them all to a surprise tea in the garden. With fine understatement, Baxter-Ellis declared it a 'ripping ending' to all their years of work with the Belgians.[142] This story about the Belgian convoy meeting the Queen of the Belgians smelling of petrol takes a central place in FANY legend.

The ending of McDougall's service was of course much more melodramatic. She explained how she was taken ill with ptomaine poisoning and exhaustion (most likely exacerbated by the stress of her mother's death), attended by the Belgian Queen's doctor, and then sent to Nurse Cavell's home under the direction of the Belgian matron that Nurse Cavell herself had trained (Edith Cavell had been executed by the Germans in 1915, inflaming anti-German feeling at the time).[143] McDougall wrote that along with her physical ailments, her nerves were shattered and she needed rest and recuperation and took it by spending time at Ardennes, Roumont and Zoute. In September McDougall left France for the last time and watched misty-eyed as the coastline receded. She recalled these past 'five crowded years of youth and life and love and death' and pondered her future: 'The boat bore me on inexorably to the doom that waited, – the doom that was spoken almost at once, as my husband greeted me at Victoria Station. "We sail for Rhodesia in three weeks".'[144] So it was with a feeling of doom (or the experience of doom filtered through the twelve or so years between the end of the war and the writing of this statement) that McDougall contemplated the closure of her war service and the beginning of her life as a married civilian woman, destined to follow her husband and his work to Rhodesia (now Zimbabwe). Again she was torn between duty to family and to organization, although this time there was no war to provide the justification for alternative gendered lives and McDougall had to face the inevitable: she was a married woman constrained by the gendered prescriptions of the time. She ends 'Five Years with the Allies' with the single exclamation 'Exile!', and the following: 'Rhodesia, far away from friends and comrades, to loneliness and a country that knew not war, nor the Gods of War, nor the brave glory of after-battle wine, the flushed recounting faces . . . [orig. ellipses]'.[145] While of course Rhodesia had seen its share of war in the context of British imperialism, to McDougall the Great War was the war to end all wars: her primary formative framework and the benchmark experience against which all experiences would be evaluated.

Endings and beginnings

Prior to their departure for Africa, McDougall and her husband attended a farewell dinner given by the Corps and were presented with a gift of a canteen of silver. McDougall made a short speech expressing 'her thanks to all who had so ably seconded her in the work of the Corps', and telling the group she 'much regretted she was unable to help in its reorganization'.[146] Note that in her choice of the word 'seconded' she implied and reminded those present of her leadership in the organization even as it slipped away from her hold. McDougall must have been aware that some of her colleagues found her a difficult personality and that her traditional notion of the Corps and its mission was to be overshadowed by more practical issues and led by more practical minds. Lillian Franklin in particular had always shown such skills and had a less sentimental approach to the organization. All McDougall's public writings speak highly and affectionately of Franklin; indeed McDougall ended her farewell report in the *Gazette* with the statement: 'Above all, [orig. emph.] my greetings go to Miss Franklin, my friend and colleague through the dark days of 1914, and who has carried the British FANYs through all difficulties to the glorious end.'[147] Everyone understood that Franklin had been the rock providing stability for the organization; even McDougall must have known this on some level. Irene Ward was very fond of Franklin and described her in this way:

Tall, broad-shouldered, strong-featured, always immaculate in her turn-out, Franklin gave an impression of sound common sense and competence. Physically strong, she was indefatigable herself, and had a quiet certainty that everyone else was the same . . . 'Boss' was tenacious to the last degree and very persistent. If she met with rebuff or opposition from Authority, she withdrew with dignity and approached the problem from another angle, and so usually achieved her aim. She had endless patience. Undemonstrative herself, she hated any form of sentimentality; but she inspired great loyalty and devotion to the Corps and not to herself . . . The most outstanding characteristic of this remarkable woman was her calmness. She was completely imperturbable. No one ever remembered seeing her fussed or visibly upset, no matter how trying the situation or how close the danger. She was no intellectual; she did not possess the knack of being amusing in general conversation; but her steadiness under all provocation was the rock upon which – in the view of many – the reputation of the Corps for courage and endurance was founded.[148]

In this way Franklin was as different from McDougall as chalk from cheese, but between the two they were able to imagine and create one of the most important women's voluntarily organizations of the period.

Like Enid Bagnold's Fanny in *The Happy Foreigner*, the FANY were personally empowered by their experiences during the war and their work after the Armistice. They learned skills and competencies in traditional areas like nursing and in the more non-traditional arenas of driving and mechanics. This work encouraged a renegotiation of their gendered identities and a realignment of social territory. They were in the forefront of such negotiations, illustrating the ways the First World War can be understood as an ideological struggle 'fought in the minds of men and women'.[149] From the organizational standpoint these realignments facilitated a bold and sometimes audacious organization committed to women's strength, leadership and autonomy, positioning femininity as central to the war effort. The FANY developed a feminine group identity or feminine collectivity grounded in traditional notions of duty and service and prided themselves on their comradeship and camaraderie. This 'sisterhood' that rivalled the brotherhood or fraternity of soldiers helped develop a collective female war experience. As Franklin wrote at the end of their war service, 'The Fannies have, I think, proved that *esprit de corps* is a much finer thing than to surround the average British girls with all sorts of rules; once establish the former and they will play the game all through.'[150] This comment is instructive in illustrating the ways the FANY operated: as an independent organization they made their own rules and gave women opportunities for training, leadership, fun and adventure; however, once established they worked within the system and did 'play the game all through'. Unfortunately this game also included a return to more traditional gender relations when the war was over.

In this way the FANY were groundbreaking in challenging the regulatory norms of gender and by living unconventional lives and doing work often coded as masculine. Through these subversive behaviours they were able to develop feminine stories of the war and claim the narrative authority of working alongside male combatants. Against the cultural myths of the time and in concert with the emerging legend of the FANY, these women 'made themselves new' and imagined new cultural possibilities. They departed into the masculine terrain of driving and mechanics that subverted traditional mythologies about gender and they entertained independent relationships with men as authority figures, wounded, and potential suitors. Through these skills they created skilled gendered performances, drawing upon and subverting traditional arrangements and crafting unconventional identities. The paradox of course was that the FANY were caught between the power they claimed through class-based patriotic femininity and the subordination that was inevitably a product of that very same claim. Ultimately, even though their war record demonstrates an inadvertent or accidental feminism that fought for the rights of women to enter and succeed in the most masculine of public spaces, their intentions were patriotic and intended to support British imperialism and military prowess. And, while their example made the case for women's full citizenship in society, the FANY did not consciously connect their desire for independence and autonomy to broader social and political gains. When the last FANY returned to England and the organization attempted to negotiate its future, it found itself in the difficult space of being poised between the militarism of its organizational identity and the genteel civilian femininity that had provided the basis for its service in the first place.

Notes

1 *Gazette* (January–April 1919), p. 4.
2 *Gazette* (October–November–December Supplement 1918), no page numbers.
3 Ibid.
4 *Gazette* (January 1920), p. 8.
5 Sharon Ouditt, *Fighting Forces, Writing Women: Identity and Ideology in the First World War* (London: Routledge, 1994), p. 30.
6 F. Tennyson Jesse, 'The First Aid Nursing Yeomanry: A Personal Impression of the FANY Camps in France – Girls Who are Doing Yeoman Service', *Vogue* (May 1916), pp. 54–5.
7 Muriel Thompson, diary (10, 11 June 1918; 7, 8 July 1918; 1 August 1918). [LC]
8 Ibid. (17 August 1918).
9 Catherine Hall, 'The Early Formation of Victorian Domestic Ideology', ch. 3 of *White, Male and Middle Class: Explorations in Feminism and History* (London: Polity, 1992), pp. 72–90.
10 FANY couple Mary Baxter-Ellis and Marjorie 'Tony' Kingston Walker went on to live a long time together: Hugh Popham, *F.A.N.Y.: The Story of the Women's Transport Service, 1907–1984* (London: Leo Cooper, 1984), p. 117. Irene Ward writes that '"Dick" and "Tony" to their numerous friends made a wonderful pair and the close harmony in which they worked was a big factor in the growth and happiness of the Corps': *FANY Invicta* (London: Hutchinson, 1955), p. 97.
11 Romantic partnerships between women during the nineteenth and early twentieth century were commonplace and thrived in the relatively gender segregated spaces of this period. See Martha Vicinus, 'They Wonder to Which Sex I Belong: The Historical Roots of the Modern Lesbian Identity', *Feminist Studies* 18: 3 (1992), 467–97; and Lillian Faderman, *Surpassing the Love of Men: Romantic Friendship and Love between Women from the Renaissance to the Present* (New York: William Morrow, 1981); *Intimate Friends: Women Who Loved Women, 1778–1928* (Chicago, IL: University of Chicago Press, 2004); Lisa Moore, 'Something More Tender Still than Friendship: Romantic Friendships in Early Nineteenth-Century England', *Feminist Studies* 18: 3 (1992), 499–520. For US accounts see Carroll Smith-Rosenberg, 'Female Worlds of Love and Ritual: Relations between Women in Nineteenth-Century America', *Signs: Journal of Women in Culture and Society* 1: 8 (1975), 1–29; and Lillian Faderman, *Odd Girls and Twilight Lovers: A History of Lesbian Life in Twentieth-Century America* (New York: Columbia University Press, 1991).
12 Ward, *FANY Invicta*, p. 45.
13 Mary Louise oberts, *Disruptive Acts: The New Woman in Fin-de-Siècle France* (Chicago: University of Chicago Press, 2002), p. 21.
14 See Ruth Brandon, *The New Women and the Old Men: Love, Sex, and the Woman Question* (London: Secker and Warburg, 1990).
15 *Gazette* (January 1920), p. 11.
16 *Gazette* (October–November–December Supplement 1918), no page numbers.
17 Ibid.
18 Ibid.

19 Ibid.

20 Ibid.

21 Beryl Hutchinson, 'St Omer Convoy', p. 30. [LC]

22 Ibid.

23 Thompson, diary (9 April 1919).

24 Hutchinson, 'St Omer Convoy', p. 33.

25 The cause for Hutchinson was clear: this 'war to end all wars' was about good and evil, and the fight was to preserve a way of life associated with British imperial relations. Hutchinson's snobbish sense of white British superiority is implicit here as she looked back on the war and wrote in hindsight: 'My generation had absorbed the idea of responsibility; our men folk had gone out in peace as in war to SERVE [orig. emph.] the Empire with its many, many people who suffered from famine and disease.' Before 'people' the adjective 'irresponsible' was bracketed off with a question mark (hand-written presumably by Hutchinson) beside it. She continued: 'Despite the sneering of modern TV and young revolutionaries that our methods were "Paternalism", we hon-estly felt that it was our destiny to supply the need': 'St Omer Convoy', pp. 33–4. And supply it they certainly did.

26 Graham Dawson, *Soldier Heroes: British Adventure, Empire and the Imagining of Mas-culinities* (London: Routledge, 1994), p. 63.

27 *Gazette* (January 1920), p. 7.

28 *Gazette* (October–November–December Supplement 1918), no page numbers.

29 Ibid.

30 Beryl Hutchinson, 'Work with the British: The Calais Convoy", p. 14. [LC]

31 Ibid.

32 *Gazette* (January 1917), pp. 5–6.

33 Pat Beauchamp (a.k.a. Waddell), *Fanny Goes to War* (London: John Murray, 1919), p. 183.

34 Grace McDougall, 'Five Years with the Allies, 1914–1919: The Story of the FANY Corps', p. 162. [IWM]

35 Thompson, diary (28 January 1918).

36 Thompson, diary (1 April 1918).

37 Thompson, diary (23, 24, 25 January 1918).

38 Thompson, diary (25 April 25 1918).

39 Beryl Hutchinson, 'My FANY Life with the Belgian Army', p. 28. [LC]

40 *Gazette* (October–November–December Supplement 1918), no page numbers.

41 *Gazette* (April 1916), p. 6.

42 Beauchamp, *Fanny Goes to War*, pp. 148–9.

43 Edith Colston (*née* Walton), 'FANY Concert Parties'. [LC]

44 Beauchamp, *Fanny Goes to War*, p. 214.

45 Ibid., pp. 214–15.

46 Ibid.

47 *Gazette* (August–September Supplement 1918), no page numbers.

48 Hutchinson, 'My FANY Life with the Belgian Army', p. 31.

49 *Gazette* (January 1920), p. 7.

50 Colston, 'FANY Concert Parties'.

51 Beauchamp Washington (a.k.a. Waddell), autobiography, p. 4. [LC]

52 Hutchinson, 'Work with the British', p. 16.

53 McDougall, 'Five Years with the Allies', pp. 129–30.

54 Beauchamp, *Fanny Goes to War*, p. 158.

55 Ibid., p. 181.
56 McDougall, 'Five Years with the Allies', p. 128.
57 Hutchinson, 'My FANY Life with the Belgian Army', p. 34.
58 *Gazette* (January 1920), p. 6.
59 Ibid., p. 5.
60 *Gazette* (November–December 1918), p. 10.
61 *Gazette* (January–April 1919), p. 4.
62 Transcribed interview, Phyllis Puckle by Peter Liddle (May 1973), p. 8. [LC]
63 McDougall, 'Five Years with the Allies', p. 280.
64 Phyllis Puckle to 'Dearest Mother' (24 November 1919). [LC; all Puckle correspondence is in the Liddle Collection]
65 Puckle to 'Dearest Mother' (undated, *circa.* early December 1918); Puckle to 'Dearest Mother' (23 December 1918).
66 Interview, Puckle, p. 8.
67 Puckle to 'Dearest Mother' (19 December 1918).
68 *Gazette* (November–December 1918), p. 8.
69 Ibid.
70 Puckle to 'Dearest Mother' (21 September 1918).
71 Puckle to 'Dearest Daddy' (31 December 1918).
72 Ibid.
73 Puckle to 'Dearest Mother' (25 January 1919).
74 Puckle to 'Dearest Mother' (2 February 1919).
75 *Gazette* (January–April 1919), p. 5.
76 Puckle to 'Dearest Mother' (7 February 1919).
77 Puckle to 'Dearest Mother' (21 February 1919).
78 Puckle to 'Dearest Molly' (20 October 1919). Molly was Puckle's sister.
79 Puckle to 'Dearest Mother'(21 September 1919).
80 Puckle to 'Dearest Mother' (9 November 1919).
81 Puckle to 'Dearest Mother' (23 August 1918). Violet O'Neill Power also refers to 'working like niggers' in her report of the Belgian military convoy Unit 5 in autumn 1918: *Gazette* (October–November–December Supplement 1918), no page numbers.
82 *Gazette* (October–November–December Supplement 1918), no page numbers.
83 *Gazette* (January–April 1919), p. 3.
84 Enid Bagnold, *A Diary Without Dates* (London: Heinemann, 1918, rep. Virago, 1978). Angela K. Smith writes about this text in *The Second Battlefield: Women, Modernism and the First World War* (Manchester: Manchester University Press, 2000) and proclaims it as modernist writing on a par with Ellen La Motte and Mary Borden (see ch. 3).
85 Anne Sebba, 'Introduction' to Enid Bagnold, *The Happy Foreigner* (London: Heinemann, 1920, rep. Virago, 1987), p. vii.
86 Enid Bagnold, excerpt from *The Happy Foreigner* manuscript titled 'The Last Night in Metz': *Gazette* (January 1920, p. 14). The heroine here is named 'Guadela' and the excerpt contains parts edited out before the final published version of the book.
87 McDougall, 'Five Years with the Allies', p. 306.
88 Ibid., p. 15.
89 Taped interview, Lady Jones (*née* Bagnold) by Peter Liddle (December 1978). [LC]
90 Bagnold, *The Happy Foreigner*, pp. 35–6.
91 Sebba, 'Introdction', p. vii.
92 Bagnold, *The Happy Foreigner*, p. 10.

93 Mc Dougall, 'Five Years with the Allies', p. 320.
94 Bagnold, *The Happy Foreigner*, pp. 19–20.
95 Ibid., p. 48.
96 Ibid., p. 291.
97 Ibid., p. 288.
98 Sebba, 'Introduction', p. xiii.
99 Bagnold, *The Happy Foreigner*, p. 292.
100 Ibid., p. 45.
101 Ibid., p. 131.
102 Smith, *The Second Battlefield*, pp. 179–92.
103 Bagnold, *The Happy Foreigner*, p. 265.
104 Smith, *The Second Battlefield*, pp. 182–3.
105 *Gazette* (January–April 1919), p. 2.
106 Ibid., p. 3.
107 McDougall, 'Five Years with the Allies', p. 268.
108 Ibid., p. 283.
109 *Gazette* (January–April 1919), p. 6.
110 McDougall, 'Five Years with the Allies', p. 306.
111 *Gazette* (January–April 1919), p. 6.
112 McDougall, 'Five Years with the Allies', p. 305.
113 Ibid.
114 Ibid., p. 306.
115 Ibid., p. 78.
116 Ibid., p. 70.
117 Ibid., pp. 97–8. In 1915 McDougall's amusements were cut short by a trip to see her
    older brother Charlie who held a commission in the 3rd Dragoon Guards. He had
    been wounded at Ypres and she was at his bedside when he died. She wrote in 'Five
    Years with the Allies' (pp. 97–8) that she saw an apparition of her father who had died
    twenty years earlier. He told her that Charlie would die as would her younger brother
    Bill, although her husband would make it through the war. Bill Smith was killed in
    January 1916 and Ronald McDougall survived.
118 Ibid., p. 99.
119 Interview, Colston.
120 Beauchamp, *Fanny Goes to War*, pp. 12–13.
121 Pat Beauchamp (a.k.a. Waddell), *Fanny Went to War* (London: Routledge, 1940), pp.
    58–9.
122 Ibid., pp. 64–5.
123 Ibid., p. 84.
124 Beauchamp, *Fanny Goes to War*, p. 17.
125 Ibid., p. 85.
126 Ibid., pp. 86–8.
127 Ibid., pp. 98–9.
128 McDougall, 'Five Years with the Allies', pp. 248–9.
129 Ibid., p. 195.
130 *Gazette* (January 1918), p. 5.
131 McDougall, 'Five Years with the Allies', p. 152.
132 Ibid., pp. 205, 209, 234.
133 Ibid., p. 206.
134 Ibid.

135 Frank Field, *British and French Writers of the First World War* (Cambridge: Cambridge University Press, 1991), pp. 119–20.

136 Rupert Brooke, *Poems* (London: Sidgwick and Jackson, 1916).

137 McDougall, 'Five Years with the Allies', p. 261.

138 McDougall, 'Five Years with the Allies', p. 300. When McDougall received the telegram about her mother's condition she was completely distraught. Her memoir reads: 'Ah God! Shall I ever forget that moment? My mother, my dear mother, and the candles burning around her, and the flowers on her breast. I knelt there and the world stopped . . .' [orig. ellipses] (p. 309). Poignantly and with great melodrama McDougall described her arrival in London, the silence and darkness in the house where her mother lay, and her crazed break-in through a window with a borrowed knife from the taxi-cab driver to get to her mother, only to find her dead.

139 Ibid., p. 307.

140 *Gazette* (January 1920), p. 4.

141 Before demobilization, however, the unit participated in an official tour of Belgium, driving journalists and other personnel around devastated Belgium. McDougall described this tour and her place in it, emphasizing her reception. She wrote how children threw her flowers and kisses and people cheered her as if she were a queen. There is slippage here in this account of her personal heroism between admiration for the Belgian royalty and her sense of herself as regal. Her account tells how she was fêted and toasted at a special banquet described as her 'little hour of triumph', and she then had tea with the Queen of the Belgians herself. The grand finale was being photographed with the Queen and receiving the autographed photo in a silver frame. She described her goodbyes with the Belgian officers and how she was mistaken for the Queen by French officers who bowed, saluted and genuflected while she passed by in her car. Indeed, this relationship with the Queen of the Belgians was of supreme importance to McDougall and was rewarded through the Queen's role as godmother to her eldest child Ronald, born several years later. For this moment the Queen represented all the gendered and class biases implicit in McDougall's understanding of the world and the war: McDougall, 'Five Years with the Allies', p. 246.

142 *Gazette* (January 1920), p. 5.

143 McDougall, 'Five Years with the Allies', p. 311.

144 Ibid., p. 312.

145 Ibid., p. 313.

146 *Gazette* (January 1920), p. 3.

147 *Gazette* (November–December 1918), p. 5.

148 Ward, *FANY Invicta*, pp. 78–9.

149 Margaret R. Higonnet and Patrice L.-R. Higonnet, 'The Double Helix' in Margaret R. Higonnet (with Jane Jensen, Sonya Michel and Margaret C. Weitz) (eds), *Behind the Lines: Gender and the Two World Wars* (New Haven: Yale University Press, 1987), p. 47.

150 *Gazette* (January 1920), p. 6.

Postscript

Grace McDougall's memoir 'Five Years with the Allies' ends with the following reflection:

There is a statue in Calais, well known to FANYs, called 'The Brave Boys of Calais', and if ever a millionaire has money to chuck about he could do worse than put up a statue in Calais, with a FANY in khaki on top and a motor ambulance in bas-relief, and engrave it with these names, as the khaki girls of Calais![1]

At this transitional historical moment when the 'khaki girls' were demobilized, the future for the Corps was somewhat uncertain. They did not receive their statue, overshadowed instead by the 'brave boys' and their story of the war. Yet, survive the FANY certainly did, rising to unparalleled service in the next war twenty years later. In the meantime, no one could take away their stories of the Great War. Although they might formally defer to the 'soldier's war' knowing the poignant sacrifices this entailed, the FANY developed a group identity or sisterhood that never subordinated their experiences and insisted they were fighting the same war as the male combatants. And certainly no one could take away their organizational success or the emotional and psychological consequences of independence and leadership on countless numbers of women.

FANY Sara 'Sadie' Talbot (*née* Bonnell), for example, reflected on these formative years when she was interviewed for a BBC Radio show in 1989 on her 101st birthday. She recalled her time with the convoy at St Omer and spoke about her courtship with her first husband Major Herbert 'Bee' Marriott, a gas victim.[2] They would visit and drink tea in one of the huts and he proposed to her in the midst of enemy fire. Although Talbot left active service with the FANY after the war and moved back into civilian life, her years with the organization were forever imprinted on her and she continued to enjoy driving and had the red herring mascot of the St Omer convoy on the front of her car. As the last known surviving FANY of the First World War and the last surviving participant in the war to have received a Military Medal, Talbot refused to admit her service was anything special. 'It wasn't courage', she said.

'I was there to do something useful. There was a job we had to get done.'[3] Still, a *Times* article juxtaposed Talbot's comments with the observation that she gave clear expression to the 'paradox presented by women by both world wars: at a terrible price, they were given a unique, and sometimes all too fleeting, taste of freedom'.[4]

This newspaper article was informed by scholarship confirming the absence of real changes in gender relations after the war, and, in terms of the employment of women, a continuity with prewar trends. However, as Penny Summerfield has emphasized in her oral history research with women workers in the Second World War, subjective experiences of the war trouble these academic accounts and highlight the ways the war was a lived experience narrated through the relationship between the self and the material practices and cultural discourses of society.[5] I started this book too late and was never able to ask the kind of questions of the FANY that Summerfield asks of her Second World War women. Indeed, one of my greatest thrills was listening to some of their voices on the oral history tapes done in the early 1970s. Even though the questions asked were not the ones I would have chosen, still it was wonderful to hear the cadence of their speech and the intensity and passion with which they spoke about their experiences. Relying only on the records left behind as well as on my own understanding of history and culture, I believe the experience of being a FANY was transformative for many and framed their understandings of themselves in the years to come. This postscript traces the lives of some of these FANY after the war and briefly summarizes the organizational development of the FANY through the Second World War.

One of the first orders of business for the peacetime FANY was the reunion dinner held in July 1919 at the Florence Restaurant in London with 118 members and guests present. The dining tables were arranged in three long lines representing the British, French and Belgians, complete with matching colours, and a table at the end running cross-wise and joining all three together, at which the special guests were seated. Toasts and speeches of recognition and gratitude were made and reminiscences shared; at one point after a flash photograph made a loud bang, the British section wailed out the 'Mournful Mary' siren 'with realism born of long experience' and a 'lusty FANY produced the inevitable hunting horn and blew the "All Clear – gone away"'. McDougall was not present due to her illness and sent a telegram with good wishes.[6] McDougall also missed the Royal Garden Party several days later to honour war workers, attended by Franklin, Hutchinson and Lowson. 'Many in the crowd', Norma Lowson said, 'wondered who the girls in khaki were who talked so long to the Royal family; perhaps they didn't know how the FANYs always manage to "get right there", whether in work or play, as their war history will show.'[7] Here Lowson demonstrates a consciousness of the FANY legend – from debut in Kipper costume to their interview at the garden party – and the centrality of these stories in that legend's creation.

These 'girls in khaki' continued their prewar tradition of being in attendance at the Naval and Military Tournament at Olympia; one enterprising member also suggested they be present at the Grand National steeplechase to replace emergency policemen stationed by the jumps.[8] These months after demobilization were a time for reflection and visioning: what might the future of the FANY look like and how might they best continue to serve? In 1919 Hutchinson considered this future of 'FANYdom' after the war. Ever the imperialist, she saw Bolshevism and Sinn Feinism as major threats and urged women to consider their role in the defence of the nation. The FANY was, she felt, 'the finest stimulant against Red Tape that the British Army has ever known'.[9]

Despite this scorn for red tape that illustrated the FANY passion for independence, negotiations began to explore the possibility of affiliation with the BRCS or with the VAD. As always, the stumbling block for the FANY was the need to maintain their autonomy and their (some might say snobbish) notion of themselves as distinct from and above other groups. In August 1920 Margaret Cole-Hamilton made the case for the future of the FANY as an Officer Training Corps for women. This idea arose after a tentative plan outlined by the War Office in July for a new Women's Reserve Army made up of VADs and the FANY. Major-General Hitchcock explained that the plan would 'more or less cut out the working classes' and 'come up more to the FANY standard'.[10] The plan met with a 'wait and see' approach from FANY Headquarters and strong feelings (unfortunately and unsurprisingly not about the blatant class rhetoric) concerning giving up the FANY name and uniform. Instead the plan encouraged Cole-Hamilton to make the case that 'a woman who by birth, education, and training is capable of leading women who are without these advantages' best serves her country by undertaking the responsibilities of an officer.[11] Muriel Thompson who spent a year after demobilization at the WRAF headquarters, was in agreement with Cole-Hamilton, as also was Betty Hutchinson who acknowledged potential problems and jealousies but made the case this way: 'Our brothers did not "shirk" like that. Many of them would have preferred to have had just a horse to groom or a gun to tend, but because they had run the cricket team at school they ran the gun team on much the same lines at the battle.'[12] Although nothing came of these tentative plans, they are instructive of the ways the FANY used their class privilege to represent themselves in this postwar period as an organization of the 'right kind of women' and align themselves with the military elite. Unfortunately, by colluding with men of privilege in positions of authority, they lost the opportunity to consolidate power for women across all classes. Even though the FANY were often at odds with the War Office, their class interests resided with this stratum of society and not with the masses of recently demobilized women war workers whom the government would just as soon see go back to their homes and stay out of men's business.

There were also organizational changes afoot with FANY structure and function. Lillian Franklin became Corps Commandant in 1920 and their Headquarters moved to 27, Beauchamp Place. Later they would move to 14 Grosvenor Crescent. In March 1920 there was a meeting of FANY officers and non-commissioned officers called to elect a representative committee from the three Allied sections. The new committee included the familiar names of Franklin, Baxter-Ellis, Hope 'Jimmie' Gamwell, Doris Russell Allen, Lowson, Peyton-Jones, Joynson, Walton, Moseley and Mordaunt. Treasurer Cluff resigned, as did Secretary 'Andy' Anderson, to be replaced by Pat Waddell.[13] FANY membership declined during the early 1920s as also did attendance at summer camps.[14] In 1926 there was a new Corps Constitution which abolished the Headquarters Committee and power became vested in the Commanding Officer with a Regimental Board of five members (consisting of the Second-in-Command, Adjutant, ex-officio Treasurer, and two others) and an Advisory Council (the Honorary Colonel-in-Chief and various patrons). In addition the FANY name was changed to Ambulance Car Corps (FANY) although this never really caught on.[15] Also in 1926, the year of the General Strike, the FANY were called out to chauffeur and help with other emergency road transport. As the only voluntary women's corps employed by the War Office, the FANY had a feather in their cap and recruitment and attendance at summer camps increased. By the late 1920s the 'nursing' aspect of the FANY had mostly disappeared; the focus was on transport and affiliation with the Army Service Corps was strengthened.

In 1932 Franklin resigned and was succeeded by Mary Baxter-Ellis; the next year HRH Princess Alice, Countess of Athlone and granddaughter of Queen Victoria, became the Corps President. Princess Alice was very active with the organization and loved by many; royal patronage also increased recruitment. In 1936 a name change was again tried and this time the Women's Transport Service (FANY) stuck, although informally it was known by its previous name. Then with uncertainties brewing in Europe, the War Office established the Auxiliary Territorial Service (ATS) in 1938 and an agreement was signed with the FANY and with the Motor Companies of the Women's Legion. The FANY were to be involved in all motor driving companies for the Army and the Women's Legion was to work with the Royal Air Force. At first the FANY was able to keep its independence, although after Dame Helen Gwynne-Vaughan took leadership of the ATS this would not last. Led by Mary Baxter-Ellis as Commandant of Motor Companies FANY-ATS, the Corps immediately provided over a thousand driver-mechanics to serve in voluntary reserve transport units. Although these were integrated into the ATS, the FANY who were not affiliated with FANY Motor Companies and therefore still independent of the ATS became known as the 'Free FANY' led by Marian Gamwell, called back from her farm in Rhodesia to take over this work.

When the Second World War broke out about 3,000 FANY-ATS served at home and abroad. In the meantime the Free FANY worked with the Poles after the German invasion of Poland and with the Red Cross in Finland (deployed at the urging of Marguerite Gripenberg [*née* Moseley Williams, married to a Finnish diplomat] with Mary 'Dicky' Runciman [Richardson] in charge). Pat Waddell, took a mobile canteen to a Polish Army camp in Brittany in the spring of 1940 and later helped support the camps for the Poles in Scotland. Waddell, now married and known as Pat Washington, wrote a book about this service titled *Eagles in Exile*.[16] A small FANY unit formed in Kenya in 1935 became the Women's Territorial Service (East Africa), a military unit of the African Colonial Forces. In addition, several thousand FANY were employed by the British Special Operations Executive (SOE) and it was these women who became most famous during the war. Their class status, education and linguistic skills facilitated the acceptance of the FANY for confidential work and encouraged their training in communications. Their duties took them all over the globe and they formed the 'backbone of the SOE', working 'in ciphers and signals, as agent-conducting officers, [and] administering the Special Training Schools'.[17] Some of these FANY were trained as agents and worked in enemy occupied regions, sending back intelligence information. Famous FANY include Violette Szabo, Andrée Borrel, Diana Rowden, Sonia Olschanesky, Noor Inayat Khan, Yolande Beekman, Elaine Plewman, Madeleine Damerment and Vera Leigh, all eventually caught and killed by the Nazis. In all, thirteen SOE FANY died in concentration camps.[18] Today the FANY is still an all-women, all-volunteer corps that specializes in communications for the Army and the City of London police. Members train in information technology, radio and electronic communications, paramedical skills, navigation and orienteering, shooting, self-defence and advanced driving. A memorial to the FANY and their war service can be found at St Paul's Church in Knightsbridge.[19]

As for the various FANY who were demobilized, a good many married and returned to civilian life. Indeed, Lady Ampthill, head of the VAD, was said to have commented in 1920 that so many engagements were being announced that FANY seemed to be expediting it [demobilization] that way.[20] Some wed officers they had met during their service with the FANY: Mary Alice White married Major Tombeur of the Belgian Army, O'Conor married Captain Ghyka, Assistant Naval Attaché to the Roumanian Legation in London and became known as Princess Ghyka, and Madge Laidlay married Major Brodie, to name a few.[21] Norma Lowson married and moved to India with her husband, as did her FANY colleague Quin.[22] The *Gazette* is full of announcements of engagements and weddings. Some like Pat Waddell and Enid Bagnold (Lady Jones) married within a few years, and others like Edith Walton, Winnie Mordaunt and Dinah 'Heasy' Heasman, some time later. Walton became 'Tony' Colston; Mordaunt, Winifred Geare; and Heasman became Dinah Kent and continued her equestrian career with a riding school in Stratford-upon-Avon.[23] As already mentioned, Marguerite Moseley Williams married a Finnish diplomat in 1928.

Many FANY went on to travel and enjoy new adventures around the globe. Grace Anderson left for Rhodesia with FANY colleague Goodliffe and planned to spend some time with McDougall 'before taking up land and settling down'.[24] In 1920 Marian Gamwell travelled to Greece to visit her brother and caught typhoid as well as malaria and influenza. 'While in Greece she startled the Athenians not a little by riding round the walls of the town on a motor bike', exclaimed a report in the *Gazette*.[25] Along with her sister Hope, she too worked on a farm in Rhodesia, but both later returned to the FANY. Gladys Marples left the organization in early 1919 to take up flying as a profession, Adèle Crocket resigned in 1920 and returned to Australia, and Gwendolyn Peyton-Jones moved to Palestine where she worked with the Ophthalmic Hospital under the order of St John.[26] Before she was married and after a respite in Italy with the American Red Cross, Marguerite Moseley Williams worked in Albania with the Boy Scouts and founded a school for street children there.[27] After her demobilization, Ida Lewis advertised herself in the *Gazette* as someone who could procure cars: 'A FANY, with brains and exceptional opportunities for obtaining privately owned second-hand cars at very reasonable prices'. She also advertised a 'charming touring car for hire, with driver. Reasonable terms. Go anywhere'.[28]

When her unit in France was demobilized, Phyllis Puckle worked for the American Committee for Devastated France driving a mobile shop and working in regional clinics, weighing babies and providing basic education on health and nutrition. Returning to England in 1922, she took a secretarial course and accepted a position as secretary-chauffeur to an anthropologist at the London School of Economics. Puckle found her position there an 'education' and a broadening of her horizon. In 1940 when the professor died she took a temporary position with the Evacuation Officer in Oxford, helping cope with the thousands of refugees from the bombing in London. A year later she joined the Naval Intelligence Department of the Admiralty and worked with them through the rest of the war. Eventually she returned to anthropology as administrative assistant to A. R. Radcliffe-Brown and Edward Evans-Pritchard and retired in 1961.[29]

Many members stayed on active service with the FANY through the decades following the Great War and most of these women did not marry. Although combining such work with the domestic responsibilities of home and family would no doubt have been difficult, these women were dedicated to working and living with other women and most likely had no desire to fall into the constraints of heterosexual marriage at this point. Lillian Franklin, as we have seen, became Corps Commandant from 1920 to 1932, receiving the MBE for her service in 1923. Despite a brief interlude away from the organization during the war, Isabel Wicks stayed affiliated and in 1923 had the rank of Lieutenant. Margaret Cole-Hamilton became a matron of a boys' school in London and took a commission in the WRAF, but returned to the FANY later.[30] Mary Baxter-Ellis took a job as Secretary with the People's League after FANY demobilization,[31] although also of course stayed with the FANY and became its Commandant after Franklin resigned. As mentioned, the Gamwell sisters held leadership positions, as also did Betty Hutchinson.

During the winter of 1919–20 Hutchinson and several colleagues went to Algiers to drive touring cars.[32] Hutchinson never married and taught driving and mechanics for the FANY through a commission in the FANY Motor Companies ATS, and as late as 1960 passed the test for the Institute of Advanced Motorists.[33] She also ran a riding school in the New Forest and took care of an ageing parent.[34] Her other interest was the scientific study of hands and palmistry (although Hutchinson did not like that term and preferred 'chirology'), and this led to her becoming a founder-member, and eventually president, of the Society for the Study of Physiological Patterns, and librarian of the International Institute for Psychic Investigation. She wrote *A Handbook on Hands* in 1953 and *Your Life in Your Hands* in 1967.

Grace McDougall of course had left for South Africa with her husband Captain Ronald McDougall and went on to establish a poultry farm in Insiza, Rhodesia.[35] She became an Honorary Officer and a Life Member of the FANY, raising her children, working on her farm and volunteering for various social service agencies as well as the Women's Institute.[36] In 1926 she published a novel titled *The Golden Bowl*, which is instructive in revealing McDougall's longing for her wartime years. Knowing something of her life history, a reader

gets the impression that those years leading the FANY were indeed a formative period and the highlight of her life. Perhaps motivated by Bagnold's *The
Happy Foreigner*, the novel begins with the demobilization of a beautiful
'khaki-clad English girl' who is identified as a FANY and named Marion
O'Hea.[37] Newly widowed after her soldier-husband is killed in the war, she has
a sizzling love affair, becomes pregnant, and then finds her husband is still
alive. She accompanies him to Rhodesia where life is crude and inhospitable
and settles down to the monotony of life on the veldt. Comparing her past
courage in the face of war and its hardships to the desolation she now feels,
Marion exclaims on her sadness and loneliness.[38] Eventually she claims back
her life and escapes to take a job as a chauffeur motoring in Europe. Heart-
broken at leaving her son with a caretaker while she works, this emotion turns
to panic on finding the child has been kidnapped. Through some complex plot
turns her husband ends up with the child and Marion starts to see him (the
husband) in a new light, finding she loves him after all. The book ends with her
resolving her dissatisfactions and living happily ever after. The plot is fascinating in the ways certain themes might have represented adjustments faced
by McDougall as a young wife and mother. Her life was not only filled with
ambition, independence, personal heroism and authority, but also with the
responsibilities of being a daughter and wife, and later a mother. Reconciling
these forces and settling into her new civilian life must have been very challenging for McDougall. In 1934 she attempted to start a FANY section in
Rhodesia (at about the same time as preparations were underway for the unit
in Kenya) but was told that the political situation in Rhodesia and its racial
problems prohibited consideration of such a plan. In addition, she was told
that 'certain re-arrangements with the standing of the Corps are being recon-
sidered [. . . and] it is difficult to see quite what the new commitments of the
Corps may be'.[39]

Eventually by the mid-1930s McDougall's children were at boarding
school in England and she too returned home, taking a course of study at the
conservative Bonar Law College and renewing her St John Ambulance Brigade
Certificate in Air Raid Precaution and First Aid for Air Raid Casualties.[40]
Living in Dorset when war broke out, McDougall offered her services to the
Director General of Medical Services at the War Office, but to no avail: this
was 1939 not 1914, and she was now a middle-aged woman.[41] McDougall also
inquired directly with the FANY-ATS about renewing her service commitment and was told she was over age.[42] McDougall referred to this as being
'thrown out' but pursued opportunities with the Emergency Nursing Services
and the Women's Services Club.[43] She worked with the YWCA in Dorset and
also helped run the YWCA Hut at Bovington Camp while its leader was away.

In her latter work McDougall poignantly inquired as to whether she might wear her FANY uniform.[44] In 1943 McDougall was living in London and working with the Women's Voluntary Services for Civil Defence.[45]

McDougall maintained contact with the FANY and helped found the Old Comrades Association in 1935 after returning from Rhodesia and finding the FANY was not represented at the Silver Jubilee Festival of the Empire.[46] Pageantry was always important to McDougall and she saw this as a definite slight against the organization. Her relationship with the Corps was often strained, however, and some members held grudges associated with her past leadership. McDougall was aware of this, writing in a letter to Marian Gamwell in 1940 that she knew how much she was disliked in the Corps, and in another correspondence she called herself a 'whipping boy' for those who followed after the war.[47] McDougall was particularly upset about an article in the *Gazette* in 1962, the year before she died. Written by Winnie Geare (*née* Mordaunt), it spoke disparagingly of McDougall's equestrian skills and her organization of the prewar camps.[48] This hurt McDougall terribly since she was so proud of her riding abilities and her love of horses. In a letter to FANY Commandant Maude MacLellan, McDougall wrote that she was 'quite taken aback by Mordaunt's outburst over me in her early memories in [the] Gazette, and rather shattered to think that thro' a lifetime anyone had such a lump of resentment'.[49] Still, McDougall attended some reunions and always stayed very proud of the FANY and its accomplishments. Unable to find a publisher for her manuscript 'Five Years with the Allies', she chose the Imperial War Museum as a safe repository in 1938.[50] She dedicated the manuscript to 'the girls who served with the FANY' and who 'proved the finest, loyalest, bravest and most unselfish women of any time' who 'should not be forgotten'.[51] McDougall died in January 1963 at the age of seventy-six years; her obituary in the *Times* was reported on 29 January, the exact day she had joined the FANY back in 1910.[52] Her son and daughter erected a memorial plaque to her life and war service at the church in Glen Tanar, Aberdeenshire, Scotland, near where she grew up.

By the 1970s many of the First World War FANY had died. When Baxter-Ellis resigned after the Second World War she lived with her partner 'Tony' Kingston Walker (her FANY second-in-command for many years). They died within months of each other twenty years later.[53] Pat Washington (Waddell) died in 1972, Margaret Cole-Hamilton and Hope 'Jimmie' Gamwell in 1973, Mary 'Dicky' Runciman (Richardson) in 1974, Marian Gamwell in 1977, Betty Hutchinson in 1981 and Edith 'Tony' Colston (Walton) at the age of ninety-four in 1982.

All those years ago when the FANY first volunteered for service, they came, as did so many of their contemporaries, from comfortable, privileged backgrounds and were thrown into the chaos of total war. Lured by the thrills of travel and adventure as well as duty to country and Empire, these young women found themselves suddenly propelled into the most masculine of all spaces. They represented an organization of economically privileged women with ties to political and military authorities, and eschewed demands for political and sexual equality in favour of aligning themselves with the elite; but while they avoided making connections between their empowerment as women and political and social enfranchisement, they did develop a profound feminine collectivity that had important consequences for their personal lives and the future of women's service in war. The FANY used traditional notions of femininity while aspiring to heights beyond their confines and therefore faced the cultural paradox of both using and reworking existing discourses on class and gender; still this negotiation and renegotiation actively constructed the organization and the women in it and reshaped the myth of war experience as inclusive of women and their stories.

Notes

1 Grace McDougall, 'Five Years with the Allies, 1914–1919: The Story of the FANY Corps', p. 263. [IWM]
2 BBC radio interview with Sara Talbot [*née* Bonnell] (June 1989). [LC]
3 *The Times* (9 September 1993).
4 Ibid.
5 Penny Summerfield, *Reconstructing Women's Wartime Lives: Discourse and Subjectivity in Oral Histories of the Second World War* (Manchester: Manchester University Press, 1998), ch. 1.
6 *Gazette* (January 1920), pp. 12–13.
7 Ibid., p. 12.
8 *Gazette* (April 1920), p. 8.
9 *Gazette* (January 1920), p. 11.
10 *Gazette* (November 1920), p. 2.
11 Ibid., p. 4.
12 Ibid., p. 5.
13 *Gazette* (April 1920), p. 3.
14 In *FANY Invicta* (London: Hutchinson, 1955, p. 103) Irene Ward writes that the total membership of the FANY in 1928 was 142 and in 1929 was 205. This number would increase exponentially as thousands of FANY served during the Second World War.
15 Hugh Popham, *FANY: The Story of the Women's Transport Corps* (London: Leo Copper, 1984), p. 51.
16 Pat Beauchamp Washington, *Eagles in Exile* (London: Maxwell, Love and Co., 1942).
17 'Background to FANY (PRVC)', fact sheet. [FA] See a FANY account of SOE work in Margaret Pawley, *In Obedience to Instructions: FANY with the SOE in the Mediterranean* (London: Leo Cooper, 1999). FANY Dorothy MacKay writes about her experiences in the Second World War in *Laughter in Khaki* (Edinburgh: Pentland, 1987). For information on women and SOE see Marcus Bonney, *The Women Who Lived for*

Danger: The Women Agents of SOE in the Second World War (London: Hodder and Houghton, 2002) and Rita Kramer, *Flames in the Field: The Story of Four SOE Agents in Occupied France* (London: M. Joseph, 1995). A good overview is W. J. M. Mackenzie, *The Secret History of SOE, 1940–45* (London: Ermin's Press, 2000).

18 'Background to FANY'; Popham, *F.A.N.Y.*, p. 114.
19 See the FANY website at www.fany.org.uk (February 2003).
20 *Gazette* (January 1920), p. 12.
21 *Gazette* (August–September Supplement 1919), p. 3.
22 *Gazette* (November 1920), p. 8.
23 *Gazette* (July 1928).
24 *Gazette* (April 1920), p. 4.
25 Ibid., p. 9.
26 *Gazette* (January–April 1919), p. 6; Gazette (January 1932), p. 2.
27 *Gazette* (January–April 1919), p. 6; *Gazette* (April 1920), p. 9; *Gazette* (August 1921), p. 13–14.
28 *Gazette* (April 1920), p. 10.
29 'Recollections of Phyllis H. Puckle', undated. [LC]
30 *Gazette* (May 1921), p. 5; Popham, *F.A.N.Y.*, p. 49.
31 *Gazette* (April 1920), p. 9.
32 Ibid.
33 Adjutant, Women's Transport Service (FANY) to Beryl Hutchinson (29 June 1960). [LC]
34 Beryl Hutchinson, 'St Omer Convoy', p. 28. [LC]
35 Grace McDougall describes her new life in Rhodesia in the *Gazette* (November 1920), pp. 9–11.
36 Grace McDougall, 'Peace and Arbitration', Address to the Women's Institute Congres, 1935. [IWM]
37 Grace McDougall, *The Golden Bowl* (London: Geoffrey Bles, 1926). One of the early prewar FANY troopers who attended the summer camps was named O'Hea.
38 Ibid., pp. 51–2.
39 Mary Baxter-Ellis to Grace McDougall (13 November 1934). [FA]
40 *Gazette* (June 1935), p. 23; Certificate, Order of St John Ambulance Brigade (31 October 1938). [IWM]
41 Grace McDougall to Director General of Medical Services (18 October 1939). [FA]
42 Mary Baxter-Ellis to Grace McDougall (25 October 1939); McDougall to Baxter-Ellis (27, 31 October 1939). [FA]
43 Ministry of Health to Grace McDougall (24 August 1939); Letter of Reference from Rhodesian Women's Working Party for McDougall (27 August 1942). [IWM]
44 Grace McDougall to Marian Gamwell (10, 26 May; 4 October 1940); Mary Baxter-Ellis to McDougall (27 May 1940). [FA]
45 Town Clerk, Borough of Poole to Grace McDougall (23 August 1943). [FA]
46 *Gazette* (June 1935); British Legion to Grace McDougall (24 August, 12 September, 14 October 1936). [IWM]
47 Grace McDougall to Marian Gamwell (4 October 1940); McDougall to Maude MacLellan (27 April 1962). [FA]
48 *The Women's Transport Service (FANY) Gazette* (Spring 1962), p. 18.
49 Grace McDougall to Maude MacLellan (27 April 1962) (hand copied by Edith Colston). Another letter with similar sentiments is McDougall to McLellan (27 May 1962). [FA]

50 Irene Ward gave her opinion of this in *FANY Invicta*: 'It is typical of Ashley-Smith's way of living that she compiled and sent to the Imperial War Museum, unknown to FANY Headquarters, an invaluable record of events from the date of joining until she sailed for Rhodesia in September 1919' (p. 34).
51 Grace McDougall to Curator, Imperial War Museum (undated, *c.* 1937). [IWM]
52 *The Times* obituary (29 January 1963).
53 Popham, *F.A.N.Y.*, p. 117.

Index

Note: 'n' after a page reference indicates the number of an endnote on that page; page references in italics refer to illustrations.

Index of FANY members

Note: 'n' after a page reference indicates the number of an endnote on that page; page references in italics refer to illustrations.